The Body of the Conquistador

This fascinating history explores the dynamic relationship between overseas colonisation and the bodily experience of eating. It reveals the importance of food to the colonial project in Spanish America and reconceptualises the role of European colonial expansion in shaping the emergence of ideas of race during the Age of Discovery. Rebecca Earle shows that anxieties about food were fundamental to Spanish understandings of the new environment they inhabited and their interactions with the native populations of the new world. Settlers wondered whether Europeans could eat new world food, whether Amerindians could eat European food and what would happen to each if they did. By taking seriously their ideas about food we gain a richer understanding of how settlers understood the physical experience of colonialism and of how they thought about the central features of the colonial project. The result is simultaneously a history of food, of colonialism and of race.

REBECCA EARLE is Professor of History at the University of Warwick. Her previous publications include *The Return of the Native: Indians and Mythmaking in Spanish America, 1810–1930* (2008) and *Spain and the Independence of Colombia* (2000).

Critical Perspectives on Empire

Editors

Professor Catherine Hall
University College London

Professor Mrinalini Sinha
Pennsylvania State University

Professor Kathleen Wilson
State University of New York, Stony Brook

Critical Perspectives on Empire is a major series of ambitious, cross-disciplinary works in the emerging field of critical imperial studies. Books in the series explore the connections, exchanges and mediations at the heart of national and global histories, the contributions of local as well as metropolitan knowledge and the flows of people, ideas and identities facilitated by colonial contact. To that end, the series not only offers a space for outstanding scholars working at the intersection of several disciplines to bring to wider attention the impact of their work; it also takes a leading role in reconfiguring contemporary historical and critical knowledge, of the past and of ourselves.

A full list of titles published in the series can be found at:
www.cambridge.org/cpempire

The Body of the Conquistador

Food, Race and the Colonial Experience in Spanish America, 1492–1700

Rebecca Earle

CAMBRIDGE
UNIVERSITY PRESS

CAMBRIDGE
UNIVERSITY PRESS

The Edinburgh Building, Cambridge CB2 8RU, UK

Published in the United States of America by Cambridge University Press, New York

Cambridge University Press is part of the University of Cambridge.

It furthers the University's mission by disseminating knowledge in the pursuit of education, learning and research at the highest international levels of excellence.

www.cambridge.org
Information on this title: www.cambridge.org/9781107693296

First published 2012
First paperback edition 2013

A catalogue record for this publication is available from the British Library

Library of Congress Cataloguing in Publication data
Earle, Rebecca.
  The body of the conquistador : food, race and the colonial experience in Spanish America, 1492–1700 / Rebecca Earle.
     p.   cm. – (Critical perspectives on empire)
  Includes bibliographical references and index.
  ISBN 978-1-107-00342-2 (hbk.)
  1. Latin America–Colonization–Social aspects.   2. Spain–Colonies–America–History.   3. Spaniards–Latin America–Attitudes–History.
  4. Latin America–Race relations–History.   5. Imperialism–Social aspects–Latin America–History.   6. Human body–Social aspects–Latin America–History.   7. Food habits–Latin America–History.
  8. Food–Latin America–Psychological aspects–History.
  9. Ingestion–Latin America–Psychological aspects–History.
  10. Latin America–Social conditions.   I. Title.
  F1411.E26 2012
  980–dc23
  2012000288

ISBN 978-1-107-00342-2 Hardback
ISBN 978-1-107-69329-6 Paperback

This book is for Gabriel and Isaac

Contents

Figures

Acknowledgements

'But are there any sources?', I was often asked when I explained that I was researching early colonial attitudes towards food. Sources in fact proved plentiful, thanks in part to the help of people such as Linda Newson and Frank Eissa Barroso, who found me documents from archives in two countries, and Jorge Cañizares Esguerra, Michael Hamerly, Jai Kharbanda, Irven Resnick, Christián Roa, James Simpson and Deborah Toner, who drew my attention to particularly useful texts. Benjamin Braude shared his knowledge of the 'African Ham', Laura Lewis advised me on colonial magic and John Elliott helped me when I was foundering in the shallow waters of Spain's sixteenth-century transatlantic trade. Leslie Tobias-Olsen and Magali Carrera assisted me in finding images and Richard Kagan discussed 'pecker checkers' over breakfast. I am also very grateful for the systemic advice offered by colleagues who read sections of this work – particularly Abel Alves, Emily Berquist, Andrea Cadelo, John Chasteen, Tony McFarlane, Jeffrey Pilcher, Claudia Stein and Guy Thompson. Many others allowed me to bend their ear about whatever bread-related con-undrum was occupying my mind at the moment. I must also thank the staff at the lovely John Carter Brown Library for making my stay in Providence so pleasant, and the Library itself for granting me a fellowship. My fellow JCB 'scholars' Ari Zighelboim and Vin Caretta listened patiently to my daily reports on the intricacies of Catholic doc-trine, and offered so much good advice that there is really no point attempting to enumerate it.

I am particularly indebted to my linguistically superior colleagues who shared their expertise in Latin, Greek and Nahuatl. Peter Pormann offered advice about medicine in the ancient world and generously translated swathes of Galen's Greek. Mary Clayton, Erica Hosselkus and Camilla Townsend deciphered bits of Nahuatl, as well as, in Cami's case, also helping me think about the project as a whole. James Muldoon translated passages of *De Indiarum Jure* and talked with me about Juan de Solórzano Pereira. And to say Andrew Laird helped me with the

Latin bits would be a travesty of his contribution to this book. To all these friends and colleagues I am deeply grateful: thank you.

The beginnings, and completion, of this project coincided with difficult moments in my own life, and I would like, finally, to thank Lizzie Collingham, Cliff, Lisa and Susan Earle, Judy Foreman, David Mond, Thomas Seidel, Jennifer Smyth and Claudia Stein for being such good friends.

Introduction: Food and the colonial experience

In November 1493 Christopher Columbus made a disagreeable discovery: things were not going well in the little Spanish colony he had founded on the Caribbean island of Hispaniola. Earlier that year, after his epochal landfall in the West Indies, Columbus had established a small outpost on the island (modern-day Haiti and the Dominican Republic) consisting of thirty-eight semi-volunteer Europeans housed in a makeshift fort. He then sailed for Spain, leaving these men to act as the vanguard of a future Spanish settlement. The admiral returned in the autumn with some 1,500 additional settlers, hoping to expand the fledgling colony. To his dismay, he found that not one of the original thirty-eight was still alive. Conflict and disease were the culprits, and the new arrivals, too, quickly began to sicken. Illness among the colonists prevented Columbus from amassing as much gold as he had anticipated, and impeded attempts to explore the island.

Why had so many Europeans fallen ill? In Columbus's view the explanation was simple but had alarming implications for the nascent Spanish colony: Europeans simply did not thrive in the very different environment of the new world. The principal cause of the dreadful ailments afflicting the small Spanish settlement was, he believed, the unfamiliar air and water of the Caribbean, which were inimical to the European constitution. The challenges the new environment posed to the European body might have implied that all attempts at settlement were doomed, but Columbus was confident that a solution could be found. Mortality, he maintained, would cease once the settlers were provided with 'the usual foods we eat in Spain'.[1] In particular, the settlers needed fresh meat, almonds, raisins, sugar and honey, as well as the wheat flour and wine that formed the backbone of the Iberian diet. Columbus was certain that these wholesome old-world

---

[1] Columbus, 'Memorial que para los Reyes Católicos dió el Almirante a don Antonio de Torres', 30 Jan. 1494, in *Los cuatro viajes del almirante*, pp. 155–68 (quotation p. 158).

foods would restore the settlers to health and allow the resumption of his enterprise.

Historians of early Spanish colonisation in the Caribbean have generally been more concerned with the precipitous decline in the region's indigenous population than with sickness among European settlers.[2] Within a decade of the establishment of this initial settlement Europeans were expressing anxiety that their newly conquered indigenous labour force might evaporate, which would leave only Spaniards and a small number of enslaved Africans to mine gold and grow food – an unpalatable prospect for colonists. Such fears were entirely justified, as by the 1530s the indigenous Taino had, in the words of one demographic historian, 'completed their course to extinction', having succumbed to the combined weight of disease, famine and overwork.[3] (We will return to the explanations settlers at the time offered to account for indigenous mortality.) In 1493, however, it was the Europeans, rather than the Taino, whose survival worried Columbus. He was convinced that the damaging effects of an unfamiliar climate and inadequate and inappropriate foods posed a serious threat to his settlers that could be surmounted only by the swift importation of healthful European food. European food, he insisted, would counteract the deleterious effects of the new-world environment and make feasible the dream of colonisation.

He was not alone in this belief. Columbus's assertion that European food was vital to the survival of such settlements forms part of a vast current of discourse that links diet to discussions of Spanish health, Indian bodies and overseas colonisation. This book examines the centrality of food to Spain's colonial endeavour. Its aim is not simply to demonstrate that Europeans were concerned to maintain adequate supplies of familiar foods, but rather to show how colonisation was as much a physical enterprise as an economic or ideological one, and to explore how ideas about food and bodies underpinned the ways Europeans understood the environment and inhabitants of the new world. For early modern Spaniards food was much more than a source of sustenance and a comforting reminder of Iberian culture. Food helped make them who they were in terms of both their character and their very corporeality, and it was food, more than anything else, that made European bodies different from Amerindian bodies. Without the right foods Europeans would either die, as Columbus

---

[2] For discussion of Spanish mortality in the ill-fated settlement see Cook, 'Sickness, Starvation and Death in Early Hispaniola'.
[3] Livi-Bacci, 'Return to Hispaniola', p. 4.

feared, or, equally alarmingly, they might turn into Amerindians. With the right foods, European settlers in the Indies would flourish and Amerindians might perhaps come to acquire a European constitution. The ability of certain crops to thrive in the Americas revealed God's providential design for humankind, and the similarities and differences between European and indigenous foodways marked out the distance Amerindians needed to travel were they to become fully civilised human beings. By paying attention to how Spanish settlers thought about food, in other words, we gain a clearer understanding of how they thought about the most fundamental features of the colonial experience.

The book's first chapters explain why Spaniards ascribed such importance to food, and how diet helped structure their understanding of the differences between themselves and Amerindians, looking particularly at the importance of humoralism, the model for understanding the human body universally embraced in early modern Europe. The later chapters consider the broader implications of these beliefs in light of the contradictory aims at the heart of Spanish colonialism, which sought simultaneously to make Amerindians like Europeans and to keep them separate, and which emerge with particular clarity from a consideration of the relationship between food, bodies and colonisation. This book in short argues that we cannot understand the nature of early modern colonialism if we do not attend to the multi-layered importance colonisers ascribed to that most quotidian of activities, eating.

Colonies, environments and diets

Many aspects of early modern colonial expansion proved unsettling for its European protagonists. The encounter with entirely new territories and peoples raised doubts about the reliability of existing knowledge and also posed theoretical and practical questions about the proper way for Europeans to interact with these new peoples and places. Far from being an enterprise based on an unquestioning assumption of European superiority, early modern colonialism was an anxious pursuit. This anxiety is captured most profoundly in the fear that living in an unfamiliar environment, and among unfamiliar peoples, might alter not only the customs but also the very bodies of settlers. Perhaps, as Columbus suspected, unmediated contact with these new lands would weaken settlers' constitutions to such an extent that they died. Or perhaps it might instead transform the European body in less destructive but equally unwelcome ways, so that it ultimately ceased to be a European body at all.

Scholars have long recognised the challenges that unfamiliar climates were believed to pose to the European body.[4] In particular, all sorts of alarming disorders were attributed to the malign impact of very hot, damp environments. This made European settlement of such regions problematic, which was ironic, because, as eighteenth-century theorists would later insist, warm climates also sapped natives' ability to govern themselves effectively, and therefore rendered them particularly suited to European conquest. European hostility towards hot climates has thus often been associated with the rise of colonial and racial ideologies. A growing body of scholarship, however, suggests that early European reactions to the *American* environment played an important role in the articulation of these ideologies not because the new world's climate was considered fatal to Europeans, but precisely because it was not. In fact, in the sixteenth and seventeenth centuries many Europeans believed that under the right circumstances they could prosper in the new world. Amerindian bodies, in contrast, seemed unable to thrive in their own native environment, for they succumbed easily to the many diseases that swept across the continent in the wake of European settlement . A number of scholars have therefore asserted that early modern colonial writers explained this apparent paradox by insisting that the bodies of Amerindians were essentially different from, and inferior to, their own. Fixed and substantial physical differences, it is claimed, were said to separate Europeans from Amerindians, which accounted for their divergent responses to the same environment. In constructing European and indigenous bodies as radically and permanently incommensurate, such studies maintain, early modern settlers laid the foundations for a racialised vision of human difference.[5]

Such research certainly highlights the dilemmas that overseas colonisation posed to Europeans, and helpfully focuses attention on the fact that early colonial actors ascribed great significance to the differences they perceived between their bodies and those of Amerindians. Nonetheless, it accords a disproportionate importance to climate as a challenge to both European and indigenous bodies. In fact, climate was but one of a number of forces believed by Europeans to affect health and character, and it assists our analysis of neither the early modern body

---

[4] See for example Kupperman, 'Fear of Hot Climates'; Lavallé, *Las promesas ambiguas*; and Harrison, *Climates and Constitutions*.

[5] See in particular Chaplin, 'Natural Philosophy and an Early Racial Idiom in North America'; Cañizares Esguerra, 'New Worlds, New Stars'; Chaplin, *Subject Matter*; Aubert, ' "The Blood of France" '; Cañizares Esguerra, *Nature, Empire, and Nation*; Greer *et al.*, eds., *Rereading the Black Legend*; and Cañizares Esguerra, 'Demons, Stars and the Imagination'.

nor the history of colonialism to isolate climate from these other forces. This book directs our attention to the role of food. When we attend to food's place within early modern discourses about human difference it becomes clear that fluidity, rather than fixity, was the hallmark of the early modern body, and that this fluidity had striking implications for the coherence of colonial ideology, as well as for our understanding of how early modern Europeans understood human difference.

Food, as this book shows, shaped the colonial body in a number of ways. To begin with, the right foods protected Europeans from the challenges posed by the new world and its environment. Spaniards believed that they would not suffer from the alien climate and unfamiliar heavens of the Indies if they ate European food. For this reason colonisers and settlers in sixteenth- and seventeenth-century Spanish America were consistently concerned about their ability to access European food-stuffs, and generations of chroniclers noted the deleterious effect of the indigenous diet on Europeans unwise enough to consume it. More fundamentally, food helped *create* the bodily differences that underpinned the European categories of Spaniard and Indian. Spanish bodies differed from indigenous bodies because the Spanish diet differed from the Amerindian diet. In the view of Europeans, it was the food that they ate, even more than the environment in which they lived, that gave Amerindians and Spaniards both their distinctive physical characteristics and their characteristic personalities. Amerindians, explained one Spanish doctor, 'don't have the same humours as us because they don't eat the same foods'.[6]

As this comment suggests, food's impact on the human body was framed in accordance with the tenets of Galenic medicine, which understood all bodies to consist of a balance of humours. Each individual possessed a particular, characteristic humoral balance, but that balance was always in uneasy equilibrium, subject to the impact of external forces, of which food was the most important. Different foods could radically alter an individual's humoral balance, which in turn could induce dramatic perturbations in both their physical and emotional condition. As one seventeenth-century Mexican writer put it, 'through eating new foods, people who come here from different climates create new blood, and this produces new humours and the new humours give rise to new abilities and conditions'.[7] Bodies were thus in a state of

---

[6] Benavídez, *Secretos de chirurgia*, pp. 26–7.
[7] Vetancurt, *Teatro mexicano*, tratado 1, chap. 6, p. 11. Vetancurt paraphrases Henrico Martínez's 1606 *Reportorio de los tiempos e historia natural desta Nueva España*, tratado 3, chap. 8, p. 283.

constant flux, in which scarcely anything was ever fixed and in which permanence was illusory. If we view the early modern body from this perspective, it becomes difficult to speak of a sixteenth-century vision of permanent embodied difference. For early modern Europeans, bodily differences were real, but by no means permanent. Bodies could alter just as easily as could diets. In this universe, the physical differences separating Europeans from Amerindians were more a function of food than of either climate or destiny.

Difference, cultures and bodies

In focusing on the ways in which Spaniards understood the physical differences that they perceived between themselves and Amerindians, I do not mean to imply that the categories of 'Spaniard' and 'Amerindian' are themselves transparent. After all, Catholic Spain was only beginning the process of political unification at the time of Columbus's first voyage, although a sense of Hispanic identity had arguably begun to emerge several centuries earlier. A number of scholars have indeed observed that the experience of overseas colonisation itself helped meld the Peninsula's diverse inhabitants into a common community of Catholic Spaniards.[8] It is, moreover, quite clear that the features that helped differentiate 'Indians' from 'Spaniards' were to a large extent socially and culturally determined. To begin with, 'Indian' was a fiscal and juridical category. In particular, paying the head tax known as the Indian tribute and possessing entitlement to the use of communal land were key markers of indigenousness for much of the colonial era. Whether an individual was subject to paying tribute or entitled to use communal land depended in part on arguments about genealogy and ancestry, but these were not the only factors on which such decisions were based. On the contrary, classifications often derived as much from clothing, language and other cultural markings as from notions of lineage. That is, individuals who embraced important features of indigenous culture were more likely to be considered Indian than those who did not, whatever their personal ancestry. In addition, tributary status might depend more on fiscal exigencies than either ancestry or appearance. European disease in the centuries after the Spanish conquest greatly reduced the size of the tribute-paying population, and as a result the officials who drew up the tax rolls might, in an attempt to

[8] On the emergence of the idea of Spain see Maravall, *El concepto de España en la Edad Media*; Herrero García, *Ideas de los españoles del siglo XVII*; Lomnitz, 'Nationalism as a Practical System'; and Herzog, *Defining Nations*.

increase revenues, include as tribute-payers individuals who themselves denied being Amerindians. Colonial archives record the many disputes occasioned by this sort of fiscally driven classification.[9]

The complex nature of what scholars loosely call 'racial' classifications has been shown with particular clarity by Douglas Cope in a now-classic study on plebeian culture in colonial Mexico City. Cope's work stressed that racial or caste identities were essentially social. They were certainly not based solely on physical appearance; as Cope noted, when individuals 'wished to convince the authorities of someone's racial status, they went beyond physical characterization', also adding information about dress, speech, occupation and name.[10] Ancestry might be discussed, but this did not necessarily provide definitive answers; the parish records in which such classifications were supposed to be recorded sometimes either omitted information on caste or contained ambiguous or contradictory classifications. Family members themselves might disagree about the caste status of other relatives; Cope cites many examples of individuals described variously as Indian and Spanish. As he observed, for plebeians 'defining race was functional rather than logical, pragmatic rather than theoretically sound'.[11] Elites sought to rely on ancestry and concepts of blood purity, but they too were intimately entangled in pragmatic colonial practices that viewed race fundamentally as a social and cultural attribute. Caste status might be proved through genealogy, but it was demonstrated on a daily basis through a mastery of Castilian and a steadfast embrace of the other emblems of Iberian culture.

These included, in addition to competence in Spanish, the use of European clothing, particular hairstyles and a range of other cultural practices. The significance of clothing to the performance of caste identity is made clear by its regular appearance in colonial lawsuits. Individuals seeking to establish their status might appeal not to the genealogies of their ancestors, but rather to the clothing that they typically wore. When in 1686 in Quito one Blas de Horta tried to demonstrate that he was not an Indian, he did not summon his parents. Rather, he produced a witness to affirm that he always wore Spanish dress.[12]

---

[9] See for example Lutz, *Santiago de Guatemala*; and Jackson, *Race, Caste, and Status*.
[10] Cope, *The Limits of Racial Domination*, pp. 5, 50, 53 (quotation, p. 56); and Lewis, *Hall of Mirrors*.
[11] Cope, *The Limits of Racial Domination*, pp. 57 (quotation, pp. 68–9).
[12] Minchom, *The People of Quito*, pp. 158, 190. Or see Schwartz and Salomon, 'New Peoples and New Kinds of People', pp. 482–94; Bauer, *Goods, Power, History*, pp. 74, 80, 110; Earle, 'Nationalism and National Costume in Spanish America'; and Martínez, *Genealogical Fictions*, pp. 104–5.

Such sartorially based classifications did not simply reflect social convention but also enjoyed semi-legal status. As one seventeenth-century Peruvian lawyer opined, people of mixed ancestry who lived 'with the Indians, wearing their clothes and following their practices', should for legal purposes be classed as Indians, although he admitted that 'in truth they are not entirely Indian'.[13] One gains a sense of the complexities involved in such classifications from the case of Nicolasa Juana, investigated by the Mexican Inquisition in the 1680s for various doctrinal lapses. An official report described her as

a white mulata with curly hair, because she is the daughter of a dark-skinned mulata and a Spaniard, and for her manner of dress she has flannel petticoats and a native blouse ... She wears shoes, and her natural and common language is not Spanish but Chocho, as she was brought up among Indians with her mother, from whom she contracted the vice of drunkenness, to which she often succumbs, as Indians do, and from whom she has also received the crime of [idolatry].[14]

Nicolasa Juana was thus simultaneously white, a mulata and an Indian, whose identity resided in both her appearance and her comportment, which was itself viewed as evidence of her indigenous ancestry. Eating, like drinking (too much, in the case of Nicolasa Juana), also played an important role in enacting caste identity. This book argues that diet was believed to help *create* the physical differences that separated Europeans from Amerindians and Africans, but in addition scholars have long recognised that certain foods were closely associated with Spanish, indigenous or African cultural identity. Guinea pig, for example, was universally labelled an 'Indian' food, and people who ate it were likely to be classed as Indians.[15] In colonial Spanish America, in other words, caste difference, although ostensibly concerned with ancestry and genealogy, was profoundly performative.

In early modern Catholic Spain, the most important social distinctions were likewise delineated as much through daily practice as through ancestry. There, concerns about difference coalesced around distinguishing 'Old Christians' (Spaniards whose families had long practised Catholicism) from 'New Christians'. New Christians were individuals

[13] Olabarrieta Medrano, *Recuerdo de las obligaciones del ministerio apostólico*, chap. 4, p. 96.

[14] Tavárez, 'Legally Indian', p. 91.

[15] See for example Francisco de Acuña, 'Relación fecha por el corregidor de los Chimbivilcas', 1586, in Jiménez de la Espada, ed., *Relaciones geográficas de las Indias: Perú*, vol. 1, p. 319; Atienza, *Compendio historial del estado de los indios del Peru*, p. 53; and Weismantel, *Food, Gender, and Poverty in the Ecuadorian Andes*. Pilcher, *¡Que vivan los tamales!*, provides a lucid discussion of the Mexican case.

of Jewish or Muslim ancestry whose conversion to Catholicism had occurred within the last few generations, and whose dedication to their new religion was considered highly suspect by Old Christians. This was in large part because many of these conversions took place in coercive contexts, such as following the pogroms that swept through various Spanish cities in 1391, or the late fifteenth-century expulsion of Muslims and Jews from Spain. Conversos (Jewish converts) and moriscos (Islamic converts) were subject to increasing harassment and regulation over the fifteenth and sixteenth centuries, which culminated in the expulsion from Spain of all moriscos in the early seventeenth century.

The differences between Old and New Christians, and between individuals with an unblemished heritage of religious orthodoxy and those with heretical or unconverted ancestors, were articulated through a language of blood purity, or *limpieza de sangre*. From the mid fifteenth century, individual Spanish towns and institutions began drawing up statutes that made proof of 'clean blood' a requirement for occupying certain positions. Individuals might be required to demonstrate their blood purity in order to attend university, join a religious order, hold municipal office or, later, emigrate to the Indies. To possess clean blood an individual needed to demonstrate that neither they nor their ancestors had been investigated by the Inquisition for heresy or, more stringently, that their family tree contained neither Jews, Muslins nor recent converts to Christianity. How far back the demand for genealogical purity went, and the stringency of the definition of purity, varied over time and from institution to institution.

As was the case with establishing one's caste in the Indies, demonstrating purity of blood in Spain required a complicated blending of genealogy and reputation. On the one hand the idea of blood purity was based on a genealogical model. Proving purity encouraged the construction of family trees and gave rise to an entire economy of genealogical experts, advisers and forgers who could assist in constructing or perhaps fabricating the required genealogy. At the same time, the bases on which these demonstrations were constructed relied not only on certified family trees but also on the individual's standing in the community. The investigations into an individual's purity thus included affidavits from neighbours and acquaintances, who reported on the individual's reputation and produced evidence that sometimes conflicted with that provided by written records. Indeed, as the historian James Casey has noted, 'before the diffusion of baptism and marriage records in the later sixteenth century it was actually rather hard to document ancestry, other than by common repute'.[16] For these reasons blood purity was 'unstable, accessible but easily lost, depending on one's reputation within the community (which was not necessarily fixed), personal relationships, and the outcome of the next probanza' or investigation, as the historian María Elena Martínez observes in her study of the concept.[17] The extension of ideas of blood purity to the Indies produced some striking modifications of the Iberian model – Amerindians, for example, on occasion succeeded in demonstrating that they possessed pure blood – but the reliance on a combination of genealogical and social evidence persisted.[18] In other words, possessing pure blood, like one's caste identity, was in part performative, enacted daily through a variety of cultural practices.

Taken together, this research into the idea of difference in the early modern Iberian world suggests that divisions between Catholic Spaniards, Jews, Amerindians and other groups were generated at least in part socially. Individuals demonstrated their Catholic or indigenous status through their daily practices and were either confirmed or rejected in these performances by the other members of their community. A substantial body of scholarship provides compelling accounts of the negotiations that these performances entailed. It also suggests that whatever the historical actors themselves may have claimed, these categories were in essence social and cultural, rather than physical. They were about reputation and were not really concerned with bodies.

What this rich corpus of scholarship explains less well is how colonial actors understood the bodies that carried out these negotiations. We tend to assume that if difference is produced through cultural production then it cannot at the same time be considered an embodied phenomenon. In fact, early modern society, at least in the Iberian world, did not classify bodies and culture as fundamentally different. Instead, the physical body was thought to be *generated* in part through the ambient culture, and in particular through diet. In other words, diet and other cultural practices were believed to have a profound physical impact on the body. The anthropologist Ann Laura Stoler's observation regarding European identity in colonial spaces that 'what is at issue here is not a shared conviction of the fixity of European identity but the protean nature of it' applies equally strongly to the European body itself.[19]

---

[16] Casey, *Early Modern Spain*, p. 142; Casey, *Family and Community in Early Modern Spain*, pp. 182–95; and Martínez, *Genealogical Fictions*.

[17] Martínez, *Genealogical Fictions*, p. 74.

[18] On indigenous claims to purity of blood see Martínez, *Genealogical Fictions*, pp. 200–26.

[19] Stoler, *Race and the Education of Desire*, p. 105.

Bodies were central to the fundamental distinctions that structured colonial society, but they were themselves understood to be the product of the cultural practices that typified the colonial world.

This book, then, considers the role of diet not merely in the display or performance of a fundamentally disembodied colonial identity, but rather in the construction and maintenance of the colonial body. It probes the space that early modern Spaniards imagined to exist between their bodies and those of Amerindians, measuring the distance that separated the one from the other and mapping the routes whereby one could begin to transform into the other. As we will see, food was central to shaping the colonial space through which those bodies moved.

Geographies, chronologies and sources

This book is deliberately broad in its geographical scope. Rather than limiting my analysis to a particular Spanish colony or a region that subsequently became an independent nation, I consider the imprecise geographical space early modern Spaniards referred to as 'the Indies'. This term embraced the western lands beyond the Atlantic claimed by Spain (and Portugal), and came to include both the Americas and the Philippines, although I will focus on the former. This generous purview means that I pay less comprehensive attention to Spanish attitudes towards specific areas or indigenous groups than some readers might prefer. Nonetheless, I believe that this approach best reflects the attitudes of the early modern actors whose mental universe I seek to understand. Early modern Spaniards themselves were extremely vague about the geographical contours of colonial space. As the literary scholar Ricardo Padrón has noted, colonial writers 'disagreed among themselves on the precise geography' of Spain's overseas possessions.[20] Many texts, including those written by people with first-hand experience of the new world, refer indiscriminately to 'the Indies' and 'the Indians', without attempting to distinguish in any way between the many different geographies and peoples encompassed by this portmanteau term. An approach based on modern geographies would not capture the mental landscapes of early colonists and colonial writers.

It should not surprise us that such people had a different understanding of American space from that reflected in modern atlases. Early modern maps of the new world were of necessity works in progress, whose secrets were jealously guarded by the Spanish state. Even people who had travelled to the new world did not always possess an overall

---

[20] Padrón, *The Spacious Word*, p. 29.

perspective on the relationship between the different regions. Most early modern Spaniards, colonists included, thus had little opportunity to frame their understanding of the Indies as a whole within a perspective provided by cartography, beyond the general sense that these lands lay to the west of Spain, and that they were extensive. An image of this mysterious space appears on the title-page of the chronicler Antonio de Herrera's 1601 *Descripción de las Indias occidentales* (*Description of the Western Indies*). (See Figure 1.) The map shows an imprecise landmass that bears only an approximate relation to the actual contours of the American continent. The northern section is labelled 'America'. The southern section positions 'Peru' in its currently recognised location along the Pacific coast of South America. The region directly beneath it, in the site occupied by Chile on modern maps, is labelled 'Brazil'. By 1601 it was of course possible to obtain far more accurate maps of the Americas than the one provided at the start of Herrera's tome; indeed the chronicle itself included a number of these, as well as precise details about the latitude of the principal Spanish colonies. My point is not that seventeenth-century Europeans still had no idea where Brazil was, but rather that in 1601 it was perfectly feasible to begin a general history of Spanish new-world colonisation with a 'map' of such inaccuracy that it functioned as little more than an icon or symbol of the Indies. My book is concerned as much with the conceptual space depicted on this map as with the actual territory through which Spanish settlers and Amerindians alike moved and interacted.

The extent to which settlers distinguished between the different inhabitants of this territory varied enormously. Writers with direct experience of the Indies at times noted the differences between, say, 'Mexicans', who possessed at least some of the signs of *policía*, or civilisation, and 'barbarous Indians' who went about totally naked and ate human flesh. Similarly, chroniclers might differentiate carefully between the languages and customs of different indigenous groups, or offer precise details about how to pronounce specific Amerindian words. Yet these distinctions were discarded with surprising ease. The same writer who on one page noted the differences between Quechua- and Aymara-speaking groups on the next might offer sweeping generalisations about 'Indians' and their habits.[21] I again follow the practice of my sources in focusing primarily on the meanings settlers ascribed to the vague but fundamentally important category of 'Indian', without, I hope, endorsing the breathtaking homogenisation that it encodes.

---

[21] See for example Acosta, *De procuranda indorum salute*; and Peña Montenegro, *Itinerario para parochos de indios*.

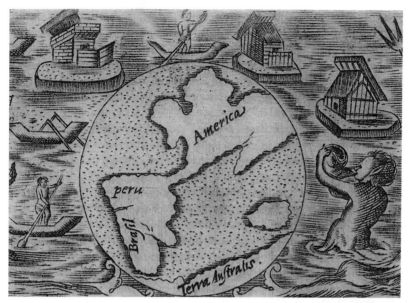

Figure 1 Antonio de Herrera, *Descripción de las Indias occidentales*, 1601 (detail of title-page). A very approximate map of the Indies.

The chronological span of this book embraces Spain's colonial experience during the sixteenth and seventeenth centuries. I concentrate on the first century of colonial rule, when Spanish responses to the novelty of the Indies generated a particularly rich body of commentary. Spanish colonisation of the Americas began with Columbus's 1492 arrival in the Bahamas, which was quickly followed by the establishment of settlements first in the Caribbean and then on the mainland. With the defeat of the Mexica empire of Central Mexico in 1521 the crown acquired control over a region that was not only densely populated but also rich in mineral and other resources, and which came to form part of the core of Spanish colonial space. The viceroyalty of Peru, established later in the sixteenth century on the ashes of the Inca empire, formed the other pole. Over the course of the century expeditions of Spaniards, often accompanied by other Europeans, as well as a number of Africans (both enslaved and free), roamed the continent, forming small settlements from Florida to Chile. By the end of the sixteenth century between 200,000 and 250,000 Spaniards had emigrated to the Indies, where they formed the apex of a hierarchical social pyramid. They were joined by nearly 100,000 enslaved Africans, brought to work on newly established sugar plantations, ranches and other economic enterprises.

In the same years the indigenous population fell dramatically. Scholars continue to debate the magnitude of the demographic collapse, but there is no doubt that it was catastrophic. One estimate suggests that the population of Central Mexico fell from precontact levels of about 25 million to perhaps 1 million in 1600. Amerindians nonetheless continued to form the majority of the population in many parts of the continent, where they provided a vital labour force for colonisers.[22]

The colonial societies that emerged across the hemisphere differed in many ways. They nonetheless shared certain features, among them a concern on the part of many Spaniards and creoles (a colonial term referring to Spaniards born in the Indies) to maintain social distance between themselves and the population of Amerindians, slaves and free people of colour who always outnumbered them. Another feature that united Spanish and creole culture across the Americas was a common understanding of how bodies functioned. Settlers were persistently concerned to protect their health by following basic and widely agreed-upon practices, which derived fundamentally from the principles of humoralism. Humoralism governed European understandings of the body throughout the early modern era, and so provides a coherence in regard to ideas about corporeality notwithstanding the many transformations undergone by Spanish and colonial society during this period.[23] As this book shows, Spanish responses to colonialism reflect, and were structured by, the vernacular body concepts that underpinned early modern epistemologies more generally.

The Body of the Conquistador is based on a disparate collection of sources, including medical handbooks, chronicles by both religious and lay writers, official and private letters, legal treatises, missionary accounts and novels. Because diet occupied such a critical role in the maintenance of the Spanish body, and in the implementation of Spain's colonial ambitions, discussion of food runs throughout early modern colonial writings. Sources as varied as geographical compendia and the plays of Lope de Vega reflect food's ability to help frame the early modern colonial universe. These texts were of course written to serve different purposes. In using them to access the attitudes of sixteenth- and seventeenth-century colonists regarding European and Amerindian bodies I have not assumed that they form part of a coherent body of discourse as regards their ostensible subjects. Chroniclers and missionaries often disagreed in their assessment of the civic capacity of

---

[22] Sánchez-Albornoz, 'The Population of Colonial Spanish America'; and Livi-Bacci, *Conquest*.

[23] Humoralism's period of dominion is discussed in Siraisi, *Medieval and Early Renaissance Medicine*; and Conrad *et al.*, *The Western Medical Tradition*.

Amerindians, and all writers wrote within the parameters of particular disciplinary and intellectual frameworks. Authors engaged in theoretical and practical debates about many different features of the early modern world. Two different handbooks on the nature of the disease the Spanish called *bubas* may differ dramatically in their recommendations regarding treatment and in their understanding of the disease's origins. Doctors also argued about whether medical knowledge was best acquired by reading Latin translations of Arabic texts based on ancient Greek writings, or whether direct contact with these Greek writings was preferable or indeed necessary. Some chroniclers believed that Amerindians were descendants of Noah's son Ham, while others maintained that they were instead the grandsons of Carthaginians or even of ancient Spaniards. Priests excoriated the behaviour of conquistadors in their chronicles and petitions, while settlers dismissed such denunciations as naive and ill-founded in equally prolix texts. Nonetheless one feature that these works share is a vision of the human body as essentially fluid and porous, in active dialogue with its environment. Indeed, it is precisely through the analysis of a wide range of sources that one has the best opportunity of uncovering the body concepts embraced by early modern Spaniards and creoles.

Overall, this book situates early European colonisation within the framework in which colonial settlers themselves understood it: the world of the mutable humoral body. As we shall see, the flexibility of both European and indigenous bodies profoundly shaped the ways in which colonists made sense of the experience of overseas colonisation. It also reveals the fundamental importance of food to the entire colonial enterprise, and helps us reconceptualise the ways in which European colonial expansion intersects with the emergence of the idea of race.

Structure

Chapter 1 explains the context out of which the Spanish colonial body emerged. It looks particularly at the importance of humoralism in providing a framework for early modern understandings of the body. The basic features of humoralism were embraced not only by the scholars who wrote guidebooks to good health and taught at the growing number of Spanish and new-world universities, but also by a wide section of the Spanish population. They therefore formed part of the intellectual baggage that all colonists took with them to the Indies. The workings of the porous humoral body provided settlers with a coherent explanation for why Amerindians had very different bodies and characters from Europeans. At the same time, the humoral body was in constant danger of transforming into something else. As this chapter shows, it was food that most effectively guarded against that danger. Appropriate food, as Columbus recognised, was thus central to the maintenance of the European body in the new world.

Chapter 2 dissects the diet that Spaniards aspired to eat, and charts the efforts of settlers to either import or cultivate these foods in the Americas. For colonists, foods such as wheat bread, wine and olive oil not only represented the familiar taste of home, but, more importantly, preserved their health in the challenging new-world environment. They also encapsulated the essential features of the civilisation that Spaniards hoped to impose on the new world. The chapter begins to unravel the connections between Christianity and the ideal Spanish diet, and to trace the links settlers perceived between their foods and the superiority of their culture. Chapter 3 situates such discussions of food and agriculture within the broader framework of colonial responses to the American environment. Although settlers varied in their opinions about the inherent healthfulness of the Indies, they generated a rich discourse affirming its suitability to the European body once it had been enriched with old-world crops. Writers advanced the most implausible claims about the ease with which European crops grew in the Indies, from which they adduced that the new world was if not the actual site of the terrestrial paradise, then at least a very close imitation. These claims formed part of a larger discourse about the providential nature of Spanish colonisation: the fertility and abundance of the new world environment both guaranteed the stability and integrity of the Spanish body, and also manifested the divine forces that favoured Spain's colonial endeavour.

The first three chapters, in other words, explain how Spanish settlers believed their bodies to function in the colonies, and also how they conceptualised the differences they perceived between their bodies and those of Amerindians, in the process revealing how distinct the humoral body was from the racialised body familiar from nineteenth-century scientific writings. These chapters emphasise the flexibility of all bodies and the centrality of old-world food to the preservation of the colonial Spanish body, and interpret colonial efforts to access that food in light of these factors. They then consider the more general significance that Spaniards ascribed to their success in cultivating these health-giving foods in the colonies.

Chapter 4 turns from a consideration of old-world foods to explore European reactions to the unfamiliar foods of the new world. Although colonists were suspicious about the impact of the indigenous diet on the European body, they nonetheless welcomed a number of new foodstuffs into their own consumption regimes, and in any event were often obliged to eat new foods whether they wanted to or not. This chapter examines Spanish responses to these foods. Colonists vacillated in their views about how much new-world food they could safely incorporate into their diet. As this chapter argues, these doubts neatly parallel the doubts that Spaniards expressed about the extent to which Amerindians themselves could be incorporated into Spanish culture. The chapter looks particularly at the dichotomy between wheat, the only grain that through the mystery of the Mass could be converted into the body of Christ, and new-world grains and roots such as maize or cassava, which were unable to undergo this sacramental transformation. Spanish doubts about what they could eat in the new world in other words reflect not only their understanding of how their bodies operated, but also a much broader uncertainty about the place of the indigenous population within Europeanised colonial space.

Chapter 5 probes these anxieties further by examining colonial efforts to convince Amerindians to adopt a European diet. Because old-world foods not merely represented old-world civilisation, but, in a profound sense, *were* that civilisation, in so far as they encapsulated the fundamental mysteries of Catholicism, it was essential for Amerindians to embrace these superior foodstuffs. Beyond this, because of the transformative potential ascribed to diet by humoralism, there was every reason to believe that consumption of an old-world diet would work profound and positive transformations on the indigenous body and character. For all these reasons writers, priests and officials repeatedly advocated that Amerindians be encouraged, or perhaps required, to consume civilised old-world foods. The attempts by colonial writers and officials to encourage Amerindians to eat European food were thus founded on the same humoral models that shaped European responses to new-world foods, but they rested on a paradox, for if it was risky, as Columbus found, for Europeans to eat unfamiliar new-world foods, it was equally risky for Amerindians to eat unfamiliar old-world foods. Indeed, colonial writers regularly ascribed the catastrophic decline in the post-contact indigenous population precisely to the excessive consumption of old-world foods. Colonial actors thus advised Amerindians to adopt a European diet, while at the same time suggesting that to do so could be fatal. The paradoxical nature of these Spanish prescriptions mirrors a larger ambiguity that lies at the heart of Spain's colonial endeavour, which aimed simultaneously to incorporate the indigenous population into European cultural space, and also to do everything possible to prevent that from happening. The chapter thus moves from a discussion of diet and bodies to a more general discussion of the contradictory aims inherent in Spanish colonisation. Food, far from being a mundane and insignificant aspect of colonial culture, proves to be central to the elaborate but unstable edifice of Spanish colonisation.

Chapter 6 returns to the relationship between race and the fluid early modern body. It probes the limits of humoral fluidity and revisits the idea that race was born out of early colonial encounters, concluding that an appreciation of the humoral body transforms our vision not only of Spain's colonial experience, but also of the emergence of the idea of race. Chapters on humoralism thus bookend the work, because humoralism provides both the necessary starting point for any understanding of food's role in the colonial project, and a better framework for understanding early modern ideas about human difference.

The Epilogue sketches the continued influence of diet, and humoralism more generally, in shaping ideas about bodies and races in eighteenth- and nineteenth-century Spanish America. It also points to the similarities between the story told here, about early modern Spanish colonialism, and the colonial projects attempted by other European powers in the same era. As the historian Joyce Chaplin has argued, if we hope to understand early European colonisation we must pay close attention to European ideas about bodies and nature.[24] To do that, we need to pay attention to how Europeans thought about food.

---

[24] Chaplin, *Subject Matter*, pp. 7–35.

1 Humoralism and the colonial body

Like virtually every other settler in Spain's newly conquered American territories, Bartolomé de las Casas wondered why Amerindians were so different from Spaniards. Las Casas, a colonist turned Dominican friar, became during the sixteenth century one of the most outspoken critics of Spanish colonisation, against which he waged a decades-long campaign conducted both in person and through thousands of pages of closely argued text. Lauded in his own lifetime as the defender of the Indians, he praised their virtue and excoriated their treatment at the hands of Spanish colonists. Las Casas played a central role in convincing the Spanish crown to restrict the authority of settlers and unequivocally affirmed the common humanity of Spaniards and Indians. Nonetheless, he never doubted that Amerindians differed from Spaniards not only in their behaviour (Amerindians were docile sheep, while Spaniards were ravening wolves) but also in their bodies. Las Casas framed these differences in the humoral language of the day: Spaniards were fierce and choleric, whereas Amerindian bodies were full of phlegmatic humours. Such dissimilarities might have seemed surprising, given that, as Las Casas maintained, Spaniards and Indians were brothers, having descended, as had all people, from Adam and Eve. Las Casas, however, offered a simple explanation: Amerindian bodies differed from Spanish bodies because they were nourished on different foods. While Europeans ate the wheat bread and wine that Columbus had hoped would restore his ailing settlers to health, Amerindians subsisted on 'roots and herbs and things from the earth and fish'.[1] This cold food generated the abundance of cold humours that characterised the indigenous body, and which consequently shaped their character. Diet, in other words, was behind the distinctive indigenous body, as well as the docile indigenous character.

---

[1] Las Casas, *Historia de las Indias*, c. 1559, book 1, chap. 164; and Las Casas, *Apologética historia sumaria*, c. 1552, chaps. 23–41; both in *Obras escogidas*, vol. I, p. 433 (quotation), vol. III, pp. 72–140 (esp. pp. 73, 86, 105–6).

Colonial texts almost invariably included some discussion of the physical qualities of Spain's new subjects, for Spaniards were fascinated by the differences (and similarities) that they detected between their bodies and those of Amerindians. This concern reflected far more than idle curiosity, or a dispassionate interest in human taxonomy: in the bodies of Amerindians colonists hoped to find clues about the ability of Europeans to thrive in the American environment. This chapter explains the importance settlers ascribed to the constitutional traits that they believed distinguished Europeans from Amerindians, by unravelling the complex web of associations that linked the fate of settlers to the bodies of Indians. As we shall see, Spanish ideas about health, bodily integrity and character, which were based fundamentally on the tenets of humoral theory, accorded a central importance to diet as a means of regulating the body. Food, more than any other factor, was what separated Amerindian bodies from Spanish bodies, but it was a fragile bulwark. This chapter outlines colonial debates about the differences – which were by no means permanent – between European and indigenous bodies, and explains the pervasive influence of humoralism in shaping colonial attitudes towards the new world, its inhabitants and its foods.

Spanish bodies, Indian bodies

The Spaniards who travelled in the Indies in the early modern era quickly determined that Amerindian bodies differed from their own in all sorts of ways. Indians were usually said to be somewhat darker skinned than Europeans, although colonial writers often observed that many were of a colour virtually indistinguishable from Spaniards. They had distinctively straight hair, and the men typically lacked beards. In addition, they suffered less from stomach ailments, were generally timid and deceitful, rarely went bald, enjoyed remarkable eyesight and almost never developed kidney-stones or gallstones. Spaniards in contrast were of a proud nature, possessed light skin and delightful beards, and were afflicted by numerous digestive disorders. Such differences were evident to all.[2] Why, however, were Amerindians and Europeans so different?

---

[2] 'It is clear', noted the German physician Nicholas Pol, 'that the climate, bodies, complexions, etc. of the Spaniards are different from those possessed by the Indians': Pol, *On the Method of Healing with the Indian Wood called Guaiac the Bodies of Germans who have Contracted the French Disease*, p. 59. My composite Spanish and indigenous bodies are drawn from Columbus, 'Diary of the First Voyage', 11 Oct., 13, 16, 24 Dec. 1492, in *Los cuatro viajes del almirante*, pp. 30, 88, 91, 106; Vespucci, 'Letter

Undoubtedly, one of the reasons that Indians and Spaniards were so different was that they lived in very different environments. Since the time of Hippocrates European writers had drawn connections between the environment in which individuals lived and their characters, and during the sixteenth and seventeenth centuries the influence of climate on the human constitution was universally acknowledged. As one Spanish scholar put it in 1608, 'people to a certain extent resemble the place where they are born'.[3] To begin with, climate was believed to shape character. Individuals living in very cold environments, for example, were likely to be hardy, fierce and stupid. Climate further played a key part in determining appearance. Writing in the early seventeenth century, the Dominican priest Gregorio García explained that Ethiopians had a dark skin because they lived in the heat of the torrid zone, although they were, like all men, the sons of Noah (who had undoubtedly been white). Prolonged residence in a hot climate had permanently altered their appearance.[4] (García, in common with most of his contemporaries, saw nothing surprising in this sort of transformation.) In addition to causing changes in skin and hair colour, climate was also believed to affect individual health, and the wrong air or temperature could provoke serious illness. Columbus, as we saw, had

on His Third Voyage to Lorenzo Pietro Francesco di Medici' (the Medici Letter), March–April 1503, in *The Letters of Amerigo Vespucci*, pp. 5–9; Peter Martyr, *De Orbe Novo*, decade 7, book 2 (vol. II, p. 258); 'Relación de las costumbres antiguas de los naturales del Pirú', *c.* 1550, in Esteve Barba, ed., *Crónicas peruanas del interés indígena*, p. 177; López de Gómara, *Historia general de las Indias*, chaps. 26, 68, 79, 193, 216 (pp. 62, 131, 149, 337, 372–3); Matienzo, *Gobierno del Perú*, pp. 16–17; Durán, *Historia de las Indias de Nueva España*, prologue to vol. I (vol. I, p. 5); López Medel, *De los tres elementos*, p. 204; Hernández, *Antigüedades de la Nueva España*, book 1, chap. 23 (p. 97); Atienza, *Compendio historial del estado de los indios del Peru*, chap. 10 (pp. 58–60); Cárdenas, *Problemas y secretos maravillosos*, book 3, chaps. 1, 9, 11 (pp. 176, 208–10, 217–19); Farfán, *Tratado breve de mediçina*, book 1, chap. 1 (pp. 1–8); Vargas Machuca, 'Descripción breve de todas las Indias occidentales', in *Milicia y descripción de las Indias*, vol. II, pp. 77–8; Dorantes de Carranza, *Sumaria relación de las cosas de la Nueva España*, p. 63; García, *Orígen de los indios del Nuevo Mundo*, book 2, chap. 5 (p. 161); Torquemada, *Monarchia yndiana*, book 14, chaps. 18–19, 24 (vol. II, pp. 609–14, 620–1); Hernández, *Quatro libros de la naturaleza*, book 3, part 1, chap. 40 (p. 133); Lázaro de Arregui, *Descripción de la Nueva Galicia*, chap. 11 (pp. 26–8); Calancha, *Corónica moralizada del orden de San Agustín en el Perú*, book 1, chap. 9 (p. 64); Cobo, *Historia del Nuevo Mundo*, book 11, chaps. 2–3 (vol. II, pp. 10–14); and Peña Montenegro, *Itinerario para parochos de indios*, book 2, tratado 1, prologue (p. 142).
[3] Bermúdez de Pedraza, *Antigüedad y excelencias de Granada*, p. 146 (quotation); Huarte de San Juan, *Examen de Ingenios, or The Examination of Mens Wits*, pp. 21–2; Cárdenas, *Problemas y secretos maravillosos*, book 3, chap. 1 (pp. 174–5); and Rocha, *El origen de los indios*, p. 69. See also Hippocrates, 'On Airs, Waters and Places', in *The Genuine Works of Hippocrates*; and Glacken, *Traces on the Rhodian Shore*.
[4] García, *Orígen de los indios*, book 2, chap. 5 (pp. 149–50).

ascribed the sickness afflicting his settlement on Hispaniola in part to the region's unfamiliar air. Some climates were inherently more healthy than others – damp, swampy places were generally viewed as dangerous – but it was considered unwise to undergo sudden alterations of environment, even from an unhealthy to a more salubrious climate. As the fifteenth-century Spanish historian Diego Rodríguez de Almela explained, 'the complexion is shaped by the air of the place where one was raised and unfamiliar air can and does make men ill'.[5] Overall, in the words of the cosmographer Henrico Martínez, a change in climate could result in a change in 'talent, vivacity and condition'.[6]

As a consequence, educated Spaniards living in the Americas were highly attuned to the potential impact of the new world's air, stars and temperature. They paid careful attention to the climate, and advised other settlers to do the same. The Spanish captain Bernardo de Vargas Machuca, for example, stipulated that 'in the Indies, people who want to stay healthy will live in the climate that their complexion demands'. Subjecting one's body to changes in temperature, on the other hand, 'cannot fail to cause illness', he warned.[7] Beyond illness, moving to a new environment was liable to provoke all sorts of other undesirable transformations as well. This fear was well expressed by the royal cosmographer Juan López de Velasco, who noted in a report from the 1570s that 'what with living under different stars and in a different climate', Spaniards who resided for a long time in the Indies 'inevitably undergo some change in the colour and quality of their persons'. He explained that:

It is moreover well known that those who are born here, and are called creoles, and whom everyone considers to be Spanish, in fact differ considerably from Spaniards in their colour and size, because they are bigger and their colour is somewhat darker as a result of the nature of the land. From this one can conclude that after many years even Spaniards who have not mixed with the natives will become like them, not simply in their bodies, but also in their spirit, for the spirit is shaped by the temperament of the body.[8]

López de Velasco's observations encapsulated many of the anxieties that overseas colonisation provoked in Europeans. As he stated, mere residence in the unfamiliar climate of the new world might transform

---

[5] Rodríguez de Almela, *Valerio de las historias escolásticas*, book 5, título 6 (p. 159).
[6] Martínez, *Reportorio de los tiempos e historia natural desta Nueva España*, p. 275.
[7] Vargas Machuca, 'Descripción breve de todas las Indias occidentales', in *Milicia y descripción de las Indias*, vol. II, p. 71.
[8] López de Velasco, *Geografía y descripción universal de las Indias*, 'De los españoles nacidos en las Indias'. Velasco here alludes to Galen's oft-cited dictum *quod animi mores* ('the faculties of the soul follow the temperament of the body').

Spaniards, body and soul, into some other sort of being. They risked becoming not only taller and darker, but also different in character. As he made clear, this transformation would be caused by the environment, not by 'mixing' with indigenous women. Many writers expressed similar concerns about the transformative effect of the new-world climate and constellations on Europeans. Spanish physician Francisco Hernández, who served as New Spain's first '*protomédico*' or chief medical officer in the same years that López de Velasco compiled his report, was one of a number who expressed comparable views. 'Let us hope that the men who are born [in Europe] and who begin to occupy those regions, whether their parents are Spanish or from some different nation, do not *in obedience to the heavens* degenerate to the point of adopting the customs of the Indians', he noted in his study of new-world *materia medica*.[9] Colonial writers were not in agreement about whether the new world's climate was intrinsically bad, but many suspected that it was unhealthy for Europeans, simply because it was different.

The clearest evidence for the deleterious impact of the American climate was provided by Amerindians themselves. Virtually all European writers believed that Amerindians had at some point in the past migrated to the Americas from the old world, although their precise place of origin and the mode of transport remained in dispute. Some maintained that Amerindians were one of the lost tribes of Israel, while others argued that they descended from the Tartars, or perhaps even from ancient Spaniards. Scholars also debated whether they had travelled to the Indies by sea or instead crossed overland from the Far East. Some writers, perplexed by the diversity of indigenous cultures, believed that different Amerindian peoples must have had different origins. Thus the ancestors of the inhabitants of Hispaniola perhaps came from Carthage, while the Peruvians might have originated in the legendary land of Ophir.[10] Evidence to support one or another position was sought in linguistic analysis, biblical exegesis and perceived

---

[9] Hernández, *Antigüedades de la Nueva España*, book 1, chap. 23 (p. 97) (my emphasis).

[10] For a pithy review of the theories current *c.* 1574 see López de Velasco, *Geografía y descripción universal de las Indias*, 'De la primera población de las Indias'. See also Cervantes y Salazar, *Crónica de la Nueva España*, chap. 2 (pp. 4–7); Herrera, *Historia general de los hechos de los castellanos en las islas y tierrafirme del mar oceano*, decade 1, book 1, chap. 6 (vol. I, pp. 269–70); García, *Origen de los indios*; Murúa, *Historia general del Perú*, book 3, chap. 1 (pp. 459–60); Torquemada, *Monarchia yndiana*, book 1, chaps. 8–11 (vol. I, pp. 24–35); Simón, *Noticias historiales*, noticia 1, chaps. 10–14 (vol. I, pp. 145–62); Salinas y Córdova, *Memorial de las historias del Nuevo Mundo*, discurso 1 (pp. 7–11); Vásquez de Espinosa, *Compendio y descripción de las Indias occidentales*, part 1, book 1 (pp. 7–30); Calancha, *Corónica moralizada*, book 1,

cultural similarities. The Jesuit priest José de Acosta for example noted that 'ignorant people commonly believe that the Indians proceed from the race of Jews because they are cowardly and weak and much given to ceremony, cunning and lying'.[11] Overall, the complexity of these debates led the Franciscan friar Gerónimo de Mendieta to dismiss the entire topic as 'extremely opaque and confusing'.[12]

One thing, however, was clear: Spaniards and Amerindians had common ancestors, since church doctrine taught that all men descended from Adam and Noah.[13] Hence it was important to explain why people who had originated in the old world now looked and behaved so differently from the Spanish. For example, Spaniards asked themselves, why did Amerindian men generally lack beards? In an extensive discussion of this question, Gregorio García, whose views on skin colour were considered in a previous paragraph, hypothesised that over time the hot climate of the new world impeded their growth. This raised the terrifying prospect that Spanish men, too, might lose their prized beards as a result of living in the same environment. Beards were considered a signal mark of manhood by sixteenth-century Spaniards. Writers insisted that they were a gift from God to beautify and adorn the male face. Beyond this, their existence correlated directly to the ability to produce semen. To lose one's beard was essentially to be unmanned.[14]

chaps. 6–7; Cobo, *Historia del Nuevo Mundo*, book 11, chaps. 11–12 (vol. II, pp. 31–6); and Lafaye, *Quetzalcóatl and Guadalupe*, pp. 139–206.

[11] Acosta, *The Natural and Moral History of the Indies*, book 1, chap. 23 (p. 69).

[12] Mendieta, *Historia eclesiástica indiana*, book 2, chap. 32 (p. 143). 'The one thing we can definitely affirm is that neither today nor in future centuries will we be able to determine by natural means from which sons or grandsons or descendants of Noah the Indians of these islands, and of Tierra Firme, and Mexico and Peru have descended', observed Reginaldo de Lizárraga (*Descripción breve de toda la tierra del Perú, Tucumán, Río de la Plata y Chile*, chap. 1, p. 4). 'It is easier to refute what is false about the Indians' origin than to discover the truth', agreed Acosta (*The Natural and Moral History of the Indies*, book 1, chap. 24, p. 71). See also Vásquez de Espinosa, *Compendio y descripción de las Indias occidentales*, part 1, book 1, chap. 5, no. 24 (p. 13); and Cobo: *Historia del nuevo mundo*, book 11, chap. 11 (vol. II, p. 32).

[13] Sahagún, *Historia general de las cosas de Nueva España*, prologue (vol. I, p. 4); Arriaga, *Extirpación de la idolatría del Piru* [1621], chap. 13 (p. 244); Avila, *Tratado de los evangelios*, vol. I, pp. 95, 295–9, 476–9; and Avendaño, *Sermones de los misterios de nuestra santa fe católica*, primera parte, sermon 4 (pp. 45–6).

[14] Huarte de San Juan, *Examen de ingenios para las ciencias*, chap. 15, part 1 (p. 326); Cárdenas, *Problemas y secretos maravillosos*, book 3, chap. 4 (p. 188); Pérez de Herrera, *Proverbios morales y consejos christianos*, book 2, enigma 8 (p. 161); Atienza, *Compendio historial*, chaps. 10, 35 (pp. 59, 133); Cadden, *The Meanings of Sex Difference*, pp. 171, 181–3; and Schiebinger, *Nature's Body*, pp. 120–5. For further discussion of the loss of the indigenous beard see Cárdenas, *Problemas y secretos maravillosos*, book 3, chap. 4 (pp. 185–9); and Ovalle, *Histórica relación del Reyno de Chile*, book 3, chap. 4 (p. 112). Spanish and indigenous sources concur that Amerindians were impressed or alarmed by the Spanish beard. See for example Las Casas, *Historia de las Indias*,

[handwritten note: as long as they ate Spanish food, they would still have their beards.]

Yet help was at hand. García affirmed that this alarming possibility was in fact remote. The new-world descendants of the Spaniards were unlikely to lose their beards, because the 'temperance and virtue that Spaniards born in the Indies inherited from their fathers and grandfathers' was continually reinforced through the consumption of Spanish food. Their constitution, he explained, was protected by 'good food and sustenance such as lamb, chicken, turkey, and good beef, wheat bread, and wine, and other nourishing foods'. This list consists almost entirely of old-world foods absent from the Indies before the arrival of Europeans. Only turkeys are indigenous to the Americas; all the other items were introduced by European settlers after 1492. Amerindian men therefore could not possibly have protected their beards from the destructive effects of the American climate, all the more so given that the foods that were available prior to the arrival of Europeans were in García's view singularly inadequate, consisting as they did of cassava, potatoes, sweet potatoes and other foods 'of very little nourishment'.[15] It was through eating this inadequate food, together with the effect of the unhealthful new-world environment, that the Indians had lost their old-world temperament. The result was the disappearance of their beards. Climate was thus important in shaping constitutions, but so too was diet.

García's belief in the transformative potential of diet was widely shared. Colonial writers throughout the sixteenth and seventeenth centuries agreed that people who travelled from Europe to the Indies were liable to undergo a variety of transformations, in accordance with the nature and celestial influence of the climate and as a result of eating new foods. In the Indies, as one writer put it, there were 'different regions, different climates, different medicines, different complexions, different foods and for this reason different subjects'.[16] A change in food, like a change in climate, was thus likely to provoke a change in character.

---

c. 1559, book 1, chap. 40 (p. 142); Yupanqui, *History of How the Spaniards Arrived in Peru*, chap. 2 (pp. 10, 18); García, *Origen de los indios*, book 2, chap. 5 (pp. 174–5); Lope de Vega, *El nuevo mundo descubierto por Cristóbal Colón*, act 3, lines 2184–5 (p. 33); Garcilaso de la Vega, *Royal Commentaries*, part 2, book 1, chap. 24 (vol. II, p. 686); and Cobo, *Historia del Nuevo Mundo*, book 11, chap. 3 (vol. II, p. 13). See also Avila, *Tratado de los evangelios*, p. 279. Some writers insisted that Amerindian men plucked out their facial hair with tweezers, which demonstrated their perversity. See for example López de Gómara, *Historia general*, chap. 26 (p. 62); and Cobo, *Historia del Nuevo Mundo*, book 11, chap. 3 (vol. I, p. 13).

[15] García, *Origen de los indios*, book 2, chap. 5 (p. 154).
[16] Miguel de Çepeda Santa Cruz, 9 Dec. 1626, Santa Fe, Archivo General de la Nación, Bogotá, Colonia Médicos y Abogados, legajo 11, fol. 853r. I am grateful to Linda Newson this reference. See also Martínez, *Reportorio de los tiempos e historia natural desta Nueva España*, tratado 3, chap. 8 (p. 283); and Huarte de San Juan, *Examen de ingenious para las ciencias*, chap. 12 (p. 239).

Diet could be controlled, but altering the climate was more difficult. If colonists in the Indies were to retain their Spanish constitution, they needed to look to their diets.

Humoral bodies

These attitudes reveal the widespread dissemination of an understanding of the human body based fundamentally on the principles of humoralism. This section sketches out its central features, for humoralism provided the framework that shaped Spanish understandings of how all bodies functioned.

Long standing European medical tradition held that good health required a balance of the four humours that governed the body: blood, phlegm, black bile and yellow bile. Each humour possessed particular qualities, being either hot or cold and either moist or dry, and was thus naturally linked to one of the four elements out of which all substances were formed. Blood was associated with hot, moist air, phlegm with cold, wet water, black bile with cold, dry earth and yellow bile with hot, dry fire. Each humour was further associated with a different season of the year, certain constellations and a variety of other categories. These may be arrayed schematically, as shown in Figure 2, which is based on a drawing from a seventh-century manuscript by Bishop Isidore of Seville.[17]

The human body was thus linked to the wider macrocosm through the doctrine of humours. Individuals possessed a particular humoral balance that helped determine their 'complexion', a term that referred equally to their character and their bodily qualities. People in whom black bile predominated were likely to be thin, dark and melancholy. Those with a predominance of blood were generally ruddy, outgoing and optimistic. Personality and physical appearance, in other words, were both manifestations of the same underlying complexion. Those in whom several humours predominated had a 'composite' complexion, in which different humours might be present in equal or unequal proportions. The system thus allowed for immense variation.[18]

Each person was born with an individual complexion, but a variety of external forces could alter their humoral makeup. Climate, or 'air', was one of these; food was another. These, together with patterns of exercise, sleeping, evacuation (which included such things as menstruation,

[17] Isidore of Seville, *De Natura Rerum*, c. 615, *Traité de la nature*, chap. 11:3 (p. 216 bis).
[18] For the basic contours of humoralism see, in addition to the sources cited below, Klibansky *et al.*, *Saturn and Melancholy*; Grangel, *La medicina española renacentista*; Siraisi, *Medieval and Early Renaissance Medicine*; and García Ballester, *La búsqueda de la salud*.

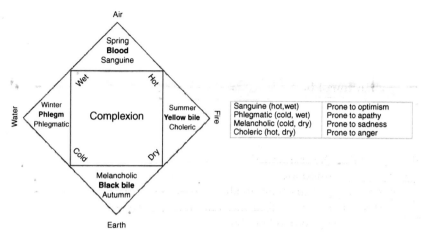

Figure 2 The humours.

purging and bloodletting, as well as excretion) and one's emotions, con-stituted the 'six non-natural things' whose impact on human health and character early modern scholars regarded as profound. Many medical treatments revolved around rectifying imbalances by modifying the influence of the non-naturals. Corrupted humours of any sort could be corrected by a bloodletting, while an appropriate purge or enema might treat an excess of yellow bile or phlegm. A melancholy disposition might respond to an adjustment in the patient's level of exercise. This signifi-cance of the six non-naturals on individual character was explained clearly by the German cosmographer Henrico Martínez, who spent a number of years in Mexico City. In his 1606 *Reportorio de los tiempos e historia natural desta Nueva España (Almanac of the Climate and Natural History of this New Spain)* Martínez asked why it was that people living under the same stars might have different complexions. The answer, he explained, was that complexion was determined by many factors, including 'the diversity of the foods with which people sustain them-selves', and their different exercise regimes and different emotional states, not to mention the fact that an individual's complexion altered during the course of their life. (The elderly were generally held to be colder and drier than the young.) These factors together explained the great variety in complexions and characters within a given region.[19]

19 Martínez, *Reportorio de los tiempos*, p. 303; Cárdenas, *Problemas y secretos maravillosos*, book 3, chap. 2 (p. 179); García, *Origen de los indios*, book 3, chap. 4 (pp. 243–6); and Cisneros, *Sitio, naturaleza y propriedades de la ciudad de México*, chaps. 9, 11, 15–17 (pp. 46r, 52r, 58v, 77–85, 108v, 114r).

Climate, in other words, was but one of a number of forces shaping the individual constitution.

As one of the six non-naturals food thus played an important role in maintaining a healthy complexion and in correcting imbalances. Indeed, for many early modern medical writers, food was the single most important factor shaping human health. The conviction that diet was the key to maintaining good health reflected long-standing medical beliefs; Aristotle had, after all, explained that food was central to health because blood, the most important fluid of all, was generated through digestion.[20] Life itself, sustained by the natural heat and radical moisture characteristic of a healthy body, was indeed entirely dependent on diet, for it was food, more than any other substance or activity, that helped maintain the body's warmth and moisture.[21] For these reasons, as the literary scholar Michael Schoenfeldt notes, 'the stomach assumed a position of particular importance in early modern regimes of mental and physical health'.[22]

Food should of course nourish the body – the best foods were those that were both easily digestible and nutritious – but it could also be used to modify and correct the complexion. In general people were advised to match their diet to their complexion; sanguine individuals, for example, should consume warm, moist foods. If, however, one's complexion needed improvement diet could provide a powerful corrective. Treatment was based on the ancient principle of *contraria contrariis curantur*: conditions are cured by their opposite. Phlegmatic people, who were excessively cold and damp, could improve their well-being by eating hot, dry foods such as black pepper. Melancholics (cold and dry, and governed by bile) were advised to eat hot, moist foods such as sugar. Food thus possessed an inherently medicinal aspect, and a change in diet, like a change in environment, could transform an individual's complexion. Men could develop a phlegmatic complexion either 'by eating phlegmy foods, or by living in a very damp region, or through being old', as the Spanish doctor Juan de Cárdenas noted in 1591.[23]

---

[20] Aristotle, *Parts of Animals*, II:iii (pp. 133–7).

[21] See for example Alvarez Miraval, *La conservación de la salud del cuerpo y del alma*, chap. 19 (p. 68r); Mexía, *Silva de varia lección*, book 4, chap. 6 (vol. II, pp. 358–66); and Vargas Machuca, *Médicos discursos y prácticas de curar el sarampion*, part 2, section 5 (p. 17).

[22] Schoenfeldt, 'Fables of the Belly in Early Modern England', p. 244. For clear and detailed analysis of the role of diet within Galenic medicine see Albala, *Eating Right in the Renaissance*; and Peña and Girón, *La prevención de la enfermedad*.

[23] Cárdenas, *Problemas y secretos maravillosos*, book 3, chap. 3 (quotation, p. 183); and Albala, *Eating Right in the Renaissance*, p. 51. 'As the philosophers say, men take on

Such transformations, however, were fraught with danger, and sudden changes of any sort were to be avoided. Spanish doctors liked to cite Hippocrates' warning that even healthy people could be harmed by an abrupt alteration in diet, and reminded readers that Aristotle himself had died from drinking cold water, rather than his usual hot beverage, while ill.[24] Only with great care should an individual use diet – or any other non-natural intervention – to alter his basic complexion, thereby acquiring a 'second nature'. Indeed, for this reason some writers argued that it was best to ensure that one's normal diet was not too limited, as otherwise the slightest disturbance in the availability of food could prove dangerous. It was better slowly to accustom oneself to a variety of foods rather than be reliant on only a handful of foodstuffs.[25]

The human body was thus in a state of continual flux, constantly responding to alterations in diet, emotion, sleeping patterns, and so forth. The complexion therefore needed to be maintained through an individualised regime of diet, exercise, purging and rest. Otherwise one humour was quite liable to transform into another, an occurrence made all the more likely by the fact that the different humours were in any event locked in a constant struggle to dominate the individual body.[26] Moreover, because of the influence of food and air on the human constitution, bodies, far from being hermetically sealed off from the outside world, were continually open to the impact of their external environment. 'All bodies are Transpirable and Trans-fluxible, that is, so open to the ayre as that it may easily passe and repasse through them', observed the English medical writer Helkiah Crooke.[27] Indeed, as Gail Kern Paster has noted in her study of humoralism in early modern England, 'solubility' was the 'sine qua non of bodily health'.[28] This

the complexion of the foods they eat', observed the novelist and physician Mateo Alemán: *Guzmán de Alfarache*, II.iii.8 (vol. V, p. 131; page reference is to the 1936 Espasa edn).

[24] Pacheco, *Question médica nuevamente ventilada si la variedad de la comida es dañosa*, p. 15; Lobera de Ávila, *Banquete de nobles caballeros*, chap. 51 (pp. 133–6); Mercado, *Diálogos de philosophia natural y moral*, dialogue 4 (p. 76v); and Albala, *Eating Right in the Renaissance*, p. 50. See also Hippocrates, 'Aphorisms', in *Hippocrates*, trans. Jones, ii.50 (vol. IV, p. 121). I am grateful to Peter Pormann for this last reference.

[25] Alvarez Miraval, *La conservación de la salud*, chap. 58 (pp. 233r–37v) and Pacheco, *Question médica*.

[26] Galen, 'On the Humours', in *Galen on Food and Drink*, p. 15; Herrera, *Obra de agricultura*, prologue (p. 6); Torquemada, *Jardín de flores curiosas*, tratado 3 (pp. 247–8); and Mercado, *Diálogos de philosophia natural y moral*, dialogue 1 (p. 9v).

[27] Crooke, *Mikrokosmographia*, p. 175; and Paster, *The Body Embarrassed*, p. 9. Or see Lobera de Ávila, *Banquete de nobles caballeros*; and Huarte de San Juan, *Examen de ingenious para las ciencias*, chap. 15, part 4, p. 367, on 'porosity' as a desirable quality.

[28] Paster, *The Body Embarrassed*, 9. See also Duden, *The Woman beneath the Skin*; and Schoenfeldt, *Bodies and Selves in Early Modern England*.

solubility, however, was capable of provoking quite dramatic transformations, such as had occurred when the ancestors of the Amerindians first migrated to the Indies. Humoral bodies were thus inherently unstable and mutable. Little wonder Spaniards in the Indies worried about their diet.

A brief history of humoralism

The origins of humoral medicine date back to the writings of ancient Greek healers, in particular Hippocrates and Galen, to whom early modern doctors constantly alluded in their own works. The corpus of Hippocratic writings – that is to say, the collection of texts by various authors produced between the fifth century BC and the first century AD and generically ascribed to the fifth-century BC physician Hippocrates – includes a very diverse range of views on medical treatment. When in later centuries writers referred to Hippocrates they generally had in mind two works: *On the Nature of Man* and *On Airs, Waters and Places*. These texts introduced the idea that good health required a balance of the four humours, and that changes in environment, diet, exercise, rest and overall attitude could alter this balance. An individualised 'regimen' aimed at correcting imbalances thus lay at the heart of Hippocratic treatment.[29] Aristotle among others developed the Hippocratic focus on the humours, which he incorporated into his general schema whereby all substances, and in particular all living things, were understood to be composed of four elements, earth, air, water and fire, which were themselves associated with the solid, the fluid, the hot and the cold. Of the humours Aristotle accorded a particular importance to blood, which he considered fundamental to determining the temperament and health of all living things.[30] Writing nearly a thousand years later Bishop Isidore of Seville reflected Aristotle's views when he asserted that the very words for health (*sanitas*) and blood (*sanguis*) were cognate so as to reflect the intimate connection between the two.[31] Blood continued to occupy a position of first among equals in early modern medicine.[32] Nonetheless, since the days of Hippocrates it was believed vital to maintain a balance between blood and the other humours.

Hippocratic ideas about humours, and much else, were further codified and interpreted by Galen, a second-century AD physician whose

[29] Hippocrates, 'Nature of Man', 'Regimen in Health', 'Humours', 'Aphorisms' and 'Regimen', in *Hippocrates*, trans. Jones.

[30] Aristotle, *Parts of Animals*, II:i–iv (pp. 107–9, 123–33, 141).

[31] Isidore of Seville, *Etymologies*, IVv4 (quotation), Xii16 (pp. 109, 232).

[32] See for example Sánchez, *Corónica y historia general del hombre*, book 2, chap. 2 (p. 99).

voluminous writings on many aspects of medicine provided the backbone for early modern humoralism. Galen, like the Hippocratic writers,
emphasised the importance of diet to the maintenance of human health,
a theme that also preoccupied Islamic healers. During the eighth to eleventh centuries humoral medicine flourished in Muslim kingdoms from
southern Spain to Persia, where scholars read and debated Greek texts
on medicine and many other topics. In particular, al-Rāzī (Rhazes)
and Ibn Sīnā (Avicenna), Persian physicians of the tenth and eleventh
centuries, greatly developed and systematised Greek humoral models. It was these scholars, along with others such as Hunayn ibn Ishāq
(Johannitius), al-Majūsī (Haly Abbas) and the Cordoban Ibn Rushd
(Averroës), who created the version of Galenic medicine that dominated medieval and early modern Europe. Avicenna's *Canon*, a collection of five books dedicated to different aspects of human health, was a
cornerstone of university education in Western Europe throughout this
period and was for this reason constantly copied and printed.[33] Rhazes,
Avicenna, Averroës and other Arab authors formed part of the corpus
of authorities whom early modern Spanish medical writers regularly
cited, alongside Galen and Hippocrates, themselves usually accessed
via translations from Arabic until the late fifteenth century. They were
joined by Christian physicians such as Arnau de Vilanova, an influential and prolific thirteenth-century Catalan doctor who taught at the
University of Montpellier, served as royal physician to three kings of
Aragon and composed dozens of widely disseminated medical texts.
Galenic medicine as it was understood in early modern Spain was thus
the creation of writers from ancient Greece, the Islamic world and
medieval Christendom.[34]

   The foundations built by these writers endured until the late seventeenth century, when new models for understanding health and the
human body began to replace the mutable humoral body. The longevity
of humoralism as an explanatory system surely owes something to that
very mutability, for as the medical historian Vivian Nutton has noted,
'it was a schema capable of almost infinite variation, unfalsifiable on
its own terms, and often corresponding to the facts of observation'.[35]
The interactions between the six non-naturals and the individual body
were indeed enormously complex – the same food might produce very

[33] Siraisi, *Avicenna in Renaissance Italy*; Conrad, 'The Arab-Islamic Medical Tradition',
   p. 115; and Peña and Girón, *La prevención de la enfermedad*, p. 70.
[34] For the contribution of Jewish physicians see Peña and Girón, *La prevención de la
   enfermedad*.
[35] Nutton, 'Medicine in the Greek World, 800–50 BC', p. 25.

different effects in different bodies, and an individual's response to the same substance would vary over the course of a single year and throughout their own lifetime. Nonetheless humoralism provided a robust system for understanding human health and character premised on an assumption of continual interaction between the body and its environment. This flexible system underpinned the ways early modern Spaniards understood both their own bodies and the bodies of the new peoples they encountered in the Indies.

Humoralism in Spain

Familiarity with humoral principles was widely disseminated among educated Spaniards in both Europe and the new world, for Catholic Spain had long engaged with the traditions of both Greek and Arab humoralism. In the eleventh and twelfth centuries Spanish scholars had played a key role in reintroducing the works of Galen and Aristotle into Western medicine by translating Arabic versions of these works into Latin, as the original Greek texts were rarely preserved in Christian libraries. At the same time, men such as the twelfth-century Gerard of Cremona began to translate the works of Avicenna and Rhazes into Latin. Gerard was based in Toledo, in the Caliphate of Cordoba, where he learned Arabic and devoted his life to translating the vast corpus of Arabic medical and scientific scholarship into Latin. Spanish scholars continued to play an important part in subsequent centuries in translating such Arabic medical texts. Catholic Spain was thus central to the dissemination of Greek and Arabic medicine across Western Europe. Not surprisingly, humoralism was firmly embedded in the medical models taught at the major Spanish universities.[36] At the University of Salamanca, established in the early thirteenth century by Alfonso IX, medicine was taught from at least the fourteenth century, and perhaps earlier. The curriculum reflected an interest in both Galenic texts and also the commentaries of Avicenna and other Arab scholars.[37] A chair of medicine was established at the University of Valencia at the

[36] See, in addition to the texts cited in subsequent footnotes in this chapter, López Piñero, *Ciencia y técnica en la sociedad española*, pp. 97–8; Grangel, *La medicina española renacentista*, pp. 41–61; Peset, 'La enseñanza de la medicina y la cirugía en el antiguo régimen'; and García-Ballester, 'The Circulation and Use of Medical Manuscripts in Arabic in Sixteenth-Century Spain', p. 184. On medieval Galenism in general see also Conrad *et al.*, *The Western Medical Tradition*; and Siraisi, *Avicenna in Renaissance Italy*.

[37] Prieto Carrasco, 'La medicina en la Universidad de Salamanca'; and García-Ballester, 'Galenism and Medical Teaching at the University of Salamanca in the Fifteenth Century', pp. 2–3.

time of its founding in 1499, and the curriculum again revolved around Avicenna and Galen; when Luis Collado took up a chair in medicine in 1547 his contract stipulated that he was to teach the works of both these scholars, for example.[38] A separate chair of Hippocratic studies was created in 1567, which reflects the growing influence of humanist medicine, with its emphasis on accessing the original Greek versions of classical medical texts, with a corresponding denigration of 'Arabised' Galenism derived from Arabic translations.[39] Indeed, in 1583 the University of Zaragoza's foundational medical statutes stated that professors must teach the works of Hippocrates and Galen, but made no mention of Avicenna or other Arab writers.[40] Notwithstanding such disputes between 'medical humanists' and 'Arabised Galenists', both accepted the fundamental framework provided by humoralism as the correct model for understanding the human body. Neither advocated a root-and-branch assault on Galenic medicine of the sort provided by the early sixteenth-century Swiss iconoclast Paracelsus, whose writings on 'chemical' medicine made little headway in the Iberian world until the last decades of the seventeenth century.[41]

Humoralism also underpinned the medical texts published in early modern Spain, which is not surprising as university-trained doctors were responsible for penning the vast majority of these works. (The historian Luis Grangel estimates that 541 such titles were printed between 1475 and 1599.[42]) Most of these works were written in Latin and were aimed at other doctors. Nonetheless, by the sixteenth century a number of vernacular health manuals were available for less learned Spanish readers who wished to understand the basic humoral principles that underpinned good health. These texts explained the all-important role of the six non-naturals in governing the body and suggested practical ways to regulate and maintain health. Sleeping first on the right-hand side, and then shifting to the left, with a final stint on the right, was regarded as most conducive to good health and digestion, for example. In regard to diet, readers were advised on what and when to eat, often in quite specific detail. Readers for instance learned that it was acceptable to dilute wine provided the ratio was not less than two parts wine to

---

[38] Grangel, *La medicina española renacentista*, p. 47.
[39] López Piñero, 'The Faculty of Medicine of Valencia'.
[40] Grangel, *La medicina española renacentista*, p. 48.
[41] López Piñero, 'Paracelsus and His Work in Sixteenth- and Seventeenth-Century Spain'; and Debus, 'Paracelsus and the Delayed Scientific Revolution in Spain'.
[42] Grangel, *La medicina española renacentista*, pp. 54–5. In the same years some 55 per cent of medical texts were printed in Latin, rather than Spanish: López Piñero, *Ciencia y técnica en la sociedad española*, p. 139.

one part water, and that the best salads combined a variety of different herbs. It was better to eat heavy, indigestible foods such as beef prior to consuming lighter, more digestible foods, rather than the other way around, and postprandial siestas were to be avoided. The dangers of overeating were constantly stressed, which in itself reveals the class of reader at which these books were aimed.

Some of these works represented entirely new compositions, with ambitions of literary quality and sometimes employing the dialogue format popular with sixteenth-century writers. Such books include Luis Lobera de Avila's 1530 *Banquete de nobles caballeros* (*The Noble Knights' Banquet*), Pedro de Mercado's 1574 *Diálogos de philosophia natural y moral* (*Dialogues of Natural and Moral Philosophy*), Francisco Nuñez de Oria's 1586 *Regimiento y aviso de sanidad* (*Regimen and Health Advice*) and Blas Alvarez Miraval's 1597 *La conservación de la salud del cuerpo y del alma* (*Conservation of Bodily and Spiritual Health*), all of which offered concrete advice grounded in humoralism, combined with learned discussions of ethics and political philosophy. Lobera de Avila's manual was reprinted a number of times, as was Nuñez de Oria's.[43] Humbler works aimed explicitly at helping men heal themselves 'without doctors when these are lacking but there is great need for them' might combine a list of specific remedies ('how you will heal a pain in the eyes and head') with a brief 'regimen' detailing the basic principles of humoral health. These regimens explained how often to take exercise, when to eat, and so on, and were often adapted freely from famous medieval health regimens, the names of whose authors usually figured prominently in the text. Particularly popular were adaptations of Arnau de Vilanova's fourteenth-century *Regimen sanitatis ad regem aragonum* (*Health Regime for the King of Aragon*), written for the Aragonese monarch Jaime II, and the medical handbook *El tesoro de los pobres* (*Treasury of Health*) ascribed to Pedro Hispano, who later became Pope John XXI.[44] Many other

---

[43] The text by Lobera de Avila was published, under a variety of titles, and in several languages, in 1530, 1531, 1542, 1551 and 1556. Nuñez de Oria's work was printed (under similarly varied titles) in 1562, 1569, 1572 and 1586. (I have cited the titles and publication dates of the particular editions I consulted.) Other examples include Jerónimo de Mondragon's 1606 Spanish translation of Arnand de Vilanova's fourteenth-century *Regimen sanitatis ad regem aragonum* (published as *El maravilloso regimiento y orden de vivir*, ed. Paniagua Arellano); López de Villalobos, 'Diálogo de las fiebres interpoladas' and 'Del calor natural', in *Libro intitulado los problemas de Villalobos que trata de cuerpos naturales y morales*; Sabuco Barrera, *Nueva filosofía de la naturaleza del hombre*; and Angeleres, *Real filosofía*.

[44] See for example *Libro de medicina llamado tesoro de los pobres*, p. iii (quotation); and Chirino, *Tractado llamado menor daño de medicina*. *El tesoro de los pobres* was printed and reprinted repeatedly; Juan Cromberger of Seville for example produced editions in 1540, 1543 and 1547. See also McVaugh, *Medicine before the Plague*, p. 145; Peña

works that were not devoted explicitly to issues of physical and spiritual health also discussed the principles of humoralism, as it formed part of the basic epistemological framework that shaped all knowledge in the early modern era. For example, Pedro Mexía's *Silva de varia lección* (*Collection of Diverse Readings*), a four-volume miscellany of instructive and entertaining facts drawn mostly from Virgil's *Georgics*, provided a clear discussion of the functioning of the four humours and their impact on the individual complexion, sandwiched between descriptions of the remarkable properties of vipers, a biography of Mohammed and other useful pieces of information. Mexía's work proved very popular and went through multiple reprintings.[45]

It is clear that ideas about the humoral body extended far beyond the university. Literate healers, whatever their academic training, could read manuals of the sort mentioned above, and there is plenty of evidence that even untrained physicians owned the works of Avicenna, in particular. Beyond this, basic humoral practices such as inspecting urine to diagnose disease or using diet to maintain good health were widely shared even by 'empirical', illiterate practitioners and by the public who consulted them. Indeed it was stipulated in the contracts that towns drew up with particular physicians that the latter would provide advice to the townspeople on diet and bloodletting, and should inspect urine, whenever requested. Ordinary people, in other words, believed these practices to be useful in maintaining good health.[46] Similarly, ideas about the causes of disease were shared by the learned and the unlettered alike. When plague struck Barcelona in 1651, the master tanner Miquel Parets reported that many people suspected that it was due in part to the position of the moon, a standard element of learned explanations of epidemic disease.[47] Spanish fishermen believed that sweating helped purge the body and maintain good health, a view with which trained doctors concurred.[48] As the medical historian José María

---

and Girón, *La prevención de la enfermedad*; and, for extensive discussion of vernacular medical texts as a genre, Solomon, *Fictions of Well-Being*.

[45] Mexía, *Silva de varia lección*, book 1, chap. 39, book 4, chap. 6 (vol. I, pp. 799–800, II:358–66). For Mexía's popularity see Fernández del Castillo, ed., *Libros y libreros en el siglo XVI*, pp. 373, 377, 390, 398, 417, 426.

[46] McVaugh, *Medicine before the Plague*, pp. 87–95, 140, 144–50, 155–6, 191–2; and Harvey, 'Oral Composition and the Performance of Novels of Chivalry in Spain', p. 90.

[47] Parets, *A Journal of the Plague Year*, pp. 23–4, 39, 41–2. The precise role of the stars in shaping health was the subject of considerable debate, as scholars sought to mesh Galenic medical models, which ascribed considerable power to astrological movements, with the Christian doctrine of free will. See Goodman, *Power and Penury*, pp. 1–49.

[48] Méndez, *Libro de ejercicio corporal*, tratado 2, chap. 10 (pp. 241–3). Or see Kagan and Dyer, eds., *Inquisitorial Inquiries*, pp. 122, 128, for lay treatment of 'salty phlegm'.

López Piñero observed, popular culture in Spain shared many suppositions with academic medicine, and folk maxims sometimes reproduced literally segments of famous Galenic texts.[49] Proverbs indeed not only endorsed basic humoral principles but also alluded directly to the central figures of Galenic medicine, while at the same time stressing the importance of diet to the maintenance of health. 'Dinner killed more people than Avicenna ever cured' runs one refrain collected in the early seventeenth century.[50] Sermons, too, disseminated ideas about the Galenic body through their frequent comparisons of sin to a bodily illness, and similar corporeal analogies.[51] Overall the idea of complexion composed of a balance of hot, cold, wet and dry, and influenced by the six non-naturals was part of the common currency of early modern Europe.[52]

Humoralism in the new world

Each bloodletting cost me a peso, and a purge ten.[53]

Humoralism was thus part of the intellectual baggage that colonists took with them to the Indies. Churchmen and other learned individuals were of course familiar with its basic principles. Indeed, Diego Alvarez Chanca, who accompanied Columbus on his second journey, probably studied medicine at the University of Salamanca and composed several medical texts in addition to an influential discovery letter.[54] Bartolomé de las Casas incorporated an extensive discussion of humoral theory, including the importance of diet, into his *Apologética historia* (*Apologetic History*), a lengthy analysis of indigenous culture and the impact of Spanish settlement.[55] Such individuals, not surprisingly, viewed nature, health and the human body in humoral terms. The *protomédico* Francisco Hernández, for example, revealed his sense of which practices should lie at the heart of medical treatment when he

---

[49] López Piñero, *Ciencia y técnica en la sociedad española*, p. 128.
[50] 'Más mató la cena que sanó Avicena': Sorapan de Rieros, *Medicina española*, pp. 95–107. 'As the wise man said, gluttony has killed many more people than has the sword': Avendaño, *Sermones*, segunda parte, sermon 24 (p. 49).
[51] García Ballester, *La búsqueda de la salud*, p. 191.
[52] For vernacular humoralism elsewhere in Western Europe see Duden, *The Woman beneath the Skin*; Lindberg, *The Beginnings of Western Science*, pp. 332–9; and Fissel, *Vernacular Bodies*.
[53] Diego Delgadillo to Juan de la Torre, 21 March 1529, Mexico, in Lockhart and Otte, eds., *Letters and People of the Spanish Indies*, p. 198.
[54] Paniagua, *El Doctor Chanca y su obra médica*, pp. 24–5.
[55] Las Casas, *Apologética historia sumaria*, c. 1552, chaps. 23–41 (pp. 72–140, esp. 73, 86, 105–6).

complained that Amerindian doctors 'at most prescribe a special diet. They never bleed anyone ... They don't understand how to adapt a remedy to the patient's specific humours.'[56] Hernández in other words took it for granted that effective, theoretically grounded medical treatment revolved around the principles of humoralism, with its emphasis on the six non-naturals and the regulation of humoral balance.

These men also imported their own libraries of medical treatises into the new world; the first professor of medicine at the University of Mexico brought over a hundred medical texts with him when he travelled to Mexico in 1562.[57] (Not surprisingly, humoralism was the central column of the medical syllabus taught at the University of Mexico and other colonial universities for the next two centuries.[58]) Similarly, members of the colonial administration consulted doctors for bloodletting and other prophylactic measures, as they would have done in Spain. Thus in 1529 Diego Delgadillo, a judge in Mexico's first Audiencia, or high court, arranged for his servants to be bled and purged a year after his arrival in Mexico, although he regarded the cost as excessive. 'Each bloodletting cost me a peso, and a purge ten,' he complained.[59] As the anthropologist George Foster has observed, in colonial Spanish America 'humoral concepts permeated the assumptions not only of physicians but of all educated and intellectual people'.[60]

In fact, in the new world, as in Spain, it was not only the highly educated who dwelt in a humoral universe. Understandings of the body based on the principles of humoralism were widely disseminated across the European and creole population. Members of the Audiencia were not the only ones who resorted to bleedings and purges when ill. Indeed one Spanish settler in the town of Tepic, in northern Mexico, observed that in such frontier regions everyone knew how to administer these basic humoral treatments.[61] (He stressed that most men could also make

---

[56] Hernández, *Antigüedades de la Nueva España*, book 2, chap. 2 (p. 110).

[57] González, 'La enseñanza médica en la ciudad de México durante el siglo XVI', p. 135. The Spanish doctor Juan Méndez Nieto similarly listed the many books he brought with him to the Indies: *Discursos medicinales*, book 2, discurso 2.

[58] Flores, *Historia de la medicina en México desde la época de los indios hasta la presente*, vol. II, pp. 71–87. For the history of medical teaching in Spanish America see Salinas y Córdova, *Memorial de las historias del Nuevo Mundo*, discurso 2 (pp. 163–82); Lanning, *The Royal Protomedicato*, pp. 34; 325–50; Risse, 'Medicine in New Spain'; Foster, 'On the Origin of Humoral Medicine in Latin America'; Foster, *Hippocrates' Latin American Legacy*, p. 152; López Piñero, *Ciencia y técnica en la sociedad española*, p. 101; and Newson, 'Medical Practice in Early Colonial Spanish America', pp. 377–86.

[59] Diego Delgadillo to Juan de la Torre, 21 March 1529, in Lockhart and Otte, eds., *Letters and People of the Spanish Indies*, p. 198.

[60] Foster, *Hippocrates' Latin American Legacy*, p. 152.

[61] Lázaro de Arregui, *Descripción de la Nueva Galicia*, chap. 16 (p. 39); and Jarcho, 'Medicine in Sixteenth Century New Spain', p. 427. See also the descriptions of

a chair, cut out a suit, castrate a steer, prepare a stew and mount a law-suit.) The Spanish captain Vargas Machuca, the author of a treatise on how to organise and run a military expedition in the Indies, similarly noted that in places where there were no doctors everyone knew how to let blood, mix medicines and administer purges. Since 'everyone is so skilled' in these matters, he explained, there was no need for his hand-book to treat the subject in any detail. He therefore concentrated on the more specific dangers posed by campaigning against Amerindians, such as poisoned arrows.[62]

Certainly it was not only trained doctors who could invoke the name of Galen. A man investigated for practising medicine without a licence in seventeenth-century Colombia assured the authorities that 'in all the cures I have effected I have always guided myself by the doctrine of Galen and other famous modern authors'.[63] Of course it was neces-sary to adapt European treatments to the specific circumstances of the Indies, but the basic model remained the same.[64] To be sure, such adaptations were sometimes viewed with suspicion by Europeans. The English priest Thomas Gage was scandalised to be prescribed a diet of roast pork after a doctor in Havana had administered a purge. As far as Gage was concerned this was completely inappropriate, for, as he pointed out to the doctor, 'the natural quality of that meat [is] to open the body'. 'I had expected some piece of mutton, or a fowl, or some other nourishing meat,' he recorded indignantly. The doctor retorted that 'what[ever] pork might work upon a man's body in other nations, it worked not there, but the contrary'.[65] Both Gage and his

medical treatment described in the emigrant letters collected in Otte, ed., *Cartas pri-vadas de emigrantes a Indias*: Hernán Ruiz to Mariana de Montedeoca, Mexico, 21 Oct. 1584; Juan de Brihuela to Pedro García, Puebla, 16 Jan. 1572; Pedro de Nájera to Diego González de Nájera, Lima, 27 March 1587; and Celedón Favalis to Simón Favalis, Los Reyes, 20 March 1587 (pp. 108, 154, 426, 432); and Fields, *Pestilence and Head Colds*.

[62] Vargas Machuca, 'Milicia indiana', in *Milicia y descripción de las Indias*, book 2 (vol. I, p. 130); and Jarcho, 'Medicine in Sixteenth Century New Spain', p. 427.

[63] Miguel de Çepeda Santa Cruz, 9 Dec. 1626, Santa Fe, Archivo General de la Nación, Bogotá, Colonia Médicos y Abogados, legajo 11, fol. 853v. For complaints about the ubiquity of such unlicensed doctors see 'R.C. que ningunas personas usen el oficio de medicina ni cirugía sin ser aprobado por el Consejo y tener para ello licencia de su majestad', Valladolid, 13 May 1538; and 'R.C. a la Audiencia del Nuevo Reino de Granada que no consienta que ninguna persona cura de cirugía ni de medicina sin que tenga los grados y licencia del protomedico', Madrid, 13 Sept. 1621; both in Konetzke, ed., *Colección de documentos para la historia de la formación social de Hispanoamérica*, vol. I, p. 183, vol. II, p. 263.

[64] Benavidez, *Secretos de chirurgia*, pp. 45–6, 52–3; Rodríguez de Almela, *Valerio de las historias escolásticas*, book 5, título 6 (p. 159); and Maravall, *Estado moderno y mentali-dad social*, vol. I, p. 476.

[65] Gage, *The English-American*, chap. 16, p. 373.

healer, in other words, felt competent to discuss and assess medical treatments.

Gage's healer, Vargas Machuca, and the other inhabitants of colonial Spanish America gained their understanding of the humoral body through a variety of means. As in Europe, sermons provided a regular opportunity to disseminate ideas about good health; priests were often quite explicit in their discussion of body management. The Dominican Pedro de Feria, for instance, explained in a published sermon that 'when a man suffers from some bodily ailment he must take a purge to expel the bad humours that cause the illness'. He continued that in like fashion, 'after a man has sinned he must take the purge of penitence to expel the sickness in his soul that is sin'.[66] Such orations thus informed listeners not only about the consequences of sin but also how to treat more mundane disorders.

In addition, doctors and other learned men published medical handbooks designed to assist literate laymen in diagnosing and treating their ailments. Mexico City, where the first printing press arrived in 1539, was a particularly important centre of publication. In contrast to the situation in early modern Spain, where more than half the medical publications were in Latin, only three of the nine medical works published in sixteenth-century Mexico were in Latin. The majority were vernacular works aimed at a lay readership. The publication of Spanish-language medical handbooks continued during the seventeenth century.[67] Such texts stated clearly that they were not aimed at learned people. Gregorio López's 1673 *Tesoro de medicina para diversas enfermedades* (*Medical Treasury for Diverse Ailments*), for example, pointed out that it was not overburdened with scholarly citations but rather confined itself to providing clear information

---

[66] Feria, *Doctrina christiana en lengua castellana y çapoteca*, pp. 101–2, 106 (quotation); Domingo de la Anunciación, *Doctrina christiana breve y compendiosa*, chap. 4 (p. 39); Sahagún, *Historia general de las cosas de Nueva España*, prologue (vol. I, p. 1); Avendaño, *Sermones*, primera parte, sermon 10 (p. 129), segunda parte, sermon 11 (p. 1); and Avila, *Tratado de los evangelios*, vol. I, p. 366. Similarly, discussions of the sin of gluttony often alluded to the corporeal harm caused by overeating: Gerson, *Tripartito del christianissimo y consolatorio doctor Juan Gerson*, n.p.; Juan de la Anunciación, *Doctrina christiana muy cumplida*, p. 187; and Baptista, *Confessionario en lengua mexicana y castellana*, p. 56.

[67] See for example Alonso López de Hinojoso's *Summa, y recopilacion de chirugia, con un arte para sa[n]grar muy util y provechosa* (1578, 1595); Agustín Farfán, *Tractado breve de medicina* (1579, 1592, 1604, 1610); Juan de Barrios, *Verdadera medicina y cirugia y astrología en tres libros* (1607); and Gregorio López, *Tesoro de medicina* (1673). (The titles of these works vary slightly from edition to edition.) See also Guerra, *Iconografía médica mexicana*; and Somolinos d'Ardois, 'Los impresos médicos mexicanos (1553–1618)'.

for non-medical readers. The book nonetheless explained the division of substances into hot, cold, wet and dry, and other elements of basic humoral theory. Juan de Barrios's 1607 manual provided a helpful description of how to identify different humoral complexions. The popularity of such works is attested by their frequent reprinting. Editions of Agustín Farfán's *Tractado breve de medicina* (*Brief Medical Treatise*), which offered practical advice on how to treat ailments ranging from impotence to toothache, were produced in 1579, 1592, 1604 and 1610.

Often these works reveal an intriguing blend of European humoralism with titbits drawn from indigenous medicine, despite the suspicion with which many religious and medical authorities viewed Amerindian healing practices. López's book, for example, explained that fever could be cured either with the juice of bitter oranges combined with sugar (two old-world ingredients), or a mixture of maize, cacao and 'alosuchitl flower', all of which were indigenous to Meso-America.[68] Indeed, ailing settlers regularly employed indigenous healers, to the disgust of licensed doctors, and resorted to semi-magical healing rituals whose potentially heretical content alarmed the Inquisition. These practices reveal clearly the continued vitality of indigenous medical models in colonial society, and also indicate that indigenous and African women, in particular, were widely believed to possess dangerous occult powers.[69] Inquisition records, however, make clear that colonists – and indeed at times the healers themselves – often understood these treatments to operate in accordance with the basic corporeal model provided by humoralism. Magical rituals worked to expel evil substances ('bad air', 'bad humours' or, in the worst case, a demon) from the body through

[68] 'Alosuchitl' was perhaps *yolloxóchitl* (*Talauma mexicana*), or *eloxóchitl* (*Magnolia schieleana*), both remedies mentioned in the *Codex Badianus*, a 1552 herbal composed by an indigenous Mexican. See López, *Tesoro de medicina*, p. 20; the Aztec herbal from the collection of Cassiano dal Pozzo, RCIN 970335, Royal Library, Windsor Castle; and Badiano, *An Aztec Herbal*.

[69] The intersection of European and indigenous medical norms is a complex and contentious topic. For discussion focusing on central Mexico see López Austin, *Human Body and Ideology*; Hassig, 'Transplanting Medicine'; Ortiz de Montellano, *Aztec Medicine, Health and Nutrition*; López Austin, 'Equilibrio y desequilibrio del cuerpo humano, las concepciones de los antiguos nahuas'; Foster, *Hippocrates' Latin American Legacy*; and Gimmel, 'Reading Medicine in the Codex de la Cruz Badiano'. For the role of women in illicit medicine see Behar, 'Sexual Witchcraft, Colonialism, and Women's Powers', pp. 190, 196–7; Few, *Women Who Lead Evil Lives*; Lewis, *Hall of Mirrors*, pp. 119–21; Silverblatt, 'The Black Legend and Global Conspiracies'; and Bristol, *Christians, Blasphemers, and Witches*, pp. 149–89.

purges and bleedings, as well as through prayers and incantations, and revealed the body to be essentially open to the influence of the external environment in much the same fashion as did more academic medicine. Supernatural illnesses might be due to a curse, but curses and spells were effective because they interfered with the body's normal humours and flows.[70]

In short, in colonial Spanish America, as in early modern Europe, the humoral body underpinned both popular and learned under-standings of health and character among the settler population. In the view of colonists, bodies were porous and mutable, in constant dialogue with their surrounding environment. They were very far from stable.

'They are delicate and feminine and of weak complexion'

Humoral theory thus provided a coherent and familiar model for explaining why Indian bodies and the bodies of Spaniards resident in the Indies were different, despite the common environment. They differed because they lived under different exercise regimes (Indians were generally acknowledged to be more active), and, critically, because they ate different foods. Spanish and creole writers regularly contrasted the typical Spanish diet with that of 'the Indians', whose varied eat-ing practices were usually homogenised into an imprecise amalgam of Caribbean and Meso-American customs, from which they drew con-clusions about the origins of the indigenous character.

Two features of the indigenous diet attracted particular attention. First, it lacked all the structural elements of the Iberian diet: wheat bread, wine, oil and meat. Chapter 2 explores the symbolic resonance of these absent foods in greater detail; here let us note simply that Spaniards invariably drew attention to the fact that Indians lacked them. In add-ition, Europeans very often remarked on the frugality of the indigenous diet. European dietary manuals and the Catholic church both warned against overeating, albeit for different reasons, and whatever their other

---

[70] See for example López de Gómara, *Historia general*, chap. 83 (p. 156); Del Río, *Investigations into Magic*, book 3, part 1, sect. 5 (p. 127); Ovalle, *Histórica relación del Reyno de Chile*, book 1, chap. 2 (pp. 21–3); Aguirre Beltrán, *Medicina y magia*, pp. 85, 87; Few, *Women Who Lead Evil Lives*, pp. 78, 80, 83 (although both Aguirre Beltrán and Few draw the opposite conclusion from my own); and Caciola, 'Mystics, Demoniacs, and the Physiology of Spirit Possession'.

flaws Amerindians were generally acknowledged to be free of the vice of gluttony. Referring to Mexican Indians the author of one chronicle noted that 'they subsist on very little food, and eat the least of all the people in the world'.[71] Spaniards, writers agreed, ate in a single day what an Indian would eat in four.[72]

Amerindians' willingness to forgo meat attracted particular comment, probably because for Catholics abstaining from meat was associated with fasting and self-deprivation. The *protomédico* Francisco Hernández, for example, observed that Amerindians in New Spain 'easily forgo meat and most content themselves with some tortillas spread with a chilli sauce, to which they usually add the fruit of a certain species of solanum called *tomamo* [tomato]'.[73] Amerindians in Guatemala were able to work for an entire week on a few dry tortillas, reported the seventeenth-century creole chronicler Francisco Antonio de Fuentes y Guzmán, who added, 'I know of no other nation as frugal as they'.[74] Those in Chile could subsist for many days on some maize flour, salt and chillies.[75] The Jesuit chronicler José de Acosta summed up the situation: the indigenous diet was 'beyond frugal'.[76] For the Spanish such restraint was all the more notable given that frugality was one of the virtues Spaniards consistently claimed as their own. As the historian and cosmographer Pedro de Medina boasted in his 1595 *Grandezas y cosas notables de España* (*Grandeurs and Notable Things of Spain*), 'the vice of gluttony has blighted Spain less than other provinces [of Europe]. On the contrary in most parts of Spain even among the richest gentlemen

---

[71] Anonymous Conquistador, 'Relación de algunas cosas de la Nueva España', 1556, in García Icazbalceta, ed., *Colección de documentos para la historia de México*; Motolinía, *Historia de los Indios de la Nueva España*, 1541, tratado 1, chap. 14, in García Icazbalceta, ed., *Colección de documentos para la historia de México*; Simón, *Noticias historiales*, noticia 1, chap. 12 (vol. I, p. 156); Cook and Borah, 'Indian Food Production and Consumption in Central Mexico Before and After the Conquest', p. 162; and Baudot, 'Amerindian Image and Utopian Project', p. 384.

[72] Peña Montenegro, *Itinerario para parochos de indios*, book 2, tratado 1, prologue; book 4, tratado 5, section 6 (pp. 142, 457).

[73] Hernández, *Antigüedades de la Nueva España*, book 1, chap. 12 (p. 71); and López Medel, *De los tres elementos*, pp. 207–8. For the rules governing fasting see Molina, *Confessionario mayor en la lengua mexicana y castellana*, pp. 66–8; Ripalda, *Doctrina cristiana*, pp. 24–5; Juan de la Anunciación, *Doctrina christiana muy cumplida*, pp. 127–32; Baptista, *Advertencias para los confessores de los naturales*, pp. 25–31; Belarmino, *Declaración copiosa de las quatro partes mas esenciales, y necesarias de la doctrina christiana*, p. 126; and, for very detailed discussion, Peña Montenegro, *Itinerario para parochos de indios*, book 4, tratado 5 (pp. 453–63).

[74] Fuentes y Guzmán, *Historia de Guatemala o Recordación Florida*, book 8, chap. 1 (vol. I, p. 288).

[75] Ovalle, *Histórica relación del Reyno de Chile*, book 3, chap. 3 (p. 110).

[76] Acosta, *De procuranda indorum salute*, book 3, chap. 20, section 2 (vol. I, p. 549).

Figure 3 Felipe de Guaman Poma y Ayala, 'The exaggerated size and stature of Spanish men and women, "great gluttons"', 1615–16. Guaman Poma, an indigenous chronicler and artist, depicts a pair of enormous Spaniards. Spaniards regarded themselves as restrained eaters, and were astonished by the fact that indigenous people ate even less than they did. Guaman Poma, in contrast, presents Spaniards simply as gluttons.

we find notable parsimony and temperance.'[77] The Indians were thus more abstemious than the most abstemious people in Europe. (See Figure 3.) Settlers often complained, however, that this abstemiousness

[77] Medina, *Primera y segunda parte de las grandezas y cosas notables de España*, part 1, chap. 11, fol. 10v; Alemán, *Guzmán de Alfarache*, part 1, book 3, chap. 10 (La Lectura/ Espasa-Calpe edn, vol. III, p. 18); Botero Benes, *Relaciones universales*, part 1, book 1 (p. 3); Herrero García, *Ideas de los españoles del siglo XVII*, p. 59; and Díez Borque, *La sociedad española y los viajeros del siglo XVII*, pp. 73–82.

? not self-indulgent

did not extend to alcohol, in contrast to Spaniards, who were not only restrained eaters but also proverbial for their sobriety.[78] This distinctive indigenous diet was offered as an ad hoc explanation for the indigenous complexion from the earliest days of the conquest. The inhabitants of the Caribbean, noted the Italian Michele da Cuneo, who accompanied Columbus on his second voyage, were 'cold people, not very lustful', which, he felt, was 'perhaps a result of their poor diet'.[79] Cuneo thus provides an early example of the view that Indians were either phlegmatic or melancholic, the complexions associated with cold. Learned men indeed generally categorised Amerindians as phlegmatic, which made them similar to women. Writers only occasionally distinguished among Amerindians, according different temperaments to different indigenous groups.[80] Spaniards, in contrast, were typically

[78] For Spanish sobriety see Durán, *Historia de las Indias de Nueva España*, vol. I, pp. 201–2; Nuñez de Oria, *Regimiento y aviso de sanidad*, pp. 9r, 16v, 19r; Recarte, 'Tratado del servicio personal y repartimiento de los indios de Nueva España', p. 363; Medina, *Primera y segunda parte de las grandezas y cosas notables de España*, part 1, chap. 11, p. 10v; Wadsworth, *The Present Estate of Spayne*, p. 74; Herrero García, *Ideas de los españoles del siglo XVII*, pp. 59–61; Taylor, *Drinking, Homicide, and Rebellion in Colonial Mexican Villages*; and Martin, 'National Reputations for Drinking in Traditional Europe'. For indigenous drunkenness see for example Acosta, *De procuranda indorum salute*, book 3, chaps. 20–2 (vol. I, pp. 545–73); López de Gómara, *Historia general*, chap. 35 (p. 73); Pedro de Ribera and Antonio de Chaves, 'Relación de la ciudad de Guamanga y sus territorios', 1586; and Pedro de Carbajal, 'Descripción fecha de la provincia de Vilcas Guaman' and 'Relación de la provincia de las Collaguas', 1586; both in Jiménz de Estrada, ed., *Relaciones geográficas de las Indias: Perú*, vol. I, pp. 187, 206, 330–1; Peñaloza y Mondragón, *Libro de las cinco excelencias del español*, p. 123; and Taylor, *Drinking, Homicide, and Rebellion*.

[79] Cuneo, 'News of the Islands of the Hesperian Ocean', 1495, p. 58.

[80] For Amerindians as phlegmatic see Cervantes de Salazar, *Crónica de la Nueva España*, book 1, chap. 16 (p. 30); Hernández, *Antigüedades de la Nueva España*, book 1, chap. 23 (p. 97); López de Velasco, *Geografía y descripción universal de las Indias*, 'Descripción de la Audiencia de la Nueva España y declaración de la tabla procedente'; 'R.C. pidiendo relación sobre que se ha advertido que los religiosos de la Compañía de Jesús querían hacer colegios', Madrid, 25 May 1583, in Konetzke, ed., *Colección de documentos para la historia de la formación social de Hispanoamérica*, vol. I, p. 550; Atienza, *Compendio historial*, chaps. 3, 35 (pp. 29–30, 131 but see also 132); 'Relación de la ciudad de Guamanga y sus terminos', 1586, in Jiménez de la Espada, ed., *Relaciones geográficas de las Indias: Perú*, vol. I, p. 185; Mendieta, *Historia eclesiástica indiana*, book 3, chap. 17, book 4, chap. 21 (pp. 222, 438); Ore, *Symbolo catholico indiano*, p. 30r; Vargas Machuca, 'Descripción breve de todas las Indias occidentales', in *Milicia y descripción de las Indias*, vol. II, p. 92; García, *Orígen de los indios*, book 2, chap. 5 (pp. 160, 163); Vásquez de Espinosa, *Compendio y descripción*, part 1, book 2, chap. 13, no. 171 (p. 50); and Calancha, *Corónica moralizada*, book 1, chap. 9 (p. 64). For Amerindians as melancholy see Durán, *Historia de las Indias de Nueva España*, vol. I, prologue (p. 5); Cisneros, *Sitio, naturaleza y propriedades*, chap. 17 (p. 112r, but see also 112v); Matienzo, *Gobierno del Perú*, p. 16; Murúa, *Historia general del Perú*, book 2, chap. 4 (p. 351); Cobo, *Historia del Nuevo Mundo*, book 11,

labelled choleric.[81] Indians, noted Ruy Díaz de Islas, a Spanish doctor who composed an early tract on the treatment of syphilis, were 'delicate and feminine and of weak complexion', and invariably died before reaching the age of forty, a situation he attributed entirely to their inadequate diet:

They do not have the habit of eating meat, as there was none in that land aside from some little animals like rabbits, which were not enough for everyone anyway, and some parrots, and as a result they ate fishes and worms that grow in the earth, and they didn't have any wine and for this reason they died so young.[82]

He noted that in contrast 'we Spaniards are of a hardier complexion, being raised on hearty foods such as meat and wine and wheat bread and hearty things'. Their different diets explained their different complexions.

chap. 4 (vol. II, pp. 15–16); and Simón, *Noticias historiales*, noticia 1, chap. 12 (vol. I, p. 156). For comparisons between Amerindians and women, see for example Díaz de Isla, *Tractado contra el mal serpentino*, fol. 40; García, *Origen de los indios*, book 2, chap. 5 (p. 161); and Lewis, 'The "Weakness" of Women and the Feminization of the Indian in Colonial Mexico'. For dissenting views or the attribution of a distinctive complexion to a particular indigenous group see Las Casas, *Historia de las Indias*, c. 1559, book 1, chap. 164 (p. 433); and Las Casas, *Apologética historia sumaria*, c. 1552, chap. 37 (p. 124); Benavidez, *Secretos de chirurgia*, pp. 26–7; Martínez, *Reportorio de los tiempos*, pp. 262, 281; Lázaro de Arregui, *Descripción de la Nueva Galicia*, chap. 11 (p. 26); Ovalle, *Histórica relación del Reyno de Chile*, book 3, chap. 3 (p. 110); and Rocha, *El origen de los indios*, p. 215.

[81] Cárdenas, *Problemas y secretos maravillosos*, book 3, chaps. 1–2 (pp. 175, 179); Calvete de Estrella, *Rebelión de Pizarro en el Perú y vida de D. Pedro Gasca*, book 2, chap. 5 (vol. I, p. 230); Medina, *Primera y segunda parte de las grandezas y cosas notables de España*, part 1, chap. 11 (p. 10r); Mendieta, *Historia eclesiástica indiana*, book 3, chap. 17, book 4, chap. 21 (pp. 222, 438); Ore, *Symbolo catholico indiano*, p. 30r; Martínez, *Reportorio de los tiempos*, pp. 262, 281; Cisneros, *Sitio, naturaleza y propriedades*, chap. 17 (p. 112v); Suarez de Figueroa, *El passagero*, p. 9; Mme d'Aulnoy, *Relation du voyage d'Espagne*, letter 3 (vol. I, p. 106); Kupperman, 'Fear of Hot Climates in the Anglo-American Colonial Experience', p. 215; and Herrero García, *Ideas de los españoles*, pp. 94–5, 97. On the differences between the Spanish and indigenous complexions see also Calancha, *Corónica moralizada*, book 1, chap. 10 (p. 68); and Vetancurt, *Teatro mexicano*, tratado 1, chap. 6 (p. 12).
 Some writers argued that Spaniards, despite being hot and dry (the qualities associated with the choleric temperament) were nonetheless of a melancholy disposition, for melancholia was an extremely complex condition that could result from a variety of humoral conditions. See Botero Benes, *Relaciones universales*, part 1, book 1 (p. 3); Joly, 'Voyage en Espagne', pp. 606–10; Pérez de Herrera, *Proverbios morales*, enigma 259 (p. 142); Klibansky *et al.*, *Saturn and Melancholy*; Herrero García, *Ideas de los españoles*, p. 65; Díez Borque, *La sociedad española y los viajeros del siglo XVII*, pp. 60–2; Soufas, *Melancholy and the Secular Mind in Spanish Golden Age Literature*; and Hillgarth, *The Mirror of Spain*, pp. 532–3.
[82] Díaz de Isla, *Tractado contra el mal serpentino*, fols. 39–40.

The importance of diet, alongside climate, in differentiating Spanish bodies from indigenous bodies was explained with great clarity by Diego Andrés Rocha in his 1681 treatise on the 'origin of the Indians'. Rocha, a Spaniard who taught law at the Peruvian University of San Marcos, and also served on the Audiencia de Lima, advanced the view that Amerindians were descended from ancient Spaniards who had travelled to the new world in the remote past. Given their common ancestry Rocha needed to explain why it was that Amerindians now differed so dramatically from Spaniards. Drawing heavily on the analysis provided a century earlier by the Dominican priest Gregorio García, he argued that this was due to 'the variation in places, climates, airs and foods,' which, he wrote,

caused this change in colour, size, gestures and faces among Americans, who did not conserve the colour of the first Spaniards who came to these Indies ... because their ancestors enjoyed different climates, different waters, different foods, which at first were not very nourishing, and it was a great achievement that they did not die of hunger until such time as they managed to cultivate fruits and other forms of food, and this is what caused the variation among peoples and in colour in accordance with the doctrine of Plato.[83]

Rocha stressed that alterations provoked solely by a change in climate occurred extremely slowly. Thus these ancient Spaniards' transformation into 'toasted and discoloured' Indians was not caused simply by the new climate, but rather by 'the lack of protection from the weather, bad foods, and over a long period'. For this reason alone creoles remained white, despite their lengthy residence in the new world. In any event, their European complexion was continually reinforced, because 'they are all raised with much care and protection and with good foods, which was not the case with the Indians and those who first came to this America'.[84] Good food trumped climate.

A change in climate could thus be managed through careful attention to diet, but the same could not be said for a change in diet. The latter, Rocha stressed, could have devastating consequences for the individual complexion, and for this reason it was essential for creoles and Europeans living in the Indies to eat appropriately. Eating the wrong food and living unprotected in the American environment had turned ancient Spaniards into Indians, and contemporary Spaniards should

---

[83] Rocha, *El origen de los indios*, p. 212. Or see Cárdenas *Problemas y secretos maravillosos*, book 3, chaps. 2, 3, 9, 11 (pp. 179, 184, 210, 219); and García, *Origen de los indios*, book 2, chap. 5, book 3, chap. 4 (pp. 148–76, 243–54). Rocha probably had Plato's *Timaeus* in mind, although neither here nor elsewhere does Plato offer an explanation for the diversity of skin colours.

[84] Rocha, *El origen de los indios*, pp. 213–14.

take care not to repeat the mistakes of their ancestors. 'Here we have seen very white men from Spain', Rocha warned, 'who, on withdrawing into the hills and eating maize and other Indian dainties, return so toasted that they resemble Indians.'[85]

As Rocha explained, food was vital to maintaining the distance between Spaniards (and creoles) and Indians. It was through eating the wrong foods that ancient Spaniards had turned into toasted and discoloured Indians, and without access to European food modern Spaniards too would sooner or later turn into Indians. European food was therefore the principal bulwark protecting the Spanish body from the rigours of the American climate. For this reason it was also the principal force preventing Spaniards from turning into Indians. 'Race', in other words, was in part a question of digestion.

Practical humoralism

These were not purely theoretical concerns of interest solely to medically trained writers. European explorers constantly complained that they fell ill when they could not eat familiar foods, and conversely asserted that only the restoration of their usual diet would heal them. Recall Columbus's 1494 letter to the Catholic monarchs with which this book began, which ascribed the demise of Spanish settlement on Hispaniola to the combined effects of climate, hunger and unfamiliar food. This in fact was the most common explanation for the fiasco in Hispaniola. The admiral's son Fernando, for example, insisted that the settlers were 'made ill by the climate and diet of that country'.[86] The Dominican priest, chronicler and political agitator Bartolomé de las Casas agreed. In his account of the settlement he recorded that the settlers fell sick because of the 'change in air and the very different location … to which must be added the rationing of supplies, which were distributed according to a strict rota, as they were brought from Spain. As for the local foods, because they were so different from ours – especially the bread – there was no hope that our men could tolerate them, and as a result they began to fall ill'.[87] Indeed, he explained, sickness among the settlers was virtually inevitable, given the region's 'more subtle air and thinner waters and different foods, all of which, in short, were so distinct from our own'.[88]

---

[85] Rocha, *El origen de los indios*, p. 212. On the yellow colour of *indianos* see also Mariscal, 'The Figure of the *Indiano*', 57.
[86] Columbus, *Life of the Admiral Christopher Columbus*, p. 122.
[87] Las Casas, *Historia de las Indias*, c. 1559, book 1, chap. 88 (p. 254).
[88] Las Casas, *Historia de las Indias*, c. 1559, book 1, chap. 154 (p. 405).

In his own discussion of the disastrous settlement in Hispaniola the Spanish chronicler and colonial official Gonzalo Fernández de Oviedo agreed that the high European death toll was due primarily to the change in diet. Oviedo, a native of Madrid, travelled to the Caribbean in the early sixteenth century to take charge of the gold-smelting operations underway in the Spanish colony of Santo Domingo. During the next three decades he composed a lengthy history of the new world, in which he drew on both his many years' residence in the Caribbean and the access to state documents made possible by his eventual appointment as Charles V's official chronicler of the Indies. The result, Oviedo's *Historia general y natural de las Indias* (*General and Natural History of the Indies*), is an idiosyncratic work that covers matters ranging from Magellan's circumnavigation of the world to the qualities of the armadillo.[89] Among many other topics it considers the reasons why the initial settlement on Hispaniola proved so unsuccessful.

In Oviedo's view the fundamental problem on Hispaniola was that 'the foods and bread of Spain are more substantial than the herbs and bad eating that they like over there'. As a consequence, the health of the settlers was so compromised that even those who survived to return to Spain died shortly thereafter.[90] He summed up the dangerous features of the new world as follows:

Beyond the incongruity that the heavens there have with those of Europe (where we were born), and the influence of the differences in the airs and vapours and nature of the land, we found in these parts no foods that were like those that our fathers gave us: the bread – of roots, the fruits – wild or unknown and unsuitable for our stomachs, the water – of a different flavour, the meats – there were none on [Hispaniola], beyond those mute rodents or a few other animals, and all very different from those of Spain.[91]

Unlike university-trained writers, Oviedo did not frame his analysis with references to Galen or Hippocrates. (Oviedo's education derived from his sojourns in various princely courts in Italy, rather than formal study.) Rather, he presented his observations as the outcome of first-hand experience in the new world, which taught him that the air, water and food of the Americas were not suited to European bodies.

[89] Gerbi, *Nature in the New World*, pp. 195, 129–406; and Myers, *Fernández de Oviedo's Chronicle of America*.

[90] Fernández de Oviedo, *Historia general y natural de las Indias*, book 2, chap. 13 (vol. I, p. 49); and López de Gómara, *Historia general*, chap. 22 (p. 57).

[91] Fernández de Oviedo, *Historia general y natural*, book 5, chap. 8 (vol. I, p. 134). Conquistadors, he noted, were obliged to 'fight in such different airs and in such strange regions, and with such different foods': *Historia general y natural*, book 23, chap. 3 (vol. II, p. 358).

Sixteenth-century Europeans indeed consistently claimed that direct experience demonstrated that the indigenous diet was unhealthy and dangerous (at least for Europeans). The conquistador Bernardo de Vargas Machuca thus reported matter-of-factly that leaders of expeditionary forces in the Indies should avoid recruiting recent arrivals from Spain, because, being unfamiliar with 'the constellation of the land [and] ... its foods', they were likely to grow sick and die.[92] The governor of the small Spanish settlement at Santa Elena, in Florida, likewise believed that reliance on new-world foods was responsible for the sickness that plagued the colony. Insisting that his subjects' shattered health would be restored only by a return to their usual diet, he arranged for supplies of wheat flour, wine and olive oil to be sent from Spain.[93] And even when they did not die Spaniards who relied on new-world foods were liable to suffer disagreeable physical disturbances that reflected serious perturbations in their underlying complexion. Madrileño Celedón Favalis regarded it as a great achievement to have stayed healthy during his journey across Panama, given that he had been forced to rely on hearts of palm and other dangerous forest fruits, but his luck ran out when he boarded ship for Peru. The voyage was beset by difficulties and the passengers were exposed to continual rainfall and reduced to eating maize tortillas, a food Favalis described as entirely unsuitable for Europeans. Specifically, it provoked fevers, a pimply rash and swellings. As a result, by the time he arrived in Lima, he informed his father in a letter from 1587, 'my body was one enormous sore'.[94] The Jesuit

---

[92] Vargas Machuca, 'Milicia indiana', in *Milicia y descripción de las Indias*, book 2 (vol. I, p. 115). Calvete de Estrella, *Rebelión de Pizarro*, book 2, chap. 5 (vol. I, p. 228) similarly noted that foods in new world were 'so insubstantial, and so different from those on which Spaniards are raised, and the nature of the air in Spain is so unlike that of this land of Peru, that those [Spaniards] who managed to escape in good health from Tierra Firme became so debilitated and sick that many of them died, and those who survived were very enfeebled and unfit for the heavy demands imposed by warfare in Peru, until they had recovered and become accustomed to its food and climate'.

[93] Petition of Pedro Menéndez Márquez, San Agustín, 15 June 1578; and Instructions for Rodrigo de Junco, San Agustín, 17 June 1579; both in Connor, ed., *Colonial Records of Spanish Florida*, vol. II, pp. 74, 234. Sailors claimed that bread made from maize or cassava made them ill: Super, 'Spanish Diet in the Atlantic Crossing', pp. 61, 69. Medical writers in Spain presumably drew in part on such reports for their own pronouncements about the dangers posed by new-world foods. Francisco Nuñez de Oria for example recorded in his 1586 dietary manual that 'that root called cassava, from which the Indians make bread, is mortal poison to those from these parts who navigate over there': Nuñez de Oria, *Regimiento y aviso de sanidad*, pp. 7v, 42r–v. The Spanish naturalist Nicolás Monardes similarly blamed the 'noughtie meates and ... raw waters' of the new world for the illnesses afflicting Spaniards in the Indies: Monardes, *Joyfull News out of the New-found Worlde*, p. 46.

[94] Celedón Favalis to Simón Favalis, Los Reyes, 20 March 1587, in Otte, ed., *Cartas privadas de emigrantes a Indias*, pp. 432–3. His fever was also due in part to constant

chronicler Bernabé Cobo, who lived for many years in Peru, summed up the situation. The Indies simply lacked 'foods suitable to sustain a Spaniard'.[95]

Wet nurses

Particularly clear evidence of the dangerous effects of new-world foods on the European constitution was offered by children suckled by indigenous wet nurses. The use of indigenous and enslaved women to nurse creole children was widespread in the Indies. Just as in Europe, all but the poorest families aspired to employ plebeian women as wet nurses. (That nursing women were advised to refrain from all sexual relations surely contributed to the popularity of wet nursing, particularly given that children were often breastfed for up to two years.) Wet nursing was nonetheless a contentious topic in both Europe and the Americas. Breast milk was a powerful substance, believed to consist of a purified form of blood. Its composition therefore reflected the lactating woman's own humoral balance.[96] To nurse from another's milk was essentially to imbibe their humours. For this reason it was widely believed that children took on the qualities of those from whom they nursed. As the Spanish doctor Blas Alvarez Miraval explained, it was largely from breast milk that children derived their 'good or bad habits, their good or bad complexion, their cleverness or doltishness, and their laudable or evil inclinations'.[97] Writers recounted stories of women nursed by dogs who were unable to restrain themselves from eating vomit, of men nursed by pigs who were given to rolling in the mud, and similarly bizarre and undesirable consequences of ingesting the wrong sort of milk. These effects made themselves felt in animals as well; sheep fed with goat's milk had coarser wool.[98] In the case of creole children nursed by indigenous or black women the effect was to endow these children with indigenous or African characteristics.

---

exposure to rain and inadequate sleeping arrangements. Explorers on Hispaniola were reported to turn an unpleasant yellow colour, a consequence of eating lizards and other 'bad and unfamiliar food': López de Gómara, *Historia general*, chap. 22 (p. 57).

[95] Cobo, *Historia del Nuevo Mundo*, book 10, chap. 1 (vol. I, p. 375).

[96] Pineda, *Primera parte de los 35 dialogos familiares de la agricultura cristiana*, dialogue 5, section 10 (vol. I, p. 115r); Alvarez Miraval, *La conservación de la salud*, chap. 9 (p. 33v); Fragoso, *Cirugía universal*, book 1, chap. 21 (p. 22); and Nieremberg, *Curiosa y oculta filosofía*, 'Oculta filosofía', book 1, chap. 65 (p. 267).

[97] Alvarez Miraval, *La conservación de la salud*, chap. 10 (p. 37r–v).

[98] Bergmann, 'Milking the Poor', p. 100; and Alvarez Miraval, *La conservación de la salud*, chaps. 9–10 (pp. 32r–38v).

Discussing the consequences of nursing a creole boy with indigenous or African breast milk, the Spanish Dominican Reginaldo de Lizárraga complained:

How will this boy turn out? He will adopt the inclinations that he absorbed from the milk on which he was nursed, and he will become like the person with whom he associated, as we see occurring every day. He who is nursed on lying milk becomes a liar. He who drinks drunken milk becomes a drunkard, and thieving milk, a thief.[99]

He recommended that for this reason the use of indigenous and black wet nurses be prohibited altogether. Writing at the turn of the seventeenth century, another Spanish priest commented that boys raised on Indian milk 'differ little from Indians'.[100] A few decades later the bishop of Popayán observed that everyone could tell the difference between Spaniards and 'those who are raised on the milk of those Indian women'. The latter, he felt, were less suitable for holding priestly office than Spaniards raised on 'good milk'.[101] Drinking indigenous breast milk provoked clear and undesirable constitutional changes, in other words.

Indigenous breast milk, like maize, was an intrinsically new-world foodstuff. Indeed, in some sense it was itself a derivative of maize, or cassava, or whatever substance formed the bulk of the nurse's diet, for the maize that nourished the woman was converted by the digestive process into blood, and hence into breast milk. Indigenous breast milk was essentially a super-concentrated form of maize (or cassava, potato, etc.). Concern over the deleterious impact of indigenous wet nurses thus reflects not simply the anxiety that these women would teach their bad habits to the children they raised. Much more seriously, colonists worried that the very nature of their children's bodies would be transformed through the ingestion of this profoundly indigenous foodstuff. In any event customs and constitution were inseparably linked; both derived, ultimately, from the individual's humoral balance. As the Guatemalan creole Francisco Antonio de Fuentes y Guzmán explained, immoral wet nurses inevitably transmitted both their humours and

---

[99] Lizárraga, *Descripción breve de toda la tierra del Perú*, p. 101; and Lavallé, *Las promesas ambiguas*, p. 48. Or see Acosta, *De procuranda indorum salute*, book 4, chap. 8, section 3 (vol. II, p. 69).

[100] Miguel de Sigüenza to the king, Manila, 24 May 1605, Archivo General de Indias, Audiencia de Filipinas, legajo 84, N. 132, fol. 3; and Lavallé, *Las promesas ambiguas*, pp. 48–9.

[101] Diego de Montoya Mendoza to Cristóbal de Moscoso, Popayán, 20 May 1635, Archivo General de Indias, Audiencia de Quito, lejano 78, N.45, fol. 2; and Lavallé, *Las promesas ambiguas*, pp. 49.

their habits to their offspring. 'We see that this milk not only corrupts and contaminates the humours but also corrupts and twists the habits and inclinations,' he observed.[102] The fear that creole children would become like their indigenous nurses, like the fear that Spaniards who subsisted on new-world starches would lose their beards, reflects the intimate relationship early modern Europeans perceived between diet and the individual constitution. Too close a familiarity with new-world foodstuffs, whether indigenous breast milk or cassava, was dangerously transformative for the European body.

Conclusions

There were thus many reasons for Spaniards to worry about what would happen to their bodies in the new world. The porous humoral body was vulnerable to the powerful influence of unfamiliar foods, just as it was subject to the astrological and climatic forces exerted by the stars and the air. A sudden change in either was liable to induce possibly fatal illness. Equally worryingly, even when it did not cause sickness, either was apt to provoke serious and unwelcome changes in the individual constitution. Travel to the Indies subjected the European body to both. It thus posed a substantial challenge to the European complexion. As one medical writer put it, 'going to the Indies is contrary to the human constitution'.[103]

Little wonder, then, that settlers viewed new-world foods such as maize and cassava with suspicion. Indeed, the theories regarding the origins of the Amerindian population provided alarming lessons about the consequences of an exclusively American diet, for it was an unfortunate combination of air and food that was held to have converted choleric, bearded Europeans into phlegmatic, beardless Amerindians. Yet while debates about the origins of the indigenous population may have been confined largely to the educated elite, fears about the practical impact of eating new-world foods were not. As we saw, writers with no medical training whatsoever regarded new-world foods as un-nourishing, and blamed them for the ill health that often struck settlers. Many sources reveal that colonists considered a diet based on new-world foods potentially damaging, and that they preferred to eat the old-world foods 'that our fathers gave us' whenever possible. Nor was it only scholars who

---

[102] Fuentes y Guzmán, *Historia de Guatemala*, book 8, chap. 2 (vol. I, p. 296); Lizárraga, *Descripción breve de toda la tierra del Perú*, p. 102; and Gemelli Careri, *Voyage du tour du monde*, vol. VI, book 1, chap. 3 (p. 35).

[103] Nuñez de Oria, *Regimiento y aviso de sanidad*, p. 7v.

believed that Spaniards would begin to transform into Amerindians if they ate the wrong foods. By way of conclusion we might consider the experiences of Jerónimo de Aguilar.

Aguilar was born in Andalusia in the late fifteenth century and travelled to the Indies sometime in the early sixteenth century. In 1511 he was sailing from Panama towards Santo Domingo when his ship was caught in a storm and foundered off the Yucatan Peninsula. Aguilar, along with several companions, was captured by local Maya Indians, with whom he lived until 1519, when he was rescued by Hernán Cortés. Following his return to Spanish society, Aguilar was offered European food, but, to the surprise of his rescuers, he ate only sparingly. When asked why he was so moderate he explained that 'after so much time he was accustomed to the food of the Indians, and his stomach would regard Christian food as foreign'.[104] Long residence among the Indians had left his stomach unable to tolerate a normal Christian diet. His digestive system had gone native; in humoral terms, he had acquired a 'second nature', and as a result, his body was not quite as Christian as it had been prior to his shipwreck. He had begun to turn into an Indian. It was to avoid such calamities that the Spanish settlers in Santa Elena, Florida, grew wheat and garbanzos alongside maize, and that writers recommended that when travelling to the Indies men would be wise to bring their own food, 'because neither wheat bread nor wine is to be found in those parts'.[105] The next chapter examines such efforts to reproduce the Spanish diet in the new world.

---

[104] Cervantes de Salazar, *Crónica de la Nueva España*, book 2, chap. 26 (p. 114). I am grateful to Deborah Toner for this reference.
[105] Benavidez, *Secretos de chirurgia*, p. 36.

'I myself would much prefer a piece of bread'

Spaniards knew that they did not want to eat the maize, cassava and other 'herbs and bad eating' that the Indies offered to settlers. These insubstantial, dangerous foods were simply not nourishing for Europeans. Instead, they longed for the healthful old-world foods they and their fathers had eaten, which suited the European constitution and savoured of civilisation itself. The colonial archive reveals the many efforts by Spanish settlers to replicate their old-world diet in the unfamiliar conditions of the new world. This chapter examines these efforts. Over the last decades scholars have become increasingly interested in European reactions to the wealth of new foodstuffs they encountered on arriving in the Americas, and the impact of new-world foods such as tomatoes, potatoes and chocolate on diets around the world is an area of innovative, ongoing research.[1] The introduction of barley and cabbages into Peru has, perhaps understandably, attracted less attention. Nonetheless, for most settlers, the successful cultivation of old-world crops in the new-world was a thousand times more important than the introduction of chocolate into Europe, and there were many who would have swapped all the pineapples in the world for a regular supply of wheat bread and red wine. The attractions of such old-world foods far exceeded their taste or even palatability. In his 1590 *Historia natural y moral de las Indias* (*Natural and Moral History of the Indies*) the Jesuit priest José de Acosta described how wheat imported from Spain

---

[1] See for example Fussell, *The Story of Corn*; Foster and Cordell, eds. *Chilies to Chocolate*; Smith *The Tomato in America*; Coe and Coe, *The True History of Chocolate*; Fresquet Febrer *et al.*, *Medicinas, drogas y alimentos vegetales del Nuevo Mundo*; Long, ed., *Conquista y comida*; Garrido Aranda, ed., *Los sabores de España y América*; Mazumdar, 'The Impact of New World Food Crops on the Diet and Economy of China and India'; Gallagher and Greenblatt, 'The Potato in the Materialist Imagination'; Jamieson, 'The Essence of Commodification'; McCann, *Maize and Grace*; Norton *Sacred Gifts, Profane Pleasures*; and Gentilcore, *Pomodoro!*. See in addition the pioneering Salaman, *History and Social Influence of the Potato*; and Crosby, *The Columbian Exchange*.

tended to deteriorate during the transatlantic voyage. The grain was inclined to spoil and as a result the imported flour was 'so damp that the bread has hardly any taste'. Nonetheless, he affirmed, 'I myself would much prefer a piece of bread no matter how hard or black it was'.[2] This chapter interprets the efforts of settlers to obtain wheat bread, olive oil, cabbages and other old-world foods, and begins to unravel the complex significance Spaniards ascribed to the success of these efforts. Further unravelling occurs in subsequent chapters.

'Day-old bread, fresh meat and aged wine keep your health fine'[3]

Early modern Spaniards knew what they wanted to eat. They wanted to eat wheat bread, with olive oil, fresh lamb and red wine. They were partial to a salad at the start of a meal, and they liked to finish their collation with a pear, some olives or perhaps a fig or two.[4] From the other side of the Atlantic colonists yearned for these old-world foods and waxed lyrical about the ingredients that made up the ideal Iberian meal. Wheat, wrote the Spanish doctor Francisco Hernández, was a 'wonderful find and gift from Mother Nature as precious as health itself'.[5] The grapevine was the 'most beneficial and necessary plant introduced and planted by the Spanish in the New World', in the view of Jesuit writer Bernabé Cobo.[6] Meat, in turn, was absolutely vital. 'Spanish people ... cannot survive without the sustenance provided by meat', insisted one viceroy.[7] Bread, wine, oil and meat provided proper nourishment for the body, and were the basis of health. 'Bread gives strength, flesh builds flesh and the rest creates blood', as the saying went.[8]

---

[2] Acosta, *Natural and Moral History of the Indies*, book 4, chap. 17 (p. 200). On *el marearse* see José Tudela de la Orden, 'Economía', in Tudela de la Orden, ed., *El legado de España a América*, vol. II, p. 680.

[3] Sorapan de Rieros, *Medicina española*, p. 36: 'Pan de ayer, carne de hoy, y vino de antaño, traen al hombre sano.'

[4] My composite meal is drawn from *Libro de medicina llamado tesoro de los pobres*, p. xxvi; Lobera de Avila, *Vergel de sanidad*, esp. pp. lviiiv–lxr; Nuñez de Oria, *Regimiento y aviso de sanidad*, pp. 229v–236r; Mercado, *Diálogos de philosophia natural y moral*, dialogue 4; Dadson, 'The Road to Villarrubia'; Pérez Samper, *La alimentación en la España del siglo de oro*, pp. 69–83; and Chabrán, 'Medieval Spain'.

[5] Hernández, 'Maize', in *The Mexican Treasury*, p. 111.

[6] Cobo, *Historia del Nuevo Mundo*, book 10, chap. 13 (vol. I, p. 391). Olives, in turn, were 'of universally acknowledged utility': book 10, chap. 14 (vol. I, p. 393).

[7] Carta del Virrey Marqués de Villmanrique to the king, Mexico, 20 July 1587, Archivo General de Indias, Audiencia de México, legajo 21, N. 19, fol. 10.

[8] Leon Pinelo, *Question moral*, part 2 (p. 47): 'El pan da fuerça, la carne carne, i lo demas sangre.'

These were essentially the same foods that the inhabitants of the Iberian Peninsula had aspired to eat in the first century AD. Catholic Spain's culinary models were largely inherited from the Greco-Roman world, in which wheat, wine and oil had constituted not only the most prestigious foodstuffs but also the very essence of civilisation. As the historian Massimo Montanari has noted, for the ancient Greeks 'grain and wine made the eater and drinker human – to the extent that for Homer the term "bread eaters" was synonymous with the word for men'.[9] In addition, stock-rearing, widespread in Roman Iberia, gave lamb, pork, goat and beef a dietary importance they perhaps lacked in Greece and Italy, and meat continued to feature prominently in the ideal Iberian diet during the Middle Ages in both Christian and Muslim Spain.[10] In his seventh-century encyclopaedia Bishop Isidore of Seville noted that 'ordinary meals' consisted of two parts: bread and wine, on the one hand, and on the other, meat or fish. He observed that bread, in particular, accompanied all meals and that 'all living creatures crave it'.[11] To lack bread was to be hungry, and wheat bread, along with wine, olive oil and a bit of meat or poultry, were what Catholic Spaniards wished to eat. These foods were redolent of health, of civilisation and of Christianity. Bread was without doubt the central, structuring element of any proper meal, and when made from wheat was universally accepted as healthy and nutritious. It was, proclaimed Gabriel Alonso de Herrera in his 1513 agricultural manual, 'more suitable for people to eat than bread made with any other grain'.[12] Just as wheat bread was the fundamental food, so wine was the essential drink.[13] Wine to begin with was supremely healthful and nourishing, as it most closely resembled blood.[14] Indeed, Bishop Isidore claimed that the reason wine was called

[9] Montanari, 'Food Systems and Models of Civilization', p. 71.

[10] Carlé, 'Alimentación y abastacimiento'; and Butzer, 'Cattle and Sheep from Old to New Spain'.

[11] Isidore of Seville, Etymologies, X.xii.15 (p. 396). On the deep longing for the elusive wheat bread, and the many substitutes invented by impoverished Europeans, see Camporesi, Bread of Dreams.

[12] Herrera, Obra de agricultura, book 1, chap. 12 (p. 32); Barrios, Verdadera medicina y cirugía, book 1, chap. 2 (p. 41bisv); Pineda: Primera parte de los 35 dialogos familiares de la agricultura cristiana, dialogue 5, section 9 (vol. I, p. 113r); Leon Pinelo, Question moral, part 2 (pp. 46–7); Albala, Eating Right in the Renaissance, p. 67; Nuñez de Oria, Regimiento y aviso de sanidad, pp. 61r–73v; Peña and Girón, La prevención de la enfermedad, p. 196; Montanari, 'Food Systems and Models of Civilization', p. 75; and Galen, 'On the Powers of Food', book 1, in Galen on Food and Drink, ed. Grant, pp. 78–108.

[13] 'If [bread] is the principal food, then [wine] is the principal drink ... Thus eating and drinking is bread and wine': Leon Pinelo, Question moral, part 2 (pp. 47–8).

[14] Albala, Eating Right in the Renaissance, pp. 74, 121; Camporesi, Bread of Dreams, pp. 30, 32; and Lobera de Avila, Vergel de sanidad, p. xxr.

vino in Latin was that it replenished the veins or *vena* with blood.[15] Early modern Spanish texts are full of encomia to wine, which was praised for its healthful, medicinal effects, provided it was drunk in moderation. 'Well-tempered wine', explained one author, 'rectifies and repairs all humours. It restores blood in those who lack it, cheers the melancholy and helps eliminate melancholia, dispels and destroys phlegm, humidifies the choleric temperament and helps purge yellow bile.'[16] Every possible complexion benefited from this wholesome beverage. Immoderate consumption of wine came in for universal criticism – the examples of Noah and Lot were cited frequently – but most writers agreed that Spaniards were less prone to the vice of drunkenness than other Europeans, and even those most outspoken in their condemnation of inebriation generally refrained from recommending total abstinence.[17] Far from being a menace to health, wine was practically a medical necessity. 'To deprive an old man or a youth of a little wine', observed one colonial official, 'is to send him straight to the grave'.[18]

More importantly, grape wine, like wheat flour, was a symbol of Christianity itself. These were the substances that through the mystery of the Mass were transformed into the very body and blood of Jesus Christ. Indeed, they were the only substances capable of undergoing this transformation. From the Middle Ages Catholic doctrine required that Communion be celebrated using only wheat bread and grape wine. Thomas Aquinas stated clearly in his thirteenth-century *Summa Theologica* that 'the proper matter for this sacrament is wheaten

---

[15] Isidore of Seville, *Etymologies*, X.xiii.2 (p. 397).

[16] Mexía, *Silva de varia lección*, book 3, chap. 16 (vol. II, p. 104, quotation); Las Casas, *Apologética historia sumaria, c.* 1552, chap. 32 (p. 106); Enriquez, *Retrato del perfecto médico*, dialogo 3, p. 169; Acosta, *De procuranda indorum salute*, book 3, chap. 22, section 2 (vol. I, p. 569); and Sánchez-Moscoso Hermida, 'Concepto científico de nutrición en un texto médico del siglo XVI', p. 230.

[17] Wine, proclaimed a seventeenth-century priest, 'is not a bad but rather a good thing, which God created, along with water, to succour mankind': Avendaño, *Sermones*, segunda parte, sermon 24 (p. 49). See also Villalón, *El scholástico*, book 2, chap. 16 (pp. 161–4); Herrera, *Obra de agricultura*, book 2, chap. 30 (pp. 92–3); Herrera, *Real filosofía*, p. 109; Mexía, *Silva de varia lección*, book 3, chaps. 16–18 (vol. II, pp. 101–23); Peñaloza y Mondragón, *Libro de las cinco excelencias del español*, pp. 141–4; Mercado, *Diálogos de philosophia natural y moral*, dialogue 4; and Torres, *Philosophia moral de príncipes*, book 11 (pp. 459–501). For Spanish sobriety see Salazar, *Veinte discursos sobre el credo*, discurso 16, chap. 5, p. 200; Mme d'Aulnoy, *Relation du voyage d'Espagne*, letter 8 (vol. II, pp. 116–17); Herrero García, *Ideas de los españoles del siglo XVII*, pp. 59–61; and, from the colonies, Durán, *Historia de la Indias*, vol. I, pp. 201–2; Mendieta, *Historia eclesiástica indiana*, p. 139; and Recarte, 'Tratado del servicio personal y repartimiento de los indios de Nueva España', p. 363. Díaz de Isla, *Tractado contra el mal serpentino*, fols. 37–8 is unusual in praising complete abstinence.

[18] Carta de Tomás López Medel, 25 March 1551, Archivo General de Indias, Audiencia de Guatemala, legajo 9A, R. 18, n. 77, fol. 1.

bread ... [and] only wine from the grape'. He explicitly ruled out the use of other grains such as barley, notwithstanding their frequent use in ordinary breads. Pomegranate or mulberry wine was similarly disqualified, despite the fact that, as Aquinas acknowledged, grapevines did not grow in all countries.[19] The Catholic church's position on the composition of the Eucharist was thus clear: only wheat and grape wine had the potential to become the body of Christ.

Grape wine was therefore, in the words of one Mexican friar, 'a most noble, useful, and necessary drink', because Christ chose it to transform into 'His most precious blood'.[20] The seventeenth-century jurist Juan de Solórzano Pereira agreed that wine 'is considered to be most worthy, for it merited conversion into the blood of Christ'.[21] (See Figure 4.) And just as wheat bread was of all breads the most nourishing for the corporeal body, so the 'bread of doctrine' sustained the Christian community.[22] The close connections between the heavenly bread and wine of the Mass and earthly wheat bread and grape wine were made explicit in many sermons and doctrinal texts. As the Augustinian priest Joan Baptista explained in his confessional manual:

[A]ll the good effects that wheat bread and grape wine work in man's body, these same effects and many more are wrought by Holy Communion in the soul that is worthy to receive this sacrament. Accordingly, just as wheat bread sustains, nourishes, heals and delights us, so this divine sacrament does all these things, and many more, for the soul that receives it with grace.[23]

As Baptista made clear, the Communion wafer was the precise spiritual equivalent of wheat bread, and each worked in similar ways to ensure health in body and soul. Wheat bread and grape wine, essential to the execution of the most important of Catholic mysteries, were therefore powerful emblems of Catholic identity, in addition to being structural elements of the Iberian diet. Olive oil, too, had a religious

---

[19] Aquinas, *Summa Theologica*, third part, question 74. Other theological texts and church legislation confirmed the necessity of wheat flour and grape wine for the celebration of this sacrament. See Rubin, *Corpus Christi*, pp. 37–49.

[20] Taylor, *Drinking, Homicide, and Rebellion*, p. 41. Or see Peña Montenegro, *Itinerario para parochos de indios*, book 3, tratado 6, section 3 (p. 349); and Leon Pinelo, *Question moral*, part 2 (pp. 46–7).

[21] Solórzano Pereira, *Política indiana*, book 2, chap. 9, section 40 (vol. I, p. 99).

[22] For 'el pan de la doctrina' see Acosta, *De procuranda indorum salute*, book 1, chap. 2, section 5 (vol. I, p. 95). Christian doctrine, explained the Franciscan friar Maturino Gilberti, is 'a most delicious daily bread': *Thesoro spiritual de pobres en lengua de Michuacan*, p. 12.

[23] Baptista, *Confessionario*, p. 83. Compare this with the Calvinist view discussed for example in Frisch, 'In Sacramental Mode', p. 85. For the relationship between earthly and heavenly bread see Bynum, *Holy Feast and Holy Fast*, pp. 31–69.

Figure 4 *Christ as the Mystic Vine*, seventeenth century. A grapevine laden with fruit grows from Christ's heart up over the cross. Christ is shown pressing the grapes into a chalice, in a graphic depiction of the Eucharistic miracle that converts wine into his blood.

significance, for consecrated olive oil was used for Baptism and other sacraments.[24]

Of course not everyone in Spain actually ate these things. To begin with, the highly esteemed wheat bread was not universally consumed. Certainly wheat was the major grain grown in early modern Spain; in 1587, for example, it constituted over 60 per cent of the total cereal and

---

[24] Beyond this, as the Spanish doctor Blas Alvarez Miraval observed, olive oil was 'very agreeable to the stomach': *La conservación de la salud*, chap. 11 (p. 41r).

legumes crop in Old Castile.[25] Nonetheless, it was beyond the reach of many Spaniards. Poorer people ate barley, oats and rye, the last described as sticking in a damaging fashion to the stomachs of those unused to it.[26] And they might accompany their rye bread not with lamb or chicken, but with a stew based on garbanzos or some lowly vegetable. Plants such as onions or turnips that grew under the ground were particularly suited to peasants, rather than individuals higher up the Great Chain of Being, whose foods should come from correspondingly elevated locations such as the top of a tree.[27] 'I have here an onion, and a little cheese, and I don't know how many crusts of bread,' says Sancho Panza to Don Quixote, 'but these are not victuals suitable for a knight as valiant as your grace'.[28] Beyond this, not everyone even ate bread. As the historian James Casey noted, many Old Castilians were reliant on 'gruel and porridge rather than bread' – on boiling rather than baking their rye, millet or barley'.[29] In Valencia and parts of Catalonia, in turn, rice formed a significant part of the diet, sometimes mixed with rye or other grains. Rice, like aubergine, was nonetheless seen as suspiciously Moorish.[30] The geographical limits of olive cultivation moreover meant that olive oil was much more widely used in Andalusia than in the more northern parts of Spain.[31] Wine was perhaps more universally consumed, but many people drank theirs heavily watered.[32] Meat, even for those who could afford it in the first place, was rarely the roast lamb or chicken that medical writers recommended as best matching the human complexion. Many Spaniards could afford only a little bacon or salt pork.[33]

[25] García Sanz, *Desarrollo y crisis del antiguo régimen*, p. 108; and Vassberg, *Land and Society*, p. 201.

[26] Herrera, *Obra de agricultura*, book 1, chap. 12 (p. 33); and Braudel, *The Mediterranean and the Mediterranean World*, vol. I, pp. 570–1, 588–9.

[27] Grieco, 'The Social Politics of Pre-Linnaean Botanical Classification'.

[28] Cervantes, *Don Quijote*, part 1, chap. 10 (p. 74); Carlé, 'Alimentación y abasticimiento', p. 279; and Ife, *Don Quixote's Diet*. Onions, explained a doctor, were a 'food for rustics': Sorapan de Rieros, *Medicina española*, p. 242. Cheese was, however, suitable as an *amuse-bouche* for the elite: Pérez de Herrera, *Proverbios morales*, enigma 73 (p. 110).

[29] Casey, *Early Modern Spain*, p. 35; and Moncada, *Restauración política de España*, 'Mudanza de alcabala util al rey', chap. 6 (p. 39v). García Sanz, *Desarrollo y crisis del antiguo régimen*, p. 109, insists that even in times of hardship most people in Castile were eating wheat.

[30] Agustí, *Libro de los secretos de agricultura*, p. 220; and Peset and Almela Navarro, 'Mesa y clase en el siglo de oro español', pp. 252–3.

[31] Carlé, 'Alimentación and abasticimiento', pp. 254, 280–2.

[32] Vicens Vives, *An Economic History of Spain*, p. 250.

[33] Lobera de Avila, *Banquete de nobles caballeros*, chap. 15 (pp. 49–52); Barrios, *Verdadera medicina y cirugía*, book 1, chap. 2 (p. 41bisv); Allard, 'Le corps vu par les traités de diététique dans l'Espagne du siècle d'or'; and Peña and Girón, *La prevención de la enfermedad*, pp. 199–214.

Yet while diet effectively differentiated the rich from the poor it also marked out other important divisions. In the Iberian Peninsula plebeian pork possessed a strong Catholic resonance, for neither Jews nor Muslims were permitted to eat it. A character in one of Lope de Vega's plays thus explains that he has hung a side of bacon on his wall 'so that the King will know that I am neither a Moor nor a Jew'.[34] Islamic teaching, moreover, forbade the consumption of any form of alcohol – although this prohibition was widely ignored, as the many Arabic paeans to wine composed in medieval Andalusia attest. As Massimo Montanari has noted, bread and wine, which had previously defined Mediterranean culture, came, along with pork, to symbolise a more specific Christian identity. Popular proverbs thus warned that too much fresh pork and young wine would send 'little *Christians*' straight to the grave.[35] Indeed, the refusal to eat pork was regarded as strong evidence of crypto-Judaism. Summoned before the Inquisition, desperate individuals insisted that they regularly ate bacon and the other meats 'which Catholics are accustomed to eat and which are forbidden to Jews'.[36] In other words, although these foods were not actually eaten by the whole of Catholic Spain, they were by 1500 powerful symbols of that culture. Such wholesome, high-status foods were what Spanish Catholics aspired to eat.

Such things were all the more important in the Indies, where the Spanish body was subjected to unfamiliar air, water and stars, and was therefore in special need of sustaining foods. Writers great and small constantly stressed the dangers posed by travel, both because of the changes it imposed on an individual's daily routine and also because of the sadness that was assumed to afflict anyone far from their natal soil, a state which was itself liable to induce illness. Sadness, after all, had long been recognised by Galenic medicine as a significant threat to health. As the Spanish jurist Juan de Solórzano Pereira, who himself spent many years in the Indies, observed, experience provided ample evidence of the 'illness, harm and death that usually result from leaving the climate and place where we were born and raised'. Love of homeland, he continued,

[34] Lope de Vega, *El primer rey de Castilla*, 1598–1603, act 3, in *Obras completas de Lope de Vega*, p. 378; and Perceval, 'Asco y asquerosidad del morisco'.
[35] Sorapan de Rieros, *Medicina española*, p. 339 (my emphasis). 'Puerco fresco, y vino nuevo, cristianillo al cementerio.'
[36] Beinart, ed., *Records of the Trials of the Spanish Inquisition in Ciudad Real*, vol. III, pp. 27, 97, 398, 442 (quotation), 451, 454, 457, 606, 614, 615, 628, 630, 652; Montanari, 'Food Models and Culinary Identity', p. 191; Vassberg, 'Concerning Pigs, the Pizarros, and the Agro-Pastoral Background of the Conquerors of Peru'; Río Moreno, 'El cerdo'; Root, 'Speaking Christian', pp. 127–9; Fernández García, 'Criterios inquisitoriales para detectar al marrano', pp. 488, 495–6; Graizbord, *Souls in Dispute*, pp. 38–9; and Kagan and Dyer, eds., *Inquisitorial Inquiries*, p. 132.

was so powerful that for many illnesses the only cure was for the patient to return home to breathe its restorative air.[37] Nostalgic expatriates were thus in particular need of familiar, sustaining foods.

It is a notable feature of Spain's early colonial expansion that it occurred in a moment in which Spanish writers were placing particular emphasis on the deep love that individuals naturally felt for their *patria*.[38] In contrast to earlier truths that had affirmed, in the words of a Roman saying, 'ubi bene ibi patria' (home is wherever one is happy), early modern thinkers increasingly insisted that travel away from one's homeland was a deeply unpleasant experience. Spaniards were thus embarking on overseas travel on an unprecedented scale at a time when conventional wisdom affirmed that prolonged absence from home was likely to induce almost unbearable homesickness. Of course great things could not be expected from those timorous souls who remained for ever at home, but venturing overseas was nonetheless recognised as an emotionally wrenching experience.[39] The affective ties that bound Spaniards to their homeland were considered so powerful that the Augustinian order abandoned its practice of allowing prelates to designate individuals to serve as missionaries, and instead determined that only men who actively sought to travel to distant parts should be sent to Asia and the new world, because even an oath of religious obedience should not compel a man to exile himself from his homeland.[40] The pain that was caused by being away from one's homeland was the subject of considerable discussion, with many writers concluding that it posed nearly as serious a risk to travellers as did changes in food, air and water.[41]

The familiar foods of home were thus doubly medicinal, for in addition to being well suited to the Spanish body they might also help

---

[37] Solórzano Pereira, *Política indiana*, book 2, chap. 8, section 42 (vol. I, p. 88); and Herrera, *Historia General*, decade 1, book 2, chap. 10 (vol. I, p. 324).

[38] For this process in Spain see Maravall, *Estado moderno y mentalidad social*, vol. I, pp. 468–76.

[39] Diego Pérez to Manuel Pérez, Panamá, 10 April 1573, in Otte, ed., *Cartas privadas de emigrantes a Indias*, p. 248; Peter Martyr to Juan Bautista de Anglería, 15 May 1488, in *Epistolario*, p. 25; Suarez de Figueroa, *El passagero*, p. 1; Salinas y Córdova, *Memorial*, p. 19r; Pérez de Herrera, *Proverbios morales y consejos christianos*, book 1, tratado 2 (p. 14); and Maravall, *Estado moderno y mentalidad social*, vol. I, p. 459.

[40] Grijalva, *Crónica de la orden de N.P.S. San Agustín*, book 1, chap. 4 (p. 27).

[41] 'The love that men feel for the land where they were born or raised forms part of their very nature ... and wise men even say that there are certain ailments that can afflict men far from the land where they were born and raised that can be cured only by returning to that land. This is because their complexions suit the air of the place where they were raised and different airs can and do make men ill; and this affects even the dead, for they say that cadavers rest more easily in the lands where their forefathers are buried than in any other', insisted Diego Rodríguez de Almela in a frequently reprinted text, *Valerio de las historias escolásticas*, book 5, título 6 (p. 159).

remedy the sadness that men far from home were likely to experience.
For the same reason slave traders, concerned for the health of their
valuable human property, made efforts to supply familiar food such as
plantains, rice, yams and couscous (often manufactured from maize) to
slaves, particularly those who were already weakened by illness. Such
measures were important, as melancholy sadness was acknowledged to
be a condition to which enslaved people, not surprisingly, were prone.
It was generally believed that providing slaves with customary foods
reduced mortality both on board ship and after arrival in the Indies,
although such concerns were often curtailed by the desire to maximise
profits.[42] Travelling Spaniards and enslaved Africans alike were liable
to fall victim to the dangerous effects of homesickness, and could alike
benefit from restorative familiar foods.

In the case of Spaniards, it was not simply that these foodstuffs helped
maintain the individual complexion. Such foods helped give them a
specifically *Spanish* complexion. Food helped make Spaniards Spanish
in several ways. To begin with, it was of course important in forging
the emotional bonds that linked a man to his homeland. Writers rhapsodised about the love individuals naturally felt for the place 'where
their body gained the strength to take its first steps, whose air formed
their first breath, *where they ate their first meals*, where they spent their
childhood and where in youth they studied and exercised'.[43] Food's significance to the construction of a specifically Spanish identity, however, transcended this general affective relationship between person
and place. As early modern Spanish writers insisted, diet, and the six
non-naturals more generally, not only explained the particular contours
of the individual complexion, but also determined the ways in which
Spaniards, as a group, differed from the inhabitants of other states and
kingdoms. Drawing on standard Galenic principles the Spanish physician Juan Huarte de San Juan for example explained (in the words of
his sixteenth-century English translator) that men differed one from

See also Bermúdez de Pedraza, *Antigüedad y excelencias de Granada*, p. 146; Maravall,
Estado moderno y mentalidad social, vol. I, p. 476; Sánchez, *Corónica y historia general del
hombre*, book 1, chap. 44 (pp. 47–8); and Casey, *Early Modern Spain*, p. 194. A man's
homeland 'is always in his heart, calling out to him', wrote Alonso Rodríguez from
Popayán to his brother, who lived near Toledo: Alonso Rodríguez to Juan Rodríguez,
Popayán, 4 Feb. 1578, in Otte, ed., *Cartas privadas de emigrantes a Indias*, p. 355.

[42] Sandoval, *De Instauranda aethiopum salute*, p. 107; Newson and Minchin, 'Diets, Food
Supplies and the African Slave Trade', pp. 533–6; Eltis *et al.*, 'Agency and Diaspora
in Atlantic History', pp. 1345–7; and Carney and Rosomoff, *In the Shadow of Slavery*,
pp. 68–9.

[43] Suarez de Figueroa, *El passagero*, pp. 1–2 (my emphasis); and Maravall, *Estado moderno y mentalidad social*, vol. I, p. 478.

another 'by reason of the heat, the coldness, the moisture, and the drouth, of the territorie where men inhabit, of the meats which they feed on, of the waters which they drink, and of the aire which they breath'. He then observed that these factors explained why Spaniards differed from Frenchmen.[44]

It was precisely in this period that the idea of a transcendent Spanish identity was beginning to emerge in the Peninsula. The Spanish state was itself under construction during the sixteenth and seventeenth centuries, and the forces driving the successive incorporation of different regions into the control of the crown of Castile had little to do with any sense of incipient nationalism. Nonetheless, despite the absence of a fully formed 'Spanish' state, the Catholic residents of the Peninsula were beginning to articulate a common identity as Spaniards which complemented, rather than replaced, regional affiliations. Thus by the early seventeenth century, the Castilian monarch Isabel I was described as having been the queen of *Spain*.[45] This common identity did not necessarily entail a desire to unite the various kingdoms into a common state, but did imply a sense of common purpose (in particular, opposition to religious heresy) and a certain shared identity that transcended regional boundaries. Thus during the early modern era the Catholic inhabitants of different parts of the Iberian Peninsula came to regard certain characteristics (sobriety, arrogance, gallantry) as typically 'Spanish' even as they affirmed that substantial differences separated, say, the Andalusian from the Galician.[46] This shared identity was reflected in the newly invented category of 'natives of the kingdom of Spain', which synthesised several older, previously separate legal categories, as the historian Tamar Herzog has shown. Natives of the kingdom of Spain were residents not only of Castile but also of Aragon and the other regions of Hapsburg Spain. It was to such people that writers alluded when they referred to *españoles*. The experience of overseas colonisation further strengthened the sense of a common Spanish identity. In Herzog's words, 'a common Spanish nativeness, which included all natives of all Spanish kingdoms, originated in Spanish America sometime at the end of the sixteenth century'.[47] Settlers indeed often failed to distinguish between the precise origins of different colonists, describing

---

[44] Huarte de San Juan, *Examen de Ingenios, or The Examination of Mens Wits*, pp. 21–2; and, for an example of Huarte's influence, García, *Origen de los indios*, book 3, chap. 4 (p. 244–5). Or see Lemnius, *The Touchstone of Complexions*, book 1 (pp. 25–31).

[45] Botero Benes, *Relaciones universales*, part 1, book 4 (p. 134).

[46] Herrero García, *Ideas de los españoles del siglo XVII*. See also Maravall, *El concepto de España en la Edad Media*; and Maravall, *Estado moderno y mentalidad social*, vol. I.

[47] Herzog, *Defining Nations*, esp. pp. 50, 54, 65 (quotation), 97, 207.

all equally as Spaniards (and Christians) – although at other times such differences might occasion bitter rivalry. In Spain itself, writers referred proudly to the overseas exploits of the Spanish – or Castilians, a term which was becoming increasingly synonymous with 'Spaniard' – without further differentiation. In short, during this period a concept of 'Spaniard' gained currency among the residents of the Peninsula and the Indies even if it did not entirely replace other identities.[48]

When early modern writers insisted that Spaniards differed from Frenchmen, they affirmed this particular vision of Spanishness, which resided in a set of shared attributes, and which derived from an at least hypothetically common culture. This common culture gave all Spaniards certain common characteristics, shaped their bodies and minds, and moulded their particular complexion. Spanishness, in other words, was as much a bodily as a political condition, and as such was in part the result of a particular diet, whose special, and superior, qualities writers were explicit in praising. As the Franciscan writer Buenaventura Angeleres observed proudly of Spain, 'if we consider its vegetables, they are of greater virtue and effectiveness than those of other parts of Europe, as we can see in its bread, wine and oil'.[49] Bread, wine and olive oil were thus markers of a Christian identity, and *Spanish* bread, wine and oil helped make men Spanish. These foods were, moreover, wholesome, nourishing and suitable for the Iberian constitution. Little wonder that this was what colonists aspired to eat.

'The bestial foods of those who lack bread and wine'

These, of course, were the very foods lacking in the new world. In 1551 Tomás López Medel, a Spanish official stationed in Guatemala, reported to the crown on the suitability of the region for Spanish settlement. In his view Guatemala lacked many of the basic necessities of civilised life. Prominent among these were the foodstuffs that ought to form the core of a Spaniard's diet. 'I found this land to be very lacking and in need of things from Spain such as wine, oil, vinegar, raisins, almonds, medicines and other necessary provisions', he wrote.[50] Colonial writers invariably drew very clear distinctions between such

---

[48] See for example Gutiérrez, *When Jesus Came, the Corn Mothers Went Away*, p. 103; I. A. A. Thompson, 'Castile, Spain and the Monarchy'; Lomnitz, 'Nationalism as a Practical System', p. 343; and Martínez, *Genealogical Fictions*, p. 141.

[49] Angeleres, *Real filosofía*, p. 123.

[50] Carta de Tomás López Medel, 25 March 1551, Archivo General de Indias, Audiencia de Guatemala, legajo 9A, R. 18, N. 77, fol. 1. Vinegar was regarded as a very healthy food: 'it is one of the tastiest things known to man, and beyond the flavour and nice taste that it gives to an infinite variety of things, it is marvellously effective in

'things from Spain' and the foodstuffs available locally. Chroniclers differentiated carefully between 'our fruits' and those 'of this land', between 'the plants that have been brought from Spain' and those 'that are native here', concluding that the Indies' lack of things from Spain posed a serious problem for settlers.[51]

Over and over Spanish officials and chroniclers expressed a combination of astonishment and dismay at the fact that the new world possessed none of the provisions necessary for a normal Iberian meal. There was neither wheat, nor grapevines, nor olives nor any proper animals. On Columbus's return from the Caribbean in 1493 the Catholic monarchs had listened in amazement to his reports of people who 'possessed neither clothes, nor writing, nor money, nor iron, nor wheat, nor wine nor any animal larger than a dog'.[52] Chroniclers felt compelled to list in detail the European foods the Americas lacked. The Indians, reported the historian Andrés Bernáldez, ate a sort of 'bread made from roots that God deigned to give those lands instead of wheat, for there is neither wheat, nor rye, nor barley, nor oats, nor einkorn, nor panic grass, nor sorghum, nor millet nor is there anything that resembles them'.[53] Such litanies of absence reflect not merely surprise but also disapproval. The presence of 'bread made from roots' in no way compensated for the absence of proper bread.[54] The conquistador Francisco de Xerez, who accompanied Francisco Pizarro on his campaigns in Peru, was explicit in his view that the absence of such foods was a measure of the

guaranteeing health and in curing several illnesses: it tempers the body's heat, soothes the stomach, and when drunk it cures hiccups and *singuito*, and its smell cures excessive sneezing': Mexía, *Silva de varia lección*, book 3, chap. 16 (vol. II, pp. 109–10).

[51] Lizárraga, *Descripción breve de toda la tierra del Perú*, chap. 54 (p. 40); Fernández de Oviedo, *Historia general y natural*, book 8, proemio (vol. I, p. 245).

[52] López de Gómara, *Historia General*, chap. 17 (p. 49).

[53] Bernáldez, *Historia de los reyes católicos*, chap. 120 (vol. II, p. 34); and Ovalle, *Histórica relación del Reyno de Chile*, book 1, chaps. 21–2 (pp. 71, 74–5). In his list of reasons why the old world was superior to the new world the official chronicler Antonio de Herrera noted that the new world not only lacked 'dogs, asses, sheep, goats, pigs, cats, horses, mules, camels [and] elephants' but also possessed neither 'orange trees, lemon trees, pomegranate trees, fig trees, nor quince trees, nor melons, nor grape vines, nor olive trees, nor sugar cane … nor wheat nor rice': Herrera, *Historia general de los hechos de los castellanos*, decade 1, book 1, chap. 5 (vol. I, pp. 267–8).

A number of colonial writers insisted that a variety of wild grape was native to the continent, a view with which modern scientists concur. See Peter Martyr, *De Orbe Novo*, decade 3; Fernández de Oviedo, *Historia general y natural*, book 4, chap. 2, book 6, chap. 49, book 8, chap. 24 (vol. I, pp. 94, 217, 262–3); López de Gómara, *Historia general*, chaps. 28, 35 (pp. 66, 73); and Hernández, *Quatro libros de la naturaleza*, book 1, part 3, chap. 39 (p. 68).

[54] Mexico, complained Beatriz de Carvallar to her father, lacked bread, other than tortillas. 'There are many other tasty things', she admitted, but this did not make up for 'the thing of not having bread': Beatriz de Carvallar to Lorenzo Martínez de Carvallar, Mexico, 10 March 1574, in Otte, ed., *Cartas privadas de emigrantes a Indias*, 85.

continent's distance from civility. Xerez observed that the achievements of the Spanish exceeded those of the Greeks and Romans, because during the latter's conquests they had been provisioned with their customary foods, whereas the Spanish had vanquished whole kingdoms 'sustaining themselves with the bestial foods of people who had never heard of bread or wine'.[55] Bestial food betokened a bestial culture, just as bread and wine betokened Christianity.

'The essential thing is to ensure that there is wheat and wine'

Since the Indies lacked these basic foodstuffs it was necessary for Spaniards to introduce them. Not only were wheat and wine resonant symbols of the entire culture that colonists hoped to transplant to the new world, but as we have seen settlers were convinced that a diet of maize and cassava put them at risk of serious illness. Settlers therefore went to great lengths to provision themselves with health-giving old-world foods, in particular the Iberian trinity of wheat bread, wine and olive oil, together with meats such as lamb and pork. These foods were always understood to function not simply as sustenance but also as necessary protection against the rigours of the unfamiliar climate. For this reason officials constantly insisted that these foods were vital for Spanish settlement. Writing from Hispaniola in 1518, treasurer Gil González Dávila for example stressed that securing an adequate supply of wine and wheat was the single most important factor to ensuring the colony's survival. 'The essential thing is to ensure that there is wheat and wine', he stated.[56] Wine was often singled out as a particular necessity.[57] The crown therefore stipulated carefully that settlers (and sailors) should always be provided with these vital foodstuffs, and conquistadors tried hard to guarantee supplies of meat, bread, wine, oil and vinegar for their men.[58]

---

[55] Xerez, *Verdadera relación de la conquista del Perú*, prologue (pp. 18–19).

[56] 'Relación de Gil González Dávila, Contador del Rey, de la despoblación de la Isla Española, de donde es vezino', 1518, in Pacheco *et al.*, eds., *Colección de documentos inéditos*, vol. I, p. 337.

[57] Fernández de Oviedo, *Historia general y natural*, book 8, chap. 24 (vol. I, p. 263); Petition of Pedro Menéndez Márquez, San Agustín, 15 June 1578; and Instrucciones for Rodrigo de Junco, San Agustín, 17 June 1579; both in Connor, ed., *Colonial Records of Spanish Florida*, vol. II, pp. 74, 234; Carta del Virrey Marqués de Villmanrique to the king, Mexico, 20 July 1587, Archivo General de Indias, Audiencia de México, legajo 21, N. 19, fol. 18; and Memorial gubernativa del Conde de Villardompardo, *c.* 1593, in Hanke, ed., *Los virreyes españoles en América*, vol. I, p. 229.

[58] Cortés, Fourth Letter, 1524, in *Letters from Mexico*, pp. 295–6, 306, 312–13; 'Instrucción ... para el buen gobierno y mantenimientos de la gente que quedó en las Indias', in Fernández de Navarrete, ed., *Coleccion de los viajes y descubrimientos que hicieron por mar los españoles desde fines del siglo XV*, doc. 115 (vol. I, p. 227); 'Relación

These supplies came at least initially from Spain. Wheat flour, wine and olive oil appear to have dominated Spanish exports to the Indies for most of the sixteenth century, although detailed statistics are difficult to find.[59] Certainly the volume of trade was substantial. On average 100,000 *arrobas* of wine were exported to the Indies every year between 1592 and 1600, for example.[60] While it is hard to estimate the total volume of Spanish wine production, this is equivalent to roughly 10 per cent of the rioja wine sold outside that region during the same years.[61] The demand for these products in the new world may have been behind the expansion of agricultural production in Andalusia and Castile in the first half of the sixteenth century, although some scholars attribute this instead to population growth in Spain itself.[62] In any event the production of cereals doubled in a number of Spanish regions, and the period saw a substantial increase in the cultivation of olives and grapevines as well.[63] New-world demand, as well as the impact of new-world silver, may also explain rising prices for these products. Between 1511 and 1559 the price of wheat in Andalusia doubled. During the same period the price of olive oil increased threefold, while that of wine increased by a factor of nearly eight.[64]

de los bastimientos que lleva la armada de Magallanes', in Fernández de Navarrete, ed., *Coleccion de los viajes y descubrimientos que hicieron por mar los españoles desde fines del siglo XV*, doc. 18 (vol. IV, p. 187); and Hamilton, 'Wages and Subsistence on Spanish Treasure Ships'. See also Alonso Ramírez to Juan García Ramírez and Pedro Sánchez to Corrales, Trinidad, 1 Jan. 1577; Segundo Martínez to Domingo Martínez, Mexico, 1 May 1572; Sebastián Pliego to Mari Díaz, Puebla, March 1581; and María de Carranza to Hernando de Soto, Puebla, 2 Oct. 1589; all in Otte, ed., *Cartas privadas de emigrantes a Indias*, pp. 69, 162, 167, 331.

[59] See the merchant letters in Lockhart and Otte, eds., *Letters and People of the Spanish Indies*, pp. 19–38; Elliott, *Imperial Spain*, pp. 189, 293; and Lynch, *Spain under the Hapsburgs*, vol. II, p. 185. Huguette and Pierre Chaunu's voluminous *Séville et l'Atlantique* provides no information on the particular merchandise exported from Spain to the Indies. I am grateful to John Elliott for his advice on this topic.

[60] Gil-Bermejo García, 'Tráfico de vinos en Sevilla para el comercio indiano', p. 319 (this figure includes the wine used as ship's rations).

[61] Ibáñez Rodríguez, 'La consolidación del vino de Rioja en el siglo XVII', pp. 42, 44, 53. 100,000 *arrobas* is roughly equivalent to 16,000 hectolitres.

[62] Ibarra y Rodríguez, *El problema cerealista en España*, pp. 17–18, 70; Vicens Vives, *An Economic History of Spain*, pp. 344–5; and Vassberg, *Land and Society in Golden Age Castile*, pp. 163–4. For a study emphasising the importance of population growth see Anés Alvarez, *Las crisis agrarias en la España moderna*.

[63] López-Salazar and Martín Galan, 'La producción cerealista en el Arzobispado de Toledo'; Gil-Bermejo García, 'Tráfico de vinos en Sevilla para el comercio indiano', pp. 324–5; and Yun Casalilla, *Marte contra Minerva*, pp. 39–40, 198–201.

[64] Vassberg, *Land and Society in Golden Age Castile*, pp. 163–4. See also Anés Alvarez, *Las crisis agrarias*, pp. 92–100; Gil-Bermejo García, 'Tráfico de vinos en Sevilla para el comercio indiano', 315–26; and Yun Casalilla, *Marte contra Minerva*, pp. 39–40. On the price revolution see Hamilton, *American Treasure*.

Despite the booming transatlantic trade in wheat flour and red wine, settlers recognised that the importation of European food would not provide a permanent solution to their dietary needs. They needed to cultivate these items themselves were their colonial outposts to survive. For this reason, in the same 1494 letter in which Columbus had asked that his ailing men be supplied with 'the usual foods we eat in Spain' he stressed that the importation of European food should last only until settlers had begun growing 'the things we sow and plant over there, that is to say wheat and barley and grapevines'.[65] This pressing need for European foods led settlers to attempt to 'Europeanise' the new-world landscape, to use the historian Alfred Crosby's terminology, by introducing old-world plants and animals (and, inadvertently, weeds and other pests).[66]

Efforts to grow wheat and other European staples were accordingly made from the 1490s, and European livestock was introduced in both the Caribbean and the American mainland from the earliest days of Spanish settlement. The instructions issued to Columbus in fact stipulated that his colonists were to be equipped with seeds and agricultural equipment precisely to encourage the cultivation of wheat and similar European crops.[67] The requirement to cultivate wheat and other such crops was made equally explicit in many of the early land grants and distributions of indigenous labourers. For example, in 1524 Hernán Cortés demanded that any Spaniard granted rights to Indian labour be obliged to raise grapevines, wheat, barley and other old-world crops.[68] In the same years Rodrigo de Albornoz, a high-ranking colonial official in New Spain, ordered that anyone allocated jurisdiction over indigenous settlements 'be required to sow a certain quantity of land with wheat', in addition to planting grapevines and other 'seeds and vegetables from Spain'.[69] Spanish settlers in Santa Elena (Florida)

---

[65] Columbus, 'Memorial que para los Reyes Católicos dió el Almirante a don Antonio de Torres', 30 Jan. 1494, in *Los cuatro viajes del almirante*, p. 158.

[66] Crosby, *Ecological Imperialism*.

[67] Columbus was specifically required to provide his settlers with 'up to 9,000 bushels of wheat ready for sowing': 'Instrucciones para la población de las islas y tierrafirme descubiertas', 23 April 1497; and the slightly different 'Cédula permitiendo al Almirante la saca ... de 550 cahices de trigo y 50 de cebada', Medina del Campo, 22 June 1497; both in Fernández de Navarrete, ed., *Coleccion de los viajes y descubrimientos que hicieron por mar los españoles desde fines del siglo XV*, docs. 104, 119 (vol. I, pp. 204, quotation, 235). Columbus brought grape vines, grain, legumes, sugar cane and stock animals to Hispaniola on his second voyage, and it was only the ill health of settlers that prevented their cultivation. He brought wheat and barley on his third voyage.

[68] 'Ordenanzas inéditas de Fernando Cortés', Temixtitan, 20 March 1524, in Alamán, ed., *Dissertaciones*, vol. I, p. 270.

[69] 'Carta del contador Rodrigo de Albornoz al emperador', 15 Dec. 1525, in García Icazbalceta, ed., *Colección de documentos para la historia de México*. Or see 'Real Cédula al virrey de la Nueva España', Valladolid, 23 Aug. 1538, in Konetzke, ed., *Colección de*

were likewise required by the terms of their *asiento* or land grant to raise sugar-cane, vineyards and olive trees.[70] By 1525 all ships leaving Spain for the Indies were obliged to carry with them seeds, cuttings and animals, again to ensure that settlers were able to recreate Spanish agricultural patterns.[71]

Various attempts were also made in the early years of Spanish settlement to induce labourers to travel from Europe to the Indies, so as to encourage the establishment of Iberian agricultural practices. Labourers were offered free passage to the Indies and grants of land and were to be supplied with the necessary tools, plants and seeds. The thirty families from the Andalusian town of Antequera who in 1520 travelled to the Indies to settle were thus equipped with 400 spades and hoes, along with many other agricultural implements, and brought with them 120 *fanegas* of wheat, 12 *fanegas* each of garbanzos, broad beans and flax, and cuttings of onion, cardoon, mustard, sesame, cabbage, parsley, cilantro, radish, watercress and hemp, as well as over a thousand olive trees, 200 quince trees, 190 plum and fig trees and 15 almond trees.[72] (A *fanega* is a unit of volume roughly equivalent to 50 litres.) As this list suggests, the intention was not simply to keep settlers supplied with wheat and wine, but to recreate an entire agricultural and culinary system, from olive trees to radishes. Lettuces, radishes and cabbages were indeed planted up and down the Indies by Spanish settlers. Bernardo de Vargas Machuca, author of a late sixteenth-century 'how-to' handbook for conquistadors, for example recommended that soldiers carry 'radish and cabbage seeds, and other vegetables to plant in case they settle or winter in a place, because that is good food'.[73] Crown officials

documentos para la historia de la formación social de Hispanoamérica, vol. I, p. 186; and Tudela de la Orden, 'Economía', pp. 665, 676.

[70] Lyon, 'Spain's Sixteenth-Century North American Settlement Attempts', p. 279; and Viñas Mey, 'Datos para la historia económica', pp. 60–1.

[71] 'Carta del contador Rodrigo de Albornoz al emperador', 15 Dec. 1525, in García Icazbalceta, ed., Colección de documentos para la historia de México; Viñas Mey, 'Datos para la historia económica', pp. 66–7; and Mörner, 'The Rural Economy and Society in Colonial Spanish South America', p. 204. Cortés had already suggested such a requirement in 1524: Fourth Letter, 1524, in Letters from Mexico, pp. 321–2.

[72] Tudela de la Orden, 'Economía', p. 676. Rodrigo de Albornoz similarly recommended that Charles V 'send three or four thousand labourers from Andalusia and Castile to settle and inhabit the land with their wives, and each one should be required to bring their tools, grapevines and trees': 'Carta del contador Rodrigo de Albornoz al emperador', 15 Dec. 1525, in García Icazbalceta, ed., Colección de documentos para la historia de México. Or see Herrera, Historia general de los hechos de los castellanos, decade 4, book 10, chap. 5 (vol. III, p. 123).

[73] Vargas Machuca, 'Milicia indiana', in Milicia y descripción de las Indias, book 2 (vol. I, p. 156). For happy discussion of the cultivation of radishes, cabbage and watercress see for example Fernández de Oviedo, Historia general y natural, book 3, chap. 11 (vol. I, p. 79); and Cobo, Historia del nuevo mundo, tomo 1, book 10, chaps. 39–40 (vol. I, p. 414–17).

were very concerned to determine which old-world plants grew well in each region, and in particular whether 'wheat, barley, wine and oil can grow there'.[74] Only those regions in which European plants grew well were considered suitable for Spanish colonisation.[75] Geographical surveys reported explicitly on this matter, and many writers detailed the old-world crops that did and did not thrive in particular regions.[76]

Initial attempts at cultivating wheat in the Caribbean were largely unsuccessful. Colonists noted that the stalks grew well but often failed to set seed, although, as we shall see, this did not prevent chroniclers from declaring the region a veritable cornucopia of European produce. Wheat did better on the mainland. According to legend it was first sown in Mexico in 1521, the same year in which the Spanish overthrew the Aztec empire.[77] By 1525 attempts were underway to establish European-style mills in Mexico City, and the sale of bread was made into a state monopoly.[78] Maintaining an adequate supply of wheat for Spaniards was a key concern of Mexican viceroys throughout the sixteenth century. At the century's end it was being grown on a large, commercial scale, often on lands that had previously produced maize.[79]

---

[74] This was question 25 in the 'Cédula, instrucción y memoria' sent to colonial officials by the Spanish crown in 1577. See Solano, ed., *Cuestionarios para la formación de las relaciones geográficas*, p. 84.

[75] See for example Asiento con Lucas Vásquez de Ayllón, 12 June 1523, Archivo General de Indias, Indiferente General, legajo 415, L.1, fol. 36.

[76] See the various *relaciones geográficas* edited by Acuña, Jiménez de la Espada, and Paso y Troncoso; Cuneo, 'News of the Islands of the Hesperian Ocean', 1495, p. 55; 'Relación de Gil González Dávila, Contador del Rey, de la despoblación de la Isla Española, de donde es vezino', 1518, in Pacheco *et al.*, eds., *Colección de documentos inéditos*, vol. I, pp. 341–2; 'Mercedes y libertades concedidas a los labradores que pasaron a las Indias', 1518, in Serrano y Sanz, ed., *Orígenes de la dominación española en América*, docs. 61–2 (vol. I, pp. 580–2); Pedro Menéndez Márquez to the Audiencia of Santo Domingo, San Agustín, 2 April 1579, in Connor, ed., *Colonial Records of Spanish Florida*, vol. II, p. 226; and Melville, *A Plague of Sheep*, pp. 32–3.

[77] Gibson, *The Aztecs under Spanish Rule*, pp. 323–5; Río Moreno and López y Sebastián, 'El trigo en la ciudad de México', pp. 33–4; and Dunmire, *Gardens of New Spain*.

[78] García Acosta, 'El pan de maíz y el pan de trigo', p. 268; Lockhart, *The Nahuas after the Spanish Conquest*, p. 188; and Río Moreno and López y Sebastián, 'El trigo en la ciudad de México', p. 36.

[79] Chevalier, *Land and Society in Colonial Mexico*, p. 59; and Gibson, *The Aztecs under Spanish Rule*, pp. 322–34. The letters of sixteenth-century Mexican viceroys report regularly on the wheat and maize harvests: Luis de Velasco to the king, Mexico, 4 May 1553, in Lockhart and Otte, eds., *Letters and People*, p. 193; Carta del virrey Martín Enríquez, Mexico, 20 Feb. 1580, Archivo General de Indias, Audiencia de México, legajo 20, N. 30, fol. 5; Carta del virrey conde de Monterrey, San Agustín, 4 Aug. 1597, Archivo General de Indias, Audiencia de México, legajo 23, N. 86, fol. 3; Carta del virrey conde de Monterrey, Mexico 28 Feb. 1598, Archivo General de Indias, Audiencia de México, legajo 24, N. 4, fol. 6; Carta del virrey conde de Monterrey, Mexico, 20 May 1601, Archivo General de Indias, Audiencia de México, legajo 24, N. 56, fol. 1; and Carta del virrey Marquez de Guadalcazar,

By the early seventeenth century Mexican-grown wheat was resupplying Spanish ships for the voyage back to Europe.[80] It was grown in Central America from 1529 and by the 1540s was cultivated in many parts of the Andes, so that by the 1550s ships trading between Mexico and Peru could provision themselves with biscuit (as well as pork) at the Peruvian end.[81] Overall, settlers cultivated wheat everywhere that the climate permitted, and it was thus only in areas such as Florida or the Caribbean, where the wet climate absolutely prevented its growth, that Spanish settlement was not accompanied by the introduction of wheat.[82]

Wine, unlike wheat, survived the sea voyage from Spain relatively successfully (provided barrels did not leak), and Spanish officials vacillated throughout the colonial era over whether settlers should be encouraged to produce their own wine, or instead should be required to purchase Spanish imports. (Colonists complained constantly that imported wines were inordinately expensive. 'They cost the very eyes from your face', was how Pedro Menéndez, the governor of Florida, put it.[83]) Ferdinand prohibited cultivation of grapes in Hispaniola in 1503, in order to prevent competition with Peninsular wines, but in 1519 the Casa de Contratación, the body regulating Atlantic trade, reversed this decision, and ordered all ships sailing to the Caribbean to oversee the planting of grapevines.[84] By the 1570s vines had been planted across South America. 'They make a great deal of very good wine from them', reported the royal cosmographer Juan López de Velasco.[85] Further prohibitions against planting were nonetheless issued in 1568, 1574 and 1595, again to prevent a decline in transatlantic trade.[86] Despite

---

Mexico, 25 Jan. 1616, Archivo General de Indias, Audiencia de México, legajo 28, N. 32, fol. 1.

[80] Mena García, 'Nuevos datos sobre bastamentos y envases en armadas y flotas de la carrera', p. 474.

[81] Recinos, *Doña Leonor de Alvarado y otros estudios*, p. 89; Meléndez, 'Aspectos sobre la historia del cultivo del trigo durante la época colonial', p. 107; Gootenberg, 'Carneros y chuño', p. 8; Borah, *Early Colonial Trade and Navigation*, p. 49; and Guzmán Pinto, 'Perspectiva urbana y cultura alimentaria, Cusco, 1545–1552', pp. 242–5.

[82] Reitz and Scarry, *Reconstructing Historic Subsistence*, pp. 47, 55; and Arnade, *Florida on Trial*, p. 9.

[83] Pedro Menéndez Márques to the king, San Agustín, 15 June 1578, in Connor, ed., *Colonial Records of Spanish Florida*, vol. II, p. 84. Or see Garcilaso de la Vega, *Royal Commentaries*, book 9, chap. 26 (vol. I, p. 598).

[84] Haring, *Trade and Navigation between Spain and the Indies*, p. 125.

[85] López de Velasco, *Geografía y descripción universal de las Indias*, 'De los árboles de las Indias'. Or see Jiménz de Estrada, ed., *Relaciones geográficas de las Indias*.

[86] Consulta del Consejo de Indias, Madrid, 2 Sept. 1584, Archivo General de Indias, Indiferente General, legajo 740, N. 282; Instrucciones al Marqués de Cañete, 1591, in Hanke, ed., *Los virreyes españoles en América*, vol. I, p. 274; Solórzano Pereira,

these periodic prohibitions successful vineyards were established in Argentina, Chile and Peru, and many colonists spoke highly of the quality of Chilean and Peruvian wine, in particular.[87] Indeed, wine became one of Peru's most important exports, second perhaps to silver.[88] Vines were planted but generally failed to prosper in Mexico.[89]

The introduction of European livestock, on the other hand, was an unequivocal triumph, as far as the Spanish were concerned. Conquistadors in the Caribbean employed a deliberate policy of introducing pigs and other animals to areas of settlement; as a result the pigs that accompanied the conquistadors to the mainland in the early sixteenth century were bred in the Caribbean. Spaniards carefully stocked even islands that they didn't intend to inhabit immediately with breeding pairs, so as to provide food for future colonists. As a result, within a few decades of colonial settlement ships returning to Spain from the Caribbean provisioned themselves generously with locally produced pork and other old-world meats. Similar practices were employed in South America; by the 1540s Spaniards were leaving pairs of horses, sheep and goats in the Argentine pampas, where they multiplied.[90] Where such measures proved insufficient the crown intervened. In entrepôts such as the Isthmus of Panama, where the demand for meat at first outstripped supply, *encomenderos* (settlers who had been assigned grants of Indian labour) were explicitly required to raise a quantity of pigs proportionate to the number of Indians they had been assigned to provision the many ships that sailed for Peru. Similar requirements obliging captains to raise pigs and other livestock were included in the

Política indiana, book 2, chap. 9, sections 14–17, 25–6 (vol. I, pp. 95–7); *Noticias sobre el Río de la Plata: Montevideo en el siglo XVIII*, ed. Martínez Díaz, chap. 8 (pp. 158–9); Haring, *Trade and Navigation between Spain and the Indies*, p. 126; and Rice, 'Wine and Brandy Production'.

[87] Acosta, *Natural and Moral History of the Indies*, book 3, chap. 22 (p. 150); and Rice, 'Wine and Brandy Production', p. 456. For the failure to implement royal decrees see 'Instrucciones al Marqués de Cañete', 1591; and 'Instrucción al virrey don Luis de Velasco', 22 July 1595; both in Hanke, ed., *Los virreyes españoles en América*, vol. I, pp. 265–6, 274–5, vol. II, pp. 23–4.

[88] Peñaloza y Mondragón, *Libro de las cinco excelencias del español*, pp. 122–3, 133–49; Murúa, *Historia general del Perú*, book 3, chap. 2 (p. 463); Lynch, *Spain under the Hapsburgs*, vol. II, p. 215; Elliott, *Imperial Spain*, p. 293; and Rice, 'Wine and Brandy Production', p. 456.

[89] Chevalier, *Land and Society in Colonial Mexico*, p. 59.

[90] Fernández de Oviedo, *Historia general y natural*, book 2, chap. 9, book 10, chap. 1 (vol. I, p. 38, vol. II, p. 184); Ovalle, *Histórica relación del Reyno de Chile*, book 1, chap. 21 (pp. 71–2); Castellanos, *Breve historia de la ganadería en el Uruguay*, p. 9; Crosby, *The Columbian Exchange*, pp. 64–121; and Río Moreno, 'El cerdo'. On ships see Super, 'Spanish Diet in the Atlantic Crossing', p. 61.

contracts issued to individual conquistadors, to ensure that their men were adequately fed.[91]

Spaniards were astonished at their own success. Writers spoke of the 'innumerable' herds of cattle, goats and sheep in South America, New Spain and the Caribbean, and speculated as to why these European animals thrived so well.[92] Scholars now attribute this success to 'ungulate eruption', which occurs when hoofed animals such as sheep or cattle are introduced into an unfamiliar environment.[93] Populations typically increase exponentially for several generations. By the seventeenth century herds of sheep, goats and cattle numbering in the hundreds of thousands roamed the continent. The result was very low meat prices. Already by the 1560s it was claimed that 'more meat was eaten and more money spent on it in one city in the Indies than ten in Spain'.[94] Spaniards in the new world were therefore able to indulge their taste for meat far more than was possible in Spain itself. Pork was particularly abundant, and perhaps for this reason settlers stressed its healthfulness over lamb more than did Peninsular writers. Similarly, lard often replaced more expensive imported olive oil in colonial cooking and household management, to the disgust of doctors, who blamed it for the dyspepsia

[91] Cédula to the governor of Tierra Firme, Valladolid, 19 Oct. 1537, Archivo General de Indias, Audiencia de Panama, legajo 235, libro 6, fol. 129; and Río Moreno, 'El cerdo', pp. 10, 17–19.

[92] Peter Martyr, De Orbe Novo, decade 3, book 7; Fernández de Enciso, Suma de geographía, p. lii; 'Relación de la Isla Española enviada al Rey d. Felipe II por el licenciado Echagoian', in Pacheco et al., eds., Colección de documentos inéditos, vol. I, p. 17; Fernández de Oviedo, Historia general y natural, book 3, chap. 11, book 6, chap. 51, book 10, chap. 9, book 4, chap. 3 (vol. I, pp. 78–9, 221, vol. II, pp. 38–9, 71); López de Gómara, Historia general, chap. 35 (p. 73); Las Casas, Historia de las Indias, c. 1559, book 1, chap. 154 (p. 610); López de Velasco, Geografía y descripción universal de las Indias, 'De los animales'; Acosta, Natural and Moral History of the Indies, book 4, chap. 33 (p. 230); Dorantes de Carranza, Sumaria relación, 50; and Cobo, Historia del Nuevo Mundo, book 10, chaps. 1–12 (vol. I, pp. 375–91). For an archaeological perspective see Reitz, 'The Spanish Colonial Experience and Domestic Animals', p. 84; and Reitz and McEwan, 'Animals, Environment and the Spanish Diet at Puerto Real', pp. 293, 332.

[93] Melville, A Plague of Sheep.

[94] Chevalier, Land and Society in Colonial Mexico, pp. 84, 92–3, 106 (quotation). See also Barrios, Verdadera medicina y cirugía, book 1, chap. 2 (p. 41bisr); and Cobo, Historia del Nuevo Mundo, book 10, chap. 5 (vol. I, pp. 385–6). Settlers often commented on this. See for example Fernando de Isla to Juan de Albear, Mexico, 22 Jan. 1590; Alonso Morales to Juan Ramiro, Puebla, 20 Feb. 1576; Alonso Herojo to Teresa González, Tunja, 10 March 1583; Andrés Chacón to Francisco Chacón, Calle de Casma, 1 Jan. 1570; Miguel de Arriba to Antón de Arriba, Cuzco, 21 Jan. 1576; and Pedro Valero to Catalina Martínez, Potosí, 1 Dec. 1576; all in Otte, ed., Cartas privadas de emigrantes a Indias, pp. 118, 159, 325, 469–70, 488, 525.

that plagued settlers.[95] (Olive trees themselves grew well in parts of Mexico, Peru and Chile, although they were never cultivated in sufficient quantities to satisfy local needs entirely.[96])

As a consequence of these endeavours settlers in Spanish America were by the end of the sixteenth century increasingly able to forgo expensive Spanish imports, as they were growing their own wheat, producing their own wine and raising their own livestock. This was a source of considerable satisfaction for colonists. Writing from Lima in the 1630s the creole chronicler Buenaventura de Salinas y Córdova reported proudly that the viceroyalty consumed annually some 200,000 sheep, 200,000 barrels of wine and 150,000 *fanegas* of wheat, all produced in Peru itself.[97]

'Wheat and wine will grow very well in this land'

Although the actual success of these agricultural ventures varied substantially from region to region, a consensus quickly emerged that European crops flourished in the new world. Confident assessments of the Indies' agricultural potential began with Columbus himself. 'We are very certain, as events themselves show, that wheat and wine will grow very well in this land', he insisted two years after his landfall in the Caribbean, although this statement could not have been based on much beyond his general optimism.[98] His confidence was echoed by writer after writer, often in the face of considerable contrary evidence.[99]

[95] Barrios, *Verdadera medicina y cirugía*, book 1, chap. 2 (p. 41bisv); Gage, *The English-American*, chap. 16 (p. 373); and Río Moreno, 'El cerdo'. On stomach ailments see Cárdenas, *Problemas y secretos maravillosos*, book 3, chaps. 1, 9 (pp. 176, 208–10); and Farfán, *Tratado breve de medigina*, book 1, chap. 1 (pp. 1–8).

[96] Acosta, *Natural and Moral History of the Indies*, p. 229; Chevalier, *Land and Society in Colonial Mexico*, p. 59; and Crosby, *The Columbian Exchange*, pp. 72–3.

[97] Salinas y Córdova, *Memorial de las historias del Nuevo Mundo*, discurso 2 (pp. 248–50); and Brading, *The First America*, p. 317. On the decline in imports see Elliott, *Imperial Spain*, p. 293; Vassberg, *Land and Society*, p. 185; Borah, *Early Colonial Trade and Navigation*, p. 80; and also DeFrance, 'Diet and Provisioning in the High Andes'.

[98] Columbus, 'Memorial que para los Reyes Católicos dió el Almirante a don Antonio de Torres', 30 Jan. 1494, in *Los cuatro viajes del almirante*, p. 158. For other enthusiastic reports see 'Mercedes y libertades concedidas a los labradores que pasaron a las Indias', 1518, in Serrano y Sanz, ed., *Orígenes de la dominación española*, doc. 61 (vol. I, pp. 580–1); López de Gómara, *Historia general*, chaps. 20, 89, 195, 208 (pp. 56, 166, 341–2, 361); Las Casas, *Apologética historia sumaria*, c. 1552, chaps. 2, 3, 5, 6, 9, 20 (pp. 9, 14, 19–20, 23, 32, 61–3); López Medel, *De los tres elementos*, pp. 13, 136, 143–5, 167–8, 183; Nuñez de Oria, *Regimiento y aviso de sanidad*, p. 40r–v; and Dorantes de Carranza, *Sumaria relación*, pp. 49–50, 60, 74, 77.

[99] See for example 'Relación de la Isla Española enviada al Rey d. Felipe II por el licenciado Echagoian', in Pacheco *et al.*, eds., *Colección de documentos inéditos*, vol. I, p. 12; 'Relación de la provincia y tierra de la Verapaz', 1574, in Acuña, ed., *Relaciones geográficas del siglo XVI: Guatemala*, pp. 207, 221; 'Deposition of Alonso Martín and

Mexico, where Spaniards had largely failed to raise grapevines, was proclaimed to be so fertile that all Spanish crops grew there in abundance.[100] In Peru everything was declared to thrive just as marvellously. 'All the produce that has been brought from Spain grows better here than it does over there', insisted a seventeenth-century Peruvian scholar.[101] If crops did not thrive it was simply because settlers had not been equipped with the appropriate supplies, or because they failed to apply themselves sufficiently to the task.[102] Colonial writers were drawn to superlatives when discussing the new world's fertility. 'All the animals, fruits, vegetables and other plants that Spaniards brought here after they discovered and settled this new world thrive with the most extraordinary abundance', rhapsodised the Jesuit writer Bernabé Cobo.[103] In letters to relatives back in Spain settlers stressed the ease with which all crops grew. 'As regards the fertility of this land I won't say anything, because you'd need to see it to believe it', Juan López Bravo wrote to his brother from Guatemala in 1603.[104] From Mexico another colonist promised his family a life of comfort made possible by the land's fertility:

Hunger is unknown in this land, because wheat and maize are harvested twice a year, and all Spanish produce grows here, and even more of the native fruits, so no one misses Spain, and poor people have a better time of it here than in Spain, because they get to give orders and don't do any work themselves and always go about on horseback.[105]

Investigation', Santa Elena, 27 Feb. 1576, in Connor, ed., *Colonial Records of Spanish Florida*, vol. I, pp. 146–74; Lázaro de Arregui, *Descripción de la Nueva Galicia*, chap. 6 (pp. 18–21); the varied reports in Jiménez de la Espada, ed., *Relaciones geográficas de las Indias: Perú*, vol. I; López de Velasco, *Geografía y descripción universal*; and Vásquez de Espinosa, *Compendio y descripción*, part 1, book 2, chap. 1, no 99 (p. 33).

[100] Anonymous Conquistador, 'Relación de algunas cosas de la Nueva España', vol. 1, p. 369; Motolinía, *Historia de los Indios de la Nueva España*, 1541, tratado 3, chap. 9; Cervantes de Salazar, 'The Environs of the City of Mexico', p. 78; and Cervantes de Salazar, *Crónica*, book 1, chaps. 5–6 (p. 14).

[101] Leon Pinelo, *Question moral*, part 2, chap. 10 (p. 63, quotation); and Zárate, *A History of the Discovery and Conquest of Peru*, p. 23.

[102] See for example 'Relación de la Isla Española enviada al Rey d. Felipe II por el licenciado Echagoian', in Pacheco *et al.*, eds., *Colección de documentos inéditos*, vol. I, pp. 13, 17; Dorantes de Carranza, *Sumaria relación*, pp. 49–50; and Lyon, 'Spain's Sixteenth-Century North American Settlement', p. 284.

[103] Cobo, *Historia del Nuevo Mundo*, prologue, book 10, chap. 1 (vol. I, pp. 6, 375 (quotation), 420); Fernández de Oviedo, *Historia general y natural*, book 3, chap. 11 (vol. I, p. 79); Murúa, *Historia general del Perú*, book 3, chap. 2 (pp. 462–3); and Vásquez de Espinosa, *Compendio y descripción*, part 1, book 2, chap. 22, no. 224 (p. 60).

[104] Sebastián Carrera to his wife, Los Reyes, 1 Nov. 1558; Juan López Bravo to Baltasar Díaz, Guatemala, 2 March 1601; and Francisco Rodríguez to Pedro Hernández, Trujillo, 19 March 1560; all in Otte, ed., *Cartas privadas de emigrantes a Indias*, pp. 37, 228 (quotation), 462.

[105] Juan Cabeza de Vaca to Elvira de Cantalejos, Mexico, 24 April 1594, in Otte, ed., *Cartas privadas de emigrantes a Indias*, p. 130.

After listing a number of European crops successfully grown in Peru the conquistador Pedro Cieza de León exclaimed '[B]ut why do I go into details, when it is believed that all the products of Spain will flourish here?'.[106]

The triumphalist story of Spain's conversion of the new world into a cornucopia of European produce quickly spread around Europe. 'The Spaniards', recorded an Italian chronicler in 1500,

report amazing things about the fertility of the island, which I can hardly repeat without blushing: they say that radishes, lettuce, and cabbages mature within fifteen days of planting, that melons and squash mature within thirty-six days, that vines produce grapes in a year, and that wheat (they were determined to try everything), planted in early February, had ripened by mid-March.[107]

Such claims gathered force in part from the desire to counter the received wisdom that the torrid zone, the region of the world that girded the Equator, in which the Indies were believed to be located, was sterile and barren, scourged by intolerable heat that prevented the generation of anything other than precious metals. Colonial writers constantly railed against this belief, which derived from the writings of ancient authorities such as Aristotle. The Spanish doctor Diego Cisneros was one of many who criticised the 'error of the ancients regarding the habitability and temperance of the torrid zone'.[108] By insisting that the new world was a cornucopia colonial writers sought to reverse the idea that the new world was all but uninhabitable.

The writings of Peter Martyr played a particularly important role in disseminating this vision of new-world plenty. Peter Martyr d'Anghiera, an Italian-born humanist who had resided at the Spanish court since the late 1480s, began in 1493 to compile disparate discovery reports into a series of letters, or 'decades', directed to an influential cardinal at the court of Pope Alexander VI, which offered both a narrative of

---

[106] Cieza de León, *Parte primera de la chrónica del Perú*, chaps. 40, 66, 70, 71 (pp. 48–9, 82–3 (quotation), 85, 87). The English translation is from Cieza de León, *The Incas*, p. 317. Or see Ovalle, *Histórica relación del Reyno de Chile*, book 1, chap. 3 (pp. 23–5); and Garcés, *De habilitate et capacitate gentium sive Indorum novi mundi nuncupati ad fidem Christi capessendam*, p. 4. I am grateful to Andrew Laird for this last reference, and translation.

[107] Coccio (Sabellico), *Book One … of the Account of the Happenings in the Unknown Regions*, 1500, p. 69. Or see Geraldini, *Itinerary to the Regions Located below the Equator*, pp. 127–8.

[108] Cisneros, *Sitio, naturaleza y propriedades de la ciudad de México*, chap. 9 (p. 50v); Torquemada, *Jardín de flores curiosas*, tratado 5 (pp. 384–6); López Medel, *De los tres elementos*, 12–16; Acosta, *Natural and Moral History*, books 1–3 (pp. 13–160); Simón, *Noticias historiales*, noticia 1, chap. 1 (vol. I, p. 109); and Cobo, *Historia del Nuevo Mundo*, book 2, chap. 3 (p. 55).

the ongoing process of European colonisation and elegant and at times acerbic commentary on indigenous mores and Spanish behaviour. His *Decades* provided one of the earliest syntheses of European knowledge about the Americas and were widely read across Western Europe.[109]

In the *Decades* Martyr presented the new world as a site of extraordinary abundance. Describing a Spanish settlement on the Colombian coast, for example, he reported:

Everything the Spaniards sowed or planted in Uraba grew marvellously well. Is this not worthy, Most Holy Father, of the highest admiration? Every kind of seed, graftings, sugar-canes, and slips of trees and plants, without speaking of the chickens and quadrupeds I have mentioned, were brought from Europe. O admirable fertility! The cucumbers and other similar vegetables sown were ready for picking in less than twenty days. Cabbages, beets, lettuces, salads, and other garden stuff were ripe within ten days; pumpkins and melons were picked twenty-eight days after the seeds were sown.[110]

Martyr, who never travelled to the new world, derived this implausible vision from conversations with settlers such as Gonzalo Fernández de Oviedo and from the writings of men such as Columbus and Ramón Pané, a Hieronymite friar who composed an early account of the Taino Indians of Hispaniola. Martyr's description of the new world's agricultural exuberance therefore reflects the opinions of these early colonisers, who, like many settlers, insisted that the Indies were a veritable Eden knee-deep in old-world foods. In short, despite the chequered success of Spanish attempts to cultivate old-world crops in the Indies, many writers, including those with direct experience of colonial society, insisted that Spanish crops flourished to a degree little short of miraculous.

Naked land

Writers often contrasted the ease and success with which Spaniards introduced their crops with an alleged neglect of agriculture by Amerindians. The Indians, writers claimed, had failed to develop the land, whereas the Spaniards had improved it by cultivating wheat and other old-world staples, and by introducing superior agricultural

---

[109] Compilations of his letters, published in stages, in Latin, appeared in 1511, 1516, 1521, 1530, 1533, 1536, 1545 and 1574 and the work was translated into Italian (1504, 1507, 1534, 1556, 1565), French (1532), German (1534, 1582), English (1555, 1577) and Flemish (1563).

[110] Peter Martyr, *De Orbe Novo*, decade 2, book 9 (quotation), decade 1, book 1, decade 1, book 3, decade 2, book 9, decade 3, book 7, decade 4, book 10. For comparison, cucumbers are generally said to take at least sixty-five days to mature. Cabbages take three to four months.

techniques. The royal cosmographer Juan López de Velasco, for example, noted in the 1570s that prior to the arrival of the Spanish 'almost everywhere the land was untended, and so little cultivated that, naked as it was, it produced only those plants and seeds that nature itself brought forth'. Spain had elevated this naked, virgin land from its savage state and was rewarded with abundant harvests of Spanish crops: 'so welcomely did it receive all the plants that have been brought from Spain that scarcely any have failed to flourish', he recorded with satisfaction.[111] (See Figure 5.) Such failings on the part of Amerindians were significant, for Spaniards were certain that skilled agriculture was an infallible indication of civilisation.

The claim that Amerindians did not cultivate their lands was first articulated by Columbus. In keeping with the admiral's uncertainty over whether he had reached the kingdom of a great Asiatic lord, he vacillated in his assessment of the landscape, which he saw variously as civilised and wild. For example, during his first voyage Columbus noted signs of indigenous agriculture, yet simultaneously asserted that the marvellous plants adorning the Caribbean landscape grew naturally, without human intervention. On 6 November 1492, while in Cuba, he reported both that 'the land [is] very fertile and planted with those yams and beans very different from our own', and also that 'it seemed to him that they did not cultivate it and that it produced fruit all year round'.[112] For Columbus, the idea that plants might grow so lushly without the need for labour made the Caribbean a virtual paradise – as we shall discuss in the next chapter – but it did not reflect well on the local inhabitants' level of civilisation. Many subsequent writers similarly maintained that Amerindians were ignorant of agriculture, or at least less learned in its arts than the Spanish. The jurist Juan de Solórzano Pereira, for example, observed that among the many things Amerindians learned from Europeans was 'the true cultivation of the soil'.[113] Whatever Amerindians had been doing with the land prior to the arrival of the Spanish, in other words, it was not proper agriculture.

Colonial writers were not unanimous in maintaining that Amerindians engaged in no agricultural activities whatsoever. Such a claim would

---

[111] López de Velasco, *Geografía y descripción universal de las Indias*, 'De los granos y semillas'. For America as naked see Montrose, 'The Work of Gender in the Discourse of Discovery'.

[112] Columbus, 'Diary of the First Voyage', 6 Nov. 1492, p. 56; and Zamora, *Reading Columbus*, pp. 51–2. See also Columbus, 'Diary of the First Voyage', 4, 30 Nov. 1492, 3, 7, 9, 13, 14 Dec. 1492, pp. 53–4, 75–7, 82–4, 86–9; Campbell, *The Witness and the Other World*, pp. 202–3; and Wey Gómez, *The Tropics of Empire*.

[113] Solórzano Pereira, *Política indiana*, book 1, chap. 8, section 7 (vol. I, p. 30).

Figure 5 Giovanni Stradano, *Vespucci Landing in America, c.* 1587–9. This image, used to make a widely circulating print, depicts the Indies as an indolent woman, roused from torpor by the technically well-equipped and fully clothed Amerigo Vespucci. The image reflects the Spanish belief that Amerindians did not engage in proper agriculture, leaving the land (here represented as a naked woman) unimproved and wild.

have been difficult to maintain in the face of overwhelming evidence to the contrary, and many colonists noted – or indeed admired – the varied forms of cultivation employed in the hemisphere. Both the conquistador Hernán Cortés and the foot soldier Bernal Díaz commented on the many cultivated fields they passed on their 1519 journey from the coastal city of Veracruz to the Mexica capital of Tenochtitlán in central Mexico. The Jesuit chronicler José de Acosta described in some detail the organisation of communal agricultural labour under Inca rule.[114] The Spanish state, moreover, implicitly acknowledged the effectiveness of indigenous agricultural practice by taxing it. For example, the government of New Spain quickly began levying tribute on the foodstuffs grown on the unusual 'floating' vegetable gardens or *chinampas* typical of the area around Mexico City, as Tenochtitlán was rechristened after 1521. *Chinampas* were constructed by mounding lake sediment into artificial islands, a technique that concentrated highly productive,

[114] Acosta, *Natural and Moral History*, book 6, chap. 15 (pp. 352–5).

nutrient-rich soil on land intended specifically for agriculture. Produce from *chinampas* played a major role in provisioning central Mexico for at least the first century of colonial rule, and local settler elites worked hard to gain control over these lucrative lands.[115] Nonetheless, even writers who recognised the ubiquity of agriculture in the indigenous world might insist that Europeans made better use of the land, or that there was something illegitimate about indigenous agricultural practices. Acosta suggested that the *chinampas* had been built with the assistance of the devil.[116]

The ability to cultivate had functioned as the mark of civilisation for European writers since the time of Aristotle. Furthermore, engaging in agriculture was in some ways a basic sign of humanity, for the obligation to labour was a consequence of mankind's sin in the Garden of Eden. From that moment the earth ceased to yield up its bounty unaided and nourishment came at the cost of sweat and toil. Only in paradise, or some very close equivalent, could men live without tilling the soil. (Whether the Indies represented such an Edenic environment will be considered in the next chapter.) But although the need for toil was a result of Eve's fatal handiwork, agricultural labour was not in itself a curse; many writers argued that it was instead a dignified and morally uplifting activity, at least for other people to engage in. The importance early modern Spanish writers ascribed to agricultural endeavours is further revealed in the frequent description of evangelisation as a form of metaphorical gardening – a matter that will be discussed in detail in Chapter 5. By presenting the evangelisation of the Indies as an agricultural process such writers very clearly dignified farming and those who succeeded at it.

Instead, it was the inability to farm successfully that reflected divine displeasure. Part of the punishment that God imposed on Cain for the murder of his brother was the perpetual failure of his attempts at cultivating the soil. 'When thou tillest the ground, it shall not henceforth yield unto thee her strength', God informed a dismayed Cain. Similar curses were contained in the edict of anathema unleashed on those who refused to denounce crypto-Jews and other evildoers. And surely it was not by chance that God favoured Jacob, the herder and farmer, over his brother Esau the hunter.[117] The fact that the Indies

---

[115] Conway, 'Nahuas and Spaniards in the Socioeconomic History of Xochimilco', pp. 62–115.

[116] Acosta, *De procuranda indorum salute*, book 2, chap. 14, section 3 (vol. I, p. 353); and Acosta, *The Natural and Moral History*, book 7, chap. 9 (p. 397–8).

[117] Gen. 3:17–23, 25:27–34, 4:12, 26:1–14; Glacken, *Traces on the Rhodian Shore*, pp. 153–4, 239–40; Freedman, *Images of the Medieval Peasant*, pp. 15–39; Fernández García, 'Criterios inquisitoriales para detectar al marrano', p. 486; and, on Cain, Braude, '"Cokkel in Oure Clene Corn"'. In the opinion of Franciscan writers Jews

lacked large domesticable animals, and therefore that many indigenous cultures had little experience of animal husbandry (the raising of llamas and other camelids in the Andes being a notable exception), provided further evidence that Amerindians were in some fundamental sense less civilised than the agriculturally adept Europeans. After all, domesticated animals were, as the chronicler Francisco López de Gómara put it, 'absolutely essential for the well-being and good ordering of human society'.[118]

Proper management of the environment was thus seen by colonial writers as a worthy and improving enterprise characteristic of a well-governed polity. It was for this reason that the chronicler Antonio de Herrera could state confidently that by teaching Amerindians how to cultivate correctly the Spanish agricultural labourers sent to the Indies would generate both abundance and 'good political order'.[119] (Engaging in wholesome agricultural pursuits would work similar transformations on idle Spanish vagabonds, who were likewise encouraged to reform themselves through farming.[120]) Indeed, it was precisely because of the importance long ascribed to agriculture as a sign of civility that the great champion of indigenous rights Bartolomé de las Casas emphasised the mastery with which Amerindians had managed their environment.[121] Failure to cultivate was, conversely, an indisputable mark of barbarism. Thus the Franciscan missionary Toribio de Motolinía could write that the Chichimecs and Otomíes 'lived savage lives', not only because they lacked houses but also because 'they neither planted crops nor cultivated the soil'. As a consequence they were forced to eat 'herbs and roots and foods they found in the fields'.[122] A culinary system not based on agriculture was fundamentally uncivilised.

People who did not cultivate the land properly did not deserve to possess it. This was the idea underpinning the principle of *res* or *terra nullius* derived from Roman law, which affirmed that individuals had a natural right to claim abandoned or unproductive lands. Such lands belonged to no one, and could thus be appropriated by anyone able

were never farmers because God had cursed them so that nothing that they planted would grow: Torrejoncillo, *Centinela contra judios*, pp. 178–9 (he refers specifically to the tribe of Ruben).

[118] López de Gómara, *Historia general*, Dedication to Charles V (p. 18).

[119] Herrera, *Historia general de los hechos de los castellanos*, decade 4, book 10, chap. 5 (vol. III, p. 123).

[120] Mörner, *La corona española y los foráneos*, pp. 29, 40.

[121] See for example Las Casas, *Apologética historia sumaria*, c. 1552, chaps. 59–60 (pp. 195–201).

[122] 'Carta de Fray Toribio de Motolinía al Emperador Carlos V', 1555, in García Icazbalceta, ed., *Colección de documentos para la historia de México*.

to put them to good use. If Amerindians did not engage in recognisable agriculture, then they did not exercise proper dominion over the lands in which they happened to reside. Failure to cultivate the soil, in other words, greatly diminished the legitimacy of any claim to ownership over it. The precise implications of this principle to Spanish colonisation of the Americas was a topic of debate among contemporary scholars, who disputed both the extent to which the lands of the Indies were truly abandoned and also whether this might justify the particular type of colonial rule imposed on the Indies. It nonetheless expressed pithily the idea that sovereignty was intimately linked to agriculture.[123] The alleged failure of Amerindians to show good husbandry thus raised questions about the legitimacy of their claims to authority over the land they had so neglected, at the same time as it revealed their fundamental lack of civilisation.

Flourishing agriculture, on the other hand, not only strengthened any claim to sovereignty but surely also betokened divine favour. In a sermon to a Quechua-speaking audience the Peruvian priest Francisco de Avila pointed out to his indigenous parishioners that because of their persistent idolatry they were scarcely capable of harvesting twenty *fanegas* of wheat a year, whereas it was God's will that the Spanish could harvest two or three thousand.[124] In the same period the theologian Francisco de Avendaño observed that Spaniards were far more successful at raising wheat, maize and sheep, because unlike Amerindians they worshipped the one true God.[125] The success of Spanish agriculture in the new world was thus not simply a fortunate development that ensured the survival of colonial outposts by providing Europeans with healthy, appropriate and culturally familiar food. It was an indication of European superiority and divine will. The next chapter looks in greater detail at the significance Spaniards ascribed to their agricultural endeavours.

[123] Hamilton, *Political Thought in Sixteenth-Century Spain*, pp. 133–4; and Pagden, *Spanish Imperialism and the Political Imagination*, esp. pp. 13–36.
[124] Avila, *Tratado de los evangelios*, vol. I, p. 473; and Silverblatt, *Modern Inquisitions*, p. 103.
[125] Avendaño, *Sermones*, primera parte, sermon 4 (p. 47).

3   Providential fertility

In the early 1530s the aged Dominican priest Julián Garcés composed an elegant Latin treatise on the capacity of Amerindians to become Christians. Appointed the first bishop of the Mexican diocese of Puebla when in his seventies, Garcés travelled to the new world in 1527, where he formed part of an influential group of missionaries deeply troubled by Spanish treatment of the indigenous population and the nature of colonial rule, matters that they successfully lobbied both the Spanish crown and the Vatican to address: Garcés's treatise probably formed the basis of Pope Paul III's 1537 declaration that Amerindians were to be considered true men. In this treatise Garcés defended the obedience and other good qualities of Amerindians, insisting that they were in every way suited to receive the Catholic faith. Like many other writers, he also commented on the astonishing frugality and simplicity of their diet, to which he in part attributed their particular talent as musicians, painters and craftsmen. The other factor that in his view explained their imitative skill was the 'clemency and temperance' of the heavens that governed America, which encouraged the development of the intellect. The clement heavens were complemented, he observed, by a fecund and bountiful earth, which brought forth European crops as easily as it did those of the Americas, so that Amerindians could enjoy 'all our fruits', as well as their own.[1]

For Garcés, as for many writers, the success of colonial agriculture reflected the fundamentally benign character of the Americas, with its pleasant climate, temperate air and gentle stars. His writings, like the rapturous accounts of colonial agriculture described in the previous chapter, form one strand of a wider debate about the new world's suitability as a site for Spanish settlement. Indeed, discussion of colonial agriculture cannot be separated from the broader questions of whether

---

[1] Garcés, *De habilitate et capacitate gentium sive Indorum novi mundi nuncupati ad fidem Christi capessendam*, p. 4. I am grateful to Andrew Laird for this reference and translation.

God wanted Spaniards to settle in the Indies, and what the physical and moral costs of this enterprise might be. Answers to these questions depended in large measure on whether the American environment was deemed safe for European bodies, for if its climate and airs were irredeemably noxious to Spaniards then all the wheat and wine in the world would not allow colonial settlements to thrive. This chapter examines Spanish responses to the new world's environment, and considers how their interpretations of the American climate reflect larger concerns about the legitimacy of their colonial endeavour.

Climate and the creole

Unfamiliar environments were always trying to the European body. In the Indies, settlers worried that the region's climate and foods might work the same transformations on their bodies that had earlier been wrought on the ancestors of the Indians, inducing alarming alterations in their very constitutions. In addition, they suspected that the combination of unfamiliar air and food was behind much of the illness that afflicted Europeans in the new world. 'One third of our people have fallen sick within the last four or five days', reported Diego Alvarez Chanca from the Caribbean in 1493, during Columbus's second voyage. This was due, the doctor believed, to both the rigours of the voyage and 'the variableness of the climate'.[2] Colonists a century later assessed the situation similarly. In Mexico, settler Alonso de Alcocer stated, 'everyone from Spain is struck with a *chapetonada*, which kills more than a third of the people who come here', although this did not stop him from encouraging his brother to undertake the journey from Madrid.[3] 'Since I came to these parts I have not enjoyed a single hour of health', complained Diego Sedeña to his nephew in 1592. In his opinion, 'this must be caused by the land being different from ours'. (Nonetheless, he too urged his relatives to hurry to Mexico.[4])

Such illness did not necessarily prove that the climate was inherently unhealthy; simply being different from the climate to which Spaniards were accustomed was sufficient to make it dangerous, as Sedeña

---

[2] Diego Alvarez Chanca to Town Council of Seville, 1493, in Olson and Bourne, eds., *The Voyages of Columbus and of John Cabot*, p. 309.

[3] Alonso de Alcocer to Juan de Colonia, Mexico, 10 Dec. 1577, in Otte, ed., *Cartas privadas de emigrantes a Indias*, p. 99. A *chapetonada* is a colloquial term for an illness specifically afflicting newly arrived Spaniards, or *chapetones*. Or see María Díaz to Inés Díaz, Mexico, 31 March 1577, in Otte, ed., *Cartas privadas de emigrantes a Indias*, p. 97.

[4] Diego Sedeño to Diego Gómez, Mexico, 22 Nov. 1592, in Otte, ed., *Cartas privadas de emigrantes a Indias*, p. 121.

implied. Everyone agreed that a change in air, like any other change to
the body's normal routine, posed a threat to health if it was not managed correctly. Travel to new environments – whether to a different
city or a different continent – which subjected the body to unfamiliar
climates and constellations, and to unusual foods, therefore required
careful attention. This was why recently captured Africans brought
from the interior to the West African slave ports were prone to suffer
from an incurable illness called *luanda*, caused by their exposure to
the coastal air, together with the bad and unfamiliar foods they were
obliged to eat.[5] Even journeys within Europe posed serious challenges
to individual health. Sixteenth-century English travellers in Spain fret-
ted about the impact of alien airs and foods in much the same manner
as did Spanish settlers in the Caribbean.[6] Any change in location, in
other words, could easily place an individual's health at risk.

It was the importance ascribed to environment (understood in the
broadest sense to include the region's climate, its waters and foods and
the stars that governed it) that explains the evolution in the colonial era
of the idea of the 'creole' – someone of European heritage born in the
Indies. The idea that creoles might differ significantly from Peninsulars
emerged in the mid sixteenth century; the first identified usage of the
term dates from the 1560s.[7] (The concept of the mestizo – a person of
mixed European and indigenous parentage – was emerging at roughly
the same time.[8]) Prior to that, and indeed for many decades subsequently, writers generally employed phrases such as 'Spaniards born in
the Indies', or failed to make any distinction at all between Spaniards
born in Europe and those born in the Indies. It was not until the seventeenth century that writers routinely emphasised the differences that
separated Spaniards and creoles. The adaptation of this word, which
hitherto had usually referred to 'acclimatised' slaves familiar with
Spanish culture, to designate the children of Spaniards born in the new
world nonetheless indicates that the distinction between 'los de acá'
(people from here) and 'los de allá' (people from there) was becoming
culturally important. As the historian Bernard Lavallé has noted, the

[5] Sandoval, *De Instauranda aethiopum salute*, p. 108. See also Zurara, *Chronica do descobrimento e conquisita de Guiné*, chap. 26 (pp. 137–8).
[6] Borde, *The Fyrst Boke of the Introduction of Knowledge*, chap. 32 (vol. II, p. 88); and
Hillgarth, *The Mirror of Spain*, pp. 13, 16.
[7] On the development of creole identity see Lafaye, *Quetzalcóatl and Guadalupe*; Lavallé,
Las promesas ambiguas; and Brading, *The First America*.
[8] Hernández, *Quatro libros de la naturaleza*, book 3, part 1, chap. 40 (p. 135); Ovalle,
Histórica relación del Reyno de Chile, book 3, chap. 5 (p. 117); Mörner, *Race Mixture in
the History of Latin America*, pp. 28–9, 54–5; Cope, *The Limits of Racial Domination*,
p. 18; and Martínez, *Genealogical Fictions*, pp. 138–9.

use of the term 'creole' to describe Spaniards born in the Indies appears to have emerged first in the Americas, rather than in Spain. It is, in other words, a colonial distinction.

Colonial writers asked themselves whether, and how, creoles might differ from their Spanish progenitors. Some, particularly those who believed that creoles adhered closely to the European diet and to European culture more generally, insisted that Spaniards and creoles varied but little in either their physiques or their personalities. The Spanish doctor Diego Cisneros for example observed, with regard to creoles and Spaniards, that 'where there is such similarity in diet the complexion and natural temperament cannot alter'.[9] Others maintained that the creole constitution varied in subtle ways from the Spanish constitution – a variation that writers almost always ascribed equally to the different lifestyle adopted by creoles and the different climate of the Indies. The simple fact of birth in the Indies, in other words, was rarely seen as a decisive factor in creating a distinctive creole constitution. Those who believed that creoles differed constitutionally from Spaniards tended to maintain that creoles were slightly more 'moist' than Peninsulars, which gave them a complex 'choleric-sanguine' complexion, in contrast to their choleric progenitors.[10] Thus in so far as creoles were believed to differ from Peninsulars these differences were not necessarily the result of some intrinsic flaw in the new world's environment, but rather were a natural consequence of following a different regimen and living under different stars.

Because conflict between creoles and Peninsulars played an important role in the deterioration of transatlantic relations that preceded the outbreak of the Spanish American wars of independence in 1810, scholars have naturally sought earlier expressions of anti-creole sentiment, and have sometimes assumed that the hostility towards creoles expressed by many Spaniards in the late eighteenth century also typified Peninsular attitudes in earlier centuries. In fact, not only did sixteenth-century writers often fail to identify any important features that differentiated creoles from Peninsulars, but any differences that were identified might be to the benefit, rather than the detriment, of the creole. Creoles were often praised for their 'rare and subtle wit', and many writers argued that they were, in general, 'frank, liberal, merry, courageous, affable, well tempered and cheerful', as a consequence of

---

[9] Cisneros, *Sitio, naturaleza y propriedades*, chap. 17 (p. 114v). As regards creoles, 'it cannot be doubted that they are truly Spanish', insisted Solórzano Pereira: *Política indiana*, book 2, chap. 30, section 1 (vol. I, p. 216).

[10] Martínez, *Reportorio de los tiempos*, pp. 281–2; and Cárdenas, *Problemas y secretos maravillosos*, book 3, chaps. 1–2 (pp. 174–5, 178–9).

the moister environment of the Indies, which moderated the Spaniard's natural choleric tendencies.[11] Furthermore, because the humid environment discouraged plants from sinking deep roots, food grown in the Indies was somewhat less nourishing than that produced in Europe. While some considered this to be a defect, others argued that it further encouraged the development of wit.[12] This was because the consumption of light, insubstantial foods was generally held to stimulate the intellect. The German cosmographer Henrico Martínez, who lived for many decades in Mexico City overseeing the drainage of several of the city's surrounding lakes, argued that this explained the keen intelligence typical of colonists raised in the Indies. 'One sees from experience', he recorded, 'that in this kingdom able and talented foreigners become even abler, and the less able improve their condition.'[13] He conceded, however, that foods grown in the Indies did not help build hearty bodies.[14] The new world's environment perhaps left Europeans ill-suited to heavy manual labour, but it also made them clever.

Some people, however, suspected that there *was* something inherently unhealthy about the American environment. The Spanish jurist Baltasar Álamos de Barrientos, for example, maintained that both the climate and its foods were not merely different but intrinsically flawed. In a political treatise addressed to Philip III he observed that in the

[11] Lope de Vega, *La Dorotea*, act 2, scene 5 (p. 54), www.scribd.com/doc/7942182/ Vega-Lope-de-La-Dorotea; and Cárdenas, *Problemas y secretos maravillosos*, book 3, chap. 2 (p. 179). See also Vargas Machuca, 'Descripción breve de todas las Indias occidentales', in *Milicia y descripción de las Indias*, vol. II, p. 194; Murúa, *Historia general del Perú*, book 3, chap. 14 (p. 515); and Herrero García, *Ideas de los españoles*, p. 316. Cárdenas noted that a creole raised in the most abandoned indigenous village would speak as if he had been raised at court, and in any event far more elegantly than a Spaniard raised in the same village: Cárdenas, *Problemas y secretos maravillosos*, book 3, chap. 2 (pp. 176–7). Of course Spaniards themselves were already known for their wit and vivacity: Villalón, *El scholástico*, book 4, chap. 17 (p. 326); and Lemnius, *The Touchstone of Complexions*, book 1 (p. 29).

[12] Cárdenas, *Problemas y secretos maravillosos*, book 1, chap. 9, book 3, chap. 1 (pp. 32–3, 175); Hernández, *Antigüedades de la Nueva España*, book 1, chap. 23 (pp. 96–7); Juan Sedeño to Diego López, Cartagena, 12 July 1580, in Otte, ed., *Cartas privadas de emigrantes a Indias*, p. 294; Torquemada, *Monarchia yndiana*, book 14, chap. 19 (vol. II, p. 613); Gage, *The English-American*, chap. 9 (p. 61); and Cañizares Esguerra, 'New Worlds, New Stars'.

[13] Martínez, *Reportorio de los tiempos*, pp. 282–3; Las Casas, *Apologética historia sumaria*, c. 1552, chaps. 24, 27 (pp. 75, 86); and Vetancurt, *Teatro mexicano*, tratado 1, chap. 6 (p. 11). Cisneros agreed that new world foods were less nourishing, but maintained that because the climate was different it was actually necessary to eat less nourishing foods: Cisneros, *Sitio, naturaleza y propriedades*, chap. 17 (p. 114v).

[14] Martínez, *Reportorio de los tiempos*, pp. 279, 296; and Calancha, *Corónica moralizada*, book 1, chap. 8 (pp. 47–8). Travellers from other parts of Europe made exactly the same criticism of food in Spain itself: Díez Borque, *La sociedad española y los viajeros del siglo XVII*, pp. 99–100.

Indies 'whether because of the climate or its air, or because of its foods, those who live there become like their surroundings, and even worse: liars, swindlers, cheats, traitors, ambitious, proud men who seek power by any means, no matter how illicit'.[15] The Franciscan priest Bernardino de Sahagún similarly believed that 'the mildness and abundance of this land and the constellations that govern it encourage vice, idleness and sensuality'. He noted that if Spanish settlers were not careful, only a few years' residence would be required for them to transform into quite different, less upstanding creatures. He added, 'this I believe is due to the climate and constellations of this land'.[16] (The Spaniard Sahagún nonetheless lived for half a century in Mexico evangelising the Nahua population, teaching Latin at the recently established Colegio de Santa Cruz de Tlatelolco and composing a vast history of the Aztec empire, without ever showing any desire to return to Europe, the new world's dangerous climate and stars notwithstanding.) Suggestions that the American environment naturally encouraged immoral behaviour did little to still the fears of wives left behind in Spain while their husbands voyaged through the Indies. Such concerns are reflected in the anxious missives penned by women to their distant husbands, in which worries about infidelity are cloaked in the language of health and hygiene. 'For the love of God look after your health because in that land too much vice will finish you off', Leonor Gil de Molina warned her settler husband from far-off Cádiz.[17]

Individuals who doubted the healthfulness of the new world often – like Sahagún – referred to the malign influence of the particular constellations that governed the region, and also mentioned its allegedly hot climate.[18] This was because a very hot, damp environment (itself, of course, a relative concept) was accepted by all Europeans as less healthy than a moderate one.[19] In addition, the influence of astral forces on human life was widely acknowledged, even though claims that the stars governed everything sailed perilously close to denying the autonomy

---

[15] Álamos de Barrientos, *Discurso político al rey Felipe III*, p. 16. See also Puente, *Tomo primero de la conveniencia de las dos monarquías católicas*, book 2, chap. 35, section 3 (p. 363), book 3, chap. 3, section 3 (p. 21); Hernández, *Antigüedades de la Nueva España*, book 1, chap. 23 (p. 97); and Martínez, *Genealogical Fictions*, pp. 201–2.

[16] Sahagún, *Historia general de las cosas de Nueva España*, book 10, chap. 27 (vol. II, pp. 486–7).

[17] Rodrigo de Ribera to Cristóbal de Ribera, Seville, 1568; and Leonar Gil de Molina to Juan de Chávez, Alcalá de los Gazules, 1576; both in Sánchez Rubio and Testón Núñez, eds., *El hilo que une*, pp. 62, 100 (quotation).

[18] For early modern criticism of new world stars see Cañizares Esguerra, 'New Worlds, New Stars'.

[19] Hippocrates, 'On Airs, Waters and Places', in *The Genuine Works of Hippocrates*; and Glacken, *Traces on the Rhodian Shore*.

of the individual will. In other words, whether or not its challenges could be mitigated through careful attention to an individual's regimen, and in particular their diet, the American environment (terrestrial and celestial) itself was regarded by some Spaniards as not only different but also inferior. It was too hot, too damp and was governed by dangerous stars. 'The night air in this land is very bad, and does me much harm', complained Sevillano Bartolomé de Morales from Mexico in 1573.[20] From such comments one might conclude the Spaniards generally viewed the American environment with distrust and suspicion.

This was not, however, the attitude most commonly expressed by early modern colonial writers. Both in private letters and published treatises creoles and Europeans were far more likely to praise the new world's environment than to excoriate it. 'This city of Mexico ... is a good and healthy land', Inés de Solís wrote to her sister in 1574.[21] 'This land is healthy and well provisioned and everyone here earns their bread and grows rich', asserted Alonso Durán from Ecuador in 1589.[22] Writing in the same years from Lima (a region not subsequently famed for its delightful climate), Alonso Martín del Campillo painted an equally appealing picture:

[T]his land ... is the best in all the known world, rich, very well provided with bread, meats, fish, fruits, and whatever there is in Spain. It never rains, nor thunders, there are no storms, and it's neither too hot nor too cold ... and to bring even greater fertility every night God sends a very fine mist, like dew, which refreshes the whole land.[23]

While everyone agreed that certain locales – whether in the Indies or in Europe – were less healthy than others, the only regions that settlers consistently denounced as completely inimical to the European body were very hot, tropical lowlands and forests. These places harboured not only hostile indigenous groups, but also dangerous snakes, insects and other fearsome creatures. Generally, only pressing commercial interests could compel Spaniards to remain in these areas. (High mountain tops where one was likely to suffer from altitude sickness

---

[20] Bartolomé de Morales to Antón Pérez, Mexico, 30 Oct. 1573, in Otte, ed., *Cartas privadas de emigrantes a Indias*, p. 72.

[21] Inés de Solís to Angela de Solís, Mexico, 25 Oct. 1574, in Otte, ed., *Cartas privadas de emigrantes a Indias*, p. 89.

[22] Alonso Durán to Juan Sánchez, Cuenca, 22 April 1589, in Otte, ed., *Cartas privadas de emigrantes a Indias*, p. 365.

[23] Alonso Martín del Campillo to Salvador Ruiz, Los Reyes, 2 Dec. 1575, in Otte, ed., *Cartas privadas de emigrantes a Indias*, p. 390. Or see Pedro de Alarcón to Ana de Alarcón, Oruro, 3 Feb. 1614, in Otte, ed., *Cartas privadas de emigrantes a Indias*, p. 544.

were not popular with settlers either.) Maritime and trading concerns thus obliged the establishment of settlements in some regions colonists might otherwise have preferred to avoid, but even hot Caribbean cities such as Cartagena were often praised as healthful and pleasant.[24] Aside from these liminal and port zones, which never constituted the heartland of colonial settlement, the landscape and climate of the Indies were routinely praised by colonial officials, individual settlers and chroniclers as comparable, if not superior, to those of Spain. Their new world, they insisted, enjoyed a temperate climate, wholesome waters and beneficent airs.

Writers found particular evidence for the beneficence of new-world nature in the ease with which European crops – like almost everything else – flourished, and in the wealth of medicinal herbs that helped preserve the bodies of settlers against the specific challenges posed by the region's unfamiliar waters and airs. Taken together, this evidence strongly suggested that the new world's environment was specially designed by God to welcome the Spanish. The new world and the Spanish constitution were thus made for each other. Spaniards, after all, were particularly suited for overseas exploits because, in the words of one chronicler, God had equipped them with a complexion that was 'the most robust and well adapted to undergoing changes in climate and environment of any people in the entire known world'.[25] In the Indies this robust, imperial constitution found an environment that in a thousand ways revealed not danger but rather the will of God.

Discussions of the new world's environment, in other words, were most often situated not in the context of denigrating America and its inhabitants, but rather of praising divine providence: God had made the American environment suitable for the Spanish body in many different ways. He ensured that the necessary old-world crops flourished, furnished the region with the very medicines needed to cure the ailments endemic in the hemisphere and on occasion even tempered the climate itself. What greater evidence could one seek that God himself supported Spain's colonial enterprise?

---

[24] See for example Miguel Hidalgo to Juan Martínez, Cartagena, 4 June 1587, in Otte, ed., *Cartas privadas de emigrantes a Indias*, p. 302. See also López Medel, *De los tres elementos*, pp. 18, 129–33, 205.

[25] This topic is listed in the book's index as 'Spain: the complexion suited to any climate': Botero Benes, *Relaciones universales*, part 2, book 4 (p. 100). See also Peñaloza y Mondragón, *Libro de las cinco excelencias del español*, p. 6; and Herrero García, *Ideas de los españoles*, p. 22.

'In what other land?'

For most writers, the fact that old-world plants and animals flourished in the new world could mean only one thing: divine forces looked favourably on Spain's presence in the Indies. 'In what other land', asked the chronicler Oviedo,

has it ever been known or heard that in such a short space of time, and in lands so far from our Europe, so much cattle and livestock should be produced, and such abundance of crops as we see with our own eyes in these Indies, brought there from across such vast oceans? This land has received them not as a step-mother, but as a truer mother than the land that sent them, for some of these things grow better and yield more here than they do in Spain.[26]

Oviedo used the success of colonial agriculture to indicate that near-miraculous forces guided Spanish settlement, for what else could explain the ease with which Iberian plants and animals thrived, so far from Europe? Clearly nature herself endorsed Spain's colonial endeavour. The abundance and fertility of the new world was thus endowed with a transcendent religious significance. Perhaps the Indies had lacked bread and wine prior to Spanish settlement, but the success with which Spanish crops now grew proved that this absolutely did not reflect any intrinsic fault in the land itself, Oviedo insisted.[27]

Indeed the ease with which European foodstuffs flourished was used by a number of writers to adduce that the new world – far from being a noxious swamp – was in fact the location of the Garden of Eden, the original site of all fertility and abundance. This was the conclusion reached by the Mexican creole Agustín de Vetancurt, for example. In the *Teatro mexicano* (*The Mexican Theatre*), Vetancurt's late seventeenth-century encomium to his homeland, he marvelled at the abundance with which European fruits grew year round. This fact, together with the region's benign climate, in his view proved beyond doubt 'that the Terrestrial Paradise is hidden in some part of this land'.[28] The following sections trace the long history of such assertions, and show how the perceived fertility of the American environment became entangled with providentialist claims about the legitimacy of Spain's colonial enterprise.

---

[26] Fernández de Oviedo, *Historia general y natural*, book 1, dedication, book 3, chaps. 8, 11, book 16, chap. 16, book 17, chaps. 3, 4, book 18, chap. 1 (vol. I, pp. 8 (quotation), 71, 79, vol. II, pp. 107, 115, 184).

[27] Fernández de Oviedo, *Historia general y natural*, book 3, chap. 11 (vol. I, p. 80).

[28] Vetancurt, *Teatro mexicano*, tratado 2, introduction, chap. 8 (pp. 17 (quotation), 42, 44). Vetancurt paraphrases Salinas y Córdova, *Memorial, informe y manifiesto*, p. 17v (see also 18r). See also Salinas y Córdova, *Memorial de las historias del Nuevo Mundo*, discurso 2 (pp. 102–15, 252–3); and Lavallé, *Promesas ambiguas*, pp. 122–3.

Although Spain's European rivals denounced Spanish imperialism as unrestrained plunder, and criticised its colonial settlements as moral cesspools, Spanish writers consistently interpreted their American endeavours as indications of the special destiny that God had reserved for their country.[29] For such writers, evidence of this destiny was scattered plentifully across the Indies, including in American nature itself. The region's ability to grow apples and wheat thus revealed far more than a simple agricultural fact.

Terrestrial paradise

In describing the new world as a veritable Garden of Eden, Vetancurt drew on long-established colonial traditions, for many writers, beginning with Columbus, entertained similar suppositions. As the philosopher George Boas has noted, although the Bible gives no hint of the fate or location of the Garden of Eden after Adam and Eve's expulsion, 'that it still existed somewhere was almost universally believed'.[30] Columbus himself consistently maintained that the earthly paradise was situated in the Indies. He first expressed this idea in 1493, during his initial voyage. While returning to Europe Columbus's fleet had been caught in a fierce storm in the Azores. This experience prompted him to contrast the stormy weather of the Azores with the calm he had witnessed in the Caribbean, where the air and ocean were always mild and temperate. He reasoned that the Indies, a temperate zone situated on the fringes of the East, must be the location of the earthly paradise.[31] Columbus subsequently refined the geography of paradise on his third voyage, when he concluded that the abundance and fertility of the land surrounding the mouth of the Orinoco River, together with what he regarded as the region's distinctive topography, indicated that he had reached one of the four rivers that flowed from the terrestrial paradise.[32] Columbus based this conclusion on his (probably second-hand) reading of 'Saint

---

[29] For a classic example see Raleigh, *The Discovery of the Large, Rich and Beautiful Empire of Guiana*.

[30] Boas, *Essays on Primitivism and Related Ideas in the Middle Ages*, p. 154.

[31] Columbus, 'Diary of the First Voyage', 15 Dec. 1492, and 21 Feb. 1493, pp. 90, 147.

[32] Columbus, 'Carta a los reyes católicos', 18 Oct. 1498, in *Los cuarto viajes del almirante*, pp. 183–6, 188; Columbus, 'Carta al papa Alexander VI', Feb. 1502, in Fernández de Navarrete, ed., *Coleccion de los viajes y descubrimientos que hicieron por mar los españoles desde fines del siglo XV*, doc. 145 (vol. II, pp. 311–13); and Las Casas, *Historia de las Indias*, *c.* 1559, book 1, chap. 90 (p. 258). Columbus believed that the ocean around the mouth of the Orinoco sloped upwards, and compared the region's topography to the top of a pear, or a woman's nipple.

Isidore and Bede and Strabo and the master of scholastic history and Saint Ambrose and Duns Scotus and all sound theologians'.[33]

The particular contours of Columbus's medieval vision of an earthly paradise were shaped not only by the writings of such Christian authorities but also by a variety of other texts, including medieval travel literature. We know that Columbus owned copies of both Marco Polo's and John Mandeville's *Travels*, and their traces are visible in many aspects of Columbus's oeuvre. Mandeville in particular specifically discussed the location of the earthly paradise, and referred repeatedly to the rivers that flowed from it. Indeed medieval maps routinely included Paradise alongside more mundane locations such as Italy. Paradise, such sources suggested, was not a wholly inaccessible destination.[34] We can see the influence of both religious and travel literature in Columbus's simultaneous identification of the West Indies as one of the mythical sites mentioned in the Bible, and also Japan. In a letter to Pope Alexander VI of 1502 he wrote of Hispaniola: '[T]his island is Tarshish, it is Cethim, it is Ophir and Uphaz and Cipango, and we have called it Española.'[35] Tarshish, Cethim (or Kittim), Ophir and Uphaz were biblical sites famed for their wealth, while Cipango, or Japan, was equally renowned for richness.[36] (As Marco Polo recorded, 'they have gold in the greatest abundance, its sources being inexhaustible'.[37]) For Columbus the West Indies were thus an amalgam of biblical and geographical loci of plenty.

Columbus's vision of the Indies as a terrestrial paradise also drew on the traditions of medieval pastoral poetry, with its evocations of a golden age free from suffering, hard work and grief. His depiction of the West Indies as a veritable land of Cockaigne, where the earth miraculously yielded food all year round without any human intervention, reflects

---

[33] Columbus, 'Carta a los reyes católicos', 18 Oct. 1498, in *Los cuarto viajes del almirante*, p. 184; and Gil, *Mitos y utopías del Descubrimiento*, p. 138. The master of scholastic history was probably Petrus Comestor.

[34] Flint, *The Imaginative Landscape of Christopher Columbus*, pp. 10–13, 161–8; Zamora, *Reading Columbus*, pp. 95–151; and Mandeville, *The Travels of Sir John Mandeville*, pp. 63, 111, 154, 169, 182–5. There is some debate about when Columbus acquired his copy of *I Millione*: Gil, *Mitos y utopías del Descubrimiento*, pp. 124–5. See also Baudet, *Paradise on Earth*.

[35] Columbus, 'Carta al papa Alexander VI', Feb. 1502, in Fernández de Navarrete, ed., *Coleccion de los viajes y descubrimientos que hicieron por mar los españoles desde fines del siglo XV*, doc. 145 (vol. II, p. 311); Gil, *Mitos y utopías del Descubrimiento*; and Campbell, *The Witness and the Other World*, p. 10. His 1502 *Libro o gavilla de autoridades, dichos, sentencias y profecias* similarly identified the Indies with Tarsis and Ophir, both of which he believed to be islands: Columbus, *Libro de las profecias*, pp. 115–23.

[36] See for example 1 Kings 10:11, 10:22; 1 Kings 22:48; 2 Chron. 9:10–21; Job 22:24, 28:16; Isa. 60:9; Jer. 10:9; Ezek. 27:6; Dan. 10:5.

[37] Polo, *Travels*, p. 207.

such influences both in its emphasis on ease and in its creation of a charming, pastoral environment.[38] From about the twelfth century, poetic descriptions of the earthly paradise had characterised it as a *locus amoenus*, a rhetorical evocation of a pleasant setting typical of classical poets such as Virgil which consisted, in A. C. Spearing's words, of:

a Mediterranean landscape ... typically set in bright southern sunlight ... but it also provides shade against the sun, and is therefore furnished with a tree or trees, often fruit-trees. The trees will be in a flowery meadow, which will provide fragrance as well as bright colours, and there will probably be birds singing in them ... In the meadow there is almost invariably a spring or brook ... and there will usually be a breeze.[39]

We find all these features in Columbus's widely disseminated 1493 *Letter Concerning the Islands Recently Discovered*, which by 1497 had been published in seventeen different editions in Spain, France, Italy, Switzerland and the Netherlands. Writing of the Caribbean islands, Columbus noted:

Many great and salubrious rivers flow through it ... All these islands are very beautiful ... and full of a great variety of trees stretching up to the stars; the leaves of which I believe are never shed, for I saw them as green and flourishing as they are usually in Spain in the month of May; some of them were blossoming, some were bearing fruit ... The nightingale and various other birds without number were singing.[40]

Water, fruits, flowers, birdsong: Columbus focused on those elements of the Caribbean landscape that best fit with the pastoral vision of an earthly paradise. Beyond these features, as literary scholar Mary Campbell has noted, the gold and spices that Columbus insistently located in the Caribbean were themselves 'part of a literary landscape generated over several centuries by the specific needs and scarcities of the actual landscape of Home. They are two items on a conventional list of paradisiacal abundance.'[41] Columbus's identification of the Indies

---

[38] Campbell, *The Witness and the Other World*, p. 10; and, for the blending of ideas of a classical Golden Age with a Christian concept of Paradise, Cooper, *Pastoral*, esp. pp. 6, 67, 92–9.

[39] Spearing, *Medieval Dream-Poetry*, p. 17; Curtius, *European Literature and the Latin Middle Ages*, pp. 195, 183–202; Boas, *Essays on Primitivism and Related Ideas in the Middle Ages*, pp. 154–74; and Glacken, *Traces on the Rhodian Shore*, pp. 130–4. According to Boas, 'we find indeed no period without its legends of wonderful undiscovered countries – usually islands – in some of which certain features of the Golden Age survived': Boas, *Essays on Primitivism and Related Ideas in the Middle Ages*, p. 154.

[40] Columbus, 'Concerning the Islands Recently Discovered in the Indian Sea'.

[41] Campbell, *The Witness and the Other World*, p. 183. On gold and Paradise see also Gen. 2:11; Columbus, 'Carta del almirante a los reyes católicos', 7 July 1503, in *Los cuarto*

with the terrestrial paradise thus synthesised a range of religious and literary traditions that located Eden in a pleasant, fertile landscape equally rich in gold and fruit trees.

This image of America as a fertile, Edenic land of plenty was reproduced by many other early colonial writers, who rhapsodised about the luxuriant and exotic flora and abundant gold. Amerigo Vespucci, writing in 1503 to Lorenzo de Medici, reported that 'great trees grow without cultivation, of which many yield fruits pleasant to the taste and nourishing to the human body; and a great many have an opposite effect ... No kind of metal has been found except gold, in which the country abounds'. The climate, he added, was very temperate. He concluded: '[I]f the terrestrial paradise is in some part of this land, it cannot be very far from the coast we visited.'[42] Gathering together such reports, alongside the news he gleaned from returning conquistadors, the humanist scholar and courtier Peter Martyr affirmed that 'our compatriots have discovered a thousand islands as fair as Paradise, a thousand Elysian regions'.[43] The idea that the Garden of Eden was located in the new world was further immortalised in Garci Rodríguez de Montalvo's popular chivalric novel *Las Sergas de Esplandián* (*The Exploits of Esplandián*) of 1510, part of whose action takes place in the fictional location of 'California', itself situated 'to the right of the Indies, near the Garden of Eden'.[44] The Spanish crown, unlike the English, did little actively to promote migration to the Indies, but such widely read texts nonetheless served as an incentive, as indeed did the many letters from individual settlers that likewise compared the Indies to paradise on earth, rich in food and gold. 'This land is a marvel, and we lack only paradise for it to be utterly heavenly', wrote a Madrileño from Lima in 1581.[45]

Consequently, as one disgruntled priest complained, by the 1540s hordes of Spaniards were converging on the Indies, believing them to be either 'the island of Ophir, from where King Solomon took fine gold' or

---

viajes del almirante, p. 201; Levin, *The Myth of the Golden Age*, p. 12; and Zamora, *Reading Columbus*, p. 137.

[42] Vespucci, 'Letter on His Third Voyage to Lorenzo Pietro Francesco di Medici' (the Medici Letter), March–April 1503, in *The Letters of Amerigo Vespucci*, pp. 10, 11.

[43] Peter Martyr, *De Orbe Novo*, decade 3, book 5. He did not believe that the Indies were the location of the *actual* Garden of Eden, but he regularly compared indigenous society to the Golden Age: *De Orbe Novo*, decade 1, books 2, 3, 6; decade 2, books 6, 9, decade 3, book 8; and Levin, *The Myth of the Golden Age*.

[44] Chevalier, *Land and Society in Colonial Mexico*, p. 25 (quotation); and Leonard, *Books of the Brave*, pp. 38–40, 57.

[45] Francisco Sanz Heredero to Juan Heredero, Los Reyes, 8 April 1581, in Otte, ed., *Cartas privadas de emigrantes a Indias*, p. 408.

'the island of Tarshish or great Japan, where there is so much gold that people gather it up in buckets'.[46] These, of course, are precisely the locations that Columbus himself identified with the Indies. His imaginative geography thus reflected a wider set of cultural associations between such semi-mythical lands, paradise and places of wealth and ease. The Dominican priest Bartolomé de las Casas, like many other clerical writers, preferred to praise the docility of the indigenous population, rather than the presence of gold, but he too labelled the Indies a fertile paradise, in his view unfortunately despoiled by greedy Spaniards.[47] The idea that the Indies were the location of either the actual terrestrial paradise or a close approximation was thus well established by the mid sixteenth century. By the seventeenth century such images had become absolutely conventional, and formed an important element of both Spanish and creole discourse on the new world. Thus a Spanish priest described the area around the city of Guatemala as a paradisiacal *locus amoenus*. It was, he wrote, 'a little piece of paradise, with many fountains and streams of fresh crystalline water, with beautiful gardens and orchards of Spanish and local fruit trees which bear fruit all the year round'.[48] The sober Spanish jurist Juan de Solórzano Pereira noted in his 1647 commentary on colonial governance that Columbus was quite justified in believing the new world to be the seat of paradise, given the region's marvellous fertility and benign climate.[49] The eccentric creole Antonio de León Pinelo penned an entire book devoted to proving that the Garden of Eden was located specifically in Peru.[50]

These traditions helped shape the language of creole patriotism, the discursive celebration of the new world that formed an important element of learned creole culture in the late seventeenth and eighteenth centuries. From the mid sixteenth century the original conquistadors and colonisers, and then their descendants, became increasingly vociferous in their claims that the crown had not rewarded them sufficiently for the immense achievement of conquering the Indies. The crown's

---

[46] Motolinía, *Historia de los Indios de la Nueva España*, 1541, tratado 3, chap. 11; and Gil, *Mitos y utopías del Descubrimiento*, p. 226.

[47] Las Casas, *Breve relación de la destrucción de las Indias Occidentales*, p. 80; Las Casas, *Historia de las Indias*, c. 1559, book 1, chaps. 44 (for a *locus amoenus*) and 54 (pp. 157, 183–4); and Las Casas, *Apologética historia*, chap. 17 (pp. 54–5).

[48] Vásquez de Espinosa, *Compendio y descripción*, part 1, book 5, chap. 6, no. 603 (p. 149).

[49] Solórzano Pereira, *Política indiana*, book 1, chap. 4, section 3 (vol. I, p. 10).

[50] León Pinelo, *El paraíso en el Nuevo Mundo*. See also Acosta, *The Natural and Moral History of the Indies*, book 2, chap. 13–14 (pp. 95, 97–8); Balbuena, *Grandeza mexicana*, chap. 4 (p. 47); Simón, *Noticias historiales*, noticia 1, chap. 10 (vol. I, pp. 146–7); Cobo, *Historia del Nuevo Mundo*, book 2, chap. 14 (vol. I, p. 86); Lavallé, *Las promesas ambiguas*, pp. 115–16; and Cañizares Esguerra, *Puritan Conquistadors*, pp. 195–8.

proposal to limit grants of encomienda (which allocated to the recipi-
ent a sometimes sizeable indigenous labour force) to two generations
was a particular bone of contention. Petitioners complained that while
the sons of the conquistadors languished in poverty, newly arrived
Spaniards, who had done nothing whatsoever to further Spain's colonial enterprise, monopolised all important posts through corruption
and their links to high-ranking Spanish officials. While at first such
complaints emerged equally from Spaniards long resident in the Indies
and their creole offspring, by the late sixteenth century, when few of
the original conquistadors and settlers remained alive, this sense of
resentment became particularly associated with creoles. Seventeenth-
century archives are full of complaints from creoles about unfair treatment in the distribution of ecclesiastical benefices and other forms of
discrimination.

Such writers not only complained about discrimination at the hands of
Peninsulars, but also insisted that their new-world birth was an advantage that Spaniards failed to appreciate. It gave creoles a knowledge of
the local environment that was infinitely more detailed and accurate
than that possessed by people born in Spain. Familiarity with indigenous languages was often offered by creole priests as a particular reason
why any discrimination in ecclesiastical appointments should benefit
creoles, rather than Spaniards. Beyond this, creole patriots embarked
on a much wider celebration of their homeland that drew heavily on
the identification of the Indies as a place of paradisiacal abundance.
Seventeenth-century writers began to compose panegyrics to their
native lands, which insisted that the Indies were uniquely blessed by
God and in no way inferior to Spain.

Antonio de la Calancha, an Augustinian monk born in Upper Peru,
was typical in his concern to vindicate creole history while at the same
time celebrating the American environment. In the 1630s he composed
an account of his order's presence in Peru in which he detailed the pious
actions of his fellow monks. In his chronicle he lauded the region's marvellous climate and general bounty in exuberant terms. 'Because its
heavens are so benevolent, its stars so favourable, its winds few and very
temperate, its waters fresh, sweet, fertile and without evil', he wrote,
'it follows that Peru is the richest and best provisioned in the entire
world, and its lands healthy, delightful and abundantly supplied with
food.'[51] His account detailed the delicious almonds that already grew all

---

[51] Calancha, *Corónica moralizada*, book 1, chap. 8 (p. 53). Such celebration was also
characteristic of the local histories composed in Spain in the same period: Kagan,
'Clio and the Crown', p. 89.

over the viceroyalty, the tasty cherries imported from Chile (and which were beginning to grow in Peru as well) and the abundance of wine, oil, honey, sugar, wheat and other crops, all of which showed that Peru had surpassed the old world in the abundance of its harvests and the fertility of its soil. He concluded that Peru could justly be considered a 'garden of delights', and perhaps even an earthly paradise. To back up this assertion he appealed to the authority of Columbus and the other early colonial writers who had first established the association between the Indies and Eden.[52]

Identification of the Indies with Eden, in short, formed an important element of colonial discourse from the earliest days of European settlement. Spanish and creole writers with a range of perspectives shared the view that the Indies could justly be described as a paradise on earth. In this they drew upon a variety of European textual traditions – from early church Fathers and classical poets to semi-fictional travel writings – which combined to form a distinct image of paradise as a place of ease, simplicity and freedom from want. In the Indies man's needs – whether for gold or for bread – were amply met by a beneficent landscape in which crops grew with little effort and nightingales sang all the while. Far from being malevolent, the new world was a veritable Eden.

Providential discovery

Actually locating the Garden of Eden in the Indies was merely an extreme version of the widely shared Spanish belief that their triumphs in the Americas revealed the hand of divine providence. Early modern Spanish writers routinely celebrated the conquest as providential: Columbus's arrival in the new world was clearly the result of divine guidance, which in turn indicated that God wanted Spaniards to discover, and colonise, the Indies. These ideas were present from the very start of American colonisation. Columbus himself saw divine forces at work in his own life, as a number of scholars have shown.[53] For example, in a letter of 1501 to the Spanish monarchs Columbus referred to the 'obvious miracle' that God worked in sending him to the Indies.[54] He

[52] Calancha, *Corónica moralizada*, book 1, chaps. 9–10 (pp. 56–67 (quotation)). Or see Fuentes y Guzmán, *Historia de Guatemala o Recordación Florida*; and Ovalle, *Histórica relación del Reyno de Chile*, book 1 (pp. 15–80).

[53] Watts, 'Prophecy and Discovery'; and Zamora, *Reading Columbus*. On early modern Spain as an agent of divine providence more generally see Herrero García, *Ideas de los españoles del siglo XVII*, pp. 15–29.

[54] Columbus, 'Carta del almirante al rey y a la reina', 1501, in *Libro de las profecías*, p. 11.

went on to add that in undertaking this journey he had relied on neither logic, nor mathematics nor maps, from which he concluded that his venture had fulfilled Old Testament prophesy.[55] The collection of biblical references compiled by Columbus around 1502 now known as the *Libro de las profecías* (*Book of Prophesies*) similarly illustrates the admiral's belief that the discovery was both divinely ordained and predicted in a variety of sacred texts. Overall, he maintained that his arrival in the new world formed part of a larger divine plan to allow the Spanish to recapture Jerusalem.

The idea that divine forces guided the discovery permeated sixteenth- and seventeenth-century Spanish literate culture. This, for example, is the underlying message of *El nuevo mundo descubierto por Cristóbal Colón* (*The New World Discovered by Christopher Columbus*), Lope de Vega's didactic comedy about Columbus's discoveries, composed at the turn of the seventeenth century. The play reviews Columbus's quest for patronage and describes his ultimate triumph in realising his vision. Lope de Vega was explicit in his explanation for Columbus's success: Columbus succeeded because he was aided by divine forces. Indeed, towards the start of the drama 'Divine Providence' and 'Christian Religion' appear before a despondent Columbus and assure him that they will support his enterprise.[56] Encouraged, he offers his services to the Catholic monarchs on condition that he be allowed to spread the gospel. 'I am certain that heaven will support such worthy and principled zeal', responds Queen Isabel.[57] The play's audience could thus conclude that Spain's by then extensive colonial settlements were the result of divine support. As further evidence that divine forces looked favourably on Spain Lope de Vega proffered the fact that Columbus's landfall in the Caribbean occurred in the same year as the defeat of the last Moorish strongholds in Andalusia.[58]

The chronicler Francisco López de Gómara was similarly explicit in linking the defeat of the Moors and the discovery of America to the divine will. Addressing Charles V in the dedication to his 1552 *Historia de las Indias* (*History of the Indies*), Gómara wrote: 'God wished the Indies

---

[55] Columbus, 'Carta del almirante al rey y a la reina', 1501, in *Libro de las profecías*, p. 15. See also Columbus, 'Carta a los reyes católicos', 18 Oct. 1498, in *Los cuarto viajes del almirante y su testamento*, pp. 169–70.

[56] Lope de Vega, *El nuevo mundo descubierto por Cristóbal Colón*. Or see Sigüenza, *Historia de la Orden de San Gerónimo*, part 3, book 1, chap. 25 (vol. II, p. 101).

[57] Lope de Vega, *El nuevo mundo descubierto por Cristóbal Colón*, act 1, lines 948–9 (p. 13).

[58] 'Sir, you have completed the conquest of Granada with great success. Now it is time to win an entire world', the play's hero tells King Ferdinand: Lope de Vega, *El nuevo mundo descubierto por Cristóbal Colón*, act 1, lines 928–9 (p. 13).

to be discovered in your reign and by your vassals, so that they should convert it to his holy law, as many wise and Christian men have affirmed. The conquests of the Indians began when those of the Moors had finished, so that Spaniards should always be battling against infidels.'[59] The conquest of the Americas, in other words, was a divinely ordained continuation of the *reconquista*. The conquest also compensated for the losses suffered by Catholicism in Europe as a result of the Reformation. Writers liked to point out that key dates in the heretical career of Martin Luther coincided with particular high points in Spain's overseas expansion, which again revealed that divine forces guided Spain's destiny. As the historian Jorge Cañizares Esguerra has noted, this meant that Spain helped compensate God for the souls lost to heresy.[60] Even the popular identification of the Indies as the mythical island of Anthilia – the origin of the term 'Antilles' – confirmed the connection between Catholic Spain's unwavering religious orthodoxy and the discovery.[61] The disappearing Island of Anthilia was one of various legendary islands believed to exist somewhere in the Atlantic. It was said that the lost island would reappear only after Catholicism reigned across the whole of the Iberian Peninsula. As early as 1493 Spanish writers were referring to the Caribbean as the 'Antillean Indies', thereby linking the Americas to the fictional island, and implying that their (re-)discovery resulted directly from Spain's defeat of the Moors, which had restored all of Spain to Christian rule.[62]

Overall, a portentous sense of the significance of Spanish victories in the new world permeates early modern Spanish writings. Around 1570

---

[59] López de Gómara, *Historia de las Indias*, dedication to Charles V (p. 19); Fernández de Oviedo, *Historia general y natural*, book 2, chap. 7 (vol. I, pp. 29–30); Peñaloza y Mondragón, *Libro de las cinco excelencias del español*, p. 25; and Zamora, *Reading Columbus*, p. 32. Chroniclers often likened Amerindians to Muslims, similarly linking the two conquests. See for example Anonymous Conquistador, 'Relación de algunas cosas de la Nueva España', 1556, chaps. 13, 15, 21, 22, 23; and Valadés, *Retórica cristiana*, part 4, chap. 11 (pp. 423–5).

[60] Mendieta, *Historia eclesiástica indiana*, book 3, chap. 1 (pp. 173–7); Torquemada, *Monarchia indiana*, book 4, prologue, book 15, prologue (vol. I, p. 373, vol. III, n.p.); Solórzano Pereira, *Política indiana*, book 1, chap. 8, section 13 (vol. I, p. 21); and Cañizares Esguerra, *Puritan Conquistadors*, p. 100.

[61] Fosse, 'Voyage à la côte occidentale d'Afrique en Portugal et en Espagne', pp. 190–1; and Vigneras, 'La búsqueda del Paraíso y las legendarias islas del Atlántico', pp. 46–7.

[62] Fosse, 'Voyage à la côte occidentale d'Afrique en Portugal et en Espagne', pp. 190–1; Vespucci, 'Letter to Pietro Sodorini', 4 Sept. 1504, in *The Letters of Amerigo Vespucci*, p. 29; Mendieta, *Historia eclesiástica indiana*, book IV, chap. 23 (p. 449); Babcock, *Legendary Islands of the Atlantic*; Olschki, *Storia letteraria delle scoperte geografiche*, pp. 34–55; Phelan, *The Millennial Kingdom of the Franciscans in the New World*, pp. 69–77; Vigneras, 'La búsqueda del Paraíso y las legendarias islas del Atlántico', pp. 46–7; and Gil, *Mitos y utopias del Descubrimiento*, pp. 81–4.

the humanist Benito Arias Montano, one of the scholars involved in the creation of the Antwerp polyglot bible (an immense compilation containing versions of the sacred text in Greek, Latin, Hebrew, Aramaic and Syriac), who also served as Philip II's librarian at the Escorial, composed a series of Latin verses based on biblical history, beginning with the expulsion of Adam and Eve from Eden and ending with the Last Judgement. A number of the poems derived from Old Testament themes drew unmistakable parallels between the ancient achievements of God's chosen people and the more recent triumphs of the Spanish. His account of the Battle of Jericho, for example, is given the evocative title 'On the Conquest of the Gentiles'. The Gentiles in question are ostensibly the Canaanites, but in the 1570s the phrase would for Spanish readers have brought other Gentiles to mind as well. The stanzas celebrating the Israelites' triumphant defeat of their Gentile enemies seem to refer as much to the achievements of Hernán Cortés as to those of Joshua. The victors are described as:

> A minute army in an unknown land,
> Overmatched in power and stature
> By the fierce giants who abounded there.
> And yet the foreigners triumphed
> Over such valiant warriors,
> So renowned and so imposing
> ...
> For their grave transgressions
> The conquered people were condemned,
> Outlawed, rigorously punished,
> And ultimately sentenced
> To lose their inheritance and lands.[63]

These lands, given by God himself to his people in recompense for their steadfast faith, and in retribution for the sins of the Canaanites, stand in unspoken but clear parallel to the lands of the Indies, whose transfer to the Spanish can thus be viewed only as the outcome of divine will. Why God chose the Spanish for this task was not difficult to discern. It was the reward for their orthodoxy and rejection of Protestantism. As one Spanish monk explained: 'I believe that God

---

[63] Arias Montano, *Humanae Salutis Monumenta*, poem 18 (pp. 218–19). The poem refers ostensibly to Josh. 5:13–6:27. I am grateful to John Chasteen for his poetic rendition. A subsequent poem on 'The Division of the Promised Land' concludes by marvelling over the speed and thoroughness of Israel's victories: 'It is astonishing that such a great empire and lordship should surrender so quickly and that scarcely having laid eyes on it pious Israel was able to triumph and destroy it': Poem 19 (pp. 220–1). Compare these poems with Cieza de León, *Parte primera de la chronica del Peru*, chap. 19 (p. 23).

uncovered those lands and placed them in the hands of Spaniards so that those numberless peoples should from them receive the Catholic faith in all its purity.'[64]

In short, when Spanish and creole writers celebrated the fertility of the new world, or, more extravagantly, insisted that the Garden of Eden itself was located in the Americas, their comments formed part of a larger celebration of the providential nature of the entire colonial venture. God wanted the Spanish to settle in the Indies, so as to spread the gospel in its most uncontaminated form. He therefore guided Columbus to the new world, and blessed its environment with many lovely features – such that numerous writers believed the region must the location of the very Garden of Eden. He made the environment as suited as possible to the Spanish constitution, moreover, by guaranteeing that their own foods grew marvellously well. The discourse of fertility, in other words, was one element of a colonial rhetoric that presented the conquest and colonisation of the Americas as part of a larger divine plan. Spaniards' mundane ability to grow wheat and radishes in Peru or Mexico was thus imbued with a powerful religious significance.

'You will not suffer the hunger and pestilence of Spain'

Europeans' ecstatic response to the perceived fertility of the new world also reflects concerns about the declining fertility of Western Europe. As scholars such as Piero Camporesi have shown, the spectre of hunger haunted both the daily lives and the imagination of early modern Europeans. 'Beset by famine, uncertain harvests, and impending doom, sixteenth-century Europeans were justifiably obsessed with food', notes the historian Abel Alves.[65] This obsession shaped the dreams that settlers brought with them to the Indies.

Wheat and other grains were in consistently short supply during the period of Spain's overseas expansion. Spain experienced repeated failed harvests, famines and dearths from the late fifteenth century to the

---

[64] Salazar, *Veinte discursos sobre el credo*, discurso 16, chap. 5 (p. 200). 'God brought the Spaniards to this land so that the priests could teach you the faith of Jesus Christ our Lord', stated Fernando de Avendaño in a sermon aimed at Quechua-speaking Indians: *Sermones*, primera parte, sermon 2 (p. 24). The constant shifting in colonial texts between the use of 'Christian' and 'Spaniard' to identify settlers similarly links the colonial process to Catholic Spain's particular religious identity.

[65] Alves, 'Of Peanuts and Bread', p. 62; Camporesi, *Bread of Dreams*; and Grove, *Green Imperialism*, pp. 16–72.

1630s. The dearths of 1486 and 1491 were followed by insufficient harvests between 1502 and 1508, which caused a serious famine in 1506. Subsequent decades saw some improvement and production increased in certain areas. From 1539, however, bad harvests occurred regularly, and the situation worsened as the century progressed. There were particular crises in 1591–2, 1597–9, 1614–16, and 1630–2. In addition an outbreak of bubonic plague in 1599 led to the death of some 10 per cent of the population in regions such as Segovia. As a result cereal production in Old Castile fell by almost 40 per cent between 1580 and 1630. The overall consequence was that the price of wheat rose steadily and Castile came increasingly to rely on imports from abroad.[66] The problems facing Castilian agriculture were evident to all, and from the 1570s analyses of its sorry state began appearing in print. Writers proposed a variety of solutions, ranging from the use of mules rather than oxen for farming work, to prohibiting agricultural workers from leaving the country.[67]

Spanish agricultural production was not starting from a particularly strong position in the first place. Stagnant between the thirteenth and fifteenth centuries, Castilian agricultural practices had not kept pace with improvements in other parts of Western Europe, nor was the situation helped in the early years of the sixteenth century by the policies of Ferdinand and Isabel, who consistently favoured grazing over agriculture. Farmers were expelled from desirable lands and crops were regularly damaged by herds of sheep.[68] Moreover, beyond the particular crises facing early modern Spanish agriculture there were other problems with the wheat-oil-wine complex underpinning the Iberian diet. The high-status wheat that stood at the centre of Mediterranean culture in fact produced a very poor yield. In early modern Spain the usual yield for wheat was only about five *fanegas* for every one sown. Even when land was well manured and left fallow farmers could at best

---

[66] Braudel, *The Mediterranean and the Mediterranean World*, vol. I, pp. 573–5, 584, 590; Elliott, *Imperial Spain*, pp. 295, 298; Lynch, *Spain under the Hapsburgs*, vol. I, p. 113; Vicens Vives, *An Economic History of Spain*, p. 304; Vassberg, *Land and Society*, pp. 198–9; García Sanz, *Desarrollo y crisis del antiguo régimen*, pp. 82, 95, 104–10; García Sanz, 'Castile, 1580–1650', p. 22; López-Salazar and Martín Galan, 'La producción cerealista en el Arzobispado de Toledo'; and Alves, 'Of Peanuts and Bread'.

[67] Such works include Juan de Valverde Arrieta, *Diálogos de la fertilidad y abundancia de España and Despertador, que trata de la gran fertilidad, riquezas, baratos, armas y caballos, que España solía tener* (1578); Lope de Deza, *Gobierno político de agricultura* (1618); Sancho de Moncada, *Restauración política de España, primera parte* (1619); and Miguel Caxa de Leruela, *Restauración de la abundancia de España, o prestantísimo, único y fácil reparo de su carestía presente* (1631). On such tracts see López Piñero, *Ciencia y técnica en la sociedad española*, pp. 302–5; and García Sanz, 'Estudio preliminar'.

[68] Vicens Vives, *An Economic History of Spain*, esp. p. 250.

hope for a yield of about ten to one.[69] Little wonder that Spaniards longed for a land where all crops flourished and cabbages ripened in ten days.

While farmers in Spain were very lucky to harvest ten *fanegas* of wheat for every one sown, farmers in the Indies were reportedly harvesting fifty. Writing from Lima, Sebastián Carrera promised his wife that 'you need only pour out the wheat and add water, and a whole field of grain shoots up, and from one *fanega* you harvest fifty'.[70] Others made far more extravagant claims. Yields of 500 *fanegas* were regularly reported from Peru. 'There are the best conditions in the world here; we all harvest 500 *fanegas* of grain from a single *fanega*, without it raining a drop the entire year, which you will think a miracle', Francisco Sanz Heredero wrote from Lima to his brother, who lived near Madrid.[71] (For comparison, the current average in New York State is about fifty-five to one.[72]) Such stories are only slightly more fantastical than the vision of Peru conjured up in one sixteenth-century comedy for a simpleton who is told that in the land of Jauja trees have trunks made of bacon, rivers run with milk and honey and the streets are paved with egg yolks. While he imagines the marvels of Jauja the hungry storytellers furtively devour the real-life casserole he is bringing to his wife.[73]

These implausible reports, which surely reflect the deep longing of individual settlers (and also their desire to lure relatives to the Indies), built on the stories and legends that Europeans told each other about a land without hunger. They also reflect the biblical descriptions of plenty familiar to settlers from sermons, which again reveals the close connections between the perceived success of colonial agriculture and a vision of the Indies as an earthly Eden. Clerical writers referred explicitly to

---

[69] Slicher van Bath, *The Agrarian History of Western Europe*, pp. 172–80, 328–33; Braudel, *Civilization and Capitalism*, pp. 120–4; Phillips, *Ciudad Real*, p. 39; Vassberg, *Land and Society*, pp. 201–3; Alves, 'Of Peanuts and Bread', p. 62; and Casey, *Family and Community in Early Modern Spain*, p. 72.

[70] Sebastián Carrera to his wife, Los Reyes, 1 Nov. 1558, in Otte, ed., *Cartas privadas de emigrantes a Indias*, p. 375.

[71] Francisco Sanz Heredero to Juan Heredero, Los Reyes, 8 April 1581, in Otte, ed., *Cartas privadas de emigrantes a Indias*, p. 407; and Garcilaso de la Vega, *Royal Commentaries*, book 9, chap. 29 (vol. I, p. 602). Salinas y Córdova, *Memorial de las historias del Nuevo Mundo*, discurso 2 (p. 247) gave similar figures, although he stressed that yields of 500 to 1 were no longer typical. At the time he wrote, the ratio was closer to 150 to 1. See also Zárate, *A History of the Discovery and Conquest of Peru*, p. 30; Murúa, *Historia general del Perú*, book 3, chap. 2 (p. 463); López de Gómara, *Historial General*, chap. 195 (p. 341); and Ovalle, *Histórica relación del Reyno de Chile*, book 1, chap. 3 (p. 24).

[72] Elizabeth Earle, personal communication, 1 October 2008.

[73] Rueda, *El deleitoso*, paso quinto (1567), in Rueda, *Pasos completos*, pp. 81–9. See also Pleij, *Dreaming of Cockaigne*.

these biblical precedents when discussing the bounty of the new world. On hearing a settler in the Mexican city of Puebla report wheat yields of a hundred to one the Franciscan missionary Toribio de Motolinía immediately recalled Genesis 26:12, in which Isaac reaped a hundred-fold harvest. Isaac's agricultural achievements reflected his special relationship to God, so Motolinía's comparison implicitly endowed Spain's colonial agriculture with an equivalent significance.[74] What then could one deduce from the fact that in Rio de la Plata, according to Bartolomé de las Casas, wheat produced a thousand *fanegas* for every one sown?[75] Who, indeed, would not choose to travel to the Indies?

The agricultural delights of the Indies are clearly captured in the writings of Juan López de Velasco, Philip II's royal cosmographer. In the 1570s López de Velasco produced a compilation of reports on the topographical and natural features of the new world intended to serve as a definitive point of reference on Spain's new possessions. The *Geografía y descripción universal de las Indias* (*Geography and Universal Description of the Indies*) drew on information provided by pilots and local officials to construct a comprehensive description of the location of bays and harbours, nautical routes, the climate, latitude and other features of the new world. It also included information on Spanish and indigenous settlements, natural resources and flora and fauna. In his descriptions of individual towns and cities López de Velasco scrupulously noted whether or not wheat and other European staples grew (often they didn't), but in his introductory overview he presented a completely one-dimensional picture of the Indies as a land of plenty. After admitting that in a few regions the soil was dry and sterile, he asserted that in general the Americas were covered with delightful green forests and fields, which yielded up a continuous supply of fresh fruit and vegetables for settlers to enjoy all the year round. Fruit, in Europe a seasonal treat, grew in such abundance that unwanted pineapples and guavas were left abandoned in huge piles. Wheat grew so well in many regions that no one bothered to plant second-class grains such as barley, oats or rye.[76] The new world was truly the land of Cockaigne: fruit lay about in heaps, and it was not necessary to eat rye, which stuck so unpleasantly to the stomach.

[74] Motolinía, *Historia de los Indios de la Nueva España*, 1541, chap. 18.
[75] Las Casas, *Apologética historia sumaria*, c. 1552, chap. 20 (pp. 62–3).
[76] López de Velasco, *Geografía y descripción universal de las Indias*, 'De la fertilidad y frutos de la tierra', 'De los árboles de las Indias', 'De los granos y semillas'. See also Calancha, *Corónica moralizada*, book 1, chap. 9 (p. 56); Garcilaso de la Vega, *Royal Commentaries*, book 9, chap. 29 (vol. I, p. 601); and Ovalle, *Histórica relación del Reyno de Chile*, book 1, chaps. 2, 22 (pp. 23–4, 75–6).

The dearth typical of early modern Spain thus imbued providential-ist accounts of new-world fertility with added meaning. Writers often drew explicit contrasts between the fertility of the Indies and the scarcity that prevailed in the old world. 'Things are much, *much* better here than in Spain', observed Oviedo.[77] The Spanish naturalist Francisco Hernández concurred. Writing of Mexico City he rhapsodised:

There is scarcely a city in the world that can be compared with Mexico in terms of the abundance of food, to say nothing of the gold, precious stones and silver, and the wealth of its markets and the fertility of the soil. What more? You will say that you are in an exceptionally fertile land, as everything is so abundant and brilliant, to nothing's detriment and with fertility and abundance in all things ... The wealth of Indian wheat, as well as our own, of vegetables and other cereals, is inexhaustible.[78]

What Hernández left implicit – that no Spaniard would starve in the Indies – was made explicit by others. 'There is no hunger in this land', Diego Martín de Trujillo promised his compatriot Alonso de Aguilar in a letter sent from Mexico in 1562.[79] 'The fertility of this land is so great that there is never any shortage of food, even for men who don't work', wrote another settler from Tunja.[80] Colonists constantly contrasted the poverty and destitution of Spain with the life of ease offered by the Indies. In Mexico, 'you will not experience the hunger and pestilence that they have over there, because this land is very healthy and well supplied with bread and meat and Spanish fruits, as well as local ones, and there is a lot to eat', Segundo Martínez promised his father, who lived in Seville.[81] 'Forget about the miseries and hardships of Spain, because

[77] Fernández de Oviedo, *Historia general y natural*, book 3, chap. 11 (vol. I, p. 79); and López Medel, *De los tres elementos*, pp. 143, 167.

[78] Hernández, *Antigüedades de la Nueva España*, book 1, chap. 23 (pp. 96–7).

[79] Diego Martín de Trujillo to Alonso de Aguilar, Mexico, 1 April 1562, in Otte, ed., *Cartas privadas de emigrantes a Indias*, p. 41.

[80] Marcos Martín to Mari Alonso de Retes, Tunja, 19 March 1580, in Otte, ed., *Cartas privadas de emigrantes a Indias*, p. 323.

[81] Segundo Martínez to Domingo Martínez, Mexico, 1 May 1572, in Otte, ed., *Cartas privadas de emigrantes a Indias*, p. 69. For 'las miserias de España' see also Diego Martín de Trujillo to Alonso de Aguilar, Mexico, 1 April 1562; Luis de Illescas to Catalina Gutiérrez, Mexico, 24 Sept. 1564; Pedro de Cantoval to Pedro de Cantoval and Diego de Cantoval, Mexico, 15 Feb. 1565; Diego Díaz Galiano to Juan Galiano, Mexico, 10 March 1571; Alonso Moreno Serrano to María Vázquez de Morales, Mexico, 1 May 1571; Juan López Tavera to Alonso García, Mexico, 30 Nov. 1572; Francisco González Gallego to Diego Sánchez, Mexico, 15 April 1585; Juan Fernández Sigurilla to Juan García Corbero, Mexico, 13 Dec. 1589; Alonso Pérez de la Mula to Diego Pérez, Mexico, 15 Dec. 1589; Alonso Martínez to Antón Rodrígeuz Salmerón, Mexico, 20 Aug. 1590; Diego Sedeño to Diego Gómez, Mexico, 22 Dec, 1592; Luis de Córdoba to Isabel Carrera, Puebla, 5 Feb. 1566; Alonso Morales to Juan Ramiro, Puebla, 20 Feb. 1576; María de Carranza to Hernando de Soto, Puebla, 2 Oct. 1589; Andrés de Arroyo to Juan Hernández, Mixteca, 14 March 1572;

a bad day here is worth more than a good one in Castile', Alonso Herojo urged his wife, Teresa González, in 1583.[82]

The attitudes of individual settlers were echoed by official chroniclers. In the same years that Segundo Martínez urged his father to travel to the Indies, the royal cosmographer López de Velasco stated clearly in an official report that in the new world one could be certain of always having enough to wear and to eat, 'because such things are never lacking in these parts'.[83] The Mercedarian friar Martín de Murúa was equally direct in his *Historia general del Perú (General History of Peru)*: 'there is no hunger in Peru'.[84] Writers recorded extravagant stories not only of miraculous wheat yields but also of spinach plants so tall that they towered over men and horses alike, of pomegranates so large that they could be used as containers for storing oil, of single radishes big enough to feed an entire party.[85] The Americas, an earthly paradise, thus welcomed the Spanish by providing them with abundant supplies of their own foodstuffs, in contrast with Spain, in the grip of shortage and hunger. It was, as Oviedo said, a true mother, not a stepmother.

Juan de Obregón to Juan de Obregón (sic), Coatzacoalcos, 15 April 1602; Hernán Sánchez to Diego Ramos, San Martín, 7 Feb. 1569; Felipe Gutiérrez to Catalina del Castillo, Guatemala, 5 April 1582; Luis de Larraga to Luisa Ramírez, Cartagena, 8 June 1581; Juan de Córdoba to Catalina Pérez, Cartagena, 27 May 1583; Miguel Hidalgo to Juan Martínez, Cartagena, 4 June 1587; Martín Domínguez to Isabel de Fuentes, Cartagena, 26 Aug. 1591; Alonso Herojo to Juan Hernández de León, Tunja, 10 March 1583; Francisco Suárez to Alonso el Harto Perea, Almaguer, 29 April 1587; Diego Cordero Osorio to his sons, Roldanillo, 1577; Alonso Martín del Campillo to Salvador Ruiz, Los Reyes, 2 Dec. 1575; Pedro García Camacho to Isabel López and Francisco López, Los Reyes, 14 April 1580; Diego de Espina to María Sánchez, El Callao, 9 April 1597; Juan Valero to Francisco Acedo, Potosí, 1 Dec. 1576; Pedro Valero to Catalina Martínez, Potosí, 1 Dec. 1576; Sebastián Carrera to Mari Sánchez, Valdivia, 22 April 1564; and Baltasar Sánchez to Gaspar Sánchez, La Plata, 22 Jan. 1578; all in Otte, ed., *Cartas privadas de emigrantes a Indias*, pp. 41, 45, 48, 58, 62, 70, 99, 110, 110, 117, 118, 119, 121, 147, 159, 167, 186, 187, 218, 224, 296, 297, 302, 309, 326, 359, 360, 390, 403, 459, 524, 525, 556, 560. Rare was the writer who compared the Indies unfavourably to Spain: Cristóbal Moreno de Vergara and Andrea López de Vergara to María de Vargas, Mexico, 8 Feb. 1574; Fernando de Isla to Juan de Albear, Mexico, 22 Jan. 1590; Antón Torijano to Catalina Ponce, Puebla, 8 April 1581; Baltasar de Valladolid to Clara de los Angeles, Santa Fe, 1 May 1591; and María de Córdoba to her sister, Lima, 27 March 1578; all in Otte, ed., *Cartas privadas de emigrantes a Indias*, pp. 75, 118–19, 164, 284, 396.

[82] Alonso Herojo to Teresa Gozález, Tunja, 10 March 1583, in Otte, ed., *Cartas privadas de emigrantes a Indias*, p. 325.

[83] López de Velasco, *Geografía y descripción universal de las Indias*, 'De los españoles que pasan a las Indias'.

[84] Murúa, *Historia general del Perú*, book 3, chap. 4 (p. 475); and Cárdenas, *Problemas y secretos maravillosos*, book 1, chap. 10 (p. 37).

[85] Zárate, *Historia del descubrimiento y conquista del Perú*, book 1, chap. 8 (p. 46); Garcilaso de la Vega, *Royal Commentaries*, book 9, chaps. 28–9 (vol. I, pp. 600–2); and Ovalle, *Histórica relación del Reyno de Chile*, book 1, chaps. 2–3 (pp. 20–5).

Indeed, the very climate was said to be undergoing a process of transformation to make it more suitable for European bodies. In 1518 Charles V's government reported optimistically that the Americas had been 'converted to the complexion of those who had gone there to settle'. The environment, the crown asserted, had actually adapted itself to match the constitution of Spanish settlers.[86] The chronicler Oviedo similarly reported that since Europeans had arrived in the Americas, the climate in the areas of Spanish settlement was becoming cooler and more temperate. In his view that was because the European presence was moderating and improving the environment. 'I have discussed this matter with several wise and learned men', he reported. Their opinion was that Spanish rule was taming the wildness of the climate, just as it was civilising the Indians.[87] Other writers ascribed such improvements directly to the introduction of Christianity. Peter Martyr reported that in Hispaniola hurricanes ceased once the sacrament of Communion began to be celebrated.[88] In any event, God in his wisdom had already moderated the most unpleasant aspects of the tropical climate. As the Jesuit writer José de Acosta remarked, 'the providence of the great god, Creator of all, has ordained that in the region where the sun always shines, and with its fire would seem to ravage everything, the most reliable and frequent winds are wonderfully cool and their coolness serves to temper the sun's ardor'.[89] (This observation was followed in Acosta's chronicle by a chapter called 'How Life in the Equatorial Region is Very Agreeable'.)

When writers such as Oviedo or López de Velasco insisted that the new world was marvellously fertile, or that the climate itself was adapting, the better to accommodate the Spanish body, they contributed to the production of a powerful discursive current affirming the

---

[86] 'Instrucciones que se dió a padre Bartolomé de las Casas, Zaragoza', 10 Sept. 1518, in Pacheco *et al.*, eds., *Colección de documentos inéditos*, vol. IX, part 2, p. 86.

[87] Fernández de Oviedo, *Historia general y natural*, book 6, chap. 46 (vol. I, p. 206). Oviedo attributed this change as well to the felling of trees and introduction of cattle, whose breath dried out the air. See also López de Gómara, *Historia general*, chap. 35 (pp. 72–4); López de Velasco, *Geografía y descripción universal de las Indias*, 'De la salubridad de las tierras'; Glacken, *Traces on the Rhodian Shore*, p. 130; and, for a modern explanation of this phenomenon, Crosby, *Ecological Imperialism*, pp. 96–7.

[88] Peter Martyr, *De Orbe Novo*, decade 7, book 9 (p. 309); and Fernández de Oviedo, *Historia general y natural*, book 6, chap. 3 (vol. I, p. 147). See also Nieremberg, *Curiosa y oculta filosofía*, 'Oculta filosofía', book 1, chap. 65 (p. 267). Another cleric asserted that the volcano at Tlaxcala ceased erupting once a consecrated host was placed in the crater: Salazar, *Veinte discursos sobre el credo*, discurso 16, chap. 5 (p. 202).

[89] Acosta, *The Natural and Moral History of the Indies*, book 2, chap. 13 (p. 95). The Jesuit writer Alonso de Ovalle noted that because parts of Chile were very cold God had equipped the region with extensive forests of firewood: Ovalle, *Histórica relación del Reyno de Chile*, book 1, chap. 2 (p. 19).

providential nature of Spanish colonisation. Spaniards needed to eat their own foods were they to thrive in the Indies, and they did not wish to be tormented by excessive heat and volcanoes. It is therefore not surprising that colonial writers repeatedly affirmed that old-world crops grew miraculously well, and that even the climate was changing in response to the Spanish presence. The environment, such accounts made clear, was welcoming and fundamentally beneficent. The more extreme version of this affirmation – that the Garden of Eden itself lay in the Indies – reflects particularly clearly the significance that such writers ascribed to these matters. God wanted the Spanish to flourish in the new world, and therefore did all that was necessary to make that possible. The fact that Spain itself was so often plagued by famine and dearth greatly increased the power of such imagery to captivate the imagination of writers and colonists alike. Out of the intersection of these different desires came a distinctive image of the Indies as a land of comfort and ease, where food grew in abundance, and where hurricanes ceased with the arrival of the host. Far from being hostile to the European body, the American environment proved to be singularly accommodating to its new residents.

New drugs from a new world

The same 1518 royal instruction that described how the climate of the Indies has already adapted to suit the Spanish complexion also noted with approval the region's overall healthfulness. 'It is almost unheard of', the order stated, 'for anyone to suffer from illness, and for that there are many remedies and treatments and good foods.'[90] While the optimistic assertion that no one fell ill in the Indies was contradicted all too frequently, the affirmation that the Americas abounded in healing remedies was widely confirmed by contemporaries. Indeed, by furnishing the old world with useful drugs and medicines, the new world provided the very means to counter any harmful effects the unfamiliar environment might induce, as the royal instruction itself pointed out. Europeans had long sought remedies in distant lands, for unlike food, which was usually best suited to the local complexion, medicines from far-off regions were often considered highly effective, and new drugs were among the items actively hunted by early explorers. This section examines the very positive reception that Spaniards accorded new-world medicines, which helped protect the Spanish body both in

---

[90] 'Instrucciones que se dió a padre Bartolomé de las Casas', Zaragoza, 10 Sept. 1518, in Pacheco *et al.*, eds., *Colección de documentos*, vol. IX, part 2, p. 86.

the Indies and in Europe. Spanish reaction to these medicaments provides further evidence that the new world's environment was seen as fundamentally welcoming; rather than posing insurmountable dangers to the European body, it proffered the very means of achieving health and well-being, at the same time as it revealed the workings of divine providence.

The Spanish response to guaiacum wood, used in the treatment of the so-called French Disease, provides an excellent example. Within a few years of Columbus's arrival in the Indies an illness that the Spanish referred to as *bubas* began to spread through Europe. The condition was characterised by large, putrid sores that spread across the body and often resulted in a painful death. Scholars continue to argue about whether this ailment was identical to modern syphilis, and also whether it was truly a new illness in Europe, but many early modern Spaniards believed that the disease was new. To the poet and doctor Francisco López de Villalobos, it was 'a pestilence never before seen in verse or prose or science or history'.[91] The illness generated enormous disagreement about its mode of transmission and ultimate cause. In his 1498 poem *Sobre las pestíferas bubas* (*On the Pestilent Pox*), which charted the unpleasant course of the disease and described a number of possible treatments, López de Villalobos reviewed the variety of explanations offered to account for the ailment. He noted that theologians described the illness as a punishment for sin, while astrologers blamed an unfortunate conjunction of Saturn and Mars. Physicians, in turn maintained it was provoked by an excess of phlegm and black bile. Whatever its cause, writers familiar with the Americas began to argue that it originated in the Indies.[92]

---

[91] López de Villalobos, *Sobre las contagiosas y malditas bubas*, stanza 3, in *The Medical Works of Francisco López de Villalobos*, p. 132. See also Calvo, *Libro de medicina*, book 3, chap. 2 (p. 150); Benavidez, *Secretos de chirurgia*, p. 10; Sandoval, *Historia de la vida y hechos del Emperador Carlos V*, book 17, chap. 15 (vol. II, p. 318); Cárdenas, *Problemas y secretos maravillosos*, book 3, chap. 5 (pp. 189, 197); and López Piñero, 'Introduction', in López Piñero, ed. *El 'Vanquete de Nobles Caballeros' (1530) de Luis Lobera de Avila*, p. 17. For Spanish texts questioning whether *bubas* was a new disease see Díaz de Isla, *Tractado contra el mal serpentino*; and Torres, *Libro que trata de la enfermedad de las bubas*. See also Crosby, 'The Early History of Syphilis'; Arrizabalaga et al., *The Great Pox*; and Stein, *Negotiating the French Pox in Early Modern Germany*. I am grateful to Claudia Stein for her advice.

[92] Fernández de Oviedo, *Historia general y natural*, book 2, chaps. 13, 14, book 10, chap. 2 (vol. I, pp. 49, 53, vol. II, pp. 9–10); Las Casas, *Apologética historia sumaria, c.* 1552, chap. 19 (pp. 58–60); Benavidez, *Secretos de chirurgia*, p. 66; Guerra, 'La mutación de las bubas desde G. Fernández de Oviedo', p. 295; and Fresquet Febrer, *La experiencia americana y la terapéutica en los Secretos de Chirurgía*, pp. 119–43. See also Díaz de Isla, *Tractado contra el mal serpentino*, prologue, p. 3; López de Gómara, *Historia general*, chap. 29 (p. 66); Calvo, *Libro de medicina*, book 3, chap. 3 (p. 156); and Fresquet

However, far from being viewed as evidence that the new world was a dangerous and insalubrious place, *bubas* were said to demonstrate both God's benevolence and also the fundamentally helpful nature of the American environment. This was because the new world also provided the cure. As the chronicler Oviedo noted, 'because *bubas* are common in all these parts, divine providence wished that this region should also furnish a remedy'.[93] The initial treatments for *bubas* – large doses of mercury applied as a paste to the skin or via a steam bath – provoked unpleasant side-effects; patients were likely to lose their teeth, for example. (Advocates of the mercury cure insisted that this was caused either by the disease itself or by failure to comply with medical advice.) Within a few decades of the disease's appearance in Europe, however, Spanish settlers in the Indies had noted that Amerindians treated *bubas* with a remedy derived from the wood of the guaiacum tree. This gentler remedy rapidly attracted a following in Europe itself, where guaiacum, drunk as a decoction in conjunction with a strict dietary regime, became the treatment of choice. (See Figure 6.) The German humanist Ulrich von Hutten, for example, composed a widely read autobiographical text in which he described his own suffering from what he called the French Disease, and then detailed how he had been cured by guaiacum.[94] Several other new-world plants, including sarsaparilla, were also advocated as effective cures.

By the 1520s large quantities of these woods were being imported into Europe for use by the growing number of sufferers who languished at home and in the new pox hospitals. Thus, whether or not the new world was believed to be the origin of the disease, it was undoubtedly the source of a cure. This of course fitted well with long-standing ideas about divine providence, which held that all aspects of the universe reflected the intentions of their creator. In fact, it is possible that the pox was described as being American in origin precisely *because* guaiacum appeared to cure it.[95] The Spanish doctor Juan Calvo summed up the situation in noting that 'it is certainly a great providence to see the

Febrer, 'La difusión inicial de la materia médica americana en la terapeútica europea', p. 337.

[93] Fernández de Oviedo, *Historia general y natural*, book 10, chap. 2 (vol. II, p. 9).

[94] Hutten, *De Morbo Gallico*. Modern scholars tend to note that Hutten died of syphilis a few years later. For the preferential use of guaiacum rather than mercury in the Hispanic world see Farfán, *Tratado breve de mediçina*, book 2, chaps. 1–4 (pp. 82–97); Vos, 'Research, Development, and Empire', p. 61; and, for a contrasting view, Risse, 'Shelter and Care for Natives and Colonists', p. 75.

[95] Munger, 'Guaiacum, the Holy Wood from the New World'.

Figure 6 Philippe Galle, *A man in bed suffering from syphilis*, 1600. The treatment of the French Disease with guaiacum wood. On the right the wood is prepared; on the left the patient sips the resultant decoction while a doctor looks on. This print is from a series depicting ingenious modern inventions, of which the guaiacum cure is one.

medicine come from the same place whence came the disease'.[96] The new-world origin of *bubas* thus provided evidence not for the malevolence of the new world's environment, but instead for the universality of divine providence.

Beyond this, as many writers of the time noted, the new world provided Europe with a wealth of other medicines, whose qualities were described and publicised across Europe in herbals and medical handbooks. Of these the most famous was composed by Nicolás Monardes. Monardes studied medicine at the universities of Alcalá and Seville in the mid sixteenth century, and wrote a number of works on topics

---

[96] Calvo, *Libro de medicina y cirugia*, book 3, chap. 9 (p. 177); López de Gómara, *Historia general*, chap. 29 (p. 66); Calancha: *Corónica moralizada*, book 1, chap. 9 (p. 61); Las Casas, *Apologética historia sumaria*, c. 1552 (p. 59); Monardes, *Joyfull News out of the New-found Worlde*, p. 10v; and Fresquet Febrer, 'La difusión inicial de la materia médica americana en la terapéutica europea', p. 337.

ranging from the properties of citrus fruits to the nature of snow. The book for which he achieved Europe-wide renown, however, was his *Historia medicinal de las cosas que se traen de nuestras Indias Occidentales que sirven en Medicina* (*Medicinal History of the Things Brought from Our West Indies That Are Useful to Medicine*), which appeared in stages between 1565 and 1574. In it Monardes detailed the healing properties of the Michoacan flower, the 'oyle of the figge tree of hell' and other new-world plants. Monardes never travelled to the Indies, but instead gathered information by interviewing returning settlers who passed through his home town of Seville. He also cultivated new-world plants from seeds and cuttings in his garden. Monardes was explicit about the value of the new world's medicinal offerings, which, he stated, 'exceede much in value and price' all the gold and silver brought out of the Indies, 'by so much as the corporall health is more excellent, and necessare than the temporall goodes'.[97] Monardes's work contributed enormously to publicising the range of medicines emerging from the new world, and within a century it had appeared in forty-two different editions, in six different languages.[98] (I quote here from the 1596 English edition, evocatively titled *Joyfull News out of the New-found Worlde*.)

Monardes's view that the new world was a veritable cornucopia of remedies was shared by many other Spanish writers. Colonial officials, in response to queries from the Spanish state, submitted hundreds of reports detailing the medicinal herbs available in their jurisdictions, using information derived from indigenous informants.[99] On a grander scale Francisco Hernández compiled an extensive account of new-world *materia medica*, which described the medical utility of thousands of plants, animals and minerals from Mexico. Hernández was a graduate of the recently founded medical faculty at the University of Alcalá, who in the 1560s became the personal physician of Philip II. In 1571 he was named the *protomédico*, or chief medical officer, of New Spain. Part of his duties was to produce a detailed study of the properties of Mexican plants and other natural objects. During his seven years in Mexico he assiduously collected information about plants and their uses from both direct study and discussion with Amerindians. His vast, unwieldy compilation, which became known as the *Rerum Medicarum Novae Hispaniae Thesaurus* (*Dictionary of Remedies from New Spain*), was brought to Spain in 1576, and immediately attracted the attention of

---

[97] Monardes, *Joyfull News out of the New-found Worlde*, p. 1v.
[98] López Piñero, *Ciencia y técnica en la sociedad española*, p. 286.
[99] See the various *relaciones geográficas* edited by Acuña, Jiménez de la Espada and Paso y Troncoso; and Barrera-Osorio, *Experiencing Nature*.

naturalists across Western Europe, interested in its analysis of new flora and fauna. Despite this interest, Hernández's complete work remained unprinted until 1651, entrammeled in a complex web of editors, printers and patrons. In 1615, however, a partial Spanish translation was composed by the Dominican priest Francisco Ximénez, and the work also circulated as printed extracts and in manuscript. Like Monardes, Hernández unequivocally affirmed the beneficent nature of new-world flora. The Indies, he stated, abounded in 'the most healthful herbs'.[100]

Hernández's contemporaries recognised that in cataloguing this floral cornucopia he was implicitly celebrating both the new world and its divine creator. José de Sigüenza, a Hieronymite friar who served as Philip II's librarian at the Escorial, where Hernández's manuscript was housed, thus praised the work as 'of no small benefit for those whose office consists in contemplating nature, and the things that God has created for the healing of men'.[101] The celebration of the new world's therapeutic plants indeed intersected with the identification of the Indies with the new Eden, for it was there that sinful man would find true health; a confluence of earthly and spiritual health in the new Jerusalem is after all the triumphant promise of the closing chapter of the Bible. The Book of Revelation describes the tree of life growing beside the river that flows from the throne of God, whose leaves 'were for the healing of the nations'.[102] The celebration of the new world as a western paradise thus melded with Hernández's botanical studies into a single vision of the Indies as a new Jerusalem.

What is of relevance here is not the broader impact of new-world drugs on European medicine – something that scholars continue to debate – but rather the ways in which colonial writers talked about them.[103]

---

[100] Hernández, *Antigüedades de la Nueva España*, book 2, chap. 2 (p. 111); López Piñero and Pardo Tomás, *Nuevos materiales y noticias sobre la Historia de las plantas de Nueva España*; López Piñero and Pardo Tomás, 'The Contribution of Hernández to European Botany and Materia Medica'; and Guerrini, 'The "Accademia dei Lincei"'. Or see Ovalle, *Histórica relación del Reyno de Chile*, book 1, chap. 2 (pp. 20–3).

[101] Sigüenza, *Historia de la Orden de San Gerónimo*, part 3, book 4, discourse 11 (vol. II, p. 590); and Vilchis, 'Globalizing the *Natural History*', p. 171.

[102] Rev. 22:1–2; and Vilchis, 'Globalizing the *Natural History*', p.171. See also Laín Entralgo, *Enfermedad y pecado*, pp. 50–75.

[103] For the European reception of new-world drugs see Talbot, 'America and the European Drug Trade'; Frequet Febrer *et al.*, *Medicinas, drogas y alimentos vegetales del Nuevo Mundo*; and Estes, 'The Reception of American Drugs in Europe, 1500–1650'. For a representative example of European interest in the suitability of new-world drugs for European bodies see Pol, *On the Method of Healing with the Indian Wood called Guaiac the Bodies of Germans who have Contracted the French Disease*; and Benavidez, *Secretos de chirurgia*, pp. 16, 26, for an example of how Spaniards and Amerindians respond differently to new-world drugs.

Regardless of the doubts that some European doctors expressed about the suitability of new-world drugs for treating Europeans, Spanish writers were generally confident that these new discoveries were therapeutically useful and that through them one could glimpse the hand of God. Nor did Spanish confidence in these new drugs remain entirely at the discursive level. Merchants imported large quantities of guaiacum, sarsaparilla, balsam and other new-world medicinal herbs into Spain. The historian J. Worth Estes estimates that in the sixteenth century American drugs were only slightly less important than dyestuffs and sugar in terms of both their volume and taxable value.[104] Overall, the abundance of health-giving and profitable herbs provided comforting evidence that whatever the challenges particular regions might pose, in general the new world's environment was fundamentally beneficent for the European body.

Conclusions

This chapter has mapped the imaginative framework within which colonial writers situated their understanding of the new world's environment. The providentialism that shaped overall Spanish interpretations of their colonial endeavour was seen to be reflected in nature itself. Giant pomegranates and wheat yields of five hundred to one were evidence that divine forces endorsed Spain's presence in the Indies. The fact that Spain itself was from the mid sixteenth century in the grip of serious agricultural crisis added additional allure to such stories of paradisiacal abundance. Further evidence for the wholesomeness of the American environment was found in the wealth of healing medicines native to the region. In short, nature in the new world, far from being hostile to the European body, was exceedingly welcoming. That colonial writers preferred to praise rather than denigrate the new world's environment is scarcely surprising, given the widespread belief that colonial settlement revealed the workings of divine providence. Would God have led them to a region utterly inimical to their constitution?

---

[104] Chaunu and Chaunu, *Séville et l'Atlantique*, vol. VI, part 2, pp. 980–1035; Estes, 'The European Reception of the First Drugs from the New World', pp. 15–19; and Estes, 'The Reception of American Drugs in Europe, 1500–1650', p. 119. Sarsaparilla was used for treating phlegmy conditions characterised by excessive cold and dampness, and for this reason was seen by some as a suitable cure for *bubas*. Balsam was used as an ointment for wounds and also for a variety of other ailments that benefited from application of a hot, dry substance. For an anthology of sixteenth-century texts discussing these and other medicinal plants, see Fresquet Febrer *et al.*, *Medicinas, drogas y alimentos vegetales del Nuevo Mundo*; and also Barrera-Osorio, *Experiencing Nature*, pp. 13–23.

And yet ... colonial insistence that the region's fertility revealed the hand of God, that the European body was proof against the rigours of an unfamiliar climate because it was amply supplied with healthful old-world food and healing medicines, that the climate itself was becoming more suitable for the European constitution – such claims only partially soothed the anxieties that the experience of overseas settlement provoked. Pastoral visions, as the literary critic Leo Marx has noted, usually entail some measure of anxiety as well as delight.[105] No matter what writers might assert, old-world crops did not thrive in all regions, as chroniclers themselves sometimes admitted, before moving quickly on to a general eulogy of the continent's fertility. Europeans did fall ill, despite the abundance of health-giving medicines, and, as we have seen, many settlers suspected that this was the result, precisely, of too close an encounter with the new world's unfamiliar airs and waters and unsuitable foods. The consoling narrative of abundance could not entirely assuage doubts that settlers would perhaps be forced into unwanted contact these things, and that this might transform them body and soul, just as writers such as Baltasar Álamos de Barrientos had alleged.

It is tempting to interpret the grandiloquent claims about miraculous wheat yields and melons that ripened a month after planting as betraying not only confidence but also anxiety, for fears about the bodily integrity of European settlers were inextricably entangled with discussions of the success of colonial agriculture. Perhaps, whatever the claims of colonial enthusiasts, settlers would not be able to rely on a continued supply of old-world food. Perhaps, despite the best efforts of colonial officials, settlers would be forced to go hungry, or else consume the region's peculiar foodstuffs. We have hitherto considered varied aspects of colonists' pressing need for familiar European comestibles, but have paid relatively little attention to their reactions to new-world foodstuffs, beyond noting that prolonged consumption of them was generally considered to be dangerous to the European constitution. The next chapter takes a closer look at settlers' responses to these worrying new-world foods.

[105] Marx, *The Machine in the Garden*; and Giamatti, *The Earthly Paradise and the Renaissance Epic*.

4   'Maize, which is their wheat'

Indians, everyone agreed, would eat anything. Dogs, worms, rats, slime: there was nothing they would not consume. 'One can scarcely find anything that escapes the voracity of those men, or which they decline to eat', complained the *protomédico* Francisco Hernández.[1] While Spaniards yearned for civilised wheat bread and health-giving wine, Amerindians guzzled an inexplicable combination of non-foods, which they persisted in consuming even after the arrival of Spaniards with their superior foodstuffs. Colonial writers had no doubt that these mistaken consumption practices revealed the fundamental backwardness of most Amerindians. After all, only uncivilised people would choose to eat such things. The connection between uncivilised foods and uncivilised peoples was captured expressively by the chronicler Oviedo, who described the disgusting fruit of the tropical mangrove tree as a 'bestial food fit for savage people'.[2]

Yet at the same time, rather disconcertingly, settlers found themselves enjoying pineapples and chocolate and chilli peppers. Even maize proved difficult to ban from their tables entirely, despite the suspicion that surrounded it. How much of the new world *was* it safe for Europeans to eat? This chapter examines colonial attitudes towards the many new foods that confronted settlers in the Indies, which were, inevitably, closely linked to their attitudes towards the new peoples who ate them. With this chapter our focus moves from European efforts to reproduce the old-world diet, and old-world bodies, in the Indies, to settler attitudes towards Amerindian foods and Amerindian bodies.

[1] Hernández, *Antigüedades de la Nueva España*, book 1, chap. 12 (p. 71); and Vargas Machuca, 'Descripción breve de todas las Indias occidentales', in *Milicia y descripción de las Indias*, vol. II, p. 91.
[2] Fernández de Oviedo, *Historia general y natural*, book 9, chap. 6 (vol. I, p. 286). See also Diego Alvarez Chanca to Town Council of Seville, 1493, in Olson and Bourne, eds., *The Voyages of Columbus and of John Cabot*, p. 312 (and the identical statement in Bernáldez, *Historia de los reyes católicos*, chap. 120 (vol. II, pp. 34–5)); and Lizárraga, *Descripción breve de toda la tierra del Perú*, chap. 84 (p. 67).

'Bestial food for savage people'

Colonists looked with disdain on many of the things eaten by Amerindians. The consumption of insects and reptiles attracted particular scorn. As the *protomédico* Hernández recorded in his extensive notes, Amerindians ate 'the most poisonous serpents ... dogs, badgers, dormice, worms, ticks, mice, lake scum'. He added that he preferred not to think about the other even more horrible plants and animals that they also consumed.[3] Writers were clear that these dietary preferences revealed an underlying bestiality, all the more so given that Amerindians persisted in eating such foods after they had been introduced to the superior European diet. In fact, the one category of things that Amerindians declined to eat were the wholesome European foods enjoyed by settlers. 'They eat porcupines, weasels, moths, locusts, spiders, worms, caterpillars, bees and ticks – raw, cooked and fried. There is not a single thing that they will not guzzle, and it is all the more astonishing that they eat such dirty animals and bugs given that they now have good bread and wine, fruits, fish and meat', exclaimed the chronicler López de Gómara in 1552.[4] Writers contrasted the filthy foods preferred by Amerindians with the nourishing foods eaten by Europeans. Oviedo, for example, noted that Amerindians in Venezuela ate revolting toads 'just as regularly as people in Europe eat bread or beef'.[5] Spaniards ate bread while Indians ate toads.

Spanish disgust at the idea of eating toads and insects surely reflects the distinctive status of these creatures within European culture. Accounts of famine, such as the oft-repeated tales of the terrible hunger that accompanied the Roman siege of Jerusalem in AD 70, which circulated through sermons and other means, located insects, rodents and toads in the category of 'un-food' which was consumed only when normal social structures had utterly collapsed. Eating such creatures

---

[3] Hernández, *Antigüedades de la Nueva España*, book 1, chap. 27 (p. 105); and Hernández, *Historia natural de Nueva España*, tratado 5, chaps. 3, 4, 12, 18, in *Obras completas*, vol. III, pp. 391, 393, 395 (but see also tratado 5, chaps. 1, 5, 7, 9, 20, 26 (vol. III, pp. 390, 392–3, 395–6) for favourable assessment of insects and larvae).

[4] López de Gómara, *Historia general*, chap. 79 (p. 151); 'Interrogatorio Jeronimiano', 1517, in Rodríguez Demorizi, ed., *Los dominicos y las encomiendas de indios de la isla Española*, p. 302; and García, *Origen de los indios*, book 3, chap. 3 (p. 222). Spaniards expressed similar complaints about the refusal of Muslims and Jews to consume pork, wine and other wholesome foods: Perceval, 'Asco y asquerosidad del morisco'.

[5] Fernández de Oviedo, *Historia general y natural*, book 13, chap. 10 (vol. II, p. 67). Oviedo noted that eating frogs, a custom he described as widespread in Europe, was perfectly civilised.

was moreover a common feature of apocalyptic visions of the end of days, and it was widely believed that the devil himself could transform into repulsive insects.[6] These animals, which appeared to generate spontaneously from putrid and rotten material, were for Europeans alarming on multiple levels. That insects and reptiles were used in various indigenous rituals and divination ceremonies merely increased their unacceptability. Such foods were thus not merely uncivilised they were also in a deep sense unchristian.[7] The Dominican priest Diego Durán for this reason recommended that the Nahua be prohibited from eating 'filthy things' such as 'dogs and skunks, badgers and mice', in part because they had once served as offerings to indigenous deities, and in part because they were absolutely revolting and dirty. Suppressing this habit would in itself help Indians to become civilised human beings, he believed.[8] Amerindians in central Mexico were similarly warned that after taking Communion they should not eat 'the disgusting things that you usually eat' such as owls, mice and the little worms that grow in maguey plants, lest they pollute this holy act. They were urged instead to eat 'good, clean foods'. Not surprisingly, wheat bread was singled out as a prime example of such good food.[9] Raw food was also a powerful marker of nature untransformed by human culture, as Claude Lévi-Strauss argued many decades ago.[10] Eating ticks – which were simultaneously raw and a horrible insect – was therefore a sin that needed to be reported in Confession.[11] And what could one say for people who subsisted entirely on raw things? The Uros Indians of Collao, near Lake Titicaca, consumed only raw

---

[6] Valadés, *Retórica cristiana*, grabado 21 (p. 488); Gil, *Mitos y utopías del Descubrimiento*, p. 33; Pouchelle, *The Body and Surgery in the Middle Ages*, pp. 168–71; Camporesi, *Bread of Dreams*, p. 156; and Pleij, *Dreaming of Cockaigne*, pp. 106–17.

[7] Peña Montenegro, *Itinerario para parochos de indios*, book 2, tratado 5, prologue (p. 190); *Instrucción contra las ceremonías y ritos que usan los indios*, chap. 4, in *Confessionario para los curas de indios*, p. 3; Avendaño, *Sermones*, primera parte, sermon 10 (p. 128); and Few, *Women Who Lead Evil Lives*, p. 85. See also Acosta, *De procuranda indorum salute*, book 1, chap. 2, section 3 (vol. I, p. 81); Cárdenas, *Problemas y secretos maravillosos*, book 3, chap. 25 (pp. 239–40); and Solórzano Pereira, *Política indiana*, book 1, chap. 5, section 15 (vol. I, pp. 16–17).

[8] Durán, *Historia de las Indias de Nueva España*, book 1, part 1, chap. 20 (p. 181). I am grateful to Jai Kharbanda for this reference.

[9] Leon, *Camino del cielo*, 132.

[10] Lévi-Strauss, *The Raw and the Cooked*; and Vitoria, 'On Self-Restraint', 1537, in *Political Writings*, p. 209.

[11] Leon, *Camino del cielo*, p. 110; Diego de Porres, 'Instrucción y orden que an de tener los sacerdotes que se ocupasen en la doctrina y conversión de los yndios en las Yndias del Piru', Archivo General de Indias, Patronato, legajo 231, n. 7, R. 8, fol. 10; and Pagden, *The Fall of Natural Man*, p. 177.

fish, meat and herbs. Not surprisingly, the Mercedarian friar Martín de Murúa characterised them as 'a bestial, brutish and uncivilised people'.[12]

This predilection for un-food was evidence that Amerindians needed the guiding hand of the Spanish. Juan Mosquera, a settler on Hispaniola, thus claimed in 1517 that if left to their own devices the island's Indians would retreat to the hills 'eating spiders and tree roots and lizards and other dirty things', discarding the more civilised practices they had learned from colonists.[13] The connection between such mistaken consumption practices and an inability to govern oneself was drawn with equal clarity by a Dominican priest in a dossier he presented to the Council of the Indies, the body charged with overseeing governance in the new world. In it he listed Amerindians' many backward habits, including their tendency to eat raw ticks, spiders and worms whenever the opportunity arose. The significance of these practices was made clear by the report's title: 'These are the characteristics of the Indians which mean they do not deserve any freedom.'[14] As the historian Anthony Pagden has observed, the inability to distinguish between the edible and the inedible was a sure sign of barbarism.[15]

Cannibalism

Cannibalism was of course the clearest example of such a category mistake. The eating of human flesh, widely reported in colonial accounts from Columbus's first voyage onwards, was for most European writers an unambiguous indication that Amerindians lacked one of the basic marks of civilisation. Columbus had at first vacillated as to whether the peoples he encountered in the West Indies were civilised subjects of the Great Khan or instead dangerous man-eaters, but a consensus soon formed that the newly discovered lands were a zone of anthropophagi. As Amerigo Vespucci reported matter-of-factly, the island peoples of the Caribbean 'slaughter those who are captured, and the victors eat

---

[12] Murúa, *Historia general del Perú*, book 3, chap. 3 (p. 470); and Botero Benes, *Relaciones universales*, part 1, book 5 (p. 151).

[13] 'Interrogatorio Jeronimiano', 1517, *Los dominicos y las encomiendas de indios de la isla Española*, ed. Rodríguez Demorizi, p. 279 (quote); and Hanke, *The First Social Experiments in America*, p. 32.

[14] Tomás Ortiz, cited in López de Gómara, *Historia general*, chap. 217 (p. 374); Peter Martyr, *De Orbe Novo*, decade 7, book 4 (pp. 274–5); and Pagden, *The Fall of Natural Man*, pp. 87, 218n.180.

[15] Pagden, *The Fall of Natural Man*, p. 87. See also Nuñez de Oria, *Regimiento y aviso de sanidad*, p. 7r.

the vanquished; for human flesh is an ordinary article of food among them'.[16] Chroniclers reported carefully on whether particular groups did or didn't consume human flesh, and the fear of being eaten permeates many conquest narratives. The expectation of meeting cannibals was such that when a party of Spaniards captured in Patagonia were prodded by their captors they immediately assumed that the Indians intended to eat them, and were gathering information about how their flesh would taste.[17] Although Spaniards sometimes grappled with the uncomfortable fact that on occasion Europeans, too, ate other people, eating human flesh quickly became associated with the new world.[18] The connection between the Indies and cannibalism, immortalised in popular prints, many different types of text and the very word 'cannibal' (a variant of the term 'Carib'), led some Europeans to believe that the concept itself originated in the new world, as the Dominican priest Bartolomé de las Casas complained.[19] 'From the moment of the Discovery', writes the historian Carlos Jáuregui in his authoritative cultural history of the new-world cannibal, 'Europeans reported the existence of cannibals everywhere, creating a sort of semantic affinity between cannibalism and the Americas.'[20] Regardless of whether any individual settler ever encountered actual incidents of cannibalism, everyone knew the continent was full of bloodthirsty cannibals. (See Figure 7.)

[16] Vespucci, 'Letter on His Third Voyage to Lorenzo Pietro Francesco di Medici' (the Medici Letter), March–April 1503, in *The Letters of Amerigo Vespucci*, p. 6. For representative texts see Columbus, 'Diary of the First Voyage', 17 Dec. 1492, 13 Jan. 1493, and 'Carta del Almirante a los reyes católicos'; both in *Los cuatro viajes del almirante*, pp. 92, 127, 173; Peter Martyr, *De Orbe Novo*, decade 2, book 1, decade 3 book 5; and Díaz del Castillo, *The True History of the Conquest of New Spain*, book 3, chaps. 51, 54, book 12, chap. 156, book 14, chap. 175, book 17, chap. 208 (vol. I, pp. 186, 196, vol. IV, p. 189, vol. V, pp. 15, 263).

[17] Fernández de Oviedo, *Historia general y natural*, book 20, chaps. 7, 12 (vol. II, pp. 246 (quotation), 254). For details on who was or wasn't a cannibal see for example Fernández de Enciso, *Suma de geographia*, pp. li, lii, liii; Federman, *Historia indiana*, p. 63; and López de Gómara, *Historia general*, chaps. 54, 57, 70, 71, 72, 89, 121 (pp. 99, 105, 135, 138, 140, 166, 222).

[18] On the varied contexts in which Europeans ate other people see Lestringant, 'Le canibale et ses paradoxes'; Camporesi, *Bread of Dreams*, pp. 40–6, 87; Cummins, 'To Serve Man'; Price, *Consuming Passions*; Heng, *Empire of Magic*; and Greer, 'Imperialism and Anthropophagy in Early Modern Spanish Tragedy'. Colonial chronicles periodically admitted to instances of cannibalism by Spanish explorers. See for example Peter Martyr, *De Orbe Novo*, decade 2, book 10; Hutten, 'Diario', vol. II, p. 368; Simón, *Noticias historiales*, noticia 2, chaps. 5–6 (vol. I, pp. 196–7, 199–202); and López de Gómara, *Historia general*, chaps. 56, 58, 73, 143, 208 (pp. 104–5, 109, 141, 251, 361). For transubstantiation as a form of cannibalism see Elwood, *The Body Broken*, pp. 34–41; Price, *Consuming Passions*, pp. 3–41; and Wandel, *The Eucharist in the Reformation*, pp. 8, 21, 3, 177, 217, 225–78.

[19] Las Casas, *Apologética histórica*, c. 1550, chap. 178, in *Obras escogidas*, vol. IV, p. 152; and Jáuregui, '"El plato más sabroso"', p. 207.

[20] Jáuregui, *Canibalia*, p. 14.

Figure 7 German woodcut of a new-world scene, c. 1505.
Befeathered Amerindians enjoy a cannibal feast. Additional body
parts hang from the rafters. The caravels visible on the horizon
suggest that such depravities will shortly be curtailed by the arrival
of Europeans.

Cannibalism was not only a dreadful sin, but also an activity that
rendered its practitioners virtually inhuman.[21] Extirpating this atro-
cious activity was thus a palpable benefit of Spanish rule, as colonial
writers liked to point out.[22] There is a substantial literature on the ways
in which Europeans used accusations of cannibalism to justify colonisation and conquest; in 1503, for example, Queen Isabel ruled that
Amerindians guilty of cannibalism could legitimately be enslaved.[23]

---

[21] 'They eat little flesh except human flesh', reported Amerigo Vespucci of the Caribbean
islanders, adding, 'herein they are so inhuman that they outdo every custom (even)
of beasts': Vespucci, 'Letter to Pier Sondarini', in *The First Four Voyages of Amerigo
Vespucci*, p. 13.

[22] Díaz del Castillo, *The True History of the Conquest of New Spain*, book 17, chaps. 208–9
(vol. V, pp. 262–70); 'Ordenanzas de su magestad hechas para los nuevos descubrimientos, conquistas y pacificaciones', 13 July 1573, in Pacheco *et al.*, eds., *Colección de
documentos inéditos*, vol. XVI, p. 183; Solórzano Pereira, *Política indiana*, book 2, chap.
15, sections 24, 30 (vol. I, pp. 189–90); and López Medel, *De los tres elementos*, p. 251.

[23] See for example Arens, *The Man-Eating Myth*; Hulme, *Colonial Encounters*; Boucher,
Cannibal Encounter; Palencia-Roth, 'The Cannibal Law of 1503'; Lestringant,
Cannibals; Barker *et al.*, eds., *Cannibalism and the Colonial World*; and Jáuregui,
Canibalia.

Here I would like to draw attention to a complementary dimension of this discourse: European insistence that cannibalism revealed a profound lack of culinary discrimination. It showed that Amerindians were unable to distinguish between things that were good to eat and things that should never be eaten. The Spanish Jesuit Bernabé Cobo, who lived for over sixty years in Mexico and Peru, thus observed that Indians 'eat every living thing, from the most noble, which is man, to the most revolting bugs and vermin'.[24] Eating spiders and eating people were thus two manifestations of this larger inability to distinguish the edible from the inedible. While Europeans ate proper food, Amerindians ate spiders and each other.

The contrast between wholesome European consumption habits and distorted indigenous ones is conveyed particularly clearly in accounts that liken Amerindian cannibalism to European meat-eating practices. Europeans often compared the ways in which Amerindians supposedly prepared human flesh to the preparation and sale of meat in the old world. 'I was once in a certain city for twenty-seven days, where human flesh was hung up near the houses, in the same way as we expose butcher's meat', remarked Vespucci.[25] Such comments highlighted the culinary dimensions of new-world anthropophagy, while at the same time stressing the differences between the diets of the new and old worlds. Presenting cannibalism as part of an ordered system of food procurement aimed to heighten rather than diminish its repulsiveness. Peter Martyr, for example, reported that in the Caribbean 'the cannibals captured children, whom they castrated, just as we do chickens and pigs we wish to fatten for the table, and when they were grown and become fat they ate them'. He added that they also salted the intestines of older persons 'just as we do hams'.[26] Pedro Cieza de León, who participated in the conquest of Peru and Colombia, claimed to have seen sausages made from human flesh hanging from the rafters of indigenous dwellings. Oviedo likewise insisted that in many parts of the Indies it was 'as

---

[24] Cobo, *Historia del Nuevo Mundo*, book 11, chap. 6 (vol. II, p. 20). 'There isn't a single type of vermin that they won't eat ... their stomachs are the tomb of human flesh, and this is their principal and most prized foodstuff, in whose absence they eat the raw flesh of other animals, not caring whether it is a viper, snake, toad or lizard', Juan de Cárdenas complained of the Chichimecs: *Problemas y secretos maravillosos*, book 3, chap. 7 (p. 200).

[25] Vespucci, 'Letter on His Third Voyage to Lorenzo Pietro Francesco di Medici' (the Medici Letter), March–April 1503, in *The Letters of Amerigo Vespucci*, p. 7. See also Nuñez de Oria, *Regimiento y aviso de sanidad*, p. 40r; and Díaz del Castillo, *The True History of the Conquest of New Spain*, book 3, chap. 51, book 17, chap. 208 (vol. I, p. 186, vol. V, p. 263).

[26] Peter Martyr, *De Orbe Novo*, decade 1.

Figure 8 Lorenz Fries, *Underweisung und uszlegunge Der Cartha Marina*, 1530 (title-page). Dog-headed new-world cannibals prepare human flesh for sale on a market stall. The accompanying text describes them as originating from 'the island of the Cannibals, which Columbus has discovered' (Johnson, *Carta Marina*, p. 111).

common to eat human flesh as in France, Spain or Italy it is to eat lamb or beef'.[27] (See Figure 8.)

---

[27] Cieza de León, *Primera parte de la chronica del Peru*, chap. 26 (p. 31); Fernández de Oviedo, *Historia general y natural*, book 5, chap. 3, book 6, chap. 9 (vol. I, p. 122 (quotation), 167–9); and Cañizares Esguerra, *Puritan Conquistadors*, pp. 90–1.

For Europeans, in other words, cannibalism was undoubtedly a monstrous act, often linked to other monstrous acts such as human sacrifice or sodomy. At the same time, it was also a profoundly mistaken consumption practice. Eating people, like eating lice, revealed a fundamentally uncivilised nature and a radical inability to distinguish between the edible and the inedible. Such things were, like the fruit of the mangrove tree, bestial food fit for savage people. Eating any of these things was a clear marker of barbarism, and people who ate frogs were likely also to eat people, and to engage in other uncivilised activities. As the Italian chronicler Giovanni Botero observed, Amerindians 'were universally bestial and barbarous, because in addition to eating frogs, lizards, worms and other filthy and disgusting things, they engage in sodomy and idolatry and eat human flesh'.[28] These misguided activities were all interlinked.

Foods such as spiders and human flesh were thus strongly marked as 'Indian'. These were things that only Amerindians were supposed to eat, thereby demonstrating their uncivilised status and need for oversight. That some settlers, particularly in more peripheral parts of the empire, in fact consumed lizards, snakes and even insects was therefore extremely worrying. The Spaniard investigated by the Mexican Inquisition in 1543 for dining 'with Indians, sitting on the floor as they do ... eating *quelites* [fresh herbs] and other Indian food and the worms they call *chochilocuyli*' was one of a number who blurred the boundary between coloniser and colonised by their failure to respect fundamental culinary frontiers.[29] Any settler who ate other people, in turn, cast serious doubt on their place within the Christian community, which is why starving conquistadors forced by necessity to eat the bodies of their companions were strongly advised to keep this information to themselves.[30]

---

[28] Botero Benes, *Relaciones universales*, part 1, books 4–5 (pp. 134 (quotation), 145, 148); Pagden, 'The Forbidden Food'; and Goldberg, *Sodometries*, pp. 179–222. 'All the inhabitants of New Spain, and even those of neighbouring provinces, eat human flesh, and esteem it over all other food ... [and] are usually sodomites, as I have said, and drink immoderately', reported the Anonymous Conquistador: 'Relación de algunas cosas de la Nueva España', chap. 24.

[29] Alberro, *De gachupín al criollo*, p. 70. See also Motolinía, *Memoriales o libro de las cosas de la Nueva España*, p. 365; Hernández, *Historia natural de Nueva España*, tratado 5, chaps. 1, 5, 7, 9, 20, 26 (vol. III, pp. 390, 392–3, 395–6); Díaz de Alpuche, 'Relación del pueblo de Dohot', 1579, p. 218; Carrasco, 'Matrimonios hispano-indios', pp. 18–19; and Melville, *A Plague of Sheep*, p. 36.

[30] On the need for secrecy see Cummins, 'To Serve Man'.

'It has a marvellous flavour'[31]

But these were not the only foods that greeted settlers in the Indies. Despite the scorn heaped on spiders and raw snakes, a number of items received a very positive reception. Pineapples and other tropical fruits were universally admired, chilli was approved for those with strong stomachs and by the late sixteenth century cacao, in the form of a chocolate drink, was widely consumed. Colonial officials carefully recorded which new-world foods were safe for Europeans to consume. Avocado, for example, was reported to be a 'very good fruit and healthy for Spaniards'.[32] Medical writers, in turn, classified these new foodstuffs according to the tenets of humoral theory, although they did not always agree in their classifications.[33]

Fruits were among the new-world foods most favoured by settlers. Sweet things were scarce in early modern Europe. There, fruit was in season only for a few months, and before the Atlantic slave trade made sugar cheap, it was difficult to preserve its flavour by any method other than drying. Honey, too, was expensive. For this reason out-of-season or imported fruits commanded high prices in Europe. In many parts of the Americas, in contrast, sweet fruits were available for pennies throughout the year. Settlers rhapsodised about the delicate flavour and tempting smells of tropical fruits, bestowing regal epithets on chirimoyas, prickly pears and avocados. 'In smell and taste this is the fruit of kings', wrote Las Casas of the mamey.[34] 'All those who have tasted it find it more delicious than any European fruit', reported an Italian traveller of the avocado.[35] But the pineapple was the true fruit of kings. Ferdinand himself, who had been presented with one imported from

[31] Fernández de Enciso, *Suma de geographia*, p. liii.

[32] 'Relación de Querétaro', 1582, in Acuña, ed., *Relaciones geográficas del siglo XVI: Michoacán*, p. 243 (quotation); Fernández de Oviedo, *Historia general y natural*, book 9, chap. 23 (vol. I, p. 297); and Motolinía, *Historia de los Indios de la Nueva España*, 1541, chap. 9.

[33] See for example Monardes, *Joyfull News out of the New-founde Worlde*; Hernández, 'Chocolate', 'Chilli', 'Maize' and 'Tomato', in *The Mexican Treasury*, pp. 107–16; Cárdenas, *Problemas y secretos maravillosos*, book 2, chap. 14 (pp. 141–2); and López, *Tesoro de medicina*.

[34] Las Casas, *Apologética historia sumaria*, c. 1552, chap. 4 (p. 17).

[35] Fernández de Oviedo, *Historia general y natural*, book 9, chap. 23 (vol. I, p. 297); Benavidez, *Secretos de chirurgia*, p. 49; and Gemelli Careri, *Voyage du tour du monde*, vol. VI, book 2, chap. 10 (p. 219, quotation). For other celebrations of new-world fruits see Zárate, *A History of the Discovery and Conquest of Peru*, p. 27; Acosta, *Natural and Moral History*, book 4, chap. 25 (p. 215); Cárdenas, *Problemas y secretos maravillosos*, book 2, chap. 11 (pp. 127–31); and Ovalle, *Histórica relación del Reyno de Chile*, book 1, chap. 22 (p. 78).

the West Indies, was said to prefer it to all others. 'I myself have not tasted it', noted the king's chaplain Peter Martyr sadly in his chronicle.[36] Charles V's official chronicler, Fernández de Oviedo, devoted an entire chapter in his general history to its praise.[37] (See Figure 9.)

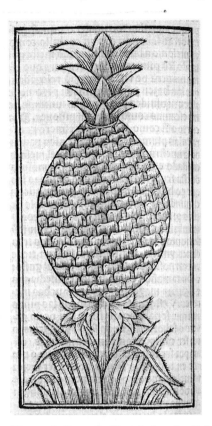

Figure 9 Gonzalo Fernández de Oviedo, woodcut of a pineapple, 1535. 'I don't believe there is anything in the world that equals it', Oviedo wrote of this fruit (Fernández de Oviedo, *Historia general de las Indias, primera parte*, book 7, chap. 13 (fol. 77v)).

[36] Peter Martyr, *De Orbe Novo*, decade 2, book 9. See also Cuneo, 'News of the Islands of the Hesperian Ocean', 1495, p. 54; Monardes, *Joyfull News out of the New-founde Worlde*, p. 90; López Medel, *De los tres elementos*, p. 157; López de Velasco, *Geografía y descripción universal de las Indias*, 'De los árboles de las Indias'; Acosta, *Natural and Moral History of the Indies*, book 4, chap. 19 (p. 204); and Gage, *The English-American*, chap. 9 (p. 95).

[37] Fernández de Oviedo, *Historia general y natural*, book 7, chap. 14 (vol. I, pp. 239–43).

With time the abundance of syrupy tropical fruits came to symbolise the grandeur and magnificence of the colonies for both residents and the newly arrived. As they did not travel well, these fruits generally needed to be eaten in the Indies; tasting and seeing them were therefore distinctively new-world pleasures.[38] Because tropical fruits were so strongly associated with the Indies, eighteenth-century genre paintings from the new world often included prominent displays, helpfully labelled with their exotic names. (See Figure 10.)

A European fondness for sweet things may similarly explain the popularity of sweet potatoes. Certainly the preferred cooking methods employed by settlers – roasting and stewing in wine – served to emphasise their honeyed qualities. The chronicler Oviedo compared them to marzipan.[39] Spicy, hot substances such as chillies were also appreciated, as they could substitute for the more expensive black pepper imported from India. Doctors affirmed that chillies were a healthy addition to most diets, but warned that it was best to toast them first; a technique they undoubtedly learned from indigenous cooks.[40] A variety of new-world meats were likewise praised by settlers and chroniclers. Iguana, manatee and llama in particular were generally described as tasty.[41] Peter Martyr observed that once they overcame their initial

---

[38] Bergamo, *Daily Life in Colonial Mexico*, p. 56; and Sheller, *Consuming the Caribbean*, p. 95.

[39] Columbus, 'Diary of the First Voyage', 4 Nov. 1492, 13 Dec. 1492, pp. 54, 87; Fernández de Enciso, *Suma de geographia*, p. li; Nicolò Scillacio, extract from *The Islands Recently Discovered in the Southern and Indian Seas*, 1494, in Symcox, ed., *Italian Reports on America*, pp. 38–9; Peter Martyr, *De Orbe Novo*, decade 1, book 1, decade 2, book 9; Fernández de Oviedo, *Historia general y natural*, book 7, chaps. 3–4 (vol. I, pp. 233–5); Nuñez de Oria, *Regimiento y aviso de sanidad*, p. 40r; and 'Description of a Voyage from Lisbon to the Island of São Thomé', c. 1540, in Blake, ed., *Europeans in West Africa*, vol. I, p. 161.

[40] Peter Martyr, *De Orbe Novo*, decade 7, book 1 (pp. 150–1); Fernández de Oviedo, *Historia general y natural*, book 7, chap. 7 (vol. I, p. 235); López de Gómara, *Historia General*, chap. 17 (p. 48); Las Casas, *Apologética historia sumaria*, c. 1552, chaps. 10, 35 (pp. 37, 118); Cervantes de Salazar, *Crónica*, book 1, chap. 6 (p. 15); Nuñez de Oria, *Regimiento y aviso de sanidad*, p. 308v; Hernández, *Quatro libros de la naturaleza*, book 2, chap. 3 (pp. 72–4); Cárdenas, *Problemas y secretos maravillosos*, book 2, chap. 10 (pp. 124–6); and Peñaloza y Mondragón, *Libro de las cinco excelencias del español*, p. 145.

[41] Fernández de Enciso, *Suma de geographia*, pp. lii–liii; López de Gómara, *Historia general*, chaps. 31, 51 (pp. 67–8, 95); Fernández de Oviedo, *Historia general y natural*, book 12, chaps. 30, 31, book 13, chaps. 3, 4, 8, 9, book 17, chaps. 9, 18, chap. 2, book 20, chap. 8, book 24, chap. 3 (vol. II, pp. 58–9, 63–4, 122, 187, 248, 396); Casas, *Apologética historia sumaria*, c. 1552, chap. 10 (p. 35); Matienzo, *Gobierno del Perú*, p. 89; López Medel, *De los tres elementos*, pp. 93, 178, 182, 187; Zárate, *A History of the Discovery and Conquest of Peru*, p. 111; López de Velasco, *Geografía y descripción universal de las Indias*, 'De los animales'; 'Descripción de la tierra del repartimiento de San Francisco de Atunrucana y Laramanti', 1586, in Jiménez de la Espada, ed., *Relaciones geográficas de las Indias: Perú*, vol. I, p. 234; and Acosta, *Natural and Moral History*,

Figure 10 Miguel Cabrera, *De Lobo y de India, Albarasado*, 1763. This indigenous woman offers the viewer a tray of carefully labelled guavas, chayotes and other tropical fruits. Her little son carries a box of chico zapotes, another of the sweet fruits that so delighted Spanish settlers.

book 4, chaps. 40–1 (pp. 243–4). 'Iguanas are edible' is the title of one section in Vargas Machuca, 'Descripción breve de todas las Indias occidentales', in *Milicia y descripción de las Indias*, vol. II, p. 148.

suspicion of iguana meat, Spaniards 'became epicures in regard to it, and talked of nothing else than the exquisite flavour of these serpents, which they found to be superior to that of peacocks, pheasants, or partridges' – information he presumably derived from the many returning settlers he interviewed when composing his popular reports on the new world.[42] Moreover, because settlers determined that sea-dwelling iguanas and manatees were fish, they were eaten on fast days by laity and clergy alike, a practice that made some recently arrived Spaniards uncomfortable. The Jesuit José de Acosta said he 'almost' felt guilty about eating a manatee on a Friday, because despite assurances that it was fish, in his view it tasted like veal.[43]

Perhaps the food most universally embraced was chocolate. Consumed as a drink it quickly become a standard element of the settler diet in Meso-America, and by the end of the sixteenth century the chocolate habit had spread across the Spanish colonies. Colonial writers were almost unanimous in their praise for the unusual frothy beverage. (Froth, an essential element of the pre-Columbian beverage, was achieved either by pouring the liquid back and forth between two containers to aerate it, or by whisking with a stick.) (See Figure 11.) The Anonymous Conquistador's views were typical. 'This drink', he reported, 'is the healthiest and most sustaining food in the world, because a single cup will by itself sustain you throughout the day, and as it is by nature cold, it is more suited to a hot climate than to a cold one.'[44] Medically trained writers shared the general approval, provided it was consumed in moderation. The Spanish doctor Francisco Hernández, for example, noted that chocolate was useful for treating liver disorders, and was in any event very tasty. Writer after writer agreed that it had a pleasant taste, once one got used to the peculiar head of foam on the top. That it constituted Europeans' first experience of caffeine perhaps also contributed to its popularity.[45]

[42] Peter Martyr, *De Orbe Novo*, decade 1, book 5; Landa, *Relación de las cosas de Yucatan*, p. 123; Fernández de Oviedo, *Historia general y natural*, book 12, chap. 7 (vol. II, pp. 32–5); and Acosta, *Natural and Moral History of the Indies*, book 4, chap. 38 (p. 240).

[43] Acosta, *Natural and Moral History*, book 3, chap. 15 (p. 133); Peña Montenegro, *Itinerario para parochos de indios*, book 4, tratado 5, section 10 (pp. 461–2); Fernández de Oviedo, *Historia general y natural*, book 12, chap. 7 (vol. II, pp. 32–5); Landa, *Relación de las cosas de Yucatán*, p. 123; and Leon Pinelo, *Question moral*, part 2, chap. 10 (pp. 75–6).

[44] Anonymous Conquistador, 'Relación de algunas cosas de la Nueva España', 1556, chap. 10 (p. 381).

[45] Fernández de Oviedo, *Historia general y natural*, book 8, chap. 30 (vol. I, p. 267–73); Cervantes de Salazar, *Crónica*, book 1, chap. 5 (p. 13); Hernández, 'Cacao', in *The Mexican Treasury*, pp. 107–9; López Medel, *De los tres elementos*, p. 153; Acosta, *Natural and Moral History*, book 4, chap. 22 (p. 210); Mendieta, *Historia eclesiástica indiana*,

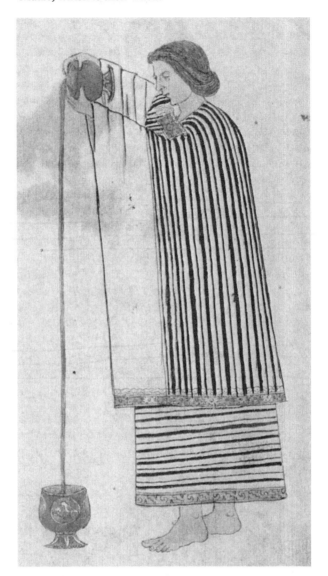

Figure 11 'Yndia Mexicana', *Codex Tudela*, *c*. 1553. Creating a froth: an indigenous woman aerates a chocolate drink by pouring it from one container to another.

Within a few decades of the establishment of colonial settlement it was being described as a drink liked by women in particular. By the early seventeenth century it had become a major expense in Mexican convents. Debates about conventual use of chocolate broke out when European priests complained that creole nuns were spoilt chocolate-guzzlers and tried to limit access to what was for Europeans still an exotic luxury. The nuns in turn attempted to justify their chocolate habit by claiming that it was an aid to fasting.[46] Similar conflicts were triggered by the custom of women in colonial Guatemala of interrupting celebration of the Mass by having their servants bring them little cups of chocolate to sip during the service. Women, complained the English priest Thomas Gage,

pretend much weakness and squeamishness of stomach, which they say is so great that they are not able to continue in the church while a Mass is briefly huddled over, much less while a solemn high Mass ... is sung and a sermon preached, unless they drink a cup of hot chocolate, and eat a bit of sweetmeats to strengthen their stomachs.[47]

Clerical suspicion of women's use of chocolate may also have reflected the fact that it was widely associated with witchcraft. Inquisition records are full of examples of women fabricating love potions and the like from chocolate mixed with menstrual blood, or other female detritus.[48]

---

p. 752; Peña Montenegro, *Itinerario para parochos de indios*, book 4, tratado 5, prologue (p. 453); Gage, *The English-American*, chap. 13 (p. 190); Coe and Coe, *The True History of Chocolate*; Jamieson, 'The Essence of Commodification'; Norton, 'Tasting Empire'; and Norton, *Sacred Gifts, Profane Pleasures*. Cárdenas recommended that the froth be removed before the drink was consumed: *Problemas y secretos maravillosos*, book 2, chaps. 7–8 (pp. 105–18).

[46] Saravia Viejo and Arenas Frutos, '¿Olla Común? El problema de la alimentación en la reforma monarcal feminina', pp. 251, 254, 259, 262; Loreto López, 'Prácticas alimenticias en los conventos de mujeres en la Puebla del siglo XVIII', pp. 485–7; Sampson Vera Tudela, *Colonial Angels*, pp. 32–3; and Forrest and Najjaj, 'Is Sipping Sin Breaking Fast?'. For debate about whether chocolate broke the ecclesiastical fast see also Leon Pinelo, *Question moral*.

[47] Gage, *The English-American*, chap. 11 (p. 161). See also Acosta, *Natural and Moral History of the Indies*, book 4, chap. 22 (p. 210); Díaz del Castillo, *The True History of the Conquest of New Spain*, book 16, chap. 201 (vol. V, p. 201); Farfán, *Tratado breve de mediçina*, book 1, chap. 6 (p. 33); Leon Pinelo, *Question Moral*, preludio primero, part 2, chap. 10 (pp. 4, 72–3); and Marradón, 'Dialogue du chocolate entre un medecin, un indien et un bourgeois', pp. 389, 402.

[48] Pedro Sánchez de Aguilar, 'Informe contra los idólatras de Yucatán', 1613, in Máynez, ed., *Hechicerías e idolatrías del México antiguo*, p. 145; Aguirre Beltrán, *Medicina y magia*, pp. 226–8; Behar, 'Sexual Witchcraft, Colonialism, and Women's Powers', pp. 190, 196–7; Lewis, *Hall of Mirrors*, pp. 119–21; Sampson Vera Tudela, *Colonial Angels*, p. 171n58; Few, 'Chocolate, Sex, and Disorderly Women in Late-Seventeenth and Early-Eighteenth-Century Guatemala'; Bristol, *Christians, Blasphemers, and Witches*, pp. 166, 169; and Restall, *The Black Middle*, pp. 266–71.

By the mid seventeenth century, in other words, chocolate was widely consumed across Spanish America, and had also developed a certain connection to women. Consumption was sustained by commercial production in Central America, the Caribbean, Brazil, Venezuela and Ecuador. The bulk of this crop went to meet new-world, rather than European, demands, for Spanish America was the major consumer as well as sole producer of chocolate. Indeed, Spanish colonial culture was responsible for its dissemination across the hemisphere: by the mid seventeenth century chocolate had been incorporated into daily life and commercial agriculture in regions far removed from its Meso-American homeland.[49] It was likewise Spanish colonists who brought chilli peppers to Florida, potatoes to Mexico and tomatoes to South America.[50]

The widespread consumption of these foods reveals something of the hybrid culinary world that had begun to develop in the Indies by the mid sixteenth century.[51] This development was due in large part to the shortage of Spanish women, which propelled settlers to rely on indigenous (and in some regions enslaved) women for many bodily needs and desires. (See Figure 12.) In 1540 there were only about a thousand Spanish women in the Indies, at a time when there were perhaps 80,000 Spanish men. A decade later Spanish women represented roughly 17 per cent of all immigrants, still far short of parity with men. Only at the end of the sixteenth century did Spanish women cease to be a rare commodity in most parts of the Indies.[52] Nor did Spanish women in the Indies necessarily wish to engage in cooking in the first place. Part of the allure of the colonies was precisely the promise – much repeated in private letters – of a life of leisure and ease. As one sixteenth-century artisan assured his relatives in Toledo, in the Americas Spanish women 'neither spin nor make clothes nor concern themselves with cooking nor with any other domestic task'.[53] Much of the food eaten by settlers was therefore prepared by indigenous women, who inevitably incorporated new-world ingredients, taste preferences and cooking techniques into the meals they prepared. For example, the form in which settlers

---

[49] Jamieson, 'The Essence of Commodification'. The cacao tree may have originated in Peru, but chocolate did not form an important part of the preconquest Andean diet: Bletter and Daly, 'Cacao and Its Relatives in South America'.

[50] Reitz and Scarry, *Reconstructing Historic Subsistence with an Example from Sixteenth-Century Spanish Florida*, p. 64; Tudela de la Orden, 'Economía', p. 692; and Long-Solís, 'El tomate', pp. 215–23.

[51] For a classic discussion of colonial hybridity see Alberro, *De gachupín al criollo*.

[52] Sánchez-Albornoz, 'The Population of Colonial Spanish America', pp. 15–16; and Socolow, *The Women of Colonial Latin America*, pp. 53–9.

[53] Alonso Hernández to Sebastián Hernández, Los Reyes, 4 Jan. 1570, in Otte, ed., *Cartas privadas de emigrantes a Indias*, p. 383.

Figure 12 José de Páez, *De Español y Negra, Mulato, c.* 1770–80 (detail). A black woman froths chocolate with a whisk in this eighteenth-century scene. Colonial kitchens were inevitably sites of culinary transculturation.

consumed chocolate was profoundly shaped by indigenous consumption practices. Both the flavour combinations and the method of preparation – including the creation of the froth – derived from indigenous practice, as the historian Marcy Norton has shown.[54] The vector of transmission was undoubtedly Meso-American women, who ground the cacao beans on a *metate*, or indigenous grindstone, and taught settlers to mix the other ingredients required for the drink. It was surely from indigenous women that settlers also learned to toast chillies, enjoy tomatoes and drink maize porridge. With time both a number of new-world dishes and a variety of indigenous preparation techniques were incorporated into the Spanish–creole world of colonial America, and settler women, too, began to employ indigenous culinary idioms. Sixteenth-century chroniclers reported on the tasty dishes Spanish women prepared from sweet potatoes and other new-world ingredients, while eighteenth-century creole recipe collections that made almost no mention of new-world ingredients might refer nonchalantly to indigenous cooking techniques. One such collection for instance instructs the cook to grind ingredients on a *metate*, heat them on a *comal* or Meso-American griddle and cook them 'until they make a sound like a cooked tamal'.[55] The outcome of this inevitable culinary transculturation was such distinctively colonial innovations as the wheat-flour tortilla.[56]

Spanish interest in eating these foods did not reflect merely the passing curiosity of travellers, or the willingness of people far from home to suspend their usual habits.[57] As we have seen, travellers were in fact the last people who ought to alter their daily routines, for in so doing they risked aggravating the already dangerous perturbations imposed by their new environment. These were things that settlers ate alongside their regular repertoire of foods because they believed them to be healthy and toothsome additions. Indeed, settlers did not eat these foods only in the Indies, but, in a number of cases, also introduced them to Spain. Considerable quantities of chocolate were imported into Spain from the late sixteenth century. Initially such imports were

---

[54] Norton, *Sacred Gifts, Profane Pleasures.*

[55] Fernández de Oviedo, *Historia general y natural*, book 7, chap. 3 (vol. I, p. 234); and *Recetario novohispano*, pp. 14, 39, 44, 45, 47, 51, 50 (quotation), 52, 55, 60.

[56] I am grateful to Jeffrey Pilcher for advice on flour tortillas.

[57] Curiosity had its place. Fernández de Oviedo noted that during the conquest of Puerto Rico Spanish soldiers tasted certain moths eaten by Amerindians, which he attributed not only to the lack of other more suitable food, but also the desire of some men to 'try things they see other people doing': Fernández de Oviedo, *Historia general y natural*, book 10, chap. 16 (vol. II, p. 108). See also Alvise da Ca' da Mosto, 'Voyages of Cadamosto', *c.* 1468, in Crone, ed., *The Voyages of Cadamosto and Other Documents*, chaps. 40, 43 (pp. 65, 72).

largely for the personal use of the importers themselves, and during the sixteenth century the chocolate habit was confined primarily to *indianos* – returning settlers, clerics and other colonials. The *indiano* with his chocolate indeed became a stock minor character in Spanish Golden Age drama.[58] Chocolate's social base began to broaden over the seventeenth century and from the 1650s thousands of *arrobas* per year were being shipped to Europe to fuel the growing demand for the beverage in Spain and other parts of the Hapsburg empire.[59] (An *arroba* is equal to 25 pounds.) (See Figure 13.) By the early eighteenth century it was consumed by a wide cross-section of the population, at least in Madrid and other large cities. Other new-world delicacies such as sweet pineapple conserve also proved immensely popular in Spain.[60]

In addition, a number of new-world foods began to be cultivated in Spain itself, which allowed them to penetrate even more deeply into the Iberian diet. As early as the 1570s the Spanish doctor Francisco Hernández could write that chilli 'was taken a long time ago to Spain, where it is highly esteemed and is cultivated in gardens and tubs as an ornament and as a useful plant'.[61] As a spice it possessed many advantages over the black pepper for which it substituted. Unlike black pepper, an expensive import, chillies could be cultivated for little cost in Spain itself, and connoisseurs proclaimed that in any event their flavour was superior.[62] Writing in Spain in 1590, the Jesuit priest José de Acosta felt no need to describe the chilli in his account of new-world plants, because 'by now this is a well-known thing, and hence not much need be said about it'.[63] Chillies, particularly in dried and smoked form, were incorporated into many dishes, from stews to sausage. (See Figure 14.)

[58] Herrero García, *Ideas de los españoles*, p. 314; and Norton, *Sacred Gifts, Profane Pleasures*, p. 160.

[59] Phillips, 'The Growth and Composition of Trade in the Iberian Empires', table 2.6 (pp. 92–3); Norton, *Sacred Gifts, Profane Pleasures*. esp. pp. 141–72; and Lindorfer, 'Discovering Taste'.

[60] Hernández, *Quatro libros de la naturaleza*, book 3, part 2, chap. 76 (p. 176); Norton, *Sacred Gifts, Profane Pleasures*; and Fattacciu, 'Cacao'.

[61] Hernández, 'Chile', in *The Mexican Treasury*, p. 109; and Hernández, *Quatro libros de la naturaleza*, book 2, chap. 3 (p. 72). See also Las Casas, *Apologética historia sumaria*, c. 1552, chap. 10 (p. 37).

[62] 'It is known in Spain, for there is no garden, nor orchard, but that it hath plenty therein of it, for the fairness of the fruit that it bringeth forth ... It is used in all manner of meats and potages, for that it hath a better taste than the common pepper hath': Monardes, *Joyfull News out of the New-founde Worlde*, p. 20.

[63] Acosta, *Natural and Moral History of the Indies*, book 4, chap. 20 (p. 206); Ríos, *Agricultura de jardines*, p. 60; Pérez Samper, *La alimentación en la España del siglo de oro*, p. 80; and López Terrada, 'Hernández and Spanish Painting in the Seventeenth

Figure 13 Antonio de Pereda, *Kitchen Scene, c.* 1650–5. A copper chocolate pot and wooden chocolate whisk lie on the broken plate at the lower right, amidst the other accoutrements of this rather disordered Spanish kitchen. Chocolate and chocolate-drinking accoutrements figure in many Seventeenth-century paintings.

As a result, seventeenth-century travellers complained that Spanish food was hopelessly spiced with 'pimentone'.[64]

Tomatoes were also introduced into Spain, where they were eaten cooked with chicken and eggs, or boiled into a sauce.[65] Since they could not survive the long sea voyage from the Indies any tomatoes eaten in Europe must have been grown there. They were evidently still sufficiently unfamiliar in the 1590s for Acosta to include a description in

Century'. By the early seventeenth century chillies had made their way into Spanish riddles and collections of household medicines, where they featured alongside onions, olive oil and vinegar: Pérez de Herrera, *Proverbios morales*, enigma 83 (p. 78); and Sabuco Barrera, *Nueva filosofía de la naturaleza del hombre*, pp. 170, 184.

[64] Hillgarth, *The Mirror of Spain*, p. 42; and Joly, 'Voyage en Espagne', p. 473.

[65] Garrido Aranda, 'La revolución alimentaria del siglo XVI en América y Europa', pp. 207–8.

Figure 14 Diego Velázquez, *Kitchen Scene with Christ in the House of Martha and Mary*, 1618. Note the dried chilli pepper on the table. It forms part of the humble, everyday meal that the young woman prepares.

his catalogue of American plants – he characterised them as 'a kind of round, juicy berry that makes a delicious sauce, and they are good to eat by themselves'.[66] By the early seventeenth century, however, they were regarded by other Europeans as a distinctive, and peculiar, feature of the Iberian diet.[67] Sweet potatoes were likewise grown in Andalusia by the 1580s, where they were reportedly used like turnips.[68] Attempts were also made to grow the highly appreciated tropical fruits, although these enjoyed only partial success.[69] The presence of these foodstuffs in the Iberian Peninsula (and elsewhere in Europe) can be traced not only in expense books and other written sources, but also in the flourishing art

[66] Acosta, *Natural and Moral History of the Indies*, book 4, chap. 20 (p. 207); and Ríos, *Agricultura de jardines*, p. 59 (for the cultivation of 'pomates').

[67] Gerard, *The Herbal or General History of Plants*, p. 346; and Garrido Aranda, 'La revolución alimentaria del siglo XVI en América y Europa', pp. 207–8.

[68] Monardes, *Joyfull News out of the New-founde Worlde*, p. 104; Nuñez de Oria, *Regimiento y aviso de sanidad*, p. 43r; Acosta, *Natural and Moral History*, book 4, chap. 18 (p. 202); Regueiro y González-Barros, 'La flora americana en la España del siglo XVI', p. 209; Pardo Tomás and López Terrada, *Primeras noticias sobre plantas americanas*, p. 160.

[69] Fresquet Febrer *et al.*, 'La presencia de los productos americanos en el *Discurso de las cosas aromáticas* (1572) de Juan Fragoso', p. 370; and López Piñero, 'The Faculty of Medicine of Valencia', p. 74.

Figure 15 Juan Sánchez Cotán, *Still Life with Game Fowl*, *c.* 1600. Note the chayote squash in the lower left corner.

of still-life painting, in which new-world fruits and vegetables regularly appear.[70] (See Figure 15.)

'A little of this fruit suffices'

None of these foodstuffs, however, were expected to form the mainstay of a Spaniard's diet whether in Spain or the Indies. On the contrary, writers insisted that these foods, tasty though they were, should be eaten only in moderate quantities. As Oviedo noted of the sweet potato,

[70] For Spanish examples see Juan Sánchez Cotán, *Still Life with Game Fowl*, *c.* 1600, Art Institute of Chicago (chayote); unknown artist, *Still Life with Basket of Fruit and Thistle*, *c.* 1615–25, Private Collection, Madrid (chillies); Diego Velázquez, *Christ in the House of Martha and Mary*, 1618, National Gallery, London (chilli); Diego Velázquez, *Old Woman Cooking Eggs*, 1618, National Gallery of Scotland (chillies); Juan van der Hamen, *Pomona and Vertumnus*, 1626, Bank of Spain Collection (tomato); Anon. *Still Life with Fruit Bowl and Sweets*, 1627, Bank of Spain Collection (tomato); Francisco de Zurburán (attributed), *Fruit in a Basket, Vegetables and Utensils on a Table*, Kredisin Foundation (chillies); and Bartolomé Murillo, *The Angels' Kitchen*, 1646, Musée du Louvre (tomato and chillies).

settlers enjoyed it because 'they don't eat it as their principle, regular sustenance, but only every now and then'.[71] Coconuts, likewise, were a splendid food, but it was similarly unwise to eat too many at once. They were, he wrote, 'food for hardy men who work a lot'. For others, 'a little of this fruit suffices, since eating it all the time, as they do in the Indies, is not for every stomach'.[72] Similarly the delightful tropical fruits could cause illness when eaten in any quantity. 'Don't eat fruit ... because you'll get very ill, and pay attention to what I am telling you because all fruit is very bad for you', Rodrigo de Prado warned his brother Pedro, who was about to join him in the Indies.[73] Pineapples in particular were said to provoke the production of yellow bile, a humour to which Spaniards were believed to be all too inclined in the first place.[74] Chroniclers and settlers alike insisted that these foods were healthy only when they were eaten in limited amounts and therefore did not constitute the core of an individual diet.

In recommending a limited consumption of fruits and vegetables, these writers consciously or unconsciously followed general European dietary advice. Galenic medicine distinguished between nourishing foods such as bread that formed the core of the individual diet, and 'medicinal foods' such as fruits which should be eaten in smaller quantities to help regulate overall health.[75] Dieticians thus advised only

<hr>

[71] Fernández de Oviedo, *Historia general y natural*, book 7, chap. 3 (vol. I, p. 234).
[72] Fernández de Oviedo, *Historia general y natural*, book 9, chap. 4 (vol. I, p. 284).
[73] Rodrigo de Prado to Pedro de Prado, Mexico, 1 March 1565, in Otte, ed., *Cartas privadas de emigrantes a Indias, 1540–1616*, p. 49. Celedón Favalis attributed his good health while in Panama to the fact that he 'ate very little fruit, which is the thing that usually causes most damage': Celedón Favalis to Simón Favalis, Los Reyes, 20 March 1587, in Otte, ed., *Cartas privadas de emigrantes a Indias*, p. 431. See also Peter Martyr, *De Orbe Novo*, decade 2, book 1; Fernández de Oviedo, *Historia general y natural*, book 8, chap. 32 (vol. I, p. 273); and Hernández, *Quatro libros de la naturaleza*, book 1, part 2, chap. 59 (p. 41). Las Casas, who unlike Oviedo thought peanuts were delicious, noted that they caused headaches if eaten in quantity: *Apologética historia sumaria*, c. 1552, chap. 10 (p. 39).
[74] 'Relación de la Isla Española enviada al Rey d. Felipe II por el licenciado Echagoian', in Pacheco *et al.*, eds., *Colección de documentos inéditos*, vol. I, p. 14; Fernández de Oviedo, *Historia general y natural*, book 7, chaps. 3, 14 (vol. I, pp. 234, 242); Cervantes de Salazar, *Crónica*, book 1, chap. 5 (pp. 12–13); Vargas Machuca, 'Descripción breve de todas las Indias occidentales', in *Milicia y descripción de las Indias*, vol. II, pp. 104–5; and Hernández, *Quatro libros de la naturaleza*, book 3, part 2, chap. 76 (p. 176).
[75] See Galen, 'On the Powers of Food', in *Galen on Food and Drink*, pp. 113–35; Lobera de Avila, *Vergel de sanidad*, p. lxr; Cisneros, *Sitio, naturaleza y propiedades*, chap. 17 (p. 115r); Nuñez de Oria, *Regimiento y aviso de sanidad*, p. 193v; and Sánchez-Moscoso Hermida, 'Concepto científico de nutrición en un texto médico del siglo XVI', p. 228. The Spaniard Reginaldo de Lizárraga noted that in Lima excessive consumption of either Spanish or local fruits caused fevers: Lizárraga, *Descripción breve de toda la tierra del Perú*, chap. 54 (p. 40).

limited consumption of fresh fruits of any sort, whether European or new world. Medical texts warned particularly against eating excessive quantities of moist fruits such as melons or apricots, which under certain circumstances could turn into poisonous humours in the stomach.[76] They similarly noted that many vegetables were liable to provoke the formation of noxious humours unless they had been prepared and eaten in the correct fashion. As one doctor put it, 'eating vegetables and falling ill are one and the same thing'.[77] Salads, for example, were regarded as a suitable start to a meal, but dieticians warned that they tended to thin the blood and were not very nourishing.[78] These views were not held only by the learned. The Barcelona tanner (and diarist) Miquel Parets initially attributed a city-wide outbreak of illness in 1651 to the consumption of 'carrots and vegetables and other bad foods which cause disease'.[79] Uncertainty about the healthfulness of new-world fruit and vegetables thus combined anxieties about the ability of Spaniards to eat American foods with broader European concerns about the place of fruit and vegetables within a healthy diet. Similar stipulations about the need for moderation were frequently repeated regarding the use of chocolate; 'immoderate' consumption of the sort to which women in particular were prone attracted sustained criticism from doctors. And no one anticipated that settlers would subsist entirely on manatee, particularly given the multitude of pigs that greeted them at every turn. In other words, neither individual settlers nor theoretically sophisticated doctors saw anything dangerous in occasionally supplementing one's diet with an avocado or a bit of chilli pepper. Naturally, Spaniards should shun spiders and human flesh – and the less said about those unable to do so, the better. The real challenge to the colonial eater was presented not by these foods but by the maize, potatoes and cassava that constituted the core of indigenous diets across the hemisphere.[80] These foods offered not a sweet (or savoury) addition to a fundamentally European diet built around wine, wheat bread and meat, but instead formed part

---

[76] Lobera de Avila, *Banquete de nobles caballeros*, chap. 23 (pp. 67–9); Mercado, *Diálogos de philosophia natural y moral*, dialogue 4 (p. 73v); Barrios, *Verdadera medicina y cirugía*, book 1, chap. 2 (p. 43r). Or see *Libro de medicina llamado tesoro de los pobres*, p. xxvi; McVaugh, *Medicine before the Plague*, pp. 145–7; Galen, 'On the Powers of Food', book 2, in *Galen on Food and Drink*, pp. 113–35; Albala, *Eating Right in the Renaissance*, pp. 96, 109–10; and Peña and Girón, *La prevención de la enfermedad*, pp. 242–74.

[77] Sorapan de Rieros, *Medicina española*, p. 234.

[78] Lobera de Avila, *Vergel de sanidad*, pp. lviiiv–lxr; Nuñez de Oria, *Regimiento y aviso de sanidad*, pp. 229v–236r; Mercado, *Diálogos de philosophia natural y moral*, dialogue 4 (p. 70–3); Sorapan de Rieros, *Medicina española*, pp. 233–45; and Albala, *Eating Right in the Renaissance*, p. 110.

[79] Parets, *A Journal of the Plague Year*, pp. 39 (quotation), 43, 128n51.

[80] See Coe, *America's First Cuisines* for details of the preconquest diet.

of entirely separate culinary systems. The next section revisits colonial reactions to these foods.

'The bread of the Indians'

As we have seen, settlers regarded a diet heavily reliant on these foods as dangerous to the European constitution. Numerous accounts ascribe illness among settlers to an unwise over-consumption of these foodstuffs, and individuals inclined towards natural philosophy could see in Amerindians themselves the dangerous consequences of too much maize or potato. As the seventeenth-century Jesuit writer Bernabé Cobo explained, these foods were not 'suitable to sustain Spaniards'.[81]

Nonetheless, there is a wealth of evidence that maize and other new-world starches in fact featured largely in the diet of many settlers. Of course these items were eaten during military campaigns, when other food was in short supply. Hungry conquistadors were overcome with joy on encountering stocks of maize, cassava or other such staples. The Peruvian chronicler Garcilaso de la Vega described how one party gobbled up a store of raw maize 'as if it were sugared almonds'.[82] But it was not only in such desperate circumstances that settlers ate these foods. Despite the suspicion with which maize and other new-world starches were viewed, it was impossible for most settlers to avoid them completely. From the earliest days of settlement colonists drank *atole* (a maize porridge), ate tortillas, and consumed other indigenous starches such as *chuño*, or freeze-dried potato, although unlike Amerindians they sometimes flavoured it with sugar.[83] Chroniclers and travellers noted the

---

[81] Cobo, *Historia del Nuevo Mundo*, book 10, chap. 1 (vol. I, p. 375).
[82] Garcilaso de la Vega, *Royal Commentaries*, book 9, chap. 24 (vol. I, p. 594); and, for particular references to joy, see Cortés, Fifth Letter, in *Letters from Mexico*, p. 361; Fernández de Oviedo, *Historia general y natural*, book 17, chap. 23 (vol. II, p. 157); and López de Gómara, *Historia general*, chap. 109 (p. 200).
[83] For varied discussion of European consumption of new-world starches see Peter Martyr, *De Orbe Novo*, decade 1, book 1, decade 2, books 1, 3, decade 3, books 2, 4; Fernández de Enciso, *Suma de geographia*, p. 72r; Federman, *Historia indiana*, pp. 40, 43, 118, 121; Las Casas, *Historia de las Indias*, *c.* 1559, book 1, chap. 111 (p. 302); López de Gómara, *Historia general*, chap. 61 (p. 116); 'Relación general de las poblaciones españoles del Perú', *c.* 1572, in Jiménez de la Espada, ed., *Relaciones geográficas de las Indias: Perú*, vol. I, p. 127; Vargas Machuca, 'Descripción breve de todas las Indias occidentales', book 2, in *Milicia y descripción de las Indias*, vol. I, p. 156; Cárdenas, *Problemas y secretos maravillosos*, book 2, chap. 14 (pp. 138–47); Mendieta, *Historia eclesiástica indiana*, book 4, chap. 38 (pp. 524–5); Leon Pinelo, *Question moral*, part 2, chaps. 9–10 (pp. 57, 63); Gage, *The English-American*, chaps. 11, 13 (pp. 166, 197–8); Peña Montenegro, *Itinerario para parochos de indios*, book 4, tratado 5, section 1 (p. 454); Gemelli Careri, *Voyage du tour du monde*, vol. VI, book 1, chap. 7 (vol. VI, p. 112); and Pilcher, *¡Que vivan los tamales!*.

widespread consumption of '*atole, pinole,* scalded plantains, butter of the *cacao,* puddings made of Indian maize, with a bit of fowl or fresh pork in them seasoned with much red biting chilli', and other local delicacies, by Spanish and creole settlers alike.[84] And from the 1570s sailors on ships returning from the Indies might be provisioned with bread made from maize or cassava in place of the regulation hardtack, although they complained vociferously that it caused all manner of digestive disturbances.[85]

The importance of such foods to the settler diet is indicated by the fact that colonists actively cultivated them for their own consumption. For example, in the Spanish settlement in Santa Elena, in Florida, colonists reported that they planted maize 'to sustain our children'.[86] Archaeology provides another perspective on this topic. Excavations of several Spanish settlements in Florida revealed the remains of a range of indigenous foodstuffs, including maize and squash. Spanish settlers there had evidently begun eating such new foods, although it is also clear that they attempted as best they could to reproduce their familiar diet. Both archaeological and written evidence shows that they planted wheat, barley, garbanzos and a range of other old-world fruits and vegetables alongside their maize and squash.[87]

Spaniards introduced these foods into the Peninsula as well. Although potatoes appear not to have been much cultivated in Spain until the seventeenth century, and cassava was not well suited to the Iberian climate, maize was being grown within a few decades of Columbus's voyages.[88] From there it spread to Italy, West Africa and beyond. By the

---

[84] Gage, *The English-American,* chap. 13 (pp. 197–8). *Pinole* is a mixture of maize and cacao.

[85] Super, 'Spanish Diet in the Atlantic Crossing', pp. 60–3.

[86] 'Deposition of Alonso Martín', Santa Elena, 27 Feb. 1576, in Connor, ed., *Colonial Records of Spanish Florida,* vol. I, p. 146; and Lyon, 'Spain's Sixteenth-Century North American Settlement', p. 288.

[87] Deagan, *Spanish St. Augustine,* pp. 151–85; Reitz and Scarry, *Reconstructing Historic Subsistence with an Example from Sixteenth-Century Spanish Florida,* p. 92; and Reitz and McEwan, 'Animals, Environment and the Spanish Diet at Puerto Real'. See also DeFrance, 'Diet and Provisioning in the High Andes'.

[88] The authors of the *relaciones geográficas* often felt the need to describe the potato, which implies that it was not familiar to Europeans. See for example 'Descripción y relación de la provincia de los Yauyos', 1586; 'Descripción de la tierra del repartimiento de San Francisco de Atunrucana y Laramanti', 1586; 'Relación de la provincia de los Collaguas', 1586; all in Jiménez de la Espada, ed., *Relaciones geográficas de las Indias: Perú,* vol. I, pp. 156, 234, 331. See also Nuñez de Oria, *Regimiento y aviso de sanidad,* p. 41v; Leon Pinelo, *Question moral,* part 2, chap. 10 (p. 63); Hawkes and Francisco-Ortega, 'The Potato in Spain'; and Albala, *Eating Right in the Renaissance,* p. 238.

1570s Hernández could claim with only a measure of hyperbole that 'it is known almost all over the world'.[89] A century later a Peruvian writer observed that 'it was brought to Spain years ago, and is the salvation of Asturias and Galicia, and a great deal is harvested in Biscay and on the coast of Granada and in Malaga, because it is so easily grown and harvested, and because it is already very well known under the name of Indian wheat I will not describe it further'.[90] In Spain, as in Italy, maize never dethroned wheat from its position of principle grain but it did make substantial inroads as a cheaper wheat substitute comparable to rye or other minor grains. The seventeenth-century French traveller Mme d'Aulnoy reported that Spanish inns served a disagreeable bread made with 'Turkish wheat', or maize. She described it as sitting in the stomach like a lump of lead.[91]

Further evidence that settlers consumed maize and other new world starches is provided by the encomia to these foods sometimes embedded in colonial accounts. For example, the Franciscan monk and Bishop of Yucatan Diego de Landa noted that except when it was cold, maize bread was 'tasty and healthy'.[92] The occasional enthusiast even proclaimed its superiority over European wheat.[93] The Spanish doctor Juan de Cárdenas not only praised *atole*, or maize porridge, as a very wholesome drink suited to all complexions but moreover asserted, against all evidence, that tortillas were easier to prepare than bread made from wheat. For these reasons maize was in his view a splendid grain deserving universal esteem.[94] (In fact, the Meso-American maize cuisine was extremely labour intensive. While women in Europe usually spent five to six hours a week making bread, women in Meso-America spent five to six hours *a day* preparing tortillas.[95])

[89] Columbus, 'Carta a los reyes católicos' (third voyage), in *Los cuatro viajes del almirante*, p. 177; Hernández, 'Maize', in *The Mexican Treasury*, p. 111; McCann, *Maize and Grace*; Warman, *Corn and Capitalism*; and Carney and Rosomoff, *In the Shadow of Slavery*.

[90] Leon Pinelo, *Question moral*, part 2, chap. 9 (p. 57).

[91] Mme d'Aulnoy, *Relation du voyage d'Espagne*, letter 3 (vol. I, p. 113).

[92] Landa, *Relación de las cosas de Yucatan*, p. 37; Mendieta, *Historia eclesiástica indiana*, book 4, chap. 38 (pp. 524–5); and Monardes, *Joyfull News out of the New-founde Worlde*, p. 104. See also Fuentes y Guzmán, *Historia de Guatemala o Recordación Florida*, book 9, chap. 1 (vol. I, pp. 305–7, quotation p. 305) for maize's healthful qualities: 'it mitigates the heat of a fever, cleanses the body and purges the stomach … it is suitable to treat all infirmities arising in either sex at any age'.

[93] Lizárraga, *Descripción breve de toda la tierra del Perú*, chap. 5 (quotation p. 6); and Cieza de León, *Parte primera de la chrónica del Perú*, chap. 66 (p. 82).

[94] Cárdenas, *Problemas y secretos maravillosos*, book 2, chap. 14 (pp. 138–47).

[95] Bauer, 'Millers and Grinders'.

Typically, such celebrations also included comments to the effect that the writer did not understand why these foods were held in low esteem by other settlers. The *protomédico* Francisco Hernández praised maize as a healthy and useful food ('let us say, finally, that toasted corn on the cob, or cooked with meat, either way is really good to eat'), but nonetheless expressed bewilderment that so few colonists chose to consume it.[96] The Spanish officer Baltasar Dorantes de Carranza, who participated in a disastrous expedition to Florida and later settled in New Spain, likewise observed that although cassava made in his view 'the best bread in the world, after our wheat', most Spaniards nonetheless preferred to provision themselves with stale wheat imported from Europe.[97] José de Acosta, who proclaimed that he would rather eat wheat bread, 'no matter how hard or black it was', was by no means unusual. Indeed, even the most enthusiastic proponents of the indigenous diet vacillated in their endorsements. Bartolomé de las Casas, for example, stated on one page of his *Historia de las Indias* (*History of the Indies*) that maize bread was healthier than wheat bread, and on another that it made settlers ill.[98] And despite his assertions that maize and chillies were healthy and useful, the *protomédico* Hernández maintained that they 'generated profuse bile [and] blood', and for this reason were probably behind the devastating epidemic of *cocoliztli* that struck Mexico City in 1576.[99]

In other words, despite such defences of maize's healthfulness and pleasant taste, many Spanish settlers, as Hernández himself indicated, preferred not to rely on such foods for their principal sustenance. It was one thing to eat an *arepa* (a maize cake) or a pineapple every now and then 'as a treat', and quite another to build your diet around them.[100] Most settlers found it difficult to avoid such foods altogether, but Spaniards who embraced the indigenous diet too enthusiastically were viewed with suspicion, like those denounced in late sixteenth-century Mexico for 'drifting about among the Indians, eating chilli and tomatoes'.[101] These were the people who ended up looking just like the

---

[96] Hernández, 'Maize', in *The Mexican Treasury*, pp. 111, 113 (quotation); and López Medel, *De los tres elementos*, pp. 153–4.

[97] Dorantes de Carranza, *Sumaria relación de las cosas de la Nueva España*, pp. 68 (quotation), 71, 73.

[98] Las Casas, *Historia de las Indias*, c. 1559, book 1, chaps. 154–5 (pp. 610, 613); and Acosta, *Natural and Moral History*, book 4, chap. 16 (pp. 197–8).

[99] Hernández, 'On the Illness in New Spain in the Year 1576 Called Cocolitzli by the Indians', in *The Mexican Treasury*, p. 84.

[100] See Acosta, *Natural and Moral History of the Indies*, book 4, chap. 16 (p. 198) on treats.

[101] Mörner, *La corona española y los foráneos*, p. 157.

Indians whose customs they unwisely imitated, and whose categorisation bewildered civil and religious authorities alike.

The daily negotiations that eating in the colonies entailed for settlers may be glimpsed in an imaginary shopping list compiled by one Mexican creole. Diego de Nagera Yanguas was a parish priest who spent many decades living and working in the town of Jocotitlán, to the northwest of Mexico City. In 1637 he published a grammar of Mazahua, the local indigenous language. His grammar included not only model admonitions on the evils of drink, but also many useful phrases and dialogues. There are phrases for motivating workmen ('Brothers hurry up look it's already late and we have done almost nothing aren't you ashamed to think what our boss will say when he gets here?'), and also a number of sections related to household management.[102] One of the latter concerns how to instruct a servant in shopping at the market. Nagera explained how to teach a servant to shop wisely and also provided a list of items one might wish to have purchased. Some of these were new-world ingredients such as chillies, tomatoes, sweet potatoes and the sweet syrup extracted from the maguey plant. The bulk of his list, however, consists of old-world foods. Nagera offered a detailed description of the best sort of wheat bread ('it should be very good, tender, white and well cooked'), and also gave the Mazahua terms for lamb, beef, bacon and a variety of other European staples.[103] This, clearly, was not only what the priest wanted to eat, but what he thought his readers might reasonably want to instruct their servants to buy.

A few years earlier another settler, Pedro de Arenas, composed a phrasebook of useful Nahuatl terms aimed at 'humble men who don't aspire to elegance and want to be able to talk with the Indians'.[104] Readers could learn how to offer words of consolation, how to reject a potential purchase as tatty and overpriced, how to sell a horse and also how to order a meal. Like Nagera, Arenas made some assumptions about what his readers would want to eat. His model phrases, like those of the priest, explained how to order 'meat, lamb, beef, veal, bacon, pork', how to ask for wine, and how to request apples and bananas. The only new-world items for which he provided specific Nahuatl translations were chillies, maguey syrup and a type of local poultry. His translation of 'pan', the Spanish for bread, however, was simply 'tlaxcalli', the generic Nahuatl term for maize tortillas.[105] Such vocabularies indicate

---

[102] Nagera Yanguas, *Doctrina y enseñanza en la lengua maçahua*, p. 92 (the original Spanish phrases are completely unpunctuated).
[103] Nagera Yanguas, *Doctrina y enseñanza en la lengua maçahua*, p. 94.
[104] Arenas, *Vocabulario manual de las lenguas castellana y mexicana*, p. 3.
[105] Arenas, *Vocabulario manual de las lenguas castellana y mexicana*, pp. 15–17, 86–90.

the parameters constraining the diet of most colonists. They aspired to wine and meat, the latter perhaps spiced with chillies, but knew that their bread was as likely to be a tortilla as a white loaf.

In general, although settlers and explorers often reported without comment that they provisioned themselves with maize and other new-world staples, when illness struck they immediately blamed the American diet. For instance, the diary of Felipe de Hutten, a German who participated in the conquest of Venezuela in the 1530s, reveals that his party relied on maize seized from locals for their food, but when a number of his companions fell ill, he recorded bitterly that maize and cassava were 'damaging not only to the sick, but also to healthy people who are not accustomed to such food'.[106] Similarly, the settlers in the Florida colony of Santa Elena, who, as we saw, grew maize as a staple crop, nonetheless reported not only that was it difficult to prepare but also that sick people 'cannot under any circumstances eat the said maize, and a number of people have died because they had no other food'.[107] In other words, even those settlers who routinely ate maize and other new-world starches suspected that they were not healthful for Europeans, particularly those who were already unwell or in a weakened condition. Slave traders held similar views regarding maize and cassava's suitability to the African body, which in some cases was equally unfamiliar with these foodstuffs. Traders preferred for this reason to feed ailing slaves on wheat bread, although the healthy were provisioned with cheaper new-world starches such as maize or cassava.[108] New-world starches, in other words, were a necessary part of life in the colonies, but they were not for that any the less dangerous for old-world bodies, particularly those already struggling to cope with the rigours of the unfamiliar environment and, perhaps, homesickness.

Bread or not bread

Europeans thus vacillated in their views about how much of the new American environment they could incorporate into their own bodies, and, by extension, into their culture. They were enthusiastic about many new-world foods, but advised against prolonged or excessive consumption. They relied on new-world starches but suspected them of causing

---

[106] Hutten, 'Diario', vol. II, pp. 356 (quotation), 367.
[107] 'Investigation into Conditions in Santa Elena', 1576, in Connor, ed., *Colonial Records of Spanish Florida*, vol. I, pp. 154 (quotation), 158, 162, 164, 168, 170, 174, 176.
[108] Newson and Minchin, 'Diets, Food Supplies and the African Slave Trade in Early Seventeenth-Century Spanish America', pp. 527–9.

illness, or worse. This uncertainly is revealed particularly clearly in their inconsistent attempts at categorising maize and other new-world carbohydrates such as cassava and potatoes. On the one hand, the Spanish quickly decided that these foods played a role in indigenous cultures equivalent to that played by wheat bread in their own. Maize, wrote the sixteenth-century Jesuit chronicler José de Acosta, was the 'bread of the Indies'.[109] Many chroniclers referred to maize as 'Indian wheat', and similarly labelled foods made from maize, cassava and potato as 'bread', regardless of the form in which they were prepared.[110] A military official, for example, described cassava root by noting simply 'it is a bread', while a Franciscan friar referred to Amerindians eating 'bread on the cob'.[111]

Such comparisons are particularly significant because of the central place that wheat bread occupied in Catholicism through its role in Holy Communion: wheat bread was the substance that became the body of Christ. For this reason wheat, in the form of bread, represented both food and Christianity itself. The arrival of wheat bread in the Indies thus stood by metonymy for the advent of Christianity. 'Since in white bread I see you descend to take possession of the Indies, I cede to your

[109] Acosta, *Natural and Moral History*, book 3, chap. 22, book 4, chaps. 16, 17, book 7, chap. 9 (pp. 151, 197–8 (quotation), 200, 202, 397).

[110] Columbus, 'Diary of the First Voyage', 13, 21, 26 Dec. 1492, 15 Jan. 1493, pp. 87, 99, 110, 130; Cuneo, 'News of the Islands of the Hesperian Ocean'; Giovanni de'Strozzi, 'Faith, Superstitions and Customs of the Island of Hispaniola'; Agostino Giustiniani, 'Psalter', 1516; and Alessandro Zorzi, 'Various Information about the Voyages'; all in Symcox, ed., *Italian Reports on America*, pp. 55, 65, 78, 108; Peter Martyr, *De Orbe Novo*, decade 1, book 1, decade 3 book 5; Fernández de Enciso, *Suma de geographia*, pp. l–liii; Fernández de Oviedo, *Historia general y natural*, book 2, chap. 13, book 5, chaps. 1, 3, book 7, preface, 1, 2, 14, book 8, chap. 40, book 10, chap. 7, book 12, chap. 10, book 16, chap. 1, book 20, chap. 1 (vol. I, pp. 48, 112, 119, 225–6, 228, 230–3, 243, 277, vol. II, pp. 15, 39, 88, 222, 225); Las Casas, *Apologética historia sumaria*, c. 1552, chaps. 3, 4, 10, 11 (pp. 14–17, 35–9, 41–2); López de Gómara, *Historia general*, chaps. 74, 195, 215 (pp. 143, 341, 370–2); Cervantes de Salazar, *Crónica*, book 1, chap. 6 (p. 14); Barrientos, 'Vida y hechos de Pero Menéndez de Avilés', chap. 28 (p. 309); López Medel, *De los tres elementos*, p. 150; Hernández, *Antigüedades de la Nueva España*, book 1, chap. 23 (p. 97, quotation); Durán, *Historia de las Indias de Nueva España*, book 1, part 1, chap. 16, book 1, part 2, chaps. 7, 20 (pp. 156, 251, 289); López de Velasco, *Geografía y descripción universal de las Indias*, 'De los granos y semillas'; 'Relación de Querétaro', 1582, in Acuña, ed., *Relaciones geográficas del siglo XVI: Michoacán*, p. 243; 'Descripción y relación de la ciudad de La Paz', 1586, in Jiménez de la Espada, ed., *Relaciones geográficas de las Indias: Perú*, vol. I, p. 344; Calvete de Estrella, *Rebelión de Pizarro en el Perú*, book 2, chap. 4 (vol. I, p. 211); Mendieta, *Historia eclesiástica indiana*, book 1, chap. 6 (p. 68); Dorantes de Carranza, *Sumaria relación*, pp. 67–73; and Cobo, *Historia del Nuevo Mundo*, book 2, chaps. 8, 11, book 4, chap. 3, book 11, chap. 6 (vol. I, pp. 69, 76–7, 159–60, vol. II, p. 21).

[111] Vargas Machuca, 'Descripción breve de todas las Indias occidentales', in *Milicia y descripción de las Indias*, vol. II, p. 161; and Torquemada, *Monarchia yndiana*, book 14, chap. 14 (vol. II, p. 599).

divine hand all rights to it', the Devil tells Christ in Lope de Vega's didactic comedy *El nuevo mundo descubierto por Cristobál Colón (The New World Discovered by Christopher Columbus)*.[112] By likening maize, cassava and potatoes to wheat bread colonial writers implicitly – and at times explicitly – dignified these new-world foods through their association with this sacred substance.

The identification of maize with wheat extended to the language of Christian prayer. 'May You give us now our daily tortillas', reads a Nahuatl translation of the Lord's Prayer from 1634.[113] Such translations of course reflected the reality that for many Nahuatl speakers, tortillas *were* their daily 'bread', but they also revealed a broader symbolic identification between wheat and new-world starches that transcends their parallel roles in the European and indigenous diets. After all, as we saw in Chapter 2, the daily bread of the Lord's Prayer and the 'doctrinal bread' of Christianity were inextricably linked. Many Eucharistic texts drew explicit parallels between the earthly food of daily life and the heavenly food of the Mass by describing the host as 'food and sustenance for the soul'.[114] If tortillas were like wheat bread, then tortillas inevitably shared some of the special spiritual qualities of wheat. Perhaps they too could represent the bread of doctrine.

For this reason bilingual catechisms on occasion used an indigenous term such as *tlaxcalli* (tortilla) to describe even the bread used in the Mass. For example, Pedro de Gante's 1553 confessional manual described the Eucharist as a 'blessed little tortilla'.[115] Similarly, in a 1680 bilingual Spanish–Chayma catechism from Venezuela, *'erepa'* (a maize cake) was the term chosen as the most suitable translation for 'bread' in the sections devoted to the Mass.[116] The Jesuit linguist Diego González Holguín likewise suggested that an appropriate Quechua translation for the consecrated host was *'tupa cocau'*, which, he explained, referred to a special variety of magical maize that the Inca gave his ambassadors to

---

[112] Lope de Vega, *El nuevo mundo descubierto por Cristóbal Colón*, act 3, lines 2780–2 (p. 41).

[113] Pareja, *Doctrina cristiana muy útil y necesaria*, p. 4v; Juan de la Anunciación, *Doctrina christiana muy cumplida*, p. 231; and Alva, *A Guide to Confession Large and Small in the Mexican Language*, p. 162 (quotation). See also Baudot, 'Los *huehuelatolli* en la cristianización de México', p. 34; and Lara, *Christian Texts for Aztecs*, 128–43.

[114] *Tercero cathecismo y exposición de la doctrina christiana*, p. 74 (quotation); Torres Rubio, *Arte de la lengua aymara*, p. 32v; Pérez Bocanegra, *Ritual, formulario e institución de curas*, p. 470; Ruyz, *Catecismo de la lengua guarani*, p. 253; Avendaño, *Sermones*, segunda parte, sermons 14, 22 (pp. 12, 43).

[115] Burkhart, *The Slippery Earth*, p. 108 (quotation); and Sahagún, 'The *Exercicio quotidiana*', vol. II, pp. 173, 179. I am grateful to Deborah Toner for these references.

[116] Tauste, 'Catecismo universal', in *Arte y bocabulario de la lengua de los indios chaymas*, pp. 175, 177.

sustain them during travel.[117] Such texts, like the very use of the term 'bread' to describe foods made from maize or cassava, implied that these foods not only served a function similar to that of wheat bread in Spanish culture, but that, more profoundly, they were in some sense equivalent to wheat.

On the other hand, perhaps the most characteristic feature of maize and other new-world starches was precisely that they were *not* wheat. Maize and cassava, those foodstuffs 'damaging not only to the sick, but also to the healthy', were not merely dangerous when eaten in quantity, but had also been repeatedly declared incapable of transformation into the body of Christ. While some new-world religious texts blurred the distinction between wheat bread and new-world starches in the way described above, a larger number stressed the fundamental difference that separated them: only wheat bread could undergo transubstantiation. Thus a 1687 Venezuelan catechism offered a clear answer to the question 'Of what material is [the Eucharist] consecrated?'. The response was 'Of true bread, *made with wheat flour and water*, and of true wine from grapes.'[118] Many other colonial texts were equally explicit that only wheat bread could become the body of Christ. Sixteenth-century sermons in Nahuatl stated clearly that the materials to be used in the Mass were 'castillan tlaxcalli' and 'castillan vino' (*Castilian* tortillas [wheat bread] and *Castilian* wine) rather than ordinary tortillas and indigenous beer.[119] A Peruvian catechism similarly admonished indigenous parishioners that they should under no circumstances confuse the host with a simple maize cake or *arepa*.[120] Maize, like cassava and all the other foods out of which Amerindians fabricated their 'breads', thus differed from wheat in this crucial way.

---

[117] Durston, *Pastoral Quechua*, p. 250.

[118] Lovera, 'Intercambios y transformaciones alimentarias en Venezuela colonial', p. 67 (my emphasis). Or see Córdoba, *Doctrina cristiana*, p. c6; Bertonio, *Confessionario muy copioso en dos lenguas, aymara y española*, p. 43; and Peña Montenegro, *Itinerario para parochos de indios*, book 3, tratado 6 (pp. 346–55).

[119] *Doctrina christiana en lengua española y mexicana*, sermon 24 (pp. 101–3, quotation); Domingo de la Anunciación, *Doctrina christiana breve y compendiosa*, chap. 3 (labelled 2) (pp. 32–3); Juan de la Anunciación, *Doctrina christiana muy cumplida*, pp. 153–7; and Baptista, *Confessionario*, pp. 76, 79, 83. I am very grateful to Erica Hosselkus for her help in deciphering Nahuatl.

[120] *Tercero cathecismo y exposición*, p. 75v. This phrase is repeated in Avendaño, *Sermones*, segunda parte, sermon 14 (p. 13). Although Catholic writers regularly constructed parallels between earthly and heavenly food, the ability to distinguish between the two was a key requirement for being allowed to take Communion. See Torquemada, *Monarchia yndiana*, book 16, chap. 20 (p. 214); and Olabarrieta Medrano, *Recuerdo de los obligaciones del ministerio apostólico*, chap. 2, section 8 (pp. 48–9).

These new-world foods not only differed from wheat, but were in some sense anti-wheat, or un-wheat. Indeed, the nomenclature used to describe maize explicitly marks the new world starch of greatest import to early modern Europe as alien and unchristian. Its name in a number of European languages (*grano turco*, *blé de turquie*, *blé sarazin*, *milho marroco*, *blat de moro*) associates it with the Islamic world, Western Europe's most visible unchristian Other.[121] Maize, itself a sacred substance within many indigenous cultures, was like wheat in that for many indigenous people it formed the core of their diet just as wheat was supposed to do for Spanish settlers, but it was at the same time utterly different because, in the view of most colonial writers, any supernatural resonance that it possessed was associated solely with its role in illegitimate indigenous rituals and ceremonies. Priests carefully chronicled and denounced the use of maize, in particular, in a variety of healing rituals and divination rites. They further recorded the superstitious ceremonies that accompanied the maize and potato harvests.[122] Even worse, they noted the consumption during certain Aztec rituals of little figures representing various deities fashioned out of maize and other seeds, which offered an uncanny parallel with Christian Communion. While some maintained that this revealed the traces of a primitive Christianity introduced by St Thomas or some other apostle in the distant past, others concluded that only the devil could be responsible for such a monstrous plagiarism of Christianity's most sacred ritual.[123] Maize in this reading was some sort of demonic anti-bread. It was for this reason that the Mexican Inquisition responded harshly

---

[121] Brandes, 'El misterio del maíz', p. 261.

[122] Durán, *Historia de las Indias de Nueva España*, book 1, part 1, chaps. 2, 4, 14, 16, 19, 20, book 1, part 2, chaps. 2, 7, 8, 11, 16, 20 (pp. 28–30, 41–5, 136–7, 153–8, 172, 179, 227–8, 252–3, 257, 266, 280, 289); 'Relación de la religión y ritos del Perú hecha por los padres agustinos', *c.* 1560, pp. 11–12, 30, 41; Sahagún, *Historia general de las cosas de Nueva España*, book 2, chap. 23 (pp. 105–7); 'Memoria de los pueblos que se yncluyen en el corregimiento de Tequisistlán', 1580, in Paso y Troncoso, ed., *Relaciones geográficas de México*, pp. 214–16; Acosta, *Natural and Moral History of the Indies*, book 5, chap. 28 (p. 316); Ruiz de Alarcón, *Tratado de las supersticiones y costumbres gentílicas*, tratado 3, chap. 1; and Gonzalo de Balsalobre, 'Relación de las idolatrías de Oaxaca', 1654, in Máynez, ed., *Hechicerías e idolatrías del México antiguo*, p. 223. For maize as a sacred substance within indigenous cultures see *Popol Vuh*, part III, chaps. 1–3 (pp. 165–73); Coe, *America's First Cuisines*, pp. 9–16; Pilcher, *¡Que vivan los tamales!*; and Taube, 'The Maize Tamale in Classic Maya Diet, Epigraphy and Art'.

[123] Acosta, *Natural and Moral History of the Indies*, book 5, chaps. 23–8 (pp. 300–18); and Jáuregui, '"El plato más sabroso"'.

when it learned of a man who had conducted a parody of the Mass using a tortilla.[124]

Colonial writers thus vacillated between labelling maize, cassava and other new world staples as the equivalent of bread, as 'Indian wheat', on the one hand, and as something profoundly unchristian, and unbreadlike, on the other. The uncertainty over whether these foods were like bread, or were on the contrary something fundamentally different from bread, may be seen in the linguistic inconstancy of José de Acosta's comment that his chronicle would show 'what sort of bread there is in the Indies and what they use in place of bread'.[125] Writers such as Acosta never resolved the conundrum of whether these Indian breads were true breads.

Men or not men

It is tempting to construct a parallel between European uncertainty over whether maize was or was not bread, and the larger question of whether the Indians were men. The news that a hitherto unknown people had been found in the Americas prompted an intense debate in Europe about the nature of the Indians, and, more specifically, their capacity to become Christians. The question was ostensibly settled in 1537 when Pope Paul III issued a bull declaring that 'the Indians are truly men and that they are not only capable of understanding the Catholic Faith but, according to our information, they desire exceedingly to receive it'.[126] Nonetheless, disputes about the character of the Indians continued for decades. While many writers defended the intelligence and religiosity of Amerindians, others insisted they were a barbarous and simple-minded people incapable of governing themselves.[127]

---

[124] Greenleaf, *The Mexican Inquisition of the Sixteenth Century*, p. 108.

[125] Acosta, *Natural and Moral History*, book 4, chap. 16 (p. 197). For comparable inconsistency see Cuneo, 'News of the Islands of the Hesperian Ocean', 1495, pp. 57, 60; and Benavidez, *Secretos de chirurgia*, p. 12.

[126] Paul III, 'Sublimus Dei'. For these disputes see Hanke, *Aristotle and the American Indians*; and Pagden, *The Fall of Natural Man*.

[127] The most influential defender of Amerindian intelligence was Bartolomé de las Casas. See for example Las Casas, *Historia de las Indias*, c. 1559, book 3, chaps. 4–5 (pp. 176–81); and *Apologética historia sumaria*, c. 1552, chap. 48 (p. 165). Or see Sahagún, *Historia general de las cosas de Nueva España*, prologue (vol. I, p. 4); and Lavallé, *Las promesas ambiguas*, pp. 79–101. For contrasting views see Diego de Porres, 'Instrucción y orden que an de tener los sacerdotes que se ocupasen en la doctrina y conversión de los yndios en las Yndias del Piru', n.d., Archivo General de Indias, Patronato, legajo 231, N. 7, R. 8, fol. 1; Carta de Tomás López a los reyes de Bohemia, Guatemala, 9 June 1550, Archivo General de Indias, Audiencia de Guatemala, legajo 9A, N. 68, R. 17, fol. 4; Carta de Tomás López Medel, 25 March 1551, Archivo General de Indias, Audiencia de Guatemala, legajo 9A, R. 18, n. 77, fol. 10; Vargas Machuca, 'Descripción breve de todas las Indias occidentales',

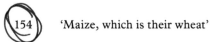

The Jesuit José de Acosta, usually an astute observer of the American scene, disagreed with those who labelled Amerindians as utterly bestial, but he nonetheless believed that before they could become Christians they needed first to learn to be men.[128]

Bread or not bread; men or not men? We would not be alone in positing a connection between these foods and the people who ate them, for colonial culture itself equated eaters and eaten. The fruit of the mangrove tree and the people who ate it were, as Oviedo insisted, equally savage. 'Indians are no more people than cassava is bread', runs an aphorism from colonial Venezuela.[129] Perhaps then these Indian breads *were* in essence identical to old-world breads. Indeed, in the late sixteenth century certain new-world churchmen disputed the doctrine that only wheat flour could be used in Communion wafers, arguing that maize, too, could serve as the basis for the host.[130] Perhaps maize, or even cassava, could become a Communion wafer and perhaps Indians had the same potential to become Christians as Europeans. Or perhaps the Indians were fundamentally Other, incapable of incorporation into the European world, just as the ersatz 'breads' of native culture could never be transformed into the true body of Christ.

Quotidian doubts about the place of new-world food in the colonial diet thus mirror larger doubts about the place of Amerindians within colonial culture. Were Amerindians barbaric spider- and man-eating savages, or were they rational beings whose own consumption

in *Milicia y descripción de las Indias*, vol. II, p. 80; and Carta del Virrey Conde de Monterrey, San Agustín, 4 Aug. 1597, Archivo General de Indias, Audiencia de México, legajo 23, N. 86, fol. 5. For the views of writers in Spain see for example Sepúlveda, *Demócrates segundo*, pp. 35, 38, 63; Álamos de Barrientos, *Discurso político al rey Felipe III*, p. 15; and Sigüenza, *Historia de la Orden de San Gerónimo*, part 3, book 1, chap. 25 (vol. II, p. 101).

[128] Acosta, *De procuranda indorum salute*, book 3, chap. 19, section 1 (vol. I, p. 539). See also proemio book 1, chap. 2, section 4, book 2, chap. 12, section 1 (vol. I, pp. 69, 89–91, 339).

[129] 'Indio no es gente, ni casabe es pan': Lovera, 'Intercambios y transformaciones alimentarias en Venezuela colonial', p. 65.

[130] In the early years of the conquest churchmen were sometimes obliged to find substitutes for scarce wine and wheat, regardless of whether they believed there was any theological basis for this innovation. See López Medel, *De los tres elementos*, p. 156; and Garcilaso de la Vega, *Royal Commentaries*, book 9, chap. 26 (vol. I, p. 598). Protestants, who viewed the Eucharist as a symbol, rather than the actual substance, of Christ's body, did not face the same doctrinal difficulties. In sixteenth-century Brazil, French Calvinists simply determined to use cassava flour and maize beer to celebrate Communion, once their supplies of wheat flour and wine gave out. Nonetheless, as Andrea Frisch has observed, they were at pains to select *analogous* substances to substitute for the missing bread and wine; they did not use seawater and parrots, two other items they also consumed. See Léry, *History of a Voyage to the Land of Brazil*, chap. 6 (p. 49); and Frisch, 'In Sacramental Mode', pp. 85–6.

practices colonists could safely imitate? Could Amerindians ever become Christians? These two questions, clearly, were interlinked, as were the 'bread of doctrine' and the daily breads that sustained settlers and Amerindians alike. Attitudes towards food both shaped settlers' responses to the colonial environment and reflected their larger concerns. The implications of these intertwinings form the subject of the next chapter.

5 'You will become like them if you eat their food'

Planting the faith

The parallels between the introduction of European foods and European religion shaped the imagination of colonial actors in the sixteenth century. Writers often spoke of 'planting' the faith, and missionaries hoped to reap a good harvest of new souls. Christianity was a tender shoot introduced into a fertile or hostile soil. Such language drew on long-standing Christian traditions, for evangelisation had for centuries been presented as a form of spiritual gardening, using imagery derived from the Bible itself. Agricultural metaphors thus permeated early modern religious writing in the Hispanic world; the Spanish Franciscan Juan de Pineda, for example, described evangelisation as 'Christian agriculture', whereby Christians planted the seeds of faith and encouraged the growth of deep roots and good fruit. At the same time, agricultural work implicitly recapitulated Christian history, for its origins lay in the Garden of Eden itself, a connection that pleased writers of agricultural treatises. Garden imagery thus permeates colonial texts, as the historian Jorge Cañizares Esguerra has observed.[1]

---

[1] Pineda, *Primera parte de los 35 dialogos familiares de la agricultura cristiana*, diálogo 1, section 16 (vol. I, p. 12); and Cañizares Esguerra, *Puritan Conquistadors*, pp. 178–214. In his teachings Jesus compared himself to a farmer, whose seeds fell variously on fertile or stony ground, or whose harvest was invaded by weeds. The good seeds in turn were the new converts: Matt. 13:3–43; Luke 8:4–15; John 4:35–8; and also Isa. 5:1–7. See also Herrera, *Obra de agricultura*, prologue (p. 7); Apuntamientos sobre la conversión y buen trato de los indios, n.d., Archivo General de Indias, Patronato, legajo 231, N. 1, R. 14. p. 1; Domingo de la Anunciación, *Doctrina christiana breve y compendiosa*, prologue (p. 2); Mendieta, *Historia eclesiástica indiana*, title of book 3 (p. 174); Murúa, *Historia general del Perú*, book 3, chap. 7 (p. 484); Sahagún, *Historia general de las cosas de Nueva España*, general prologue, book 3, prologue (vol. I, pp. 1, 143); Acosta, *De procuranda indorum salute*, for example book 1, chap. 3, sections 1–2, book 11, chap. 17, section 1 (vol. I, pp. 97–9, 219–23); Torquemada, *Monarchia yndiana*, book 15, prologue, chap. 7, book 16, prologue (vol. I, n.p., vol. III, pp. 12, 157); Ríos, *Agricultura de jardines*, p. 19; Deza, *Gobierno político de agricultura*, part 1 (p. 11); Belarmino, *Declaración copiosa de las quatro partes mas esenciales*, prologue; Peñaloza y Mondragón, *Libro de las cinco excelencias del español*, p. 164; Peña Montenegro, *Itinerario para parochos*

By now it should be clear that in colonial Spanish America injunctions to tend the vineyards and wheat fields of the Lord were both metaphorical and literal. Europeans were constantly enjoined by the crown not only to catechise the Indians but also to plant wheat and vines wherever possible. Wheat after all represented both 'el pan de cada día', the daily bread of the Lord's Prayer, and 'el pan de la doctrina', the 'doctrinal bread' of the Christian faith. Bartolomé de las Casas captured well wheat's multivalent importance when he reported with satisfaction that wheat grown in Hispaniola had been used by fellow Dominicans to prepare both bread and 'very good hosts'.[2] The interconnections between earthly and spiritual sustenance are similarly apparent in the image that introduces Antonio de la Calancha's 1638 *Corónica moralizada del orden de San Agustín en el Perú* (*Moralising Chronicle of the Augustinian Order in Peru*). Calancha's chronicle combined a history of the Augustinian order in Peru (a history in which Calancha, an Augustinian monk, himself participated), with a celebration of creole culture in Lima and other colonial cities. Its title-page offers an elaborate tableau of religious scenes that includes, alongside images of Baptism, the Annunciation and religious instruction, the figure of a priest harvesting wheat.[3] (See Figure 16.) The harvest scene captures both dimensions of Calancha's text. In the vignette the farmer-priests are accompanied by an indigenous figure carrying a sack of harvested grain, while a group of other Indians separate from these agrarian activities hovers menacingly in the background. A snake draped over a nearby tree recalls man's original expulsion from the Garden of Eden but the flourishing wheat field demonstrates that this ominous reptile had failed to impede the spread of Christian agriculture to the Indies. The image evokes both Calancha's description of the unstinting and heroic efforts by Augustinian missionaries to convert Peru's indigenous population to Catholicism, and also his account of the success Europeans enjoyed in introducing old-world crops to the Andes. The vignette, like the chronicle it introduces, celebrates simultaneously Spain's evangelical and [agri]cultural achievements, for the two were intertwined.

de indios, book 2, prologue, book 2, tratado 4, section 1, book 2, tratado 7, section 1 (pp. 141, 177–8, 203); and Agustí, *Libro de los secretos de agricultura*, prologue.
[2] Las Casas, *Apologética historia sumaria*, c. 1552, chap. 2 (p. 12). For a seamless transition from the need to evangelise to the need to cultivate European crops see 'Mercedes y libertades concedidas a los labradores que pasaron a las Indias', 1518, in Serrano y Sanz, ed., *Orígenes de la dominación española*, doc. 61 (vol. I, p. 580).
[3] Calancha, *Corónica moralizada*, title-page; and Cañizares Esguerra, *Puritan Conquistadors*, pp. 155–7.

Figure 16 Antonio de la Calancha, *Corónica moralizada del orden de San Agustín en el Perú*, 1638 (detail of title-page). A scene of Christian agriculture adorns the title page of Calancha's colonial chronicle.

This chapter examines the implications of the view that European foodstuffs represented both salvation and proper sustenance for prescriptions to reform indigenous culture and mores. In particular, it considers the interconnections between European attempts to evangelise the Amerindian population and to transform their dietary habits. These two activities, far from being separate undertakings, were as profoundly linked as were the loaves and hosts made from the Dominican wheat celebrated by Las Casas. Europeans envisioned a root-and-branch transformation of indigenous culture from one based on the worship of Lord Maize Cob to one built around a god made flesh in a wheaten wafer. The consequences expected to follow from this revolution were wide-ranging, spiritually, culturally and corporeally. At the same time, as this chapter also shows, the transformations entailed in this vision were profoundly disquieting for colonists, priests and officials alike, for they implied, ultimately, the complete elision of the very differences that separated colonisers and colonised. The chapter's closing sections contemplate this paradox.

A European diet for Indians

If evangelisation was an agricultural endeavour, the crop that priests and missionaries hoped to harvest was wheat. The Jesuit writer José de Acosta made this clear when he listed the stages of a successful evangelisation campaign. After the seed was planted, he explained, shoots would appear, which, with cultivation, would sprout into 'abundant ears of wheat; that is to say, the faith'.[4] Faith *was* wheat. Other colonial writers were equally explicit in equating evangelisation not simply with agriculture but specifically with the cultivation of wheat. The Dominican priest Diego Durán, writing in the 1570s, like Acosta presented wheat as the desired outcome of successful evangelisation. 'Never', he explained,

will we succeed in teaching these Indians to know the true God, if we do not first eradicate and totally remove from their memory their superstitions, ceremonies and false cults to the false gods whom they worship, just as it is not possible to grow a good field of wheat in mountainous and shrubby soil if you have not first completely removed all the roots and stumps that it naturally produces.[5]

Evangelisation could thus be seen, specifically, as a process of substitution, whereby the unwholesome 'roots and stumps' of indigenous idolatry were replaced by the nourishing wheat of Christianity.

Durán advised a wholesale uprooting and other writers were no less direct. Confessional manuals noted that it was pointless to preach the gospel to Amerindians before eradicating their superstitions, 'just as it would be pointless to sow grain in a thicket before you had levelled and cleared it'.[6] Such metaphors encoded a series of literal prescriptions; as we have seen, colonists were regularly enjoined to plant both the faith and the grain that represented it. What then are we to make of these repeated recommendations that the Indians' unwholesome plantings be uprooted and destroyed? What, in particular, ought Amerindians to eat? If their bad roots were to be dug up and replaced with fields of wheat, what then should they consume? It should come as no surprise that these agricultural metaphors were accompanied by

---

[4] Acosta, *De procuranda indorum salute*, book 2, chap. 15, section 3 (vol. I, p. 207).

[5] Durán, *Historia de las Indias de Nueva España*, vol. I, prologue (vol. I, p. 3). 'The Devil has sown this cockle and error over the wheat fields of the evangelical truth of the resurrection', noted another priest regarding the Nahua belief that husbands would join only their first wife in the afterlife: Baptista, *Advertencias*, p. 56.

[6] *Confessionario para los curas de indios*, proemio (p. 2, quotation); and Grijalva, *Crónica de la orden de N.P.S. San Agustín*, book 1, chap. 6 (p. 46).

persistent recommendations that Amerindians adopt the dietary habits of Europeans alongside their religion.

In the mid sixteenth century Tomás López Medel wrote a series of letters to the Spanish monarchs in which he emphasised the necessity of teaching local Amerindians to adopt Spanish customs. López Medel, a Spanish-born lawyer and cleric, served on the Audiencias of Guatemala and New Granada, experiences upon which he later drew when composing a treatise on the new world's climate and environment. Between 1550 and 1556 he was based in Central America, which had only recently been incorporated into Spain's colonial orbit. From there he reported periodically on the spiritual and temporal well-being of the province of Guatemala, and offered prescriptions for improvement. Among his suggestions was that the local Maya be obliged to 'raise cattle, plough and cultivate the earth and grow European plants and wheat'.[7]

This would certainly have represented a substantial change in indigenous Meso-American agricultural practices, which revolved around the cultivation of maize. Maize, grown primarily on communally owned village lands, was cultivated by hand, using digging sticks rather than the plough, which allowed steeply sloping small plots to be exploited effectively. It was complemented by crops of beans, squash, chillies and also fruit trees such as cacao, which were grown for trade and tribute. The only domesticated animals were dogs, turkeys and bees, none of which were raised on a large scale. The introduction of European crops, animals and agricultural methods entailed major alterations to Meso-American farming practices, and were generally unpopular among indigenous people.[8] Stock-rearing in particular was greeted with hostility. Although chickens quickly infiltrated indigenous households, stock-herding remained an activity dominated by Europeans and mestizos well into the nineteenth century.[9] While the occasional Maya cacique might own a small herd, ranching was inherently incompatible with indigenous agricultural practices. The animals tended

---

[7] Carta de Tomás López Medel, 25 March 1551, Archivo General de Indias, Audiencia de Guatemala 9A, R. 18, N. 77, fol. 10. Similarly, the bishop of Michoacán, Vasco de Quiroga, stipulated in the regulations for his 'hospitals' (utopian indigenous communities to be run by priests) that Indians were to cultivate 'livestock such as sheep, goats, cows, pigs ... and cattle': 'Reglas y ordenanzas para el gobierno de los hospitales de Santa Fe de México y Michoacán', c. 1534, in Quiroga, *Don Vasco de Quiroga. Documentos*, p. 256. Or see Vargas Machuca, 'Milicia indiana', book 4, in *Milicia y descripción de las Indias*, vol. II, p. 54.

[8] Whitmore and Turner, 'Landscapes of Cultivation in Mesoamerica on the Eve of the Conquest'.

[9] Landa, *Relación de las cosas de Yucatán*, chaps. 21, 32, 50 (pp. 37, 57, 133); and Cook and Borah, 'Indian Food Production and Consumption', p. 170n79.

to trample maize fields, which were not generally fenced, so whatever profits an individual rancher might accrue were at the expense of the community. Numerous colonial documents record conflict between villagers and ranchers over marauding livestock.[10] Wheat cultivation also received a lukewarm reception among many indigenous groups, both in Guatemala and beyond. Not only did wheat produce a much lower yield than maize or potatoes, but it required a costly investment in equipment and draught animals at all stages of the production process, from ploughing to threshing. That it was sometimes taxed more heavily than maize served as a further disincentive to undertaking its cultivation. Beyond this, precisely because wheat was so redolent of Iberian civilisation it was a natural target for anti-Spanish sentiment. For this reason the indigenous leaders of the 1680 Pueblo Revolt in New Mexico – a substantial uprising against colonial rule in this peripheral region – ordered their followers to 'burn the seeds which the Spaniards sowed and to plant only maize and beans, which were the crops of our ancestors'.[11] Similarly, when a group of Maya attacked the Spanish settlement of Valladolid during the conquest, they reportedly killed not only all the Spanish dogs, cats and chickens, but also 'everyone who had eaten the Spaniards' bread'.[12]

López Medel's suggestion that the Maya take up ranching and begin growing European crops therefore envisioned a substantial transformation in indigenous farming practices. Nonetheless, his recommendations went much farther. In his view it was not sufficient simply for Amerindians to grow European crops. They also had to eat them. Indeed, not only their diet but their entire approach to body management needed radical readjustment. Specifically, he recommended that officials should do everything possible to ensure that Indians adopted 'our customs in eating, drinking, dressing, cleanliness and personal conduct ... and finally our language'. They should further be obliged to wear shoes, to sit at table and to comport themselves with modesty.[13] (See Figure 17.) López Medel was explicit about the good consequences

---

[10] For the Mexican case see Melville, *A Plague of Sheep*; and Fariss, *Maya Society under Colonial Rule*, pp. 182, 277. Various royal orders therefore ruled that livestock ranches needed to be located at some distance from indigenous villages: Solórzano Pereira, *Política indiana*, book 2, chap. 11, section 21 (vol. I, p. 105).

[11] Gutiérrez, *When Jesus Came, the Corn Mothers Went Away*, p. 136. I am grateful to Deborah Toner for this reference. See also Gibson, *The Aztecs under Spanish Rule*, p. 323; and Bauer, *Goods, Power, History*, pp. 87–90.

[12] Díaz de Alpuche, 'Relación del pueblo de Dohot', 1579, in Asensio, ed., *Colección de documentos inéditos relativos al descubrimiento, conquista y organización de las antiguas posesiones españoles de ultramar*, p. 202.

[13] Carta de Tomás López a los reyes de Bohemia, Guatemala, 9 June 1550, Archivo General de Indias, Audiencia de Guatemala, legajo 9A, N. 68, R.17, fols. 5, 9

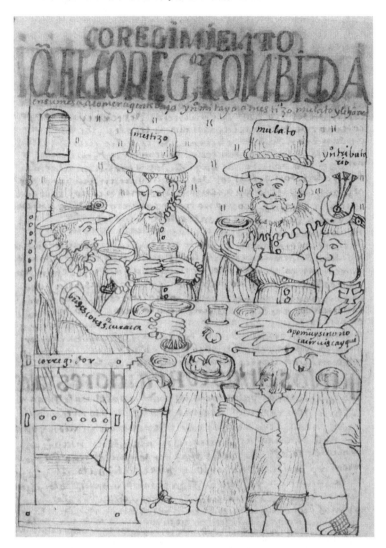

Figure 17 Felipe de Guaman Poma y Ayala, 'The royal administrator and his low-status dinner guests: the mestizo, the mulatto and the tributary Indian', 1615–16. Eating at a table: the scene depicts the table behaviour that López Medel hoped Amerindians could be persuaded to adopt, although the Amerindian artist of this image was critical of his imagined subject, a colonial administrator, for socialising with plebeians.

that would ensue were such a policy implemented. Through eating European food, and generally embracing European culture, Indians would acquire 'all the elements of *policía*'.

Policía, a term that simultaneously encodes ideas of rationality, civility and political order, can be loosely translated as the state of being civilised. John Minsheu's sixteenth-century Spanish–English dictionary glossed the term as 'policy or cunning dealing in matters, dealing in state matters, fineness, neatness, trimness'.[14] This was what Amerindians largely lacked, although chroniclers sometimes noted that certain indigenous polities had attained a level of *policía* prior to the arrival of Europeans. To live in *policía* entailed, generally, dwelling together in an organised fashion, subject to recognisable laws that were themselves rational and just, and following customs that displayed urbanity and culture. All sorts of Spanish practices were lauded as contributing the Amerindians' general level of *policía*, from the clothing and dietary habits that López Medel hoped the Maya would embrace, to European agricultural techniques and approaches to urban planning. Through adopting such practices, Amerindians would become not simply more civilised, but also more human, for it was the capacity to live in *policía* that distinguished men from beasts. Were the Maya to live according to the precepts that López Medel recommended, they would begin, he affirmed, to be men.[15]

López Medel's different prescriptions were not simply a disjointed assemblage of recommendations. Rather, they were profoundly interconnected. The inability of Amerindians to dress and eat properly was part of their larger inability to manage themselves, and to live in *policía*. In his own communication with the crown another official made such interconnections clear when he stated that:

[R]egarding the good treatment of the said Indians we are at present trying very hard and taking a great deal of care over instructing them in matters concerning both our faith and also their food and dress, but despite this their numbers diminish every day because just as they are incompetent in matters concerning the faith so they are also in things that concern their health.[16]

(quotation); and Carta de Tomás López Medel, 25 March 1551, Archivo General de Indias, Audiencia de Guatemala, legajo 9A, R. 18, N. 77, fol. 10.

[14] Minsheu, *A Dictionary in Spanish and English*, 'Policía'; and Lechner, 'El concepto de "policía"'.

[15] Carta de Tomás López Medel, 25 March 1551, Archivo General de Indias, Audiencia de Guatemala, legajo 9A, R. 18, N. 77, fols. 6, 10.

[16] Andrés de Haro al rey, Puerto Rico, 21 Jan. 1518, Archivo General de Indias, Patronato, legajo 176, R. 1, fol. 2.

Failure to manage their bodies through appropriate dress and diet paralleled their inability to become Christians. All three characteristics – dress, diet and religion – needed to be transformed were Amerindians to become true men. It was to effect such transformations that colonial officials began to implement the set of policies know as *reducción*, the process of reorganising indigenous peoples into new settlements, new lifestyles and new mindsets, which began in the earliest days of colonial rule. As the anthropologist William Hanks has pointed out, *reducción* entailed not only the concentration of Amerindians into centralised towns so as to facilitate colonial surveillance, but also a larger project of transforming indigenous attitudes, behaviour and language so that they conformed to *policía cristiana*, or Christian civilisation. López Medel's prescriptions provide a clear example of *reducción*'s totalising ambitions.[17]

As with his suggestion that the Maya adopt Spanish agriculture, López Medel's advice regarding their diet and comportment entailed significant modifications. The Franciscan Diego de Landa noted around the time that López Medel was penning his recommendations that the Mayan diet centred on maize, which was eaten in a variety of manners together with chillies, vegetables, fish, chocolate and other local products. In the 1540s Landa joined the Franciscan mission to the recently colonised Yucatan Peninsula, where he served for some fifteen years, during which time he mastered Mayan and familiarised himself with many aspects of the Maya world. His experiences there provided the basis for his *Relación de las cosas de Yucatán* (*Account of the Things of the Yucatan*), one of the first European accounts of Maya culture, which he composed in the 1560s following a return to Spain to face charges that he had in various ways mistreated the indigenous population. In his *Relación* Landa made no reference whatsoever to the cultivation or consumption of wheat or other European crops, which had evidently penetrated hardly at all into Maya culinary practices, although he did mention that chickens and pigs had been incorporated into the local diet. Landa noted many other troubling differences between Maya and Spanish culture as well. Men preferred to dress in a length of fabric wrapped around their hips, while women liked to file their teeth into sharp points. Men and women alike bathed too frequently, with little concern for modesty, and men in particular tended to drink too much.[18] Beyond this, Landa and the other missionaries who formed part of the vanguard of Spanish settlement naturally focused on the need to instil

[17] Hanks, *Converting Words*.
[18] Landa, *Relación de las cosas de Yucatán*, chaps. 18–33, 49–50 (pp. 31–60, 126–35).

Catholic sentiments in this pagan people. The new settlements established through the process of *reducción* were organised around a series of missions (staffed by a minute number of clergy), and sustained efforts were made to convince the Maya to adopt the new religion. When in the 1560s Landa discovered that certain supposedly Christianised Maya were continuing to follow traditional religious practices he embarked on a ferocious investigation that resulted in the execution of over 150 Amerindians, and the torture of thousands more. In addition, the Maya language itself was subject to a process of linguistic *reducción*, the better to enable it to express the mysteries of the Catholic faith.[19] Clearly, were the Maya to adopt European religious, sartorial, hygienic, culinary and aesthetic values, and to embrace a transformed version of their own language, they would need to alter many of their cultural practices.

Nonetheless, in the opinion of colonial writers, the consequences would be highly beneficial, not only for Amerindians' spiritual well-being, but also for their corporeal health. Most profoundly, the adoption of a European diet and European practices of bodily maintenance would transform the indigenous body itself. The Franciscan friar Bernardino de Sahagún explained this clearly in a sermon delivered in Nahuatl to an indigenous audience in the mid sixteenth century. Sahagún, the author-editor of a vast encyclopaedia of life in preconquest Mexico, stated explicitly in this homily that Amerindians should emulate European consumption practices. Specifically, they should eat 'that which the Castilian people eat, because it is good food, that with which they are raised, they are strong and pure and wise'. He continued, advising them on the details of this superior diet: 'raise Castilian maize [wheat] so that you may eat Castilian tortillas [wheat bread] ... Raise sheep, pigs, cattle, for their flesh is good. May you not eat the flesh of dogs, mice, skunks, etc. For it is not edible. You will not eat what the Castilian people do not eat, for they know well what is edible.' Sahagún then extended a ringing promise to his congregation. 'You', he told them, 'will become like them if you eat their food, and if you are careful with your bodies as they are.'[20]

The consequences that would accrue from a European diet are here set forth unequivocally. Amerindians would not merely become more civilised but would actually become like the Spanish were they to eat their foods. Similar assertions were made by another sixteenth-

---

[19] Clendinnen, *Ambivalent Conquests*; and Hanks, *Converting Words*.

[20] Bernardino de Sahagún, 'Siguense unos sermones de dominicas y de sanctos en lengua mexicana: no traduzidos de sermonario alguno sino sopuestos nuevamente a la media de la capacidad de los indios', 1563, cited in Burkhart, *The Slippery Earth*, p. 166.

century writer, who commented that, as a result of eating a specifically European diet and sleeping under a roof, the indigenous inhabitants of the Mexican village of Citlaltepec were well on the way to acquiring a European constitution. 'Their complexion has almost been converted into ours, because they have been given beef and pork and lamb to eat, and wine to drink, and they now live under roofs', he reported.[21] Just as a diet of inadequate new-world foods had in the past transformed the Indians into the pusillanimous, phlegmatic beings that they now were, so a return to nourishing European foods (in particular wine and European meats) would restore the healthful old-world complexion they had lost over the centuries.[22] The connection between diet and the current condition of the Indians was explained clearly in the Spanish jurist Juan de Solórzano Pereira's 1629 justification of Spain's American empire, *De Indiarum Jure* (*On the Laws of the Indies*). In this text Solórzano, who served in the colonial administration in both Spain and Peru, explained that Amerindians were savage not 'from birth or lineage or from the air of their native place', but rather from 'a depraved education over a long span of time and from the practice, harshness and lack of instructions in their way of life and from the *poor quality of the food they consume*'.[23] Indians should thus be encouraged to adopt the healthy diet of Europeans, for this in itself would improve their level of civility and *policía*.

It was for this reason that the Spanish regularly noted that one of the benefits Amerindians derived from the conquest, in addition to salvation, was access to European food. A 1573 royal order thus stated that Europeans should regularly remind Amerindians that they themselves benefited from colonisation because through it they had been introduced to 'bread and wine and oil and many other foods'.[24] The humanist scholar Juan Ginés de Sepúlveda similarly claimed that the introduction of wheat and other old-world foodstuffs amply compensated the

---

[21] The author of this report ascribed this view to the local Indians themselves, but the use of the humoral term 'complexion' strongly suggests that this notion originated with the report's European author. 'Descripción del pueblo de Citlaltepec', 1579, in Acuña, ed., *Relaciones geográficas del siglo XVI: México*, vol. II, p. 200.

[22] For other recommendations to feed Indians more meat see 'Interrogatorio Jeronimiano', 1517, in Rodríguez Demorizi, ed., *Los dominicos y las encomiendas de indios*, pp. 342.

[23] Juan de Solórzano Pereira, *De Indiarum Jure* (1639), book 2, chap. 8, para. 87, cited in Muldoon, *The Americas in the Spanish World Order*, p. 59 (my emphasis). I am grateful to James Muldoon for his advice on Solórzano. See also Peña Montenegro, *Itinerario para parochos de indios*, book 2, tratado 8, section 8 (p. 225).

[24] 'Ordenanzas de su magestad hechas para los nuevos descubrimientos, conquistas y pacificaciones', 13 July 1573, in Pacheco *et al.*, eds., *Colección de documentos inéditos*, vol. XVI, p. 183 (quotation); Landa, *Relación de las cosas de Yucatan*, chap. 52

Indians for any losses suffered as a result of the conquest. It was true, he conceded, that colonists annually exported a great deal of silver to Spain, but its value was nothing compared to the benefits Amerindians derived from the knowledge of wheat.[25] Spaniards liked to list the plants and animals with which they had enriched the hemisphere, creating an implicit balance sheet greatly in Spain's favour.[26] Writers also noted transformations in indigenous dress and diet, which likewise spoke eloquently to the benefits that Amerindians themselves derived from colonisation. The cosmographer Juan López de Velasco, for example, recorded with satisfaction in the 1570s that most Amerindians 'now wear clothes and shoes, and cover their heads, and thrive with the meat and other foods and drinks that Spaniards use', although he conceded that they seemed unable to imitate Spaniards' sober drinking habits. Beyond this, he noted over-optimistically, 'they all dedicate themselves to raising livestock and growing wheat and other Spanish crops'.[27] Overall, many colonists and advocates of colonialism were certain that Amerindians had either already benefited, or would do so, from adopting a European diet, which would reverse the destructive effects of centuries of bad food, and help restore the old-world complexion once enjoyed by their ancestors. The introduction of old-world foods into the Indies thus was not only essential to Spaniards who needed such foods to stay healthy, but was also one of the palpable benefits that Amerindians themselves derived from the conquest, along with Christianity. Europeans could justly pride themselves on planting not only the faith, but also wheat, grapevines and other Spanish crops, whose fruits were enjoyed by Spaniard and Amerindian alike.

Indians die on a European diet

In maintaining that Amerindians could acquire a European complexion by eating Spanish food and caring for their bodies as Spaniards

---

(pp. 137–8); and Domingo de la Anunciación, *Doctrina christiana breve y compendiosa*, chap. 2 (p. 33).

[25] Sepúlveda, *Demócrates segundo*, p. 78. This is repeated in Cobo, *Historia del Nuevo Mundo*, book 10, chap. 1 (vol. I, p. 376). See also Ovalle, *Histórica relación del Reyno de Chile*, book 1, chap. 22 (p. 75).

[26] López de Gómara, *Historia general*, dedication to Charles V, chap. 35 (pp. 18–19, 72–4); Herrera, *Historia general de los hechos de los castellanos*, decade 1, book 1, chap. 5 (vol. I, pp. 267–8); Cobo, *Historia del Nuevo Mundo*, book 10, chap. 43 (vol. I, p. 420); and Solórzano Pereira, *Política indiana*, book 1, chap. 4, section 17 (vol. I, p. 12).

[27] López de Velazco, *Geografía y descripción universal de las Indias*, 'De los pueblos y gobierno de los indios'. Or see Díaz del Castillo, *The True History of the Conquest of New Spain*, book 17, chap. 209 (vol. V, p. 269).

did, these writers reflected the basic humoral beliefs that underpinned European understandings of the body. Bodies were shaped by their innate complexion, but the body itself was in constant dialogue with the environment, continually modified by the foods it ingested, by the evacuations it emitted, by its levels of exertion and all the other factors that worked to shape and mould the human constitution. Amerindians, as we have seen, acquired their particular character and constitution through this process – this, after all, was probably how Amerindian men lost their manly beards. It made sense to suppose that by reversing this trajectory the indigenous constitution would be brought more closely to resemble that of Europeans.

This seemingly logical expectation, however, contradicted basic elements of the same humoral theory that underpinned it. Indians were advised to adopt a European diet so as to acquire (or restore) a European complexion, yet it was widely believed that an abrupt change of diet could have devastating consequences for an individual's constitution. Even the shift from a bad to a good diet was fraught with danger, and should be undertaken only with great care. Sixteenth-century medical writers often quoted Hippocrates and Galen, who had explained how habitual practices – including diet – came to constitute a 'second nature' to which the body would naturally become accustomed, and which it was therefore very unwise to alter.[28] 'Changing your habits can be lethal', ran the saying.[29] Indeed, as we saw, changes in diet were specifically blamed for illness and death among European settlers in the new world. If it was so dangerous for Europeans to eat Indian food, what would happen to Indians who ate European food?

In fact, many writers believed that it was precisely the adoption of European food, together with the excessive movement from one climate to another imposed by the colonial system, that explained the extraordinarily high mortality rates that afflicted Amerindians after the advent of colonisation.[30] This explanation was first offered in the 1510s to account for the decimation of the indigenous population in the Caribbean. In Hispaniola, settlers blamed the wave of epidemics

---

[28] See for example Lobera de Avila, *Banquete de nobles caballeros*, chap. 51 (pp. 133–6); and Pacheco, *Question médica nuevamente ventilada*, p. 12. The concept derives from Hippocratic Aphorism ii, 5, on which Galen also commented. I am grateful to Peter Pormann for his advice about this.

[29] 'Mudar costumbre es a par de muerte': Bernáldez, *Historia de los reyes católicos*, chap. 43 (vol. I, p. 125); *Refranes famosísimos y provechosos*, chap. 10 (p. viii); Valdés, *Diálogo de la lengua*, p. 264; and Cárdenas, *Problemas y secretos maravillosos*, book 3, chap. 7 (p. 202).

[30] On postconquest demography see Livi-Bacci, *Conquest*.

that nearly exterminated the Taino people in large part on their adoption of European dietary habits, whose impact was augmented by the dangerous shifting between different environments that resulted when enslaved natives left their villages to mine gold. Illness among Amerindians was thus attributed to precisely the same forces that were believed to be behind the ill health afflicting Spanish settlers on the island: the consumption of unfamiliar foods alongside the impact of unfamiliar airs and waters. Colonists reported that when Amerindians came to Spanish settlements to work they ate European food, and as a consequence sickened and died. 'Many of them die from eating unfamiliar foods, because our foods are very different from the ones they have in their own towns', explained one settler. In their lands Amerindians ate 'fish and roots and poisonous things of very little nourishment', noted another colonist, whereas when they served in Spanish settlements they ate pork and beef. 'Thus they sicken and die because of the change from one land to another, together with the change in foods', he affirmed.[31] Likewise, the Spanish geographer and former conquistador Martín Fernández de Enciso observed that certain Caribbean Indians, whose usual diet consisted solely of fish and cassava, 'die if they are taken to other places and given meat to eat'.[32] The combination of a new diet with travel to unfamiliar climates thus produced devastating consequences in the indigenous population, in the view of settlers.

The Spanish doctor Juan de Cárdenas offered similar explanations as to why the Chichimec Indians, who in their own environment were hardy and robust, fell ill and died when incorporated into colonial society. He attributed their mortality to various causes, first among them 'the change in food, in that they are deprived of the natural sustenance on which they were raised, which, although it is very bad in itself, is for them healthy and very good, as they are accustomed to it, unlike our food which harms them'. Dreadful though the Chichimec diet was (Cárdenas explained that it consisted largely of raw meat), it was better suited to their complexion than was European food. 'As our food is foreign and harmful to them, it does not give them strength to resist illness', he concluded. In keeping with basic humoral principles, Cárdenas also observed that changes in their level of exercise and their

[31] 'Interrogatorio Jeronimiano', 1517, in Rodríguez Demorizi, ed., Los dominicos y las encomiendas de indios de la isla Española, pp. 284–5 (quotation), 305, 307, 324, 343; and Cook, 'Sickness, Starvation and Death', p. 382.

[32] Fernández de Enciso, Suma de geographía, p. lii; and Bartolomé de las Casas, 'Relaciones que hicieron algunos religiosos sobre los excesos que había en Indias y varios memoriales', 1517, in Pacheco et al., Colección de documentos inéditos, vol. VII, p. 47.

unhappy emotional state following incorporation into colonial society exacerbated their ill health. He noted in particular the bad effects produced by 'the sad rage and melancholy that overcomes them, on finding themselves among men whom they loathe so much'.[33] As doctors since Galen had warned, perturbations in the six non-naturals could have devastating consequences for the individual constitution.

Spaniards of course understood that illness, and often epidemic disease, was the proximate cause of indigenous mortality. The question was why Amerindians were so susceptible to illness in the first place.[34] As these examples suggest, the answers usually drew in a straightforward way on basic humoral concepts; writers did not postulate that indigenous bodies were fundamentally different from European bodies, or offer explanations that made distinctions between the ways that indigenous and European bodies functioned. On the contrary, Indian bodies were understood to work in accordance with the same principles that explained the working of European bodies. For this reason abrupt movement from one climate to another, like changes in diet, was frequently blamed for illness among Amerindians. Peter Martyr, for example, noted that of the ten native interpreters taken from the Caribbean to Spain after Columbus's second voyage, 'only three survived; the others having succumbed to the change of climate, country and food'.[35] The Dominican priest Reginaldo de Lizárraga likewise observed that when Peruvian Indians from mountainous regions moved to the lowlands they sickened, 'as occurs everywhere'.[36] Travel, in other words, was just as dangerous for Amerindians as it was for Europeans. Indeed, given Amerindians' feeble constitution (itself the result of their poor diet), it was probably more dangerous. For this reason the crown in 1528 prohibited Spaniards from transporting Amerindians to Europe, even if the Indians were travelling voluntarily. This decision was necessary because, as the legislation explained, 'the majority of those Indians die, because these parts are different from their own kingdoms, and are contrary to their nature, and because they are of

---

[33] Cárdenas, *Problemas y secretos maravillosos*, book 3, chap. 7 (p. 202–3). On sadness causing epidemic disease among Amerindians see also Martínez, *Reportorio de los tiempos*, tratado 3 (p. 261).

[34] After describing the devastation wrought by smallpox among Amerindians the official chronicler Antonio de Herrera observed that 'no one born in Europe falls ill': Herrera, *Historia general*, decade 1, book 1, chap. 5 (vol. I, p. 268).

[35] Peter Martyr, *De Orbe Novo*, decade 1, book 2.

[36] Tomás López Medel and the bishop of Quito, Hordenanças [1559], in López Medel, *Visita de la gobernación de Popayán*, p. 234; Lizárraga, *Descripción breve de toda la tierra del Perú*, chap. 19 (p. 16), chap. 81 (p. 6); and Ovalle, *Histórica relación del Reyno de Chile*, book 3, chap. 5 (pp. 117–18).

feeble complexion'.[37] The Mexican viceroy the Conde de Monterrey similarly explained that the vast movement of Indians set in motion by colonialism placed them at risk of falling ill 'from the change in climate and other inconveniences'.[38]

For this reason moving Amerindians into the new colonial settlements or *reducciones* established with the aim of facilitating evangelisation and the management of indigenous labour was often criticised as counter-productive because the resettled Indians tended to die. While some colonists and officials supported this venture on the grounds that the resettled Indians would be easier to govern and evangelise, others complained that, far from increasing Spanish control over indigenous labour it actually reduced the size of the labour force because Amerindians didn't respond well to being moved. The factors offered to explain mortality among congregated Indians were those offered to explain ill health in any traveller: the combination of a new climate (and diet) with a nostalgia for home, which provoked dangerous melancholy passions. Congregated Indians in New Spain were thus said to sicken 'as they miss the nature of the climate in which they were born and raised, and despair at having to leave the lands that they used to cultivate'.[39] This was exactly what happened to Spanish settlers in the Indies. As the chronicler Antonio de Herrera noted, they too fell ill not only from the change to a different climate and food, but also because they were saddened 'to find themselves so far from their own lands'.[40] Amerindian bodies, in other words, operated according to exactly the same principles that shaped the operation of all bodies.

[37] Order of Charles V, Toledo, 4 Dec. 1528, cited in Trueba, *Sevilla: tribunal de océanos*, pp. 101–3; and Vigneras, *The Discovery of South America and the Andalusian Voyages*, p. 92.

[38] Hernando de Santillan, 'Relación del orígen, descendencia, política y gobierno de los incas', *c.* 1563, in Esteve Barba, ed., *Crónicas peruanas de interés indígena*, clause 115 (p. 144); Alonço de Villanueba, 'Relación del pueblo de Çicab', 1579; and Giraldo Díaz de Alpuche, 'Relación del pueblo de Dohot', 1579; both in Asensio, ed., *Colección de documentos inéditos relativos al descrubimiento, conquista y organización de las antiguas posesiones españoles de ultramar*, pp. 202, 209–10; Acosta, *De procuranda indorum salute*, book 3, chap. 18, sections 1, 3, 5 (vol. I, pp. 529, 531, 535); Carta del virrey conde de Monterrey, Mexico, 20 May 1601, Archivo General de Indias, Audiencia de México, legajo 24, N. 56, fol. 3 (quotation); Botero Benes, *Relaciones universales*, part 1, book 5 (p. 151); Lizárraga, *Descripción breve de toda la tierra del Perú*, chaps. 19, 81 (pp. 16, 64); Peña Montenegro: *Itinerario para parochos de indios*, book 2, tratado 1, section 10 (p. 151); and Solórzano Pereira, *Política indiana*, book 2, chap. 8, section 39, book 2, chap. 15, section 40 (vol. I, pp. 88, 128). Conversely, when the climate, food and water of the new environment were similar to that of their homeland, Indians could safely be moved: Pedro Sánchez de Aguilar, 'Informe contra los idólatras de Yucatán', 1613, in Máynez, ed., *Hechicerías e idolatrías del México antiguo*, p. 195.

[39] Vivero, *Tratado ecónomico político*, p. 34.

[40] Herrera, *Historia General*, decade 1, book 2, chap. 10 (vol. I, p. 324).

When writers sought explanations for epidemics and population decline that lay outside the indigenous body itself, they tended to recur to the supernatural. Divine wrath, probably provoked by the persistence of idolatry, was the most popular of such explanations. Abuse by settlers trailed considerably behind these factors as an explanation. Many colonists indeed claimed that Amerindians worked *less* hard under Spanish rule, and blamed mortality in part on this life of unaccustomed ease. José de Acosta summed up the current orthodoxy when he observed in the 1590s that 'people attribute [the decline in the indigenous population] to various causes, some to the fact that the Indians have been overworked, *others to the changes of food and drink that they adopted after becoming accustomed to Spanish habits,* and others to the excessive vice that they display in drink and other abuses'.[41]

Adopting Spanish food and drink was thus a risky undertaking for Amerindians. The very European meats that Spaniards so often encouraged Indians to eat were specifically blamed as a particular cause of illness. The Franciscan chronicler Gerónimo de Mendieta noted that because Indians had begun eating 'meat and the other victuals that we Spaniards eat', they now suffered from constant sneezing. Meat, he explained, 'generates gross, superfluous humours of the sort that we ourselves generate, and for this reason they now sneeze just as we do'.[42] In a 1517 report into the decline of the indigenous population on Hispaniola colonists similarly agreed that one of the precipitating factors was the consumption of old-world meat by Amerindians. As the settler Juan de Anpies observed, when Indians went to work for Spaniards they ate meat, whereas in their own lands they ate different foods. 'Everyone knows that this is why those Indians are falling ill and so many of them are dying', he concluded.[43] The official chronicler

---

[41] Acosta, *Natural and Moral History*, book 3, chap. 19 (pp. 143–4, my emphasis). Acosta endorsed the latter view. For discussion of other factors see also Fernández de Oviedo, *Historia general y natural*, book 3, chap. 6, book 17, chap. 4 (vol. I, p. 67–9, vol. II, p. 116); 'Relación de Zapotitlán', 1579, in Acuña, ed., *Relaciones geográficas del siglo XVI: Guatemala*, p. 42; Feria, *Doctrina christiana en lengua castellana y çapoteca*, pp. 63–5; Murúa, *Historia general del Perú*, book 3, chap. 2 (p. 464); Sandoval, *De Instauranda aethiopum salute*, 196; Avendaño, *Sermones*, primera parte, sermon 2 (p. 24), sermon 6 (p. 75); Phelan, *The Millennial Kingdom*, pp. 92–6; and Cook, *Born to Die*, pp. 1–14, 66. The Peruvian creole Buenaventura de Salinas y Córdova believed that indigenous mortality was a divine punishment of the *Spanish*, because it deprived them of a labour force: Salinas y Córdova, *Memorial, informe y manifiesto*, p. 40r.

[42] Mendieta, *Historia eclesiástica indiana*, book 4, chap. 35 (pp. 508–9)

[43] 'Interrogatorio Jeronimiano', 1517, in Rodríguez Demorizi, ed., *Los dominicos y las encomiendas de indios de la isla Española*, pp. 305 (quotation), 324. See also Fernández de Enciso, *Suma de geographía*, p. lii. Consumption of old-world meats is repeatedly blamed for indigenous mortality in the *relaciones geográficas*. Their authors ascribed this belief to Amerindians themselves, but as these men tended also to blame the

Antonio de Herrera similarly noted in his early seventeenth-century history that one of the causes of indigenous mortality was the consumption of European foods, and specifically meat, together with European wine. He blamed this increased consumption of meat and wine on lax government by local indigenous leaders, who allowed their subjects to succumb to 'the vice of eating meat and getting drunk, which is the cause of the many very widespread diseases that have consumed so many of them'.[44] Meat, which colonial officials described as vital to Spanish health, was for Amerindians a fatal vice.

The wine singled out by Herrera was also identified by many other writers as a particular source of illness and mortality among Amerindians. Wine was virtually a medical necessity for Spaniards – recall the plaintive remark of Tomás López Medel that 'to deprive an old man or a youth of a little wine is to send him straight to the grave'.[45] For Amerindians, however, it was, many writers insisted, a poison, which in an ironic twist they received from the very people who should have been offering them health and salvation.[46] By giving Amerindians wine, Spaniards were sending them straight to the grave, the very effect of *withholding* wine from Spaniard. As doctors regularly reminded their patients, the same foods could produce dramatically different effects on different constitutions. For this reason the crown repeatedly prohibited the sale of wine to Amerindians.[47]

Other staples of the European diet were regarded as equally toxic for Amerindians. Salt, described by the conquistador Bernardo de Vargas Machuca as one of the most important provisions for European expeditions, was similarly said to be mortal poison to certain Amerindians. Vargas Machuca reported on one group that was completely unable to tolerate the condiment. 'If they are made to eat it', he observed,

increased comfort and leisure Amerindians allegedly enjoyed under colonial rule, it seems likely that these ideas were European rather than indigenous in origin. See 'Relaciones de Aculma, Tequizistlan, Tepexpa, and Ocopetlayuca', 1580; and 'Relación de las minas de Tasco', 1581; all in Paso y Troncoso, ed., *Relaciones geográficas de México*, pp. 217, 224, 227, 231, 258, 278.

[44] Herrera, *Historia general*, decade 1, book 1, chap. 5 (vol. I, p. 268).

[45] Carta de Tomás López Medel, 25 March 1551, Archivo General de Indias, Audiencia de Guatemala, legajo 9A, R. 18, N. 77, fol. 1.

[46] Carta del Virrey Marqués de Villmanrique al rey, Mexico, 20 July 1587, Archivo General de Indias, Audiencia de México, legajo 19, fols. 4, 6, 18; Carta del Virrey Conde de Monterrey al rey, Mexico, 25 April 1598, Archivo General de Indias, Audiencia de México, legajo 24, N. 8, fols. 2, 14; Peñaloza y Mondragón, *Libro de las cinco excelencias del español*, p. 123; and Solórzano Pereira, *Política indiana*, book 2, chap. 25, sections 38–9 (vol. I, p. 192).

[47] *Recopilación de leyes de los reynos de las Indias*, Book 6, tit. I, ley 36, Book 6, tit. XII, ley 7, Book 7, tit. I, ley 26 (vol. II, pp. 197, 301, 350).

'they vomit up their insides, and because it contains salt, if they eat our food they suffer fatal attacks of the bloody flux.' (Obliging these people to eat salt was evidently a long-established Spanish practice, for Vargas Machuca insisted that this information was the fruit of considerable practical experience.[48]) The same foods which Europeans regarded as vital to their own survival – in particular wine and meat – were thus positively lethal for Amerindians. Nonetheless, these were the foods Amerindians were being encouraged to eat so as to acquire a European complexion and greater *policía*? Indeed, the recommendation that Amerindians eat these foods was offered by the very people who acknowledged that these same foods were bad for them. In the 1517 investigation into indigenous mortality on Hispaniola, for example, one settler (Marcos de Aguilar) simultaneously recommended that Indians be provided with European meats, and opined that the introduction of pork and beef into the indigenous diet was one of the reasons why so many were dying.[49] In short, Indians should adopt a European diet, but doing so might kill them.

Dream of Hispanicisation

This paradox hints at the contradictory desires to assimilate and differentiate that lay at the heart of Spain's colonial enterprise. On the one hand, generations of colonial officials yearned for the Amerindian population to adopt 'our customs' not only in eating but also in dressing, hygiene, language and religion. The centrality of evangelisation to the colonial endeavour had of course been set forth from the earliest days of the conquest, but Spanish ambitions extended far wider. Many colonial writers considered evangelisation and Hispanisation to be mutually supportive enterprises. It was hoped that were Amerindians to adopt Spanish culture (in particular the Castilian language) this would assist in their evangelisation, and also that were Amerindians successfully evangelised this would speed their adoption of other features of Spanish culture. For example, royal orders repeatedly asserted that Amerindians should be taught Castilian so that they would embrace both Christianity and a Spanish lifestyle. Were they to master Spanish

---

[48] Vargas Machuca, 'Descripción breve de todas las Indias occidentales', in *Milicia y descripción de las Indias*, vol. I, p. 91. On salt's virtues see also Sorapan de Rieros, *Medicina española*, pp. 265–72.

[49] 'Interrogatorio Jeronimiano', 1517, in Rodríguez Demorizi, ed., *Los dominicos y las encomiendas de indios*, p. 343. The meats he had in mind were clearly European, as settlers stated that by the 1510s there were virtually no edible indigenous animals left on the island.

they would more easily understand Catholicism and also all the other things that 'they ought to learn about how to live'.[50] And once they became Christians 'it will be a small step for them to acknowledge the authority of those who are governing them, and to pay their taxes and tributes like any other people with a King and ruler', in the words of one seventeenth-century friar.[51] The desire to Christianise was thus inherently linked to a Hispanising and colonising project. In general, most early modern colonial writers reiterated that Indians should be introduced to both Christianity and Spanish culture, and saw the two as closely linked, just as the introduction of wheat to a wheatless continent was both a metaphor and a concrete agricultural policy.[52]

---

[50] 'R.C. que los indios se les enseñe la lengua castellana', Valladolid, 7 June 1550, in Konetzke, ed., *Colección de documentos para la historia de la formación social de Hispanoamérica*, vol. I, p. 272. See also 'R.C. que se pongan en policia los indios', Valladolid, 23 Aug. 1538; 'R.C. sobre el enseñar a los indios la lengua castellana', Valladolid, 7 June 1550; 'R.C. para que desde la niñez los indios aprendan y hablen la lengua castellana', Madrid, 16 Jan. 1590; 'Consulta del Consejo de Indias sobre las causas porque pareció se debía ordenar que los indios hablasen la lengua castellana', Madrid, 20 June 1596; 'R.C. que se ordene poner maestros para los indios que voluntariamente querían aprender el castellano', Toledo, 3 July 1596; 'R. carta al virrey de la Nueva España ... sobre que los indios aprenden la lengua castellana', Denia, 16 Aug. 1599; 'R.C. al arzobispo de Quito que procure encaminar como a los indios se les enseñe la lengua castellana', Madrid, 12 June 1638, 'R.C. que se enseñe a los indios la lengua española', Madrid, 7 July 1685, 'R.O. que se cumple lo dispuesto sobre la enseñanza del castellano a los indios', Madrid, 20 July 1686; 'R.C. al obispo de la Puebla de los Angeles sobre la enseñanza de la lengua castellana a los indios', Madrid, 10 Nov. 1689; and 'R.C. al virrey y Audiencia de México ordenandoles lo que han de ejecurar para facilitar que los indios aprendan la lengua española', Buen Retiro, 25 June 1690; all in Konetzke, ed., *Colección de documentos para la historia de la formación social de Hispanoamérica*, vol. I, pp. 186, 273–4, 603, vol. II, pp. 38–40, 41, 62, 358, 766, 780–2, 817–18, 831–3. Many clerics argued that it was unreasonable to expect Amerindians to grasp the complexity of Catholic doctrine when it was taught to them in Spanish, and for this reason recommended that priests instead learn indigenous languages. The many catechisms and *doctrinas* written in indigenous languages speak to this clerical concern that royal ambitions, although laudable, were unrealistic. For discussion of linguistic policy see for example Acosta, *De procuranda indorum salute*; Solórzano Pereira, *Política indiana*, book 2, chap. 26 (vol. I, pp. 191–7); and Durston, *Pastoral Quechua*. I am grateful to Michael Hamerly for this last reference. For the evangelical imperative see *Recopilación de leyes de los reynos de las Indias*, vol. I, pp. 1–10. Only a few clerics advocated Christianisation without Hispanisation: see Phelan, *The Millennial Kingdom*, pp. 86–91.

[51] Sigüenza, *Historia de la Orden de San Gerónimo*, part 3, book 1, chap. 25 (vol. II, p. 104, quotation); Acosta, *De procuranda indorum salute*, book 3, chap. 24 (vol. I, p. 587); and Liss, *Mexico under Spain*, p. 44.

[52] Colonial writers found it difficult to separate the discussion of new-world grains from larger discussions of the evangelisation of the Indies. It was for this reason that the Franciscan priest Bernardino de Sahagún interrupted the description of maize in his sixteenth-century *Historia general de las cosas de la Nueva España* with an apparent digression on whether the gospel had been preached in the Indies prior to 1492. In fact, the two subjects were intimately linked, for the absence of wheat in the Indies

Spaniards were at first optimistic about the speed with which this transition would occur. In 1525, a colonial official in the recently conquered territory of New Spain wrote to Charles V to recommend that he send three or four thousand agricultural labourers from Andalusia and Castile to settle in the region. Each labourer should be assigned several hundred Indians whom they were to instruct in Spanish agricultural practices, and in Spanish customs more generally. The official, Rodrigo de Albornoz, believed that since Amerindians were intelligent they would quickly understand – and, crucially, adopt – 'the manner in which we live in Spain'. He was certain this process would take less than two years.[53] Such confidence waned over subsequent decades in the face of contrary evidence, and clerics and officials began increasingly to lament that Amerindians resisted adopting the most basic aspects of Spanish culture. Their failure to learn Spanish was a particular source of complaint. (The extent to which indigenous groups in different parts of the hemisphere did embrace aspects of Spanish culture is a topic of continued historical debate.[54])

When Spaniards spoke of the 'manner in which we live in Spain', they had in mind an entire constellation of beliefs, practices and activities, which ranged from Catholicism to particular naming practices, and in which diet and eating habits played an important role. In his 1567 *Gobierno del Perú* (*Government of Peru*) the colonial official Juan de Matienzo provided a catalogue of European customs that Peruvian Indians should be obliged to adopt so as to acquire *policía*. Matienzo had trained as a lawyer in Valladolid, where he worked for several decades as a judge. In 1560 he travelled to Peru to take up a position in the Audiencia of Charcas and Lima, which he held until his death in 1579. He produced a number of works of jurisprudence and political economy, including the *Gobierno del Perú*, which set forth his ideas about the most effective way of governing Spain's Andean colony. He was quite specific about the need to inculcate Spanish habits in the indigenous population. Indians, for example, should abandon 'the habit of eating together en masse in the plaza' and should instead eat each in their own house, 'like rational men'.[55] (Spaniards presumably objected

spoke directly to the question of whether the region had any prior knowledge of Christianity: Sahagún, *Historia general de las cosas de Nueva España*, book 11, chap. 13 (vol. II, pp. 627–9).

[53] 'Carta del contador Rodrigo de Albornoz al emperador', 15 Dec. 1525, in García Icazbalceta, ed., *Colección de documentos para la historia de México*.

[54] For classic studies see Gibson, *The Aztecs under Spanish Rule*; Lockhart, *The Nahuas after the Spanish Conquest*; and Spalding, *Huarochirí*.

[55] Matienzo, *Gobierno del Perú*, p. 53.

particularly to communal banqueting in part because it played an important role in cementing the reciprocal relationships that bound together Andean society.[56]) Matienzo also insisted that Amerindians should wear Spanish clothing. This would bring multiple benefits:

> Wearing Spanish clothing not only is not bad, but indeed is good for many reasons. Firstly, because they will thereby grow to love us and our clothes; secondly because they will thereby begin to be more like men … thirdly, being dressed as Spaniards they will be ashamed to sit together in the plaza to eat and drink and get drunk and fourthly, because the more they spend, the more silver they will extract from the earth, and that much more Spanish merchandise will be sold, which will all be to the benefit of the treasury.[57]

Writing a century later, the jurist Juan de Solórzano Pereira agreed that Indians should learn Spanish, 'so that they learn to love us more'. They should likewise adopt Spanish habits 'in dressing, and in clothing and other laudable customs'.[58] (See Figure 18.) Overall, many settlers believed that contact with Spanish customs, and Spanish people, played an important role in civilising and Christianising the indigenous population. For this reason Ferdinand and Isabel actively encouraged settlers (both male and female) to intermarry with Amerindians, and many priests recommended that Amerindians reside in Spanish settlements. Such Indians, proclaimed numerous voices, were more intelligent, more civilised and more Catholic than those left to their own devices.[59]

Two republics

Here then is a clear programme for Hispanisation. Nonetheless, theorists such as Homi Bhabha have reminded us of the discomfort caused to colonisers by too close an imitation of their ways by wily colonised people. The colonial mimic, as Bhabha phrased it, is almost the same but not quite, *almost the same but not white.* Colonial mimicry, in other words, creates a disturbing approximate resemblance between coloniser and colonised. It must for this very reason be rejected, prohibited, circumvented or denied, for otherwise it would constitute a menace to the entire colonial project, since by imitating the forms of colonial authority the colonial mimic implicitly challenges their legitimacy. This

[56] See for example Cummins, *Toasts with the Inca.*
[57] Matienzo, *Gobierno del Perú*, pp. 69–70.
[58] Solórzano Pereira, *Política indiana*, book 1, chap. 8, section 7, book 2, chap. 26, sections 40, 42 (vol. I, pp. 30, 196 7, quotation p. 196).
[59] See for example Peña Montenegro, *Itinerario para parochos*, book 4, tratado 4, section 3 (p. 444); Olabarrieta Medrano, *Recuerdo de los obligaciones del ministerio apostólico*, chap. 4 (pp. 95, 97); and Mörner, *La corona española y los foráneos*, pp. 21–5.

Figure 18 Felipe de Guaman Poma y Ayala, 'Creolized Indians spend their time singing and amusing themselves, rather than serving God', 1615–16. Amerindians dressed in Spanish clothes: the indigenous artist disapproved of these Europeanised Amerindians, whose embrace of European clothing would have pleased Juan López de Velasco. The man sports Spanish garb, while the woman wears a hybrid outfit that combines European lace cuffs with Andean garments such as the *lliclla*, or cloak, which is fastened with a decorated *tupu* or pin.

is why colonial discourse typically disputes the ability of the colonised
fully to imitate the colonisers. As Bhabha writes, 'it is as if the very
emergence of the "colonial" is dependent for its representation upon
some strategic limitation or prohibition *within* the authoritative discourse itself'.[60] Bhabha's analysis of colonialism relies on a model of
racial difference rather different from the body concepts that Spanish
American settlers took with them to the Indies. Nonetheless, his specu-
lation on the unsettling effect of colonial resemblance captures well a
fundamental feature of the Spanish colonial dilemma. Colonisers hoped
to transform indigenous society, and indigenous people, into more civilised polities and more civilised people, yet the idea that Amerindians
might become like Europeans evoked profound ambivalence. The art
historian Carolyn Dean has labelled this the coloniser's quandary: 'the
paradoxical need to enculturate the colonized and encourage mimesis
while, at the same time, upholding and maintaining the difference that
legitimizes colonization'.[61]

Colonial ambivalence helps explain the fact that Spanish demands
that Amerindians adopt European customs were regularly undercut by
legislation intended to preserve the distance between colonisers and
colonised. For example, sumptuary laws, retained in colonial Spanish
America for centuries after they were abandoned in Europe, struggled
to maintain clear hierarchies that *mestizaje* and the fluidities of colonial
culture rendered increasingly imprecise: colonial legislation at times
actually criminalised attempts by native peoples to 'adopt our customs
in dressing'. Most Amerindian women were expressly prohibited from
wearing Spanish dress, and Amerindians, blacks and mulattos were
regularly ordered to dress with the modesty befitting their lowly status.
That these laws were routinely ignored was a source of persistent complaint by local officials and private individuals alike.[62]

Indeed, challenges to the colonial system (real or perceived) were
often blamed precisely on ill-advised attempts at incorporating
Amerindians into European culture. For example, following the 1692
riot in Mexico City that had seen the city's indigenous population rise
up in protest against maize shortages, European and creole observers

[60] Bhabha, 'Of Mimicry and Man', p. 127; Bhabha, 'Signs Taken for Wonders'; Young,
Colonial Desire; and also Pagden, *European Encounters with the New World*, pp. 42–7.
[61] Dean, *Inka Bodies and the Body of Christ*, p. 47; and Dean and Leibsohn, 'Hybridity
and Its Discontents'. See also Goldberg, *Sodometries*, pp. 203–8.
[62] See for example 'Ordenanzas para el bueno gobierno de los indios en las Provincias de
Soconusco y Verapaz', 29 Sept. 1628, in Konetzke, ed., *Colección de documentos para
la historia de la formación social de Hispanoamérica*, vol. II, p. 321; and Earle, 'Luxury,
Clothing and Race in Colonial Spanish America', pp. 222–3.

attributed the unrest in part to the injudicious blurring of caste divisions. Teaching Indians to speak Spanish was the first step towards total societal breakdown, in the view of one outraged priest. Indeed, once an Indian learned Spanish he wasn't really an Indian at all: 'they learn Spanish and become ladinos [acculturated Indians]', the priest complained. Far from being a desirable outcome, this was a disaster. Equally, the widespread use of Spanish clothing by the city's indigenous inhabitants in his view led directly to disorder. Allowing Indians to wear a European-style cape was particularly pernicious, 'because it seems this infuses them with pride and with their blankets they are more humble and obedient'.[63] The very practices – wearing Spanish clothes and speaking Castilian – that Juan de Solórzano Pereira believed would encourage Amerindians to 'love us more' were here blamed for causing a riot. Colonists were thus divided in their assessment of whether the adoption of Spanish practices by the indigenous population was pernicious or beneficial to the maintenance of colonial order, and indeed to the well-being of Amerindians themselves.

It was precisely because of concerns that contact with Spaniards was damaging to indigenous spiritual and temporal health that the Spanish crown made persistent attempts throughout the colonial period to prevent Spaniards and Amerindians from coming into contact with each other at all, aside from those circumstances in which it was strictly necessary. Spaniards were thus repeatedly prohibited from inhabiting, or even visiting, indigenous villages. Indeed, there was a substantial current of thought maintaining that anyone, from acculturated slaves to the children of Amerindians and Spaniards, with sufficiently close ties to the Hispanic world should be prohibited from residing in these villages. Moreover, Amerindians who lived in Spanish cities were often expected to confine themselves to certain neighbourhoods, in which they, rather than Spaniards, were to exercise municipal control. Overall, colonial legislation sought to divide Spaniards and Amerindians into two separate 'republics': the Spanish Republic and the Indian Republic. The idea of establishing these two republics began to emerge as early as the 1530s, although the evolution of an actual system of legislation was to occupy the Spanish crown for over a century and questions such as whether certain Spaniards should be exempt from the residential

---

[63] Fray Bernabe Nuñez de Paez, Informe, Doctrina de San Pablo, 4 July 1692, Archivo General de la Nación, Mexico City, Historia, vol. 413, fols. 10, 11, 13; Cañeque, *The King's Living Image*, p. 227; Cope, *The Limits of Racial Domination*, pp. 125–60; and Lewis, *Hall of Mirrors*, p. 27. I am grateful to Francisco Eissa Barroso for the material from the AGN.

prohibition were never fully resolved. The system nonetheless formed part of the colonial law code until the end of Spanish rule in the early nineteenth century. The programme evolved together with the process of *reducción* or *congregación*, which was intended to concentrate the sometimes dispersed indigenous population into well-defined settlements that were modelled on Spanish towns but which were at the same time part of the process of establishing a separate indigenous republic. From the late sixteenth century many Amerindians were forcibly resettled in these new villages, not only to facilitate colonial control and evangelisation but also to create settlements free of the disruptive influence of Spaniards, blacks and mulattos.[64]

The determination to keep Amerindians and Spaniards separate was in part a response to the precipitous decline in the indigenous population, and in part a result of the lobbying by priests such as Bartolomé de las Casas, who spent much of the period from the 1520s to the 1560s urging the crown to curb abuses of the indigenous population by settlers. Las Casas harboured well-founded concerns that the model of governance employed in early colonial Spanish America would lead inexorably to the extermination of the entire indigenous population. Beyond this, Las Casas, like many of the other clerics involved in the early evangelisation of the Indies, believed that Amerindians could best be converted to Catholicism by limiting indigenous contact with Spaniards to carefully selected priests and friars. The consequence of such lobbying was not only the gradual evolution of the concept of the two republics but also the proclamation in 1542 of the so-called New Laws, which prohibited the enslavement of Amerindians and outlawed a variety of common coercive practices, while at the same time affirming the indigenous population's status as free vassals of the Castilian

---

[64] See for example 'Instrucción al virrey don Luis de Velasco', 22 July 1595, in Hanke, ed., *Los virreyes españoles en América*, vol. II, pp. 25, 29; 'R.C. que no vivan españoles entre indios', Tomar, 8 May 1581; 'R.C. para que en los pueblos de indios no vivan españoles, mulatos, negros ni mestizos', Madrid, 18 Feb. 1587; 'R.C. para que el virrey de la Nueva España pueda fundar villas donde se recogan y vivan los españoles que se entresacaren de con los indio', Madrid, 20 Oct. 1598; 'R.C. para que se guarde lo que esta ordenado cerca de que no residan españoles en ningun lugar de indios', Cervera, 21 March 1626; 'Consulta del Consejo de Indias sobre las proposiciones que hizo el capitán Andrés de Deza pidiendo que los españoles puedan vivir libremente en pueblos de indios', Madrid, 17 Jan. 1628; 'R.C. que entre los indios no vivan españoles, mestizos, ni mulatos', Zaragoza, 30 June 1646; and 'R.C. a la Audiencia de Santa Fe sobre el cumplimiento de las cédulas en qe se dispone que los españoles y mestizos no vivan entre los indios', Madrid, 23 Dec. 1665; all in Konetzke, ed., *Colección de documentos para la historia de la formación social de Hispanoamérica*, vol. I, pp. 535, 572–3, vol. II, pp. 58, 287, 308, 401, 532; Mörner, *La corona española y los foráneos*; and Martínez, *Genealogical Fiction*, pp. 99–101.

crown. Grants of entitlement to indigenous labour were limited to the lifetime of the current holder, and individuals who forced Amerindians to carry excessive loads or engage in pearl-fishing were to be executed. The New Laws, enormously unpopular with Spanish settlers, formed part of the larger body of legislation designed to protect Amerindians from the abuses believed to follow from unmediated contact with Spaniards. Both the laws prohibiting Spaniards from residing in indigenous villages and the New Laws referred to the 'vexations' and 'injuries' that Spaniards caused to Indians by demanding labour and other services from them, and gave no indication that contact with Spaniards would increase Amerindians' level of *policía*. On the contrary, such legislation implied that the impact of Spaniards on Amerindians was entirely negative. Thus while some colonists maintained that the most civilised Amerindians were those who enjoyed most 'conversation' with Spaniards, others countered that, in the words of one Jesuit writer, 'the Indians with the most depraved customs are those who have most contact with Spaniards'.[65]

Spanish colonial legislation, in other words, failed to resolve the contradiction between the 'many royal orders' that urged Amerindians to imitate Spanish mores, including dietary practices, and the equally persistent efforts to limit contact between Spaniards and Amerindians. This was not merely because the crown sought to reconcile different interest groups, or because policy-makers were thoughtless or erratic. It is also because the aims that lay at the heart of the colonial endeavour were inherently contradictory.

Conclusions

'With their blankets they are more humble and obedient': this observation, as much as the demand that Indians imitate Spaniards 'in dressing, and in clothing and other laudable customs', characterises the colonising vision, for colonialism relies on a dream of unity combined with an insistence on distance. Maintaining the separation between colonisers and colonised was as much a requirement of the enterprise as was the elimination of that separation by teaching the Indians to live 'like rational men'. Thus Europeans simultaneously recommended

Acosta, *De procuranda indorum salute*, book 1, chap. 11 (vol. I, p. 171); Díaz de Alpuche, 'Relación del pueblo de Dohot', 1579, p. 213; and Mörner, *La corona española y los foráneos*, esp. pp. 27–36. For the new laws see 'Leyes y ordenanzas nuevamente hechas por S. M. para la gobernación de las indias, y buen tratamiento y conservación de los indios', 1542, in García Icazbalceta, ed., *Colección de documentos para la historia de México*.

that Amerindians should eat 'that which the Castilian people eat' and suspected that European food was lethal for the indigenous constitution. They longed for Amerindians to become like the Spanish, and were filled with anxiety when they attempted to do so. The uncertainties that characterised European opinions about whether Amerindians should adopt the European diet, and conversely whether Europeans could thrive in the new world, reflect precisely this tension. To survive, Europeans needed to be able to eat the foods of the new world, or at least to succeed in cultivating their own crops in the colonial environment, but they did not wish to turn into Indians. Indians needed to learn to eat wholesome European foods, but if they thereby acquired a European complexion what possible justification remained for their subordination to Spanish rule? Food thus provides a surprisingly effective vehicle for examining the unstable foundations of colonial ideology. Ambivalence about whether Europeans could eat maize, and whether maize was like wheat, reflect deeper European doubts about whether they could live in the Indies, and whether Indians could or should become part of the Hispanic world. Colonists in other parts of the world harboured similar doubts about the consequences of culinary hybridity, for similar reasons.[66]

Food is both a daily necessity and a potent symbol, and is therefore particularly effective at capturing anxieties about status in virtually any social context. For this reason anthropologists have long noted its power to represent far more than simple nourishment.[67] But in the context of early modern Spanish America food was uniquely meaningful for settlers because of its importance in shaping the human body itself. Food, more than any other factor, was responsible for the constitutional differences that separated Spaniards from Amerindians. Food created the indigenous and Spanish bodies, and food could turn one into the other. Spanish anxieties about whether they could cultivate their crops in the Indies were thus about far more than mere culinary nostalgia. Spanish stipulations that Amerindians should or should not eat European foods likewise went beyond a simple yearning for cultural homogeneity. These concerns spoke directly to Spanish worries about the physical integrity of their bodies, and about the maintenance or dissolution of the most fundamental of colonial divisions: that between the bodies of the colonisers and the colonised.

---

[66] Collingham, *Imperial Bodies*, discusses the situation in British India.
[67] See for example Lévi-Strauss, *The Raw and the Cooked*; or Douglas, 'Deciphering a Meal'.

Therefore the hybridity that has often been identified as one of the most dynamic aspects of colonial culture and society was for many colonisers a source of anxiety, rather than satisfaction. This was not merely because it provoked anxieties about the blurring of divisions between Europeans and Amerindians by potentially making Amerindians more like settlers. As we have seen, colonisers were also worried by the consequences of Europeans adopting indigenous habits, including those concerned with diet and body management. Members of the Inquisition and colonial officials were not alone in expressing concern about such things; individual settlers denounced their neighbours for using peyote, engaging in African or indigenous healing rituals and showing a suspicious enjoyment of dirty Indian food. That such transgressions occurred frequently made them all the more disturbing.[68] The indigenous women with whom many settler men associated were thus dangerous not simply because they introduced Amerindian blood into 'Spanish' genealogies. They indigenised the very bodies of their men through the foods that they fed them. (See Figure 19.) Digestion, particularly in the world of humours, is after all 'a very literal assimilation of something that is not part of one to the essence of one's body', as the literary scholar Michael Schoenfeldt has observed.[69] Colonisers in short feared that they could not make the Indies their own without ceasing to be themselves.

Concerns about hybridity were not unique to colonial Spanish America. Ann Laura Stoler, for example, has demonstrated that in the Dutch East Indies it was not only acculturated natives who were seen as threats to the integrity of European identity. 'What was "dangerous"', she writes, 'was as much those legally defined as European – that noxious "middle-race" inside the borders of this amorphous European community – as those clearly external to it.'[70] In the Dutch East Indies, as in Spanish America, too close a familiarity with the indigenous world – its culture, its bodies – was seen to undermine an always shaky European identity. In sixteenth- and seventeenth-century Spanish America fears about the instability of colonial identity were powerfully magnified by the body concepts that underpinned all

---

[68] See, for example, Aguirre Beltrán, *Medicina y magia*; Alberro, *De gachupín al criollo*, pp. 70–3, 122–5; Gruzinski, *The Mestizo Mind*; Lewis, *Hall of Mirrors*; and Norton, *Sacred Gifts, Profane Pleasures*, pp. 118, 131–2, 231–5. For debate about the social function of 'eating like an Indian' see also Rodríguez-Alegría, 'Eating Like an Indian', as well as the comments that follow that article.

[69] Schoenfeldt, *Bodies and Selves in Early Modern England*, p. 26.

[70] Stoler, *Race and the Education of Desire*, p. 47.

Figure 19 *De Español y de Mestiza, Castiza*, late eighteenth century. This Spanish man troubles the boundaries between Europeans and colonial subordinates through his association with a mixed-race woman and his consumption of the chillies she prepares for him on her *metate*. His unkempt appearance further proclaims his dangerously liminal position.

understandings of corporeal identity. As Gail Kern Paster has noted, 'for the humoral body *all* boundaries were threatened because they were – as a matter of physical definition and functional health – porous and permeable'.[71]

The mutability of the humoral body was both a problem and opportunity for colonialism. Spaniards *had* to believe that Amerindians could become like them, given that evangelisation was the principle justification for the entire colonial endeavour, and their understanding of how bodies worked made this an achievable goal.[72] At the same time, they had compelling reasons for denying that such transformations were possible. The outcome was an understanding of the indigenous body that emphasised its fluxability while insisting on the obstacles to its full transformation into a European body. The contradictory expectations that Amerindians should both become like Europeans and remain forever separate, like the doubts about what would happen to Europeans who adapted too well to the colonial environment, thus reflect both the

[71] Paster, *The Body Embarrassed*, p. 13.
[72] On this point see Martínez, *Genealogical Fictions*, pp. 206–8.

deep contradictions that underpinned most colonialisms, and also the humoral world of early modern Europe.

The last chapter returns to the questions raised in the introduction concerning the origins of racial thinking. It considers the tensions between fixity and fluidity encoded in the humoral body, and re-examines the limits to the malleability typical of the early modern body.

The cradle of race?

'The history of racism as we know it today began to be articulated right then, in the sixteenth century, and there, in the Atlantic world.'[1] So begins an authoritative investigation into the origins of racial thinking. In contrast to an older scholarship that located the invention of race in the eighteenth and nineteenth centuries, such studies find its roots to lie in the period that saw the beginnings of European overseas colonisation and the Atlantic slave trade, and the rise of a militant Catholicism in the Iberian Peninsula. The idea that these events were responsible for the articulation of a racialised view of human society seems inherently plausible. After all, they generated an intense discussion not only of the nature of the new peoples Europeans encountered in their travels across the globe, but also of the larger question of whether Europeans had the right to impose their rule over them. In Spain the early modern era also witnessed a focused assault on the autonomy of Jewish and Muslim communities, and a growing insistence that people of Jewish or Islamic heritage were profoundly different from 'old' Christians.

Little wonder that many scholars now identify the sixteenth and seventeenth centuries as the period when Europeans first began to view the world in terms of race, understood as a belief that certain physical and cultural characteristics were indelibly fixed in the body. A rich and varied corpus of research has argued that Jewish, African and indigenous bodies (in particular) were 'racialised' during the medieval and early modern era, as European ideas of human difference based on religious divisions began to give way to 'the concept of race as we understand it today'.[2] Inspired in part by the path-breaking work of

---

[1] Greer et al., 'Introduction', in Greer et al., eds., Rereading the Black Legend, p. 2.
[2] Greer et al., 'Introduction', in Greer et al., eds., Rereading the Black Legend, p. 3. For these debates see also Bartlett, The Making of Europe; Chaplin, 'Natural Philosophy and an Early Racial Idiom in North America'; Cañizares Esguerra, 'New Worlds, New Stars'; Chaplin, Subject Matter; Journal of Medieval and Early Modern Studies 31:1

Edward Said, such research links the development of colonial regimes of power to the othering of conquered and defeated peoples in Europe and overseas, and traces the discursive framework that helped justify colonialism and religious conquest through a systematic insistence on the physical and moral inadequacies of the expelled and the colonised. The result, in the words of the historian Jorge Cañizares Esguerra, was 'a discourse of scientific racism that long predated the one invented in the late eighteenth and early nineteenth centuries in Europe'.[3]

For all their inherent plausibility, however, claims that a discourse of scientific racism can be identified in the early modern period fit awkwardly with the ways in which early modern Europeans (and their overseas relations) understood bodies to work. The vernacular humoralism that provided the epistemic framework for all theories of bodily difference was posited on fluidity, not fixity. In the Indies, as we have seen, settlers regarded the differences that separated Spanish from indigenous bodies as significant, but impermanent. They reflected the differences between Spanish and indigenous culture, at the same time as they hinted at the possibility of transformation. Far from being innate and indelible, bodily characteristics – whether skin colour or personal character – were seen as fluxable and subject to change. Permanence was not a central feature of the humoral body. The complexion, everyone agreed, 'can and often does change over time or as a result of various external forces'.[4] This understanding of the human body makes it difficult to speak of an early modern idea of race, in so far as race is concerned with supposedly permanent and indelible bodily traits, whose significance is located precisely in their immutability. How could anything be fixed in this world of flux?

Perhaps, however, this mutability had its limits. Were all bodies as fluid as those of Spanish Catholics or Amerindians? Or on the contrary was the growing hostility towards Jews, Muslims and their descendants reflected in a new, 'racialised' discourse about the Jewish or Muslim body? After all, the 'purity of blood' restrictions that swept over early modern Spain were premised on the idea that certain 'taints' – Muslim, heretical or Jewish ancestry – could never be erased, and remained

(2001), special issue: *Race and Ethnicity in the Middle Ages*; Isaac, *The Invention of Racism in Classical Antiquity*; Aubert, '"The Blood of France"'; Cañizares Esguerra, *Nature, Empire, and Nation*; and Eliav-Feldon *et al.*, eds., *The Origins of Racism in the West*. See also Wilson, *The Island Race*, pp. 11–15.

[3] Cañizares Esguerra, 'New World, New Stars', p. 68; Sweet, 'The Iberian Roots of American Racist Thought', p. 166; Silverblatt, 'Foreword', pp. x–xi; and (for a slightly different chronology) Cañizares Esguerra, 'Demons, Stars and the Imagination'.

[4] Torquemada, *Jardin de flores curiosas*, tratado 3 (pp. 247–8).

for ever in the blood. And how might the belief that the blackness of Africans was due to a divine curse limit the ability of the African body to transform? This chapter explores Spanish understandings of such apparently intractable bodies. In so doing it situates the early modern humoral body within a history of race or, rather, within a history that we usually approach via the idea of race.

I approach this topic via an examination of religion and the confessional body. For early modern Catholics the humoral body was at all times also a religious body, governed not only by its humours but also by the divine will. The chapter therefore begins with a discussion of the relationship between physical and spiritual health, which provides the necessary framework for a subsequent consideration of the sinful bodies of Jews and other tainted beings. We will see that even as Catholic writers insisted on the distinctiveness of the African or Jewish body, their understanding of that distinctiveness was powerfully shaped by the idea of the mutable humoral body. Readers will determine for themselves whether they find the language of race helpful in understanding these early modern body concepts. In the end, my aim is not to pronounce on the origins of race, for as the historian David Nirenberg has warned, such debates all too easily disintegrate into unproductive definitional disputes.[5] Rather, I want to insist that if we wish to understand how early modern European actors made sense of human difference in their newly expanded world, we must understand how they thought about the forces that shaped all bodies.

Souls and bodies

The early modern body was embedded in a web of humours, fluxes and flows. These operated according to the principles of the natural world, but early modern Spaniards knew that that world was itself shaped by a far more powerful force. God himself ultimately determined all things, including matters of sickness and health. Since God was the prime cause of everything that occurred in the world, divine will was behind all bodily states; human science could achieve nothing on its own. When asked if he was 'the man known for healing quartan fevers', one doctor replied 'only God can heal. I do no more than treat them.'[6] It was for

[5] Nirenberg, 'El concepto de raza en el estudio del antijudaísmo ibérico medieval'; and Nirenberg, 'Race and the Middle Ages', pp. 71–87. See also the discussion in Martínez, *Genealogical Fictions*, pp. 1–17.

[6] Méndez Nieto, *Discursos medicinales*, book 1, discurso 13 (p. 125). 'Every cure proceeds from the ultimate good', stated Arnau de Vilanova in the late thirteenth century: Laín Entralgo, *Doctor and Patient*, pp. 88—91, quotation p. 88. See also Laín Entralgo, *Enfermedad y pecado*.

this reason that the sick prayed for the restoration of shattered health, and that Confession should precede any medical treatment. Indeed, sometimes prayers were the only thing a doctor could offer to an ailing patient.[7] This did not, however, mean that nature operated according to no rules; on the contrary, these rules were designed and set into motion by God himself, and it was often possible to discern their functioning. Early modern writers therefore stressed the interconnections that linked medicine and religion. God, explained the Spanish doctor Andrés Laguna, was the 'most excellent chief physician and Rector of the entire world'. Conversely, the clergy provided medicine for the soul. Medical treatment and human health, in other words, reflected a universe shaped by divine forces.[8]

Illness could thus generally be ascribed to humoral imbalance, but a cure might be effected through either medical treatment or prayer. And just as prayer might be rewarded with health, so evil deeds could be punished with illness or disability. Wicked actions, like the wrong food, could provoke catastrophic responses in the individual constitution, although in the case of transformations caused by sin the mechanism was direct, rather than indirect, divine action. For example, the sinful acts committed by parents could mark their offspring, particularly if the sin occurred during conception or pregnancy.[9] Of course, sin was capable of provoking far more dramatic transformations than those usually induced by eating the wrong food. A 1678 pamphlet relayed the cautionary tale of a 'very beautiful damsel whose profanity and blasphemy led God to take away her beauty, by replacing her face, hands, eyes and hair with those of different beasts'. Divine punishment might also consist in a change of skin colour. A seventeenth-century ballad recounts how two youths who failed to show proper respect for the host had their skin miraculously transformed from white to black. Conversely, sinful Saracens who kissed fragments of the True Cross lost their blue and black skin, which became shiny white, according to a medieval legend.[10]

---

[7] On the need for prior Confession see García Ballester, *La búsqueda de la salud*, pp. 159–65; and Farfán, *Tratado breve de mediçina*, for repeated exhortations that the most important thing to offer the gravely ill was Confession. 'Who can doubt', Farfán asked, 'that God sends us illness because of our sins': book 1, chap. 2 (p. 10).

[8] Fresquet Febrer, 'La difusión inicial de la materia médica americana en la terapeutica europea', p. 337 (quotation); Sahagún, *Historia general de las cosas de Nueva España*, prologue (vol. I, p. 1); Avendaño, *Sermones*, segunda parte, sermon 12 (p. 5); and Salazar, *Veinte discursos sobre el credo*, proemio.

[9] See for example Nieremberg, *Curiosa y oculta filosofía*, 'De la curiosa filosofía', book 2, book 3, chap. 10 (pp. 39–62, 70–1); and Huet, *Monstrous Imagination*.

[10] García de Enterría, 'El cuerpo entre predicadores y coperos', pp. 242–3 (quotation); and Hahn, 'The Difference the Middle Ages Makes', p. 14.

Black skin, in other words, might result not only from the force of the sun's rays or from diet, but also from evil deeds. In the latter case it was not simply an accidental corporeal quality, but instead a mark of sin. The idea that black skin, like any other distinctive bodily mark, might indicate its bearer's spiritual state thus reflects the larger epistemic framework that explained the workings of all bodies. It also indicates that Europeans sometimes associated dark skin with a larger spiritual darkness, the various saintly Africans who populated the medieval Christian pantheon notwithstanding. Thus black skin either revealed that an individual possessed a particular complexion, or that they had committed some dreadful sin, or perhaps both. What then was the meaning ascribed to the dark skin of certain Africans?

The curse of Ham

The dominant explanation for dark skin was humoral, and derived from the writings of ancient scholars such as Aristotle and Pliny. Drawing on these standard texts, early modern writers explained how the heat of the sun dries up the body, producing a burnt, bilious residue that darkens the skin. This was the model to which the Dominican priest Gregorio García for example referred when he explained in an early seventeenth-century text that Ethiopians were black because they lived in the heat of the torrid zone. Over time they had lost the white colour of their ancestor Noah, and their new black skin became 'connaturalised', or innate. García regarded this process as quite straightforward and unproblematic, and many others advanced identical explanations.[11] It is worth recalling, as the literary scholar Mary Floyd-Wilson notes, that analogous reasoning was deployed to explain the very white skins of people dwelling in exceptionally cold regions. In this case the excessive moisture of their environment led to an accumulation of heavy, damp humours, which were reflected in an unnaturally pale skin. Both very pale and very dark skin were deviations from a balanced norm.[12]

This was not, however, the only explanation available. Perhaps blackness was instead caused by the curse, described in Genesis, which Noah pronounced on his son Ham. Ham earned this curse by failing to cover

[11] García, *Origen de los indios*, book 2, chap. 5 (pp. 149–50). Or see Antoine Malfante to Giovanni Marione, 1447, in Crone, ed., *The Voyages of Cadamosto*, p. 86; Zurara, *Chronica do descobrimento e conquisita de Guiné*, chap. 2 (p. 10); Columbus, 'Carta a los reyes católicos', 18 Oct. 1498, in *Los cuarto viajes del almirante*, pp. 181–2; Acosta, *Natural and Moral History of the Indies*, book 2, chap. 11 (p. 92); and Avendaño, *Sermones*, primera parte, sermon 9 (p. 104).

[12] Floyd Wilson, *English Ethnicity and Race in Early Modern Drama*, pp. 23–47.

his father's exposed genitals as Noah lay asleep in a drunken stupor. Far from showing appropriate filial respect, Ham mocked his progenitor. On awaking Noah cursed Ham, by condemning Ham's son Canaan to be the 'slave of slaves'.[13] The suggestion that dark African skin was caused not by the earthly workings of the humours, as writers since Pliny had affirmed, but rather by a mysterious biblical curse afflicting not an individual but an entire people seems to mark the African body as fundamentally different from (and inferior to) the bodies of Europeans. A number of scholars have therefore pointed to this association as an important step in the racialisation of the African body.

The historian Benjamin Braude has shown that the association between a distinctive African body and the curse of Ham developed in the early modern era. The Bible itself makes no connection between Noah's curse and dark skin. Neither did Europeans prior to about 1400 posit any consistent link between the curse of Ham, dark skin and Africa, which was in any case a poorly conceptualised location.[14] Indeed, many medieval writers believed that if anyone was the offspring of Ham it was the European peasant. From the fifteenth century, however, such connections began to be asserted more regularly. Some scholars have suggested that Portuguese and Spanish writers were in the vanguard of employing the story of the curse of Ham to explain the dark skin of Africans, perhaps because of their involvement in slaving expeditions brought them into closer contact with Sub-Saharan Africa. Such contacts certainly contributed to the formation of new geographies, and led Europeans to consider whether and how West African peoples differed from the more familiar 'Moors' who inhabited the Mediterranean's southern shores. Europeans had however long been aware of the (at least hypothetical) existence of dark-skinned 'Ethiopians', as visual artefacts ranging from religious statuary to illuminated manuscripts reveal.[15]

The new web of associations linking Ham, slavery, dark skin and Africa was loosely knit, and the earliest examples hint at how it was constructed. The fifteenth-century chronicler Gomes Eanes de Zurara, who composed an early account of Portuguese exploration along the West African coast, for instance speculated that the blackness of certain Guineans might be caused by the curse that Noah placed on his son *Cain*. Zurara in other words confused Noah's son Ham with Adam's

---

[13] Gen. 9:20–27.
[14] Braude, 'The Sons of Noah'. For a contrasting view see Russell-Wood, 'Before Columbus', p. 154.
[15] Devisse, *The Image of the Black in Western Art*, vol. II.i; and Devisse and Mollat, *The Image of the Black in Western Art*, vol. II.ii.

son Cain, who murdered his brother Abel. This confusion, not infre-
quent in medieval texts, surely reflected the similarities between the
Portuguese words for Ham and Cain (*Cam* and *Caim*).[16] It also reminds
us that early modern writers often possessed only a shaky recollection
of scripture. More importantly, however, such amalgamations of Ham
and Cain help explain how the story of Noah's curse was transformed
to provide an explanation of blackness. The biblical account of Noah's
drunkenness does not imply that his curse induced any sort of physical
change in its victims. There is thus no scriptural basis for affirming
that the curse manifested itself in a darkened skin, or any sort of bodily
transformation whatsoever. Those cursed were condemned to slavery,
but this condition was not proclaimed in their appearance. The Old
Testament story of God's curse of *Cain*, however, refers explicitly to
a visible mark. On discovering that Cain had killed his brother God
cursed him, and 'set a mark' upon him, so that he might be recognised
everywhere.[17] God's cursing of Cain thus placed a visible, physical
(albeit unspecified) mark on Cain's body. In amalgamating the curses
placed on Ham and Cain early modern writers subtly transformed the
two stories into a single account that linked a condemnation to perpetual slavery with a visible, bodily transformation.

In any event, in early modern Spain some Jewish, Muslim and
Christian writers began to associate Ham's curse specifically with
darkened skin. The Carmelite priest Antonio Vásquez de Espinosa, for
example, explained in an early seventeenth-century text that this curse
was responsible for the dark colour of people in Ethiopia and Guinea,
although he added that the region's 'constellation and climate' probably contributed as well.[18] The dark skin of Africans, in other words,
might have resulted not only from the usual workings of the six non-
naturals, but also from the direct intervention of divine forces. Perhaps
it was therefore permanent. The sixteenth-century Franciscan Juan de
Torquemada thus described the African's dark skin as a 'perpetual sanbenito', an indelible mark of shame.[19] Some philosophers indeed began
to assert that, contrary to the claims of earlier scholars, the descendants
of Africans transported to colder climates did not develop a lighter skin

[16] Zurara, *Chronica do descobrimento e conquisita de Guiné*, chap. 16 (p. 93); Braude,
'The Sons of Noah', pp. 128–9; Friedman, *The Monstrous Races in Medieval Art and
Thought*, pp. 100–5; and Freedman, *Images of the Medieval Peasant*, pp. 89–91.

[17] Gen. 4:15.

[18] Vásquez de Espinosa, *Compendio y descripción de las Indias occidentales*, part 1, book 1,
chap. 3, no. 17 (pp. 10–11). See also Sweet, 'The Iberian Roots of American Racist
Thought'; Freedman, *Images of the Medieval Peasant*, pp. 86–104; and Schorsch, *Jews
and Blacks in the Early Modern World*, pp. 135–65.

[19] Torquemada, *Monarchia indiana*, book 14, chap. 19 (vol. II, p. 612).

or give birth to lighter children, although this was a novel suggestion for which there was little consensus.[20] To be sure, the alleged persistence of dark skin in colder climes did not necessarily mean that the African body was fundamentally different from other bodies; it might reveal merely that the innate complexion of Africans was particularly strong. After all, everyone knew that different men did not pass their qualities on to their offspring with equal ease, some complexions being weaker than others. Perhaps the African complexion was simply unusually robust.

The powerful nature of African blood is indicated visually in the eighteenth-century artistic genre known as casta painting. Casta painting, a distinctive Spanish American art form, depicts the outcome of sexual encounters between different sectors of the colonial population, organised by 'caste', or, if one prefers, race. A typical picture might depict a Spanish man, an indigenous woman, and their baby, each labelled with a nomenclature describing their particular caste or race. (In this example, the threesome would be captioned: 'A mestizo is born from a Spanish man and an Indian woman.') The paintings were usually produced in series of sixteen, and include three characteristic sub-cycles, built around pairings between Spaniards and Amerindians, Spaniards and Africans and Amerindians and Africans. The Spaniard–Amerindian cycle, for example, shows a progression starting with a Spaniard and an Indian, as described above, and then showing the outcomes of encounters between, first, a mestizo and a Spaniard, which produces a 'castizo', and then a castizo and a Spaniard, which produces another Spaniard. (See Figure 20.) Casta paintings are certainly not transparent windows on to past mentalities. Despite their captivating realism they represent an overly schematic, elite vision of the outcome of different sexual pairings; the tidy classifications of different castes do not mirror perfectly the daily realities of colonial life.[21] Moreover, in some ways they reflect a later, eighteenth-century effort to classify and taxonomise the inhabitants of colonial space. Nonetheless, they illustrate well certain sixteenth- and seventeenth-century ideas about the relative mutability and immutability of different types of body.

As Figure 20 demonstrates, casta series classify the offspring of sexual liaisons between Spaniards and certain other groups as Spanish: specifically, the children of a Spaniard and someone with one quarter

[20] See for example León Pinelo, *El paraíso en el Nuevo Mundo*, book 5, chap. 14 (vol. II, pp. 526–7); Stuurman, 'François Bernier and the Invention of Racial Classification', p. 5; and Kidd, *The Forging of Races*, esp. pp. 67–9.
[21] Carrera, *Imagining Identity in New Spain*; and Katzew, *Casta Painting*.

Figure 20 Juan Rodríguez Juárez, *De Castiso y Española Produce Español*
c. 1725. The painting shows a Spanish woman, her castizo husband
and their Spanish son. The husband's partial indigenous ancestry has
not prevented him from fathering a Spaniard.

indigenous ancestry are labelled Spanish. These children, in other
words, were not simply *like* Spaniards; they *were* Spaniards. In this
regard casta paintings do reflect a larger social reality, which permitted
some mixed children to blend into the Hispanic world, particularly if
they were legitimate and adopted the norms of Spanish colonial culture. As one seventeenth-century writer noted, rather tautologically,
'*Spaniards* who descend in part from Indians' were usually considered
Spanish.[22] In the world of the casta painting, however, encounters with
other groups led to children ever more removed from Spanishness. In
particular no encounter between a Spaniard and the descendants of
Africans was ever shown as resulting in Spanish offspring. The children
of a Spanish man and a black woman were mulattos, and the offspring
of Spaniards and mulattos were moriscos, but the offspring of Spaniards

---

[22] García, *Origen de los indios*, book 3, chap. 4 (pp. 240–2, quotation p. 240; my
emphasis). See also Martínez, *Genealogical Fictions*, pp. 142–66, 217–18.

and moriscos were not Spanish. Instead, admixtures involving 'black' blood were presented as descending into an incomprehensible jumble infinitely removed from the clarity offered by the Spaniard-Mestizo-Castizo-Spaniard cycle. (See Figure 21.) Some casta series, moreover, situate these confusing mixed couples in debased and violent social settings, in a further affirmation that liaisons with certain castes (and certain women) led inexorably to degradation.

These paintings thus depict well the early modern belief that, for whatever reason, blackness ('a perpetual sanbenito') was difficult to overcome and that African blood was a powerful force. To return to the story of the curse of Ham, the early modern application of this legend to the African body seems to suggest that these bodies might differ in fundamental ways from those of Europeans, who were unencumbered by divine curses. The visual world of the casta painting depicts precisely this sentiment in its 'clearly marked routes to whitening and civilization, and clearly marked routes to darkening and degeneration'.[23] Casta paintings, however, capture only very imperfectly a more complex colonial reality. In fact, colonists and officials were not in agreement that the descendants of Spaniards and Africans would never be considered Spanish, or white. Recall the case, mentioned in the Introduction, of Nicolasa Juana, 'a *white* mulata with curly hair, because she is the daughter of a dark-skinned mulata and a Spaniard'.[24] While most agreed that African ancestry was a taint, it was not necessarily indelible. In the mid seventeenth century the bishop of Quito explained clearly in a clerical manual that small amounts of indigenous *or* African blood were insignificant, and therefore did not prevent an individual possessing some African heritage from being considered Spanish either in the eyes of the law or in the estimation of the community.[25]

Beyond this, many individuals of African heritage were able to escape the strictures of their condition either by obtaining special privileges from the crown, or through more informal means. Thus in 1578 Sebastián Toral, a former slave who had been among the first old-world settlers in the Yucatan Peninsula, succeeded in removing himself and his family from the mulatto tribute rolls, in recognition of his services to the crown. Instead he and his children were taxed as Spaniards, the first step towards being regarded as altogether Spanish.[26] Scholars have moreover identified many cases in which an individual's caste status

[23] López Beltrán, 'Hippocratic Bodies', p. 283.
[24] Tavárez, 'Legally Indian', p. 91 (my emphasis).
[25] Peña Montenegro, *Itinerario para parochos*, book 3, tratado 10, sections 5–7 (pp. 403–4).
[26] Restall, *The Black Middle*, esp. pp. 6–9, 105–9.

Figure 21 Miguel Cabrera, *De Español y Albina, Torna Atras*, 1763. The pale skin of this Spaniard's wife belies her partial African heritage, which reveals itself in the dark complexion of their 'throw-back' daughter.

changed over the course of their lifetime; modified or deleted entries in baptismal and marriage records bear witness to such transformations. It was by no means unknown for someone to be reclassified from mulatto to mestizo, or indeed white. By the late eighteenth century the Bourbon crown itself introduced a procedure whereby individuals could petition to be exempted from the ignominy associated with mixed birth, thereby becoming legally white. Hundreds of petitions of 'gracias al sacar', as the procedure was called, were submitted to the crown, which viewed the measure as a relatively unproblematic way of raising revenue. As the historian Ann Twinam has shown, although the measure provoked some unrest in the Indies, objections overwhelmingly centred on whether it was socially desirable to allow such movement. In virtually all cases – she has located one exception – objections to the procedure did not question the basic premise that mulattos or other people of mixed race could become white. Instead, the question was whether they *should*. In general, petitioners and officials agreed that 'pardo-ness and mulatto-ness were not permanent conditions but might be changed'.[27] While such transformations were by no means the norm, they point to a greater flexibility in the way in which colonial society treated people of African descent than that suggested by the rigid taxonomies of casta paintings.

Were African bodies considered intrinsically different from those of Europeans? And might this mean that Africans, cursed with their different bodies, could legitimately be enslaved by Europeans? In general, early modern Spaniards hesitated in drawing such large conclusions from the story of the curse of Ham, even though they did not hesitate to enslave many thousands of Africans. To begin with, the lives of men such as Toral suggest that African bodies might perform roles supposedly restricted to Europeans and creoles, regardless of how these bodies acquired their colouring. In addition, the 'curse of Ham' explanation for dark skin was by no means accepted universally. Many, as we have seen, attributed the dark skin of Ethiopians and Guineans simply to the African heat. Others doubted that anyone could truly understand the mystery of skin colour. After puzzling over the conundrum of black skin. The chronicler Francisco López de Gómara concluded that variations in skin colour were a mysterious act of God beyond the reach of natural explanation.[28] The Spanish theologian Francisco de Avendaño adopted a similarly cautious approach in his discussion of why Cush, another of Ham's sons, had been black. He noted that while some attributed this to Noah's curse, others believed it was the result of

[27] Minchom, *The People of Quito*, pp. 158–70; Twinam, 'Racial Passing'; and Twinam, 'Purchasing Whiteness', p. 145 (quotation).

[28] López de Gómara, *Historia de las Indias*, chap. 216 (pp. 372–3); and Torquemada, *Monarchia yndiana*, book 14, chap. 19 (vol. II, pp. 613–14). I am grateful to Christián Roa for the reference to López de Gómara. Or see Purchas, *Purchas His Pilgrimage*, book 6, chap. 14 (p. 546); Braude, 'The Sons of Noah', pp. 135–8; and Kidd, *The Forging of Races*, p. 76.

maternal imagination. Perhaps, Avendaño speculated, Cush's mother had thought of something very black at the moment of conception, or perhaps she had desired and been denied a dark snack during pregnancy, either of which would have been sufficient to produce a black child, since, as scholars agreed, the power of the maternal imagination was almost unlimited.[29] Furthermore, even individuals like Zurara who ascribed the black skin of Guineans to a biblical curse did not necessarily regard it as a satisfactory justification for their enslavement. Zurara preferred to view Guineans not as mysterious, cursed beings, but rather as a peculiar variety of infidel Moor. In his view, they could be enslaved not because of their dark skin, but because they resisted conversion to Christianity, a justification universally accepted in the early modern Iberian world. Nor did Zurara believe that all Guinean 'Moors' were truly black in the first place. Although he blandly ascribed their black skin to Noah's curse, he also insisted that skin colour varied considerably among them.[30]

In general, however, discussions of the African body placed far less emphasis on its ability to transform than those concerned with the indigenous body. While transforming Amerindians into civilised beings was at least theoretically a central ambition of the colonial endeavour, transforming Africans into Europeans was nobody's project. The great majority of the roughly 200,000 Africans brought to the Spanish Indies in the first century and a half of colonialism arrived as unfree labourers, whose distinctive physical qualities were considered an advantage, not a defect to be remedied.[31] The belief that the African body was less mutable – whether expressed through the idea that the African complexion was particularly robust, or through the notion that dark skin reflected a divine curse – meshed well with the roles which most Africans were expected to perform in colonial society. At the same time, the vernacular humoralism that shaped European understandings of all bodies undermined attempts to construct African bodies as radically different.

[29] Avendaño, *Sermones*, primera parte, sermon 9 (p. 105). Or see Sandoval, *De Instauranda aethiopum salute*, pp. 24, 33. On maternal imagination see Huet, *Monstrous Imagination*; Cadden, *The Meanings of Sex Difference in the Middle Ages*; and Finucci, 'Maternal Imagination and Monstrous Birth', pp. 41–77.

[30] Wolf, 'The "Moors" of West Africa and the Beginnings of the Portuguese Slave Trade' (note that Wolf translates *Caym* as Ham, rather than Cain). On the varied colour of Africans see also Antoine Malfante to Giovanni Mariono, 1447, in Crone, ed., *The Voyages of Cadamosto*, pp. 86–7; and Sandoval, *De Instauranda aethiopum salute*, pp. 20–3, 91. On legitimate grounds for enslavement see Sandoval, *De Instauranda aethiopum salute*, pp. 20–3, 91, 97–104; Russell-Wood, 'Before Columbus', p. 155; Schorsch, *Jews and Blacks in the Early Modern World*, pp. 156–7; and Blumenthal, *Enemies and Familiars*.

[31] Sánchez-Albornoz, 'The Population of Colonial Spanish America', pp. 15–16.

Most likely, if the curse of Ham played some role in making Africans dark, it was, as Vásquez de Espinosa proposed, because it worked in harmony with the rays of the sun. In practice, the idea that African bodies bore the curse of Ham operated alongside, rather than in competition with, the broader explanatory model provided by Christian humoralism, which explained the functioning of all human bodies. This meant that, cursed or not, the African body, like all bodies, was composed of a balance of humours, and was prone to illness or transformation when subjected to a different regimen, even if writers preferred not to dwell on the latter possibility. This is why slavers sought to feed ailing captives familiar food, and also why, as the Augustinian friar Antonio de la Calancha observed, Africans born or raised in the benign climate of the Indies differed notably in talent and ability from those who lived in Spain or West Africa.[32]

Amerindians and the sons of Ham

Could the curse of Ham explain the distinctive Amerindian body? As we have seen, unravelling the ancestry of Amerindians occupied the minds of many early modern writers, who identified them variously as the descendants of Carthaginians, Spaniards, Scythians or one or another old-world people. The 'toasted' colour of some Amerindians, together with their manifestly sinful and immoral behaviour, prompted some colonial writers to consider whether Amerindians might instead be the descendants of Ham. The Franciscan creole Buenaventura de Salinas y Córdova, for example, maintained that Amerindians were of a 'toasted, ashy or reddish' colour because they were the sons of Ham. Very unusually, he explicitly ruled out explanations that ascribed this colour to the heat of the sun, the climate or the governing constellations, and he declined to discuss diet at all.[33] That is, some early modern writers wondered whether certain aspects of the distinctive Amerindian body might be due not to the standard humoral features that shaped all bodies, but rather to some more mysterious (and perhaps permanent) divine force.

The problem with the sons of Ham theory was that it hung largely on a single feature of the indigenous body: skin colour. As far as most colonial writers were concerned, Amerindians varied substantially in colour among themselves. That is, they did not all possess the dark

---

[32] Calancha, *Corónica moralizada*, book 1, chap. 10 (p. 68).
[33] Salinas y Córdova, *Memorial de las historias del Nuevo Mundo*, discurso 1 (pp. 11–12). See also Solórzano Pereira, *Política indiana*, book 1, chap. 5, section 35 (vol. I, p. 19).

skin understood to have resulted from Noah's curse. Many chroniclers described Amerindians as ranging in colour from 'toasted' to 'brownish' (*moreno*), the latter being the term often used by other Europeans to describe Spaniards themselves, who were certainly not the sons of Ham. (Perhaps not by coincidence seventeenth-century Spanish writers increasingly insisted on their own whiteness.[34]) Beyond this, it was regularly observed that Indians in some regions were practically white. In any event, those who were brown probably owed their colour more to the darkening effects of heat, alongside peculiar habits such as frequent bathing, than to any intrinsic quality, whatever its origin.[35] It was therefore difficult to maintain that their colour revealed them to be the sons of Ham. This was one of the reasons offered by Antonio de la Calancha, for instance, for rejecting the sons of Ham theory. Calancha, like his contemporary Salinas y Córdova, was a Peruvian creole who after taking religious orders composed a chronicle of colonial settlement in the Andes. In contrast to Salinas y Córdova, however, Calancha did not believe that Amerindians were the sons of Ham, in part, as he explained, because they were not uniformly 'toasted' in colour. Those who lived in the mountains, he noted, were nearly white. Calancha instead advanced the opinion that Amerindians were descendants of the Tartars, with whom he believed they shared many characteristics.[36]

Other savants refrained from labelling Amerindians the sons of Ham, but nonetheless expressed uncertainty about why some people had darker skins than others, just as writers discussing the dark skin of Africans had done. Perhaps the Amerindians' colour was due to extrinsic factors such as diet, or was instead intrinsic to their nature. This was a difficult matter to resolve. The Jesuit scholar Bernabé Cobo concluded in his 1653 *Historia del Nuevo Mundo* (*History of the New World*) that he could not possibly determine whether the Indians' character and appearance was the result of their 'natural complexion' or their food and drink. This, he suggested, was a question best left to

---

[34] See for example Cobo, *Historia del Nuevo Mundo*, book 11, chap. 2 (vol. II, pp. 11–12); and Martínez, *Genealogical Fictions*, pp. 249, 268. On the colour of Spaniards see Joly, 'Voyage en Espagne', pp. 606, 609; Cobo, *Historia del Nuevo Mundo*, book 11, chap. 2 (vol. II, pp. 11–12); Mme d'Aulnoy, *Relation du voyage d'Espagne*, letter 3 (vol. I, p. 108); and Martínez, *Genealogical Fictions*, pp. 249, 268.

[35] For white Amerindians see Columbus, 'Diary of the First Voyage', 13 Dec. 1492, in *Los cuarto viajes del almirante*, pp. 88, 91; Peter Martyr, *De Orbe Novo*, decade 1, book 6; Las Casas, *Historia de las Indias, c.* 1559, book 1, chap. 54 (p. 184); Zárate, *A History of the Discovery and Conquest of Peru*, p. 27; and Lizárraga, *Descripción breve de toda la tierra del Perú*, chap. 71 (p. 54). See also López de Velasco, *Geografía y descripción universal de las Indias*, 'De la disposición y suerte de los indios'; and Landa, *Relación de las cosas de Yucatán*, chap. 31 (p. 55).

[36] Calancha, *Corónica moralizada*, book 1, chap. 6 (pp. 36–7).

philosophers.[37] Most often, writers affirmed the conventional wisdom that differences in skin colour were due to 'the variation in places, climates, airs and foods'.[38] Thus, although early modern writers both in Spain and the new world sometimes alluded to the story of the curse of Ham to help explain why certain people possessed dark skin, this explanation neither dethroned the larger humoral model, nor appeared very compelling when used in isolation. Those who deployed the curse of Ham theory tended instead to frame explanations that drew on both humoralism and religious teaching about the physical consequences of sin. The seventeenth-century Jewish writer Avraham ben Shmuel Gedalia thus hypothesised that Noah's curse consisted in exiling Ham's descendants to a very hot climate, where their skin naturally darkened in accordance with standard Galenic tenets.[39] The Jesuit writer Alonso de Sandoval similarly speculated that God had given the children of Ham a hotter complexion, so that their skin darkened in keeping with long-standing humoral principles.[40]

Intrinsic qualities

Sandoval was the author of an unusual seventeenth-century handbook aimed at helping clergy evangelise the newly enslaved Africans who were arriving in their thousands at Spanish American ports each year. In his text Sandoval vigorously affirmed the common humanity of all men and criticised the cruelty that typified the Atlantic slave system. Although he was not particularly concerned with the question of why some Africans had black skin, he did meditate briefly on this topic towards the start of his manual. After rehearsing various arguments, including the possibility (mentioned above) that Ham's children had particularly hot complexions, he concluded that it was impossible to determine whether their colour derived from 'the will of God, or the particular qualities that are intrinsic to these people'.[41] Sandoval's suggestion that the African's dark skin might be due to some intrinsic quality, like Bernabé Cobo's question about whether Amerindians' 'natural complexion' was fundamentally different from the natural complexion of Spaniards, reminds us of a central feature

---

[37] Cobo, *Historia del Nuevo Mundo*, book 11, chaps. 2–4 (vol. II, pp. 10–16).

[38] Rocha, *El origen de los indios*, p. 212 (quotation); Cárdenas, *Problemas y secretos maravillosos*, book 3, chaps. 2, 3, 9, 11 (pp. 179, 184, 210, 219); and Garcia, *Origen de los indios*, book 2, chap. 5, book 3, chap. 4 (pp. 148–76, 243–54).

[39] Schorsch, *Jews and Blacks in the Early Modern World*, pp. 144–5.

[40] Sandoval, *De Instauranda aethiopum salute*, p. 26.

[41] Sandoval, *De Instauranda aethiopum salute*, p. 26.

of humoralism, which has a bearing on early modern understandings of bodily difference. This is that each person possessed their own natural complexion. That complexion resulted from 'the disposition of their bodies and the influence of the heavens and the other forces in operation', in the words of the humanist writer Pedro Mexía.[42] What, however, created this 'disposition of the body' in the first place? The factors that shaped the individual disposition were complex, but they derived in significant measure from the qualities that a child inherited from their parents. Children whose parents possessed more innate heat would themselves be hotter than average, for example, and many writers noted that children tended to resemble their parents in skin colour and other characteristics.[43] This meant that different groups of people were likely to have distinctive, definable characteristics. For example, Spanish men were generally choleric and were likely to pass these qualities on to their sons, all other things being equal. Humoralism, in other words, was perfectly compatible with an idea of heredity.

At the same time, as we have seen, a distinctive and inherited complexion could transform into something else. The consumption of particular foods, or other changes in regimen, might induce a 'second nature', since new customs could radically alter the body. Indeed, even the transmission of characteristics from one generation to the next was shaped by external factors such as food, since the qualities of semen were determined in part by the father's diet. The particular characteristics that a man might transmit to his children – far from being fixed – thus varied in accordance with what he ate. In his widely read treatise on character the Spanish doctor Juan Huarte de San Juan therefore explained in great detail what a man ought to eat in order to engender intelligent, handsome sons. (Chicken breast was strongly recommended; beef and sausage were to be avoided.[44]) Similarly, the mother's diet played a central role in determining the character of her children. For this reason medical handbooks devoted considerable attention to the diet of pregnant noblewomen, since incorrect foods could impede the transmission of the mother's noble qualities to her unborn offspring. Blue blood could be thus undermined not only by misalliances but also by too many turnips.[45] In addition, a child might resemble not its actual

---

[42] Mexía, *Silva de varia lección*, book 4, chap. 6 (vol. II, p. 362).

[43] Huarte de San Juan, *Examen de ingenios para las ciencias*; Cadden, *The Meanings of Sex Difference*, pp. 34–5, 53, 80–1, 96, 123, 127–8; and García Ballester, *La búsqueda de la salud*, p. 151.

[44] Huarte de San Juan, *Examen de ingenious para las ciencias*, chap. 15, part 3 (p. 352); Pineda, *Primera parte de los 35 dialogos familiares de la agricultura cristiana*, dialogue 5, section 9 (vol. I, p. 114r); and Cadden, *The Meanings of Sex Difference*, p. 197.

[45] Grieco, 'The Social Politics of Pre-Linnaean Botanical Classification', p. 137.

father, but rather the man to whom the mother's thoughts turned at the instant of conception – perhaps someone depicted in a painting that hung in the parental bedroom, or the man she truly loved or even the husband to whom she was at that moment being unfaithful.[46]

The world of the humoral body thus embraced a sense of heredity and the idea that certain characteristics were likely to be passed from one generation to another. At the same time, even heredity was subject to the powerful forces of the non-naturals. The very characteristics that parents transmitted to their children depended in part on the quality of their diet around the time of conception, and on the emotions of the mother. Heredity was a porous process, and whatever complexion an individual had inherited was itself liable to change. Indeed, such transformations in an individual's underlying complexion were said to occur 'all the time'.[47] For this reason it is not really accurate to argue, as some scholars have done, that early modern Spaniards regarded characteristics such as skin colour or overall appearance as 'genetically fixed qualities'.[48]

Of course certain sorts of transformations were considered more likely, or feasible, than others. Early modern ideas about sexual difference offer a clear example of the possibilities and limits of malleability. As a number of scholars have demonstrated, medical and religious writers concurred that under certain circumstances women could turn into men. All that was required was a sufficient increase in bodily heat. Women after all differed from men fundamentally in possessing less natural heat, which prevented their sexual organs from maturing and left them subject to a range of ailments associated with excessive cold and damp. With enough heat women's nature would transform. In an anthology of 1643 the Spanish Jesuit Juan Eusebio Nieremberg for example discussed several cases of women who turned into men after giving birth.[49] It was to precisely such ideas that one Elena, or Eleno, de Céspedes appealed when s/he was arrested in Toledo in the 1580s, charged with sodomy and impersonating a man. Céspedes insisted that although she had been born with woman's parts, on giving birth she acquired a male member the length and size of a thumb. In her

[46] Finucci, 'Maternal Imagination and Monstrous Birth'.
[47] Torquemada, *Jardín de flores curiosas*, tratado 3 (p. 248).
[48] Sweet, 'The Iberian Roots of American Racist Thought', p. 144.
[49] Torquemada, *Jardín de flores curiosas*, tratado 1 (pp. 122–3, 187–90); Huarte de San Juan, *Examen de ingenios para las ciencias*, chap. 15, part 1 (pp. 315–16); Pineda, *Primera parte de los 35 diálogos familiares de la agricultura cristiana*, dialogue 6, section 37 (vol. I, p. 163r); and Nieremberg, *Curiosa y oculta filosofía*, 'De la curiosa filosofía', book 2, chap. 17 (pp. 54–5).

defence she referred explicitly to Pliny and other ancient authorities who explained the processes that allowed this sort of transformation. The Inquisition disputed the veracity of Céspedes's account, but they did not deny that under some circumstances women could turn into men.[50] Indeed, because women's porous bodies were more open to the external environment than men's they were more prone than men to suffer such transformations. Thus, while no one denied that the differences between men and women were deep-seated and real, the barriers that separated one from another were not necessarily unbreachable.

Were there any limits to this apparently boundless mutability? Dark Ethiopian skin was perhaps one ancestral taint that resisted erasure, whether because the African complexion was particularly powerful, or because God had set his mark upon that people. But could certain sins mark the body so powerfully that *nothing* would remove their trace, even many generations hence? Precisely such concerns underpinned the anxiety, pervasive in the Catholic culture of early modern Spain, provoked by the figure of the Jew.

Alien bodies in Europe

Hostility towards Jews increased steadily in early modern Spain for reasons that remain somewhat opaque. From the late fourteenth century Jews were subject to growing harassment, and during the fifteenth century a number of Spanish towns and institutions passed laws excluding Jews, and Jewish converts, from holding office. These laws were justified on the grounds that the persistence of Jewish religious ritual constituted an inherent insult to the Catholic faith, and also that Jews engaged in various unsocial practices that imperilled the well-being of the Christian population. The formation of the Inquisition in 1480 helped consolidate these disparate initiatives, for the Holy Office paid considerable (although by no means exclusive) attention to reports of Judaizing. The increasingly restrictive purity of blood statutes were designed to impede the access of Jews, Muslims and their offspring to positions of power and prestige, although in this they were never entirely successful. More sweepingly, the expulsion of all practising Jews in 1492, the forced conversion of Muslims in the years between 1499 and 1526 and then the expulsions in 1609–10 of all Islamic converts, or moriscos, sought to reverse the centuries of uneasy coexistence

---

[50] Burshatin, 'Written on the Body'; and Kagan and Dyer, eds., *Inquisitorial Inquiries*, pp. 36–59. See also Laqueur, *Making Sex*; and Caciola, 'Mystics, Demoniacs, and the Physiology of Spirit Possession in Medieval Europe'.

that had hitherto characterised the Iberian Peninsula, and to impose a homogenous Catholic identity on the region's inhabitants. Jews were permitted to remain in the Peninsula after 1492 if they converted to Catholicism, but many Catholics harboured grave doubts about the sincerity of these conversions. Fears that these converts secretly persisted in their earlier faith permeated early modern Catholic Spain.

But who were these crypto-Jews? How could one tell them from good Catholics? There is an enormous amount of evidence indicating that in practice Spanish Catholics found it very difficult to distinguish between these categories. Indeed, it was for this reason that from the thirteenth century various legal codes had stipulated that Jews (and Muslims) must wear distinctive, identifying garments and coiffures. The Fourth Lateran Council explained clearly the motive for such legislation. 'In some provinces', the Council stated in 1215, 'difference in dress distinguishes the Jews or Saracens from the Christians, but in certain others such a confusion has grown up that they cannot be distinguished by any difference.'[51] Not surprisingly, in the absence of special clothes, cultural practices were the central indicator of confessional belief during the early modern era, as many denunciations to the Inquisition reveal. Individuals who were seen to light candles on Friday nights, or to bath with excessive frequency, were likely to attract disapproving attention, as were those who refused to eat pork, or who displayed a suspicious lack of familiarity with basic prayers. People detained by the Inquisition on charges of Judaizing were thus likely to be quizzed on their eating habits, their knowledge of the Catholic faith and their reported remarks to neighbours. Inquisitors did not generally scrutinise the bodies of detainees, beyond determining whether men were circumcised, itself virtually incontrovertible evidence of Jewish or Islamic faith.[52] In practice, then, Jewishness was not a condition easily read through the body.

At the same time it could not be completely divorced from the body. How could the physical body be separated from its cultural milieu, since that milieu had an impact on the body itself? What one ate, or how one lived one's life, was likely to be reflected in one's constitution

---

[51] *The Canons of the Fourth Lateran Council*, 1215, canon 68; Bartlett, 'Symbolic Meanings of Hair in the Middle Ages', pp. 46–7; Nirenberg, 'Religious and Sexual Boundaries in the Medieval Crown of Aragon', pp. 142–3; Black, *Perfect Wives, Other Women*, pp. 40–4; Russell-Wood, 'Before Columbus', p. 151; and Bristol, *Christians, Blasphemers, and Witches*, p. 301.

[52] Beinart, *Conversos on Trial*, pp. 11–13, 61, 80, 205, 212–13, 219, 223, 248; Nirenberg, 'Religious and Sexual Boundaries in the Medieval Crown of Aragon', pp. 146–6; Pardo Tomás, 'Physicians' and Inquisitors' Stories'; Kagan and Dyer, eds., *Inquisitorial Inquiries*, pp. 119–51; and Richard Kagan, personal communication (March 2010).

and complexion. For this reason Jewish religious practices might be
expected to leave an imprint on the bodies of their practitioners, making them Jewish. The very language of blood purity, which framed
the debate about the place of the convert in Catholic society, located
Jewishness clearly within the body. Jews, it was said, possessed corrupt,
infected blood, which made them blind to reason and so very difficult
to convert to Christianity.[53] Of course *limpieza de sangre* was in part a
metaphorical concept, but as a metaphor it derived its power from its
base in the very real world of humours and flows.

Indeed, the explanations offered for the most distinctive corporeal sign
of Jewish identity (other than circumcision) reveal clearly the role of vernacular humoralism in shaping Catholic understandings of Jewishness.
Jewish men, it was said, suffered from periodic rectal bleeding. This
belief appears to have been widely disseminated across the Catholic
population in both Spain and the Indies. A witness summoned by the
Inquisition in the Caribbean city of Cartagena thus volunteered the
information that a suspected Jew experienced mysterious anal bleeding,
knowledge that subsequently formed a key part in the Inquisition's case
against him.[54] Many Catholic writers agreed that Jewish men tended to
suffer from haemorrhoidal flows resembling a woman's menstruation.
'Every month', noted one doctor, 'many of them suffer a flowing of
blood from their posterior, as a perpetual sign of infamy and shame.'[55]
This, he suggested, was in fact a characteristic shared more generally
by all men of impure blood. The religious errors of Jews and other heretics were reflected in their disgusting bodily infirmities. While medical
writers usually viewed periodic bleedings – whether from the nose or
the anus – as wholesome and purgative, in Jewish men they became a
pathology.[56] This bleeding was moreover responsible for the distinctive
bad smell (the *foetor Judaicus*) said to characterise Jews.[57]

Why were Jewish men afflicted in this way? Explanations offered a
typical combination of humoral and religious factors, and thus situated
this peculiar ailment within the larger framework employed to explain

---

[53] See in particular García Guillén, 'Judaism, Medicine and the Inquisitorial Mind in
Sixteenth-Century Spain', pp. 381–2; and Graizbord, *Souls in Dispute*, p. 119.
[54] Schorsch, *Swimming the Christian Atlantic*, pp. 131–40.
[55] Juan de Quiñones, cited in Beusterien, 'Jewish Male Menstruation', p. 454.
[56] For a clear discussion of medical (and to some extent popular) attitudes towards male
menstruation in early modern Europe see Pomata, 'Menstruating Men'.
[57] Gavilan Vela, *Discurso contra los judios*, chap. 18 (pp. 301–9); Torrejoncillo, *Centinela
contra judios*, pp. 168–72, 178–83, 186; Graizbord, *Souls in Dispute*, p. 59; Caro Baroja,
Los judios en la España moderna y contemporánea, vol. I, p. 91; Cid, 'Judios en la prosa
española del siglo XVII', pp. 218–19, 238; and Schorsch, *Jews and Blacks in the Early
Modern World*, pp. 179–80.

the functioning of all bodies. 'Jewish male menstruation' was probably the result of the haemorrhoids that afflicted Jewish men because they ate bad foods that engendered gross blood, because they spent too much time sitting down and also because the hatred which Christians directed towards them made them fearful. All of these things caused an accumulation in melancholy humours, which naturally purged themselves through smelly, periodic rectal bleeding. In addition, this affliction was probably divine retribution for the shameful cry of 'Let his blood be on us, and on our children' uttered by the Jews before Pontius Pilate when he absolved himself of the death of Jesus.[58] The Jewish body thus acquired its distinctive form in part through the direct action of an outraged deity and in part through the accumulation of malignant humours, humours that resulted in significant measure from diet. Food, that most powerful substance, was in part behind the Jewish condition. The early sixteenth-century Spanish chronicler Andrés Bernáldez thus attributed the Jews' bad smell equally to the oily food they preferred to eat and the fact that they had not been baptised.[59] Excessively oily 'Jewish' dishes such as stewed aubergines thus helped create the smelly Jewish body at the same time as they signalled Jewish identity.[60]

The converso physician Juan Huarte de San Juan accorded a similar importance to diet in shaping the Jewish complexion. In his widely read and translated *Examen de ingenios* (*An Examination of Men's Wits*), an extended essay on human character, he explained why it was that Jews possessed particularly keen intellects. This was due, he believed, to the distinctive characteristics of the manna-based diet their Old Testament ancestors had consumed in the desert following their flight out of Egypt. Manna, Huarte maintained, was an especially delicate foodstuff, which permanently altered the stomachs of the Israelites, who had hitherto been accustomed to coarser foods such as garlic, onions and leeks. The delicate manna provoked the over-production of yellow bile, which in turn endowed Israelites with a choleric disposition and a correspondingly sharp intelligence. The consequences of this special

[58] Matt.7:25; Gordonio, *Lilio de medicina*, book 5, chap. 21 (p. 262); Torrejoncillo, *Centinela contra judios*, pp. 168–9, 180; Trachtenberg, *The Devil and the Jews*, pp. 50–1; Biller, 'Views of Jews from Paris around 1300', pp. 192–202; Ruderman, *Jewish Thought and Scientific Discovery in Early Modern Europe*, p. 290; Kruger, 'Becoming Christian, Becoming Male?', p. 23; Beusterien, 'Jewish Male Menstruation in Seventeenth-Century Spain', p. 453; and Cid, 'Judios en la prosa española del siglo XVII', pp. 218–19, 238.

[59] Bernáldez, *Historia de los reyes católicos*, chap. 43 (vol. I, pp. 126, 134); and Trachtenberg, *The Devil and the Jews*, pp. 47–50.

[60] On the aubergine as a morisco or converso food see Beinart, ed., *Records of the Trials of the Spanish Inquisition in Ciudad Real*, vol. III, p. 433; and Cervantes, *Don Quijote*.

diet were so powerful that its effects were felt even 3,000 years later, among Spanish Jews who had never themselves eaten manna. Huarte compared the constitutional effects of eating manna to those caused by cases of extreme fright, which, he believed, could affect even a man's great-grandchildren. If the effects of fright on the complexion took over a hundred years to dissipate, it was not surprising that those of eating manna, a miraculous substance created directly by God, should persist for thousands of years. Huarte nonetheless believed that little by little Spain's Jews were losing their keen wits, which would inevitably deteriorate with the passage of time.[61] For Huarte, Jewishness was an embodied condition, but it was also inherently mutable.

It was precisely because confessional identity was in part a physical condition that Christian legislators and theologians worried about the corrupting effect of conversa and morisca wet nurses on Christian children, for breast milk, like semen, derived from blood. As we saw in Chapter 1, breastfeeding was a powerful mechanism for transmitting characteristics, not simply because the child would become familiar with the nurse's cultural habits but because the milk itself contained a concentrated form of the nurse's own humours. For this reason Spanish texts ranging from law codes to domestic manuals advised against or prohibited outright the use of Jewish and Islamic converts to nurse Christian children. Writers alerted readers to cases in which men of pure blood became Judaizers because they had been suckled by Jewish wet nurses. Similar fears were expressed that children fed by morisca wet nurses would become 'amoriscados', or moorified.[62] In the Indies concerns about religious contamination focused on indigenous wet nurses, who might similarly transmit not only their particular complexion but also their tendency towards idolatry to the unfortunate children they nursed. This was why creoles and mestizos, so often suckled by these women, 'display some signs of the idolatry they imbibed from this milk', as one colonial official put it. The same process helped explain the disturbing persistence of idolatry among Amerindians themselves.[63] Such concerns point to the essentially fluxable nature of the humoral body, and to the profound connections that linked body and character. The bodies, and attitudes, of Christian children, who had surely

---

[61] Huarte de San Juan, *Examen de ingenios para las ciencias*, chap. 12 (pp. 239–51).
[62] García Guillén, 'Judaism, Medicine and the Inquisitorial Mind', p. 384; Bergmann, 'Milking the Poor'; Martínez, *Genealogical Fictions*, p. 55; and Edwards, 'The Beginnings of a Scientific Theory of Race?', pp. 186–8.
[63] Juan de Mañozca, 1625, cited in Lavallé, *Las promesas ambiguas*, p. 49 (quotation); Peña Montenegro, *Itinerario para parochos de indios*, book 2, tratado 4, section 1 (p. 176); Acosta, *De procuranda indorum salute*, book 5, chap. 9, section 9 (vol. I, p. 255); and Arriaga, *Extirpación de la idolatría del Piru* [1621], chap. 1 (p. 195).

inherited a Christian constitution from their parents, could undergo a radical transformation through ingestion of tainted breast milk. Eating the wrong foods placed one at risk of becoming a Jew or a Moor. Christian faith required a Christian body. Mistaken practices, both doctrinal and corporeal, could endanger that body, making it less Christian. This is what had happened to Jerónimo de Aguilar, marooned among the Indians for a decade, whose stomach could no longer tolerate Christian food. But could the reverse transformation occur? Christian children might become *amoriscados* through drinking morisca breast milk; could suckling from the breasts of Old Christians redeem impure blood? The very suggestion was repellent, given that numerous injunctions expressly prohibited Christians from working as wet nurses or domestics in the homes of Jews or Muslims.[64] Nonetheless, it seems that Christian writers did believe that imbibing Christian milk would have a transformative effect on the Jewish body, although they were disturbed by the circumstances required for this to occur. The thirteenth-century French Dominican Vincent of Beauvais indicated as much in his *Speculum doctrinale* (*Mirror of Doctrine*), a comprehensive manual of scholastic knowledge that includes various pronouncements on proper relations between Christians and Jews, which was reprinted repeatedly through the sixteenth century. Vincent decried the supposed Jewish custom of requiring Christian wet nurses to discard their breast milk for three days after taking Communion, lest it taint their charges. Jews, he claimed, insisted that communicant nurses pour their milk into the latrine, a practice he found particularly offensive.[65] Whether Jews actually imposed such strictures on Christian wet nurses is beside the point; Vincent's assertions reflect his (and presumably his readers') belief that consumption of Christian milk might work to Christianise Jewish children. It was because they did not want their children to become Christian that Vincent's fictional Jews required Christian women to desecrate the body of Christ, present in their milk, in this way. In ascribing this notion to Jews, Vincent hoped to strengthen his overall argument that contact with Jews was degrading to Christians, and also to highlight the validity of the doctrine of the Real Presence, which insisted that Christ's body was truly present in the Eucharist, and therefore in these nurses' milk. His arguments gained force, however, because they drew on an underlying understanding that all bodies, even Jewish ones, were mutable. It was presumably also for this reason that during the 1609–10

[64] See for example Third Lateran Council, canon 26 (1179).
[65] Vincent of Beauvais, *Speculum doctrinale*, book 9, chap. 37. I am grateful to Irven Resnick for this reference, and to Andrew Laird for deciphering the Latin for me.

expulsion of Muslim converts the Spanish crown considered requiring that all nursing morisco children remain in Spain, to be fed and cared for by Old Christians. It was forced to abandon this plan on practical grounds, but the intention was undoubtedly to redeem these infants from their mistaken religious heritage through an appropriate upbringing and appropriate food.[66]

Fundamentally, what was required for Jews to lose their Jewishness was for them sincerely to embrace Christianity and abandon the dirty and unchristian habits that impeded their conversion and actively reinforced their Jewish constitution. Many Catholics appear to have believed that this was an almost impossible enterprise, particularly for Jewish men, who were constitutionally obdurate. In this regard Jews were perhaps like Africans, who found it similarly difficult to shed their dark skins. For Prudencio de Sandoval, the bishop of Pamplona, these two conditions were alike in that both were very deeply engrained. 'Who can deny', he stated, 'that bad faith and ingratitude endure in the descendants of the Jews, just as the accidental fact of their blackness persists in blacks?'. [67] Sandoval did not, however, assert that these qualities were indelible. Indeed, by describing blackness as an Aristotelian 'accident', Sandoval underlined its superficiality, for, as Aristotle had explained, accidental qualities were those properties extrinsic to a thing's nature.

Were Jews truly to embrace Christianity, questions would nonetheless remain about their relationship to Old Christians, whose ancestors had converted in the more distant past. As the historian María Elena Martínez has noted, purity of blood requirements that demanded an individual possess no 'tainted' ancestors whatsoever were premised on an utterly inflexible model of heredity. By insisting that the stain of Jewish, Muslim or heretical ancestry persisted undiminished across generations the concept of blood purity pointed towards a more rigid model of inheritance, in which certain traits endured more or less intact across time. In practice, few investigations of blood purity were able to probe further back than the great-grandparents, but in theory, *any* Jewish, Muslim or heretical ancestor might be sufficient to destroy the purity of an entire lineage.[68] At the same time, the idea that Jewishness was indelibly rooted in the constitution flew in the face of fundamental Christian doctrine, which insisted on the essential redeemability of all

---

[66] Boronat y Barrachina, *Los moriscos españoles y su expulsión*, vol. II, pp. 522–50.
[67] Sandoval, *Historia de la vida y hechos del Emperador Carlos V*, book 29, chap. 38 (vol. III, p. 319); and Martínez, *Genealogical Fictions*, p. 158.
[68] Martínez, *Genealogical Fictions*, pp. 52–8, 83, 202–3.

people – a fact that opponents of the blood purity laws did not hesitate to point out.[69]

The suggestion that impure blood passed unaltered from one generation to the next might be viewed as evidence that early modern Spaniards were beginning to construct the Jew as an immutable physical type endowed with specific and permanent characteristics. For this reason a number of scholars see Spanish or, more broadly, Western European Christian ideas about Jews as an early manifestation of racial thinking.[70] The fact that in this period the Spanish term 'raza' was closely associated with religious impurity (and in particularly Jewish or Muslim identity) further points to the close links between blood purity and the idea of embodied, permanent difference.[71] Martínez has indeed argued that the concept of blood purity provided the framework for the elaboration of the colonial caste system, with Amerindians occupying the position of the old world's Jews and conversos, and Africans that of Muslims and moriscos. Old-world categories of impurity, she suggests, were transformed in the new world into categories of colour.

It is clear that the features that distinguished Jews from Catholic Spaniards were considered to be very deeply rooted, and highly resistant to change. But even deeply rooted characteristics were not necessarily permanent. Amerindians were evidence of that, for they had clearly lost many of the qualities of whatever old-world people they had descended from. Specifically, this was precisely what savants who viewed Amerindians as the descendants of Jews believed had happened. The Dominican priest Gregorio García thus maintained that certain Amerindian peoples were the descendants of Jews, but that they now looked different from their old-world ancestors because over time they had lost the special *naturaleza*, or nature, that Jews possessed as a result of eating manna. This transformation, he explained clearly, was the result of the 'different heavens, different air, different climate, different waters and different and less nourishing foods' that distinguished the new world from the old.[72] God had given the Jews a special appearance and character, but their Amerindian descendants had lost this complexion through the workings of the six non-naturals. These

[69] Kamen, *The Spanish Inquisition*, pp. 117–36.
[70] Kruger, 'The Bodies of Jews in the Late Middle Ages'; Kruger, 'Conversion and Medieval Sexual, Religious and Racial Categories', pp. 158–79; and Elukin, 'From Jew to Christian?', pp. 171–89.
[71] Covarrubias, *Tesoro de la lengua castellana*, 'Raza' (letter R, p. 3r).
[72] García, *Origen de los indios*, book 3, chap. 4 (pp. 248–51, quotation p. 248).

Amerindians were *not* Jews, even though they descended directly from them, in García's view. In similar fashion, the Franciscan writer Juan de Torquemada, who maintained that Amerindians bore the curse of Ham, believed that their bodies had nonetheless been modified by the new world's climate and insubstantial food.[73] Thus even characteristics due directly to divine intervention – manna, a curse – might gradually transform under the combined weight of climate, diet and other external forces.

All bodies in early modern Spain and its colonial possessions bore the traces of the ambient culture through which they moved, at least as far as Spaniards were concerned. Religious beliefs left their impact on the body, and a change in bodily practices might alter an individual's religious convictions. Christians should therefore shun Jewish wet nurses, lest their faith weaken. Jews emitted a specially unpleasant smell because they ate smelly food, because they were melancholy and because they had not undergone the transformative experience of Baptism. Africans were most probably black because the hot African sun dried up their humours, and those raised in the Indies had a livelier complexion than those dwelling in cold climates. Amerindians looked quite different from Jews because they ate potatoes and maize. Early modern bodies, in short, were generated by the cultural practices of the early modern world.

Conclusions

Scholars concerned with locating the origins of race often distinguish between systems of difference based on permanent characteristics such as physical appearance and those based on potentially changeable ones. In general only the former are considered examples of racial thinking. As the historian Kathleen Wilson has explained, race in its modern sense is usually understood to concern 'fixed, inherent difference, articulated through and signified primarily by physical appearance and the "science of surfaces"'.[74] This in particular is the definition (implicit or explicit) underpinning most arguments that race emerged in the early modern era.[75] Yet if race is defined as a system of difference

---

[73] Torquemada, *Monarchia yndiana*, book 14, chaps. 18–19 (vol. II, pp. 609–14).

[74] Wilson, *The Island Race*, pp. 11—15, quotation p. 11; Fredrickson, *Racism*, pp. 5–13; and Isaac, *The Invention of Racism in Classical Antiquity*, pp. 1–51.

[75] See for example Chaplin, *Subject Matter*, p. 14; Greer *et al.*, 'Introduction', in Greer *et al.*, eds., *Rereading the Black Legend*, pp. 2–3; Cañizares Esguerra, *Nature, Empire, and Nation*; Sweet, 'The Iberian Roots of American Racist Thought', p. 166; Silverblatt, 'Foreword', pp. x–xi; and Isaac *et al.*, 'Introduction', in Eliav-Feldon *et al.*, eds., *The Origins of Racism in the West*, pp. 10–12.

based on physical characteristics that are claimed to be fixed and permanent, then the early modern Hispanic world provides little evidence for the existence of racial thinking. This is because cultural practices were believed to leave a physical imprint on the body. Physical characteristics, therefore, were not in general considered immutable. Any system of differentiation premised on the idea that the physical body was unchangeable will thus fail to capture the way early modern Spaniards thought about their bodies and those of others. Perhaps the idea that the dark skin of Sub-Saharan Africans was imposed directly by God, or that Jewish blood endured for ever, hints at a move toward greater fixity, but, as we have seen, there was little consensus on these matters.

One response would be to argue that the first glimmerings of racial thinking appeared in this period, although it was not until many decades later that a fully elaborated model of race emerged. This approach in other words interprets the quest for the origins of race as a search for the moment when Europeans and their overseas descendants (in particular) began to believe in fixed physical types. The difficulty is that it is not clear that such a belief was ever truly hegemonic even at the height of nineteenth-century scientific racism. Although powerful voices insisted throughout those years that enormous, unbreachable chasms separated the white race from all others, many harboured doubts about how firmly whiteness was fixed in the individual constitution. Fear of degeneration and racial decline haunted European colonial projects from the Caribbean to the Dutch East Indies. Nor was it even necessary to leave Europe to find heart-breaking examples of racial degeneration, in the view of many nineteenth-century social reformers. No one, however, would claim that race did not exist as a meaningful social category in this period.[76] This suggests that racial thinking is concerned not so much with a belief in indelible, embodied differences, as with a desire to believe in them.

A second response would be to assert that in its essence racial thinking is not actually concerned with the physical body at all. Perhaps we should understand race simply as the notion that certain groups of people are naturally superior to others. By blurring the boundaries between systems of difference revolving around physical characteristics

---

[76] For a critique of indelibility see Stoler, 'Racial Histories and Their Regimes of Truth'; Stoler, *Carnal Knowledge and Imperial Power*; and also McClintock, *Imperial Leather*.

and those concerned, say, with class or levels of education, we certainly gain insight into the fundamental processes that produce all social hierarchies. After all, as the anthropologist Peter Wade has observed, the widespread belief that culture is itself innate and inherited renders tenuous any division between systems of difference based on culture and those based on the physical body.[77] At the same time, to describe race simply as an ideology which naturalises hierarchical power structures transforms it into a category so far removed from the body as to risk losing touch with its own historical genealogy, for racial thinking, whatever its origin, has always expressed itself in terms of embodied characteristics, whether these are understood to be physical or cultural. I believe we must pay closer attention to how different societies understood the idea of embodiment. We should neither minimise the role of the physical body in constructing hierarchies of difference nor assume that physical characteristics were always considered permanent or heritable. Neither should we suppose that cultural practices remain external to the body. This book has shown how early modern Spaniards elaborated hierarchical models of physical difference that were not based on the belief that bodily characteristics were necessarily inherited in a fixed manner across the generations. Armed with these models Spaniards in the new world constructed lasting social hierarchies that served the interests of colonial rule without resorting to the idea that the bodies of the colonisers and colonised were incommensurately different.

The challenge is to understand how models of physical difference were constructed without treating their constituent elements, in particular the body itself, as trans-historical categories. This book explores the dynamic relationship between overseas colonisation and the bodily experience of eating in the early modern Hispanic world, asking how the colonisers thought about their bodies and those of the native peoples they aspired to rule. By taking seriously their ideas about food, and by tracing the implications of those ideas through other areas of colonial discourse, we gain a richer understanding of how settlers understood the physical experience of colonialism and of how they thought about some of the central features of the colonial project. In his analysis of European responses to the new world the historian Anthony Pagden commented that frequently there is 'relatively little at stake in dietary

---

[77] Wade, 'Afterword: Race and Nation in Latin America'. For race as a naturalisation of hierarchies of difference see the illuminating discussion in Cadelo-Buitrago, 'Luxury, Sensibility, Climate and Taste'.

customs'.[78] For early modern Spaniards, certainly, a great deal was at stake.

The Epilogue examines the afterlife of the humoral body in the eighteenth and nineteenth centuries, and also points to its significance in understanding colonial encounters beyond the Hispanic world.

[78] Pagden, *European Encounters with the New World*, p. 186.

Epilogue

'It's all a question of humours,' said the public prosecutor gloomily.[1]

Humoralism provided a framework for understanding bodily difference throughout the early modern era. It shaped the ways in which Spanish settlers framed the experience of overseas colonisation, and helped give diet an exceptional importance in the maintenance of the colonial order. Because of its centrality to models of the body across Western Europe, concerns about the corporeal effects of travel, and in particular of eating new foods, were widely expressed not only by Spanish colonists but also by many other categories of traveller. Europeans living in the hot climate of Equatorial Africa thus imported quantities of wheat flour and wine from Spain, in order to protect their health. 'If the ships which bring these goods did not come, the white merchants would die, because they are not accustomed to negro food', explained a Portuguese pilot who left a short account of the nascent sugar industry in São Tomé.[2] Travel in Spain itself posed significant dangers to the non-Spanish. Writers warned that English pilgrims travelling to Santiago de Compostela risked falling ill from 'eatynge of frutes and drynkynge of water', and English troops campaigning in northern Spain complained that the region's cider made them ill.[3]

Fears about the transformative effects of new foods haunted colonial settlements in regions outside Spanish America as well. Colonists in India suspected that too close an encounter with the foods and practices of the region would darken the skins, and perhaps characters, of Europeans.[4] Settlers in early seventeenth-century Virginia reported cautionary tales of Englishmen who, on living with local Amerindians,

[1] Eça de Queiroz, *The Maias*, p. 79.
[2] 'Description of a Voyage from Lisbon to the Island of São Thomé', *c.* 1540, in Blake, ed., *Europeans in West Africa*, vol. I, p. 157.
[3] Borde, *The Fyrst Boke of the Introduction of Knowledge*, chap. 32 (vol. II, p. 88, quotation); Howell, *Instructions for Forreine Travell*, part IV, p. 5; and Hillgarth, *The Mirror of Spain*, pp. 13, 16.
[4] Collingham, *Imperial Bodies*.

had become virtually indistinguishable from them 'in complexion and habit'.[5] Others suspected that mortality among Native Americans was due at least in part to their adoption of the European diet, much as Spanish settlers had done. Overall, as the historian Joyce Chaplin has noted, English settlers 'wondered whether Indians could eat English foods or the English subsist on an Indian diet'.[6] And like Spanish settlers, English colonists too found it reassuring that old-world crops could be cultivated in the new world, and saw the workings of divine providence in the existence of useful medicinal plants that helped counter the dangerous effects of the new world's climate and airs. Thus the early eighteenth-century savant Hugh Jones observed that although colonists in Virginia were prone to illness caused by sudden changes in temperature and the excessive consumption of the native fruits, 'the goodness of God has furnished us with a perfect catholicon for that sickness' in the form of local medicinal barks.[7]

Humoralism, and the mental universe it supported, structured the bodily experience of overseas travel and colonisation for settlers from many parts of Europe, and beyond. During the period in which it provided the fundamental framework for Western understandings of the body its influence can be discerned in many venues, from the plays of Shakespeare to Islamic travel guides.[8] That influence diminished gradually over the eighteenth century, such that by the mid nineteenth century humoralism had become an obsolete paradigm, discarded in favour of newer models premised on the circulation of blood, the germ theory of disease and similar innovations. When a character in a late nineteenth-century Portuguese novel attributes human behaviour to the humours, he reveals himself as intellectually stagnant, hopelessly mired in an out-of-date world.[9] Three centuries earlier he would have uttered a truism whose validity was affirmed by everything from popular proverbs to the writings of medical experts.

Nonetheless, while in both Spanish America and Europe the language of humours and flows gradually gave way to new ways of talking

---

[5] Hamor, *A True Discourse of the Present Estate of Virginia*, p. 44.

[6] Chaplin, 'Natural Philosophy, pp. 239—45, quotation p. 239. See also Kupperman, 'Fear of Hot Climates'; Eden, 'Food, Assimilation and the Malleability of the Human Body in Early Virginia'; and Finch, '"Civilized" Bodies and the "Savage" Environment of Early New Plymouth'; and Parrish, *American Curiosity*, esp. pp. 77–102.

[7] Jones, *The Present State of Virginia*, pp. 84–5 (quotation); Isaac, *The Transformation of Virginia*, pp. 46–52; and Egan, *Authorizing Experience*, pp. 22–4, 49–57.

[8] See for example Paster, *The Body Embarrassed*; Schoenfeldt, *Bodies and Selves in Early Modern England*; Floyd Wilson, *English Ethnicity*; and Qusta ibn Luqa, *Qusta ibn Luqa's Medical Regime for the Pilgrims to Mecca*.

[9] Eça de Queiroz, *The Maias*, p. 79.

about the body, the legacy of humoralism – or better, the way of thinking about the body expressed by humoralism – was long-lived. The idea of the individual complexion, with its associated regimen, persisted well into the eighteenth century, and even nineteenth-century savants and statebuilders attributed far-reaching transformative powers to food. 'The social problem for the Indian race', proclaimed the Mexican positivist Justo Sierra in 1889, 'is one of nutrition and education.' 'Let them eat more meat and less chilli', he recommended, and 'the Indians will transform themselves.'[10]

The idea of the mutable humoral body was never wholly abandoned in Spanish America. The popularity of Lamarckian models of evolution, with their emphasis on the inheritance of acquired characteristics, like the ideas about hot and cold that permeate folk medicine in many parts of the continent, point to the deep roots that vernacular humoralism sank in the Americas.[11] Food lay at the centre of the humoral system, as it lies at the centre of much human activity. We do well to attend to the immense importance of such ordinary human activities in our attempts to understand the past.

[10] See for example Feijoo, 'Régimen para conservar la salud'; Caldas, 'El influxo del clima en los seres organizados'; Sierra, 'México social y político, apuntes para un libro', p. 126 (quotation); Bulnes, *El porvenir de las naciones latinoamericanas*, pp. 19–20; and, for a clear discussion of the role of diet in redeeming the Mexican Indian, Pilcher, *¡Que vivan los tamales!*. I am grateful to Andrea Cadelo and Mauricio Nieto for their advice about Caldas.

[11] Stepan, *'The Hour of Eugenics'*, pp. 64–101. There is debate about whether preconquest Mexica medicine already possessed its own hot–cold dichotomy. Nonetheless, anthropological studies strongly suggest that twentieth-century folk medicine in many parts of the continent represents a blending of European and indigenous traditions. See Comas *et al.*, *El mestizaje cultural y la medicina novohispana del siglo XVI*; López Austin, *Human Body and Ideology*; Foster, 'On the Origin of Humoral Medicine'; Foster, *Hippocrates' Latin American Legacy*; and Ortiz de Montellano, *Aztec Medicine, Health and Nutrition*.

Bibliography

UNPUBLISHED SOURCES

ARCHIVO GENERAL DE INDIAS, SEVILLE, SPAIN

Audiencia de Filipinas, legajo 84.
Audiencia de Guatemala, legajo 9A.
Audiencia de México, legajos 20, 21, 23, 24, 28.
Audiencia de Panama, legajo 235.
Audiencia de Quito, legajo 78.
Indiferente General, legajos 415, 740.
Patronato, legajos 176, 231.

ARCHIVO GENERAL DE LA NACIÓN, BOGOTÁ, COLOMBIA

Colonia: Médicos y Abogados, legajo 11.

ARCHIVO GENERAL DE LA NACIÓN, MEXICO CITY, MEXICO

Historia, vol. 413.

ROYAL LIBRARY, WINDSOR CASTLE

Aztec herbal from the collection of Cassiano dal Pozzo, RCIN 970335.

DISSERTATIONS

Cadelo-Buitrago, Andrea, 'Luxury, Sensibility, Climate and Taste in the Eighteenth-Century Worldwide Racialisation of Difference', Ph.D. dissertation, University of Warwick, 2012.
Conway, Richard, 'Nahuas and Spaniards in the Socioeconomic History of Xochimilco, New Spain', Ph.D. dissertation, Tulane University, 2009.

PUBLISHED SOURCES

Note: the original publication date for printed sources is listed in square brackets after the publication date of the edition I consulted, in cases where these are significantly different. For works that were composed at a date earlier than the edition I have consulted, but that were not published at that time, I have listed the approximate date of composition after the title.

Acosta, José de, *De procuranda indorum salute*, trans. L. Pereña, V. Abril, C. Baciero, A. García, D. Ramos, J. Barrientos and F. Maseda, 2 vols. (Madrid, 1984 [1588]).

Natural and Moral History of the Indies, trans. Frances López-Morillas, Duke University Press (Durham, NC, 2002 [1590]).

Acuña, René, ed., *Relaciones geográficas del siglo XVI: Guatemala*, Universidad Nacional Autónoma de México (Mexico City, 1982).

Acuña, René, *Relaciones geográficas del siglo XVI: México*, 3 vols., Universidad Nacional Autónoma de México (Mexico City, 1986).

Acuña, René, *Relaciones geográficas del siglo XVI: Michoacán*, Universidad Nacional Autónoma de México (Mexico City, 1987).

Aguirre Beltrán, Gonzalo, *Medicina y magia: el proceso de aculturación en la estructura colonial*, Instituto Nacional Indigenista (Mexico City, 1973).

Agustí, Miguel, *Libro de los secretos de agricultura, casa de campo, y pastoril. Traducido de lengua catalana en castellano* (Madrid, 1695).

Alamán, Lucas, ed., *Dissertaciones*, 3 vols., Editorial Jus (Mexico City, 1969 [1844–49]).

Álamos de Barrientos, Baltasar, *Discurso político al rey Felipe III al comienzo de su reinado*, ed. Modesto Santos, Anthropos (Madrid, 1990 [1598]).

Albala, Ken, *Eating Right in the Renaissance*, University of California Press (Berkeley, 2002).

Alberro, Solange, *De gachupín al criollo, O cómo los españoles de México dejaron de serlo*, El Colegio de México (Mexico City, 1992).

Alemán, Mateo, *Guzmán de Alfarache*, 5 vols., Espasa (Madrid, 1936 [1595]).

Guzmán de Alfarache, ed. Samuel Gili y Gaya, 3 vols., La Lectura/Espasa-Calpe (Madrid, 1926–36 [1595]).

Allard, Jeanne, 'Le corps vu par les traités de diététique dans l'Espagne du siècle d'or', in Redondo, ed., *Le corps dans la société espagnole*.

Alva, Bartolomé de, *A Guide to Confession Large and Small in the Mexican Language, 1634*, ed. Barry Sell and John F. Schwaller, University of Oklahoma Press (Norman, 1999).

Alvarez Miraval, Blas, *La conservación de la salud del cuerpo y del alma* (Medina del Campo, 1597).

Alves, Abel, 'Of Peanuts and Bread: Images of the Raw and the Refined in the Sixteenth-Century Conquest of New Spain', in Francisco Javier Cevallos-Candau, Jeffrey Cole, Nina Scott and Nicomedes Suárez-Araúz, eds., *Coded Encounters: Writing, Gender and Ethnicity in Colonial Latin America*, University of Massachusetts Press (Amherst, 1994).

Anés Alvarez, Gonzalo, *Las crisis agrarias en la España moderna*, Taurus (Madrid, 1970).

Angeleres, Buenaventura Angela, *Real filosofía, vida de la salud temporal* (Madrid, 1692).

Anonymous Conquistador, 'Relación de algunas cosas de la Nueva España', 1556, in García Icazbalceta, ed., *Colección de documentos para la historia de México*.

Aquinas, Thomas, *Summa Theologica*, trans. Fathers of the English Dominican Province, online edition copyright © 2008 by Kevin Knight, www.newadvent.org/summa.

Arenas, Pedro de, *Vocabulario manual de las lenguas castellana y mexicana*, ed. Ascensión H. de Léon-Portilla, Universidad Nacional Autónoma de México (Mexico City, 1982 [1611]).

Arens, William, *The Man-Eating Myth*, Oxford University Press (New York, 1979).

Arias Montano, Benito, *Humanae Salutis Monumenta/Monumentos de la salud del hombre, desde la caída de Adán hasta el juicio final*, ed. Benito Feliú de San Pedro, Editorial Swan (Madrid, 1984 [1571]).

Aristotle, *Parts of Animals*, trans. A. L. Peck, Heinemann (London, 1961).

Arnade, Charles, *Florida on Trial, 1593–1602*, University of Miami Hispanic American Studies (Coral Gables, 1959).

Arriaga, Pedro José de, *Extirpación de la idolatría del Piru* [1621], in Esteve Barba, ed., *Crónicas peruanas de interés indígena*.

Arrizabalaga, Jon, Montserrat Cabré, Lluís Cifuentes and Fernando Salmón, eds., *Galen and Galenism: Theory and Medical Practice from Antiquity to the European Renaissance*, Ashgate (Aldershot, 2002)

Arrizabalaga, Jon, Roger French and John Henderson, *The Great Pox: The French Pox in Renaissance Europe*, Yale University Press (New Haven, 1997).

Asensio, José María, ed., *Colección de documentos inéditos relativos al descrubrimiento, conquista y organización de las antiguas posesiones españoles de ultramar*, second series, vol. 13:2, *Relaciones de Yucatán* (Madrid, 1900).

Atienza, Lope de, *Compendio historial del estado de los indios del Peru*, 1583, ed. J. Jijón y Caamaño, published as an appendix to *La Religión del imperio de los Incas*, Escuela Tipográfica Salesiana (Quito, 1931).

Aubert, Guillaume, '"The Blood of France": Race and Purity of Blood in the French Atlantic World', *William and Mary Quarterly*, third series, 61:3 (2004).

Aulnoy, Mme d' (Marie-Cathérine), *Relation du voyage d'Espagne*, 3 vols. (The Hague, 1692).

Avendaño, Fernando de, *Sermones de los misterios de nuestra santa fe católica, en lengua castellana y la general del inca, impugnandose los errores particulares que los indios han tenido* (Lima, 1648).

Avila, Francisco de, *Tratado de los evangelios que nuestra madre la iglesia propone en todo el año* ([Lima], [1648]).

Babcock, William, *Legendary Islands of the Atlantic: A Study in Medieval Geography*, American Geographical Society (New York, 1922).

Badiano, Juan, *An Aztec Herbal: The Classic Codex of 1552*, trans. William Gates, Dover Publications (Mineola, 2000).

Balbuena, Bernardo de, *Grandeza mexicana*, Universidad Nacional Autónoma de México (Mexico City, 1992 [1604]).

Baptista, Joan, *Advertencias para los confessores de los naturales* (Sanctiago Tlatilulco, 1600).

Confessionario en lengua mexicana y castellana con muchas advertencias muy necessarias para los confessores (Santiago Tlatilulco, 1599).

Barker, Francis, Peter Hulme, and Margaret Iverson, eds., *Cannibalism and the Colonial World*, Cambridge University Press (1998).

Barrera-Osorio, Antonio, *Experiencing Nature: The Spanish American Empires and the Early Scientific Revolution*, University of Texas Press (Austin, 2006).

Barrientos, Bartolomé, 'Vida y hechos de Pero Menéndez de Avilés', 1568, in *Menéndez de Avilés y la Florida. Crónicas de sus expediciones*, ed. Juan Carlos Mercado, Edwin Mellen Press (Lewiston, 2006).

Barrios, Juan de, *Verdadera medicina y cirugía y astrología en tres libros* (Mexico City, 1607).

Bartlett, Robert, *The Making of Europe: Conquest, Civilization and Cultural Change, 950–1350*, Penguin Books (Harmondsworth, 1994).

'Symbolic Meanings of Hair in the Middle Ages', *Transactions of the Royal Historical Society*, sixth series, 4 (1994).

Baudet, Henri, *Paradise on Earth: Some Thoughts on European Images of Non-European Man*, Yale University Press (New Haven, 1965).

Baudot, Georges, 'Amerindian Image and Utopian Project: Motolinía and Millenarian Discourse', in René Jara and Nicholas Spadaccini, eds., *Amerindian Images and the Legacy of Columbus*, University of Minnesota Press (Minneapolis, 1992).

'Los *huehuelatolli* en la cristianización de México: Dos sermones en lengua náhuatl de fray Bernardino de Sahagún', *Anales de literatura hispanoamericana* 9 (1980).

Bauer, Arnold, *Goods, Power, History: Latin America's Material Culture*, Cambridge University Press (2001).

'Millers and Grinders: Technology and Household Economy in Meso-America', *Agricultural History* 64:1 (1990).

Behar, Ruth, 'Sexual Witchcraft, Colonialism, and Women's Powers: Views from the Mexican Inquisition', in Asunción Lavrin, ed., *Sexuality and Marriage in Colonial Latin America*, University of Nebraska Press (Lincoln, 1989).

Beinart, Haim, *Conversos on Trial: The Inquisition in Ciudad Real*, Magnes Press (Jerusalem, 1981).

Beinart, Haim, ed., *Records of the Trials of the Spanish Inquisition in Ciudad Real*, 4 vols., Israel Academy of Sciences and Humanities (Jerusalem, 1985).

Belarminio, Roberto, *Declaración copiosa de las quatro partes mas esenciales, y necessarias de la doctrina christiana*, trans. Bartolomé Jurado Palomino (Lima, 1649).

Benavídez, Pedrarias de, *Secretos de chirurgia, especial de las enfermedades de morbo gallico y lamparones y mirrarchia* (Valladolid, 1567).

Bergamo, Ilarione da, *Daily Life in Colonial Mexico*, trans. William Orr, University of Oklahoma Press (Norman, 2000).

Bergmann, Emilie, 'Milking the Poor: Wet-Nursing and the Sexual Economy of Early Modern Spain', in Eukene Lakarra Lanz, ed., *Marriage and Sexuality in Medieval and Early Modern Iberia*, Routledge (London, 2002).

224   Bibliography

Bermúdez de Pedraza, Francisco, *Antigüedad y excelencias de Granada* (Madrid, 1608).
Bernáldez, Andrés, *Historia de los reyes católicos D. Fernando y Doña Isabel*, c. 1500, 2 vols. (Seville, 1870).
Bertonio, Ludovico, *Confessionario muy copioso en dos lenguas, aymara y española con una instrucción acerca de los siete sacramentos de la sancta yglesia, y otras varias cosas* (Juli, 1612).
Bethell, Leslie, ed., *The Cambridge History of Latin America*, 11 vols., Cambridge University Press (1984).
Beusterien, John, 'Jewish Male Menstruation in Seventeenth-Century Spain', *Bulletin of the History of Medicine* 73:3 (1999).
Bhabha, Homi, 'Of Mimicry and Man: The Ambivalence of Colonial Discourse', *October* 28 (1984).
'Signs Taken for Wonders: Questions of Ambivalence and Authority under a Tree outside Delhi, May 1817', in *The Location of Culture*, Routledge (London, 1994).
Biller, Peter, 'Views of Jews from Paris around 1300: Christian or "Scientific"?', in Diana Wood, ed., *Christianity and Judaism*, Blackwell (Oxford, 1992).
Black, Georgina Dopico, *Perfect Wives, Other Women: Adultery and Inquisition in Early Modern Spain*, Duke University Press (Durham, 2001).
Blake, John William, ed., *Europeans in West Africa, 1450–1560*, 2 vols., Hakluyt Society (London, 1942).
Bletter, Nathaniel, and Douglas Daly, 'Cacao and Its Relatives in South America: An Overview of Taxonomy, Ecology, Biogeography, Chemistry and Ethnobiology', in Cameron NcNeil, ed., *Chocolate in Mesoamerica: A Cultural History of Cacao*, University Press of Florida (Gainesville, 2006).
Blumenthal, Debra, *Enemies and Familiars: Slavery and Mastery in Fifteenth-Century Valencia*, Cornell University Press (Ithaca, 2009).
Boas, George, *Essays on Primitivism and Related Ideas in the Middle Ages*, Octagon Books (New York, 1978 [1966]).
Boronat y Barrachina, Pascual, *Los moriscos españoles y su expulsión*, 2 vols., Imprenta de Francisco Vives y Mora (Valencia, 1901).
Borah, Woodrow, *Early Colonial Trade and Navigation between Mexico and Peru*, University of California Press (Berkeley, 1954).
Borde, Andrew, *The Fyrst Boke of the Introduction of Knowledge*, ed. James Hogg, 2 vols., University of Salzburg (1979 [1547]).
Botero Benes, Juan, *Relaciones universales*, trans. Diego de Aguiar (Valladolid, 1603).
Boucher, Philip, *Cannibal Encounter: Europeans and Island Caribs, 1492–1763*, Johns Hopkins Press (Baltimore, 1992).
Brading, David, *The First America: The Spanish Monarchy, Creole Patriots, and the Liberal State, 1492–1867*, Cambridge University Press (1991).
Brandes, Stanley, 'El misterio del maíz', in Long, ed., *Conquista y comida*.
Braude, Benjamin, 'The Sons of Noah and the Construction of Ethnic and Geographical Identities in the Medieval and Early Modern Periods', *William and Mary Quarterly* 54:1 (1997).
Braude, Pearl, '"Cokkel in Oure Clene Corn": Some Implications of Cain's Sacrifice', *Gesta* 7 (1968).

Braudel, Fernand, *Civilization and Capitalism, 15th–18th Century*, vol. I, *The Structures of Everyday Life: The Limits of the Possible*, trans. Siân Reynolds, Collins (London, 1981).
The Mediterranean and the Mediterranean World in the Age of Philip II, trans. Siân Reynolds, 2 vols., Collins (London, 1972).
Bristol, Joan Cameron, *Christians, Blasphemers, and Witches: Afro-Mexican Ritual Practice in the Seventeenth Century*, University of New Mexico Press (Albuquerque, 2007).
Bulnes, Francisco, *El porvenir de las naciones latinoamericanas ante las recientes conquistas de Europe y Norteamérica* (n.p., 1899).
Burkhart, Louise, *The Slippery Earth: Nahua–Christian Moral Dialogue in Sixteenth-Century Mexico*, University of Arizona Press (Tucson, 1989).
Burshatin, Israel, 'Written on the Body: Slave or Hermaphrodite in Sixteenth-Century Spain', in Josiah Blackmore and Gregory Hutcheson, eds., *Queer Iberia: Sexualities, Cultures and Crossings from the Middle Ages to the Renaissance*, Duke University Press (Durham, 1999).
Butzer, Karl, 'Cattle and Sheep from Old to New Spain: Historical Antecedents', *Annals of the Association of American Geographers* 78:1 (1988).
Bynum, Carolyn Walker, *Holy Feast and Holy Fast: The Religious Significance of Food to Medieval Women*, University of California Press (Berkeley, 1987).
Caciola, Nancy, 'Mystics, Demoniacs, and the Physiology of Spirit Possession in Medieval Europe', *Comparative Studies in Society and History* 42:2 (2000).
Cadden, Joan, *The Meanings of Sex Difference in the Middle Ages*, Cambridge University Press (1993).
Calancha, Antonio de la, *Corónica moralizada del orden de San Agustín en el Perú* (Barcelona, 1638).
Caldas, Francisco José de, 'El influxo del clima en los seres organizados', *Semanario del Nuevo Reyno de Granada* 22–30 (Santa Fé, 1808).
Calvete de Estrella, Juan Cristóbal, *Rebelión de Pizarro en el Perú y vida de D. Pedro Gasca*, c. 1593?, 2 vols. (Madrid, 1889).
Calvo, Juan, *Libro de medicina y cirugia que trata de las llagas en general y en particular* (Barcelona, 1592).
Campbell, Mary B., *The Witness and the Other World: Exotic European Travel Writing, 400–1600*, Cornell University Press (Ithaca, NY, 1989).
Camporesi, Piero, *Bread of Dreams: Food and Fantasy in Early Modern Europe*, trans. David Gentilcore, Polity Press (Cambridge, 1989).
Cañeque, Alejandro, *The King's Living Image: The Culture and Politics of Viceregal Power in Colonial Mexico*, Routledge (New York, 2004).
Cañizares Esguerra, Jorge, 'Demons, Stars and the Imagination: The Early Modern Body in the Tropics', in Eliav-Feldon *et al.*, eds., *The Origins of Racism in the West*.
Nature, Empire, and Nation: Explorations of the History of Science in the Iberian World, Stanford University Press (2006).
'New Worlds, New Stars: Patriotic Astrology and the Invention of Indian and Creole Bodies in Colonial Spanish America, 1600–1650', *American Historical Review* 104:1 (1999).
Puritan Conquistadors: Iberianizing the Atlantic, 1550–1700, Stanford University Press (2006).

The Canons of the Fourth Lateran Council, 1215, www.fordham.edu/halsall/basis/lateran4.html.

Cárdenas, Juan de, *Problemas y secretos maravillosos de las Indias*, Ediciones Cultura Hispánica (Madrid, 1945 [1591]).

Carlé, Maria del Carmen, 'Alimentación y abastacimiento', *Cuardernos de Historia de España* 61–2 (1977).

Carney, Judith, and Richard Rosomoff, *In the Shadow of Slavery: Africa's Botanical Legacy in the Atlantic World*, University of California Press (Berkeley, 2009).

Caro Baroja, Julio, *Los judios en la España moderna y contemporánea*, 3 vols., Ediciones Arion (Madrid, 1961).

Carrasco, Pedro, 'Matrimonios hispano-indios en el primer siglo de la colonia', in Seminario de Historia de las Mentalidades, ed., *Familia y poder en Nueva España*, Instituto Nacional de Antropologia e Historia (Mexico City, 1991).

Carrera, Magali, *Imagining Identity in New Spain: Race, Lineage, and the Colonial Body in Portraiture and Casta Paintings*, University of Texas Press (Austin, 2003).

Casey, James, *Early Modern Spain: A Social History*, Routledge (London, 1999).

Family and Community in Early Modern Spain: The Citizens of Granada, 1570–1739, Cambridge University Press (2007).

Castellanos, Alfredo, *Breve historia de la ganadería en el Uruguay* (Montevideo, 1971).

Cervantes de Salazar, Francisco, *Crónica de la Nueva España*, c. 1560, Hispanic Society of America (Madrid, 1914).

'The Environs of the City of Mexico', in *The Dialogues of Cervantes de Salazar*, trans. Minnie Lee Barrett Shepard, University of Texas Press (Austin, 1953 [1554]).

Cervantes Saavedra, Miguel de, *Don Quijote*, trans. Edith Grossman, Vintage (London, 2005 [1605/1615]).

Chabrán, Rafael, 'Medieval Spain', in Melitta Weiss Adamson, ed., *Regional Cuisines of Medieval Europe: A Book of Essays*, Routledge (New York, 2002).

Chaplin, Joyce, 'Natural Philosophy and an Early Racial Idiom in North America: Comparing English and Indian Bodies', *William and Mary Quarterly*, 3rd series, 54:1 (1997).

Subject Matter: Technology, the Body, and Science on the Anglo-American Frontier, 1500–1676, Harvard University Press (Cambridge, 2001).

Chaunu, Huguette, and Pierre Chaunu, *Séville et l'Atlantique*, 8 vols., École Pratique des Hautes Études (Paris, 1955–9).

Chevalier, François, *Land and Society in Colonial Mexico: The Great Hacienda*, trans. Alvin Eustis, ed. Lesley Byrd Simpson, University of California Press (Berkeley, 1963).

Chirino, Alfonso, *Tractado llamado menor daño de medicina* (Seville, 1547 [1406]).

Cid, Jesús Antonio, 'Judios en la prosa española del siglo XVII (imperfecta síntesis y antología minima)', in Iacob Hassán and Ricardo Izquierdo Benito, eds., *Judíos en la literatura española*, Universidad de Castilla-La Mancha (Cuenca, 2001).

Cieza de León, Pedro de, *The Incas*, trans. Harriet de Onís, University of Oklahoma Press (Norman, 1959).

Parte primera de la chrónica del Perú (Seville, 1553).

Cisneros, Diego, *Sitio, naturaleza y propriedades de la ciudad de México* (Mexico City, 1618).

Clendinnen, Inga, *Ambivalent Conquests: Maya and Spaniard in Yucatan, 1517–1570*, Cambridge University Press (1987).

Cobo, Bernabé, *Historia del Nuevo Mundo*, 1653, in *Obras*, ed. Francisco Mateos, 2 vols., Editorial Atlas (Madrid, 1956).

Coccio, Marcantonio (Sabellico), *Book One … of the Account of the Happenings in the Unknown Regions*, 1500, in Symcox, ed., *Italian Reports on America*.

Coe, Sophie, *America's First Cuisines*, University of Texas Press (Austin, 1994).

Coe, Sophie, and Michael Coe, *The True History of Chocolate*, Thames & Hudson (London, 1996).

Collingham, E. M., *Imperial Bodies: The Physical Experience of the Raj, c. 1800–1947*, Polity Press (Cambridge, 2001).

Columbus, Christopher, 'Concerning the Islands Recently Discovered in the Indian Sea', 1493, ed. Matthew Edney, University of Southern Maine, www.usm.maine.edu/~maps/columbus/.

Los cuatro viajes del almirante y su testamento, ed. Ignacio Anzoátegui, Espasa (Madrid, 1971).

Libro de las profecías, c. 1502, ed. Juan Fernández Valverde, Alianza (Madrid, 1992).

Columbus, Fernando, *Life of the Admiral Christopher Columbus*, trans. Benjamin Keen, Rutgers University Press (New Brunswick, NJ, 1959).

Comas, Juan, Enrique González, Alfredo López Austin, Germán Somolinos and Carlos Viesca, *El mestizaje cultural y la medicina novohispana del siglo XVI*, Universitat de València (1995).

Confessionario para los curas de indios (Lima, 1585).

Connor, Jeannette Thurber, ed., *Colonial Records of Spanish Florida*, 2 vols., Florida Historical Society (Deland, 1925).

Conrad, Lawrence, 'The Arab-Islamic Medical Tradition', in Conrad *et al.*, eds., *The Western Medical Tradition*.

Conrad, Lawrence, Michael Neve, Vivian Nutton, Roy Porter and Andrew Wear, *The Western Medical Tradition, 800 BC to AD 1800*, Cambridge University Press (1995).

Cook, Noble David, *Born to Die: Disease and New World Conquest, 1492–1650*, Cambridge University Press (1998).

'Sickness, Starvation and Death in Early Hispaniola', *Journal of Interdisciplinary History* 32:3 (2002).

Cook, Sherburne, and Woodrow Borah, 'Indian Food Production and Consumption in Central Mexico Before and After the Conquest (1500–1650)', *Essays in Population History*, vol. III, *California and Mexico*, University of California Press (Berkeley, 1979).

Cooper, Helen, *Pastoral: Medieval into Renaissance*, D. S. Brewer (Ipswich, 1977).

Cope, Douglas, *The Limits of Racial Domination: Plebeian Society in Colonial Mexico City, 1660–1720*, University of Wisconsin Press (Madison, 1994).

Córdoba, Pedro de, *Doctrina cristiana para instrucción i información de los indios* (Mexico, 1544).

Cortés, Hernán, *Letters from Mexico*, trans. Anthony Pagden, Grossman (New York, 1971).

Covarrubias, Sebastián de, *Tesoro de la lengua castellana, o española* (Madrid, 1611).

Crone, G. R., ed., *The Voyages of Cadamosto and Other Documents on Western Africa in the Second Half of the Fifteenth Century*, Hakluyt Society (London, 1937).

Crooke, Helkiah, *Mikrokosmographia A Description of the Body of Man* (London, 1615).

Crosby, Alfred, *The Columbian Exchange: Biological and Cultural Consequences of 1492*, Greenwood Press (Westport, 1972).

'The Early History of Syphilis: A Reappraisal', in *The Columbian Exchange*.

Ecological Imperialism: The Biological Expansion of Europe, 900–1900, Cambridge University Press (1986).

Cummins, Thomas, 'To Serve Man: Pre-Columbian Art, Western Discourses of Idolatry, and Cannibalism', *RES: Anthropology and Aesthetics* 42 (2002).

Toasts with the Inca: Andean Abstraction and Colonial Images on Quero Vessels, University of Michigan Press (Ann Arbor, 2002).

Cuneo, Michele da, 'News of the Islands of the Hesperian Ocean', 1495, in Symcox, ed., *Italian Reports on America*.

Curtius, Ernst Robert, *European Literature and the Latin Middle Ages*, Routledge and Kegan Paul (London, 1953).

Dadson, Trevor, 'The Road to Villarrubia: The Journey into Exile of the Duke of Híjar, March 1644', in Trevor Dadson, R. J. Oakley and P. A. Odbur de Baubeta, eds., *New Frontiers in Hispanic and Luso-Brazilian Scholarship: Como Se Fue el Maestro*, Edwin Mellen Press (Lewiston, 1994).

Deagan, Kathleen, *Spanish St. Augustine: The Archaeology of a Colonial Creole Community*, Academic Press (New York, 1983).

Dean, Carolyn, *Inka Bodies and the Body of Christ: Corpus Christi in Colonial Cuzco, Peru*, Duke University Press (Durham, 1999).

Dean, Carolyn, and Dana Leibsohn, 'Hybridity and Its Discontents: Considering Visual Culture in Colonial Spanish America', *Colonial Latin American Review* 12:1 (2003).

Debus, Allen, 'Paracelsus and the Delayed Scientific Revolution in Spain: A Legacy of Philip II', in Allen Debus and Michael Walton, eds., *Reading the Book of Nature: The Other Side of the Scientific Revolution*, Thomas Jefferson University Press (Kirksville, 1988).

DeFrance, Susan D., 'Diet and Provisioning in the High Andes: A Spanish Colonial Settlement on the Outskirts of Potosí, Bolivia', *International Journal of Historical Archaeology* 7:2 (2003).

Del Rio, Martín, *Investigations into Magic*, ed. and trans. P. G. Maxwell-Stuart, Manchester University Press (2000 [1599]).

Devisse, Jean, *The Image of the Black in Western Art*, vol. II, *From the Early Christian Era to the 'Age of Discovery'*, part i, *From the Demonic Threat to the Incarnation of Sainthood*, trans. William Grander Ryan, Harvard University Press (Cambridge, 1979).

Devisse, Jean, and Michel Mollat, *The Image of the Black in Western Art*, vol. II, *From the Early Christian Era to the 'Age of Discovery'*, part ii, *Africans in the Christian Ordinance of the World (Fourteenth to the Sixteenth Centuries)*, trans. William Grander Ryan, Harvard University Press (Cambridge, 1979).

Deza, Lope de, *Gobierno político de agricultura*, 1618, ed. Angel García Sanz, Instituto de Estudios Fiscales (Madrid, 1991).

Díaz de Alpuche, Giraldo, 'Relación del pueblo de Dohot', 1579, in Asensio, ed., *Colección de documentos inéditos relativos al descrubrimiento, conquista y organización de las antiguas posesiones españoles de ultramar*.

Díaz de Isla, Ruy, *Tractado contra el mal serpentino que vulgarmente en España es llamado bubas* (Seville, 1539).

Díaz del Castillo, Bernal, *The True History of the Conquest of New Spain*, c. 1568, trans. Alfred Percival Maudslay, 5 vols. Cambridge University Press (2010).

Díez Borque, José María, *La sociedad española y los viajeros del siglo XVII*, Sociedad General Española de Librería (Madrid, 1975).

Doctrina christiana en lengua española y mexicana (Mexico City, 1550).

Domingo de la Anunciación, *Doctrina christiana breve y compendiosa por via de diálogo entre un maestro y un discipulo, sacada en lengua castellana y mexicana* (Mexico City, 1565).

Dorantes de Carranza, Baltasar, *Sumaria relación de las cosas de la Nueva España*, 1604, ed. José María de Agreda y Sánchez, Jesus Medina Editor (Mexico City, 1970).

Douglas, Mary, 'Deciphering a Meal', in *Implicit Meanings: Essays in Anthropology*, Routledge (London, 1975).

Duden, Barbara, *The Woman beneath the Skin: A Doctor's Patients in Eighteenth-Century Germany*, trans. Thomas Dunlap, Harvard University Press (Cambridge, 1991).

Dunmire, William, *Gardens of New Spain: How Mediterranean Plants and Foods Changed America*, University of Texas Press (Austin, 2004).

Durán, Diego, *Historia de las Indias de Nueva España e islas de la Tierra Firme*, ed. Angel Garibay, 2 vols., Porrua (Mexico City, 1967 [1570]).

Durston, Alan, *Pastoral Quechua: The History of Christian Translation in Colonial Peru, 1550–1650*, University of Notre Dame Press (2007).

Earle, Rebecca, 'Luxury, Clothing and Race in Colonial Spanish America', in Maxine Berg and Elizabeth Eger, eds., *Luxury in the Eighteenth Century: Debates, Desires and Delectable Goods*, Palgrave (Basingstoke, 2003).

'Nationalism and National Costume in Spanish America', in Mina Roces and Louise Edwards, eds., *The Politics of Dress in Asia and the Americas*, Sussex Academic Press (Eastbourne, 2007).

Eça de Queiroz, José Maria de, *The Maias*, trans. Margaret Jull Costa, Dedalus (Sawtry, 2007 [1888]).

Eden, Trudy, 'Food, Assimilation and the Malleability of the Human Body in Early Virginia', in Lindman and Tarter, eds., *A Center of Wonders*.

Edwards, John, 'The Beginnings of a Scientific Theory of Race? Spain, 1450–1600', in Yedida Stillman and Norman Stillmann, eds., *From Iberia to Diaspora: Studies in Sephardic History and Culture*, Brill (Leiden, 1999).

Egan, Jim, *Authorizing Experience. Refigurations of the Body Politic in Seventeenth-Century New England Writing*, Princeton University Press (1999).

Eliav-Feldon, Miriam, Benjamin Isaac and Joseph Ziegler, eds., *The Origins of Racism in the West*, Cambridge University Press (2009).

Elliott, John, *Imperial Spain, 1469–1716*, Penguin Books (London, 1990 [1963]).

Eltis, David, Philip Morgan and David Richardson, 'Agency and Diaspora in Atlantic History: Reassessing the African Contribution to Rice Cultivation in the Americas', *American Historical Review* 112:5 (2007).

Elukin, Jonathan, 'From Jew to Christian? Conversion and Immutability in Medieval Europe', in James Muldoon, ed., *Varieties of Religious Conversion in the Middle Ages*, University Press of Florida (Gainesville, 1997).

Elwood, Christopher, *The Body Broken: The Calvinist Doctrine of the Eucharist and the Symbolization of Power in Sixteenth-Century France*, Oxford University Press (1999).

Enriquez, Henrico Jorge, *Retrato del perfecto médico* (Salamanca, 1595).

Estes, J. Worth, 'The European Reception of the First Drugs from the New World', *Pharmacy in History* 37 (1995).

'The Reception of American Drugs in Europe, 1500–1650', in Varey *et al.*, eds., *Searching for the Secrets of Nature*.

Esteve Barba, Francisco, ed., *Crónicas peruanas del interés indígena*, Editorial Atlas (Madrid, 1968).

Farfán, Agustín, *Tratado breve de mediçina y de todas las enfermedades que a cada passo se ofrecen* (Mexico City, 1592).

Fariss, Nancy, *Maya Society under Colonial Rule: The Collective Enterprise of Survival*, Princeton University Press (1984).

Fattacciu, Irene, 'Cacao: From an Exotic Curiosity to a Spanish Commodity. The Diffusion of New Patterns of Consumption in Eighteenth-Century Spain', *Food and History* 7:1 (2010).

Federman, Nicolás, *Historia indiana*, trans. Juan Friede, Aro-Artes Gráficas (Madrid, 1958 [1557]).

Feijoo, Benito Jerónimo, 'Régimen para conservar la salud', in *Teatro crítico universal*, vol. I, discurso 6 (Madrid, 1778 [1726]), Biblioteca Feijoniana, www.filosofia.org/bjf/bjft106.htm.

Feria, Pedro de, *Doctrina christiana en lengua castellana y çapoteca* (Mexico City, 1567).

Fernández de Enciso, Martin, *Suma de geographia que trata de todas las partes y provincias del mundo: en especial de las Indias* (Seville, 1530).

Fernández de Navarrete, Martín, ed., *Coleccion de los viajes y descubrimientos que hicieron por mar los españoles desde fines del siglo XV*, 5 vols., Imprenta Nacional (Madrid, 1837–59?).

Fernández de Oviedo, Gonzalo, *Historia general de las Indias, primera parte* (Seville, 1535).

Historia general y natural de las Indias, ed. Juan Pérez de Tudela Bueso, 5 vols., Editorial Atlas (Madrid, 1959 [1535–57]).

Fernández del Castillo, Francisco, ed., *Libros y libreros en el siglo XVI*, Fondo de Cultura Económica (Mexico City, 1982 [1914]).

Fernández García, María de los Angeles, 'Criterios inquisitoriales para detectar al marrano: los criptojudíos en Andalucía en los siglos XVI y XVII', in Ángel Alcalá, ed., *Judíos. Sefarditas. Conversos. La expulsión de 1492 y sus consecuencias*, Ambito (Valladolid, 1995).

Few, Martha, 'Chocolate, Sex, and Disorderly Women in Late-Seventeenth and Early-Eighteenth-Century Guatemala', *Ethnohistory* 52:4 (2005).

Women Who Lead Evil Lives: Gender, Religion, and the Politics of Power in Colonial Guatemala, University of Texas Press (Austin, 2002).

Fields, Sherry, *Pestilence and Head Colds: Encountering Illness in Colonial Mexico*, Columbia University Press (Gutenberg e-book, 2008).

Finch, Martha, '"Civilized" Bodies and the "Savage" Environment of Early New Plymouth', in Lindman and Tarter, eds., *A Center of Wonders*.

Finucci, Valeria, 'Maternal Imagination and Monstrous Birth: Tasso's *Gerusalemme liberata*', in Finucci and Brownlee, eds., *Generation and Degeneration*.

Finucci, Valeria, and Kevin Brownlee, eds., *Generation and Degeneration: Tropes of Reproduction in Literature and History from Antiquity through Early Modern Europe*, Duke University Press (Durham, 2001).

Fisher, Andrew, and Matthew O'Hara, eds., *Imperial Subjects: Race and Identity in Colonial Latin America*, Duke University Press (Durham, 2009).

Fissel, Mary, *Vernacular Bodies: The Politics of Reproduction in Early Modern England*, Oxford University Press (2004).

Flandrin, Jean-Louis, Massimo Montanari and Albert Sonnenfeld, eds., *Food: A Culinary History from Antiquity to the Present*, trans. Clarissa Botsford, Columbia University Press (New York, 1999).

Flint, Valerie, *The Imaginative Landscape of Christopher Columbus*, Princeton University Press (1992).

Flores, Francisco, *Historia de la medicina en México desde la época de los indios hasta la presente*, 2 vols. (Mexico City, 1886).

Floyd Wilson, Mary, *English Ethnicity and Race in Early Modern Drama*, Cambridge University Press (2003).

Forrest, Beth Marie, and April Najjaj, 'Is Sipping Sin Breaking Fast? The Catholic Chocolate Controversy and the Changing World of Early Modern Spain', *Food and Foodways* 15 (2007).

Fosse, Eustache de la, 'Voyage à la côte occidentale d'Afrique en Portugal et en Espagne (1479–1480)', ed. R. Foulché-Delbosc, *Revue Hispanique* (Paris, 1897).

Foster, George, *Hippocrates' Latin American Legacy: Humoral Medicine in the New World*, Gordon and Breach (Amsterdam, 1994).

'On the Origin of Humoral Medicine in Latin America', *Medical Anthropological Quarterly*, new series, 1:4 (1987).

Foster, Nelson, and Linda S. Cordell, eds., *Chilies to Chocolate: Food the Americas Gave the World*, University of Arizona Press (Tuscon, 1992).

Fragoso, Juan, *Cirugía universal aora nuevamente añadida con todas las dificultades, y questiones, pertenecientes a las materias de que se trata* (Madrid, 1627).

Fredrickson, George, *Racism: A Short History*, Princeton University Press (2002).

Freedman, Paul, *Images of the Medieval Peasant*, Stanford University Press (1999).

Fresquet Febrer, José Luis, 'La difusión inicial de la materia médica americana en la terapéutica europea', in Fresquet Febrer *et al.*, *Medicinas, drogas y alimentos vegetales del Nuevo Mundo.*

La experiencia americana y la terapéutica en los Secretos de Chirurgia (1567) de Pedro Arias de Benavides, Universitat de València (1993).

Fresquet Febrer, José Luis, María Luz López Terrada and José Pardo Tomás, 'La presencia de los productos americanos en el *Discurso de las cosas aromáticas* (1572) de Juan Fragoso', in Fresquet Febrer *et al.*, *Medicinas, drogas y alimentos vegetales del Nuevo Mundo.*

Fresquet Febrer, José Luis, María Luz López Terrada and José Pardo Tomás, *Medicinas, drogas y alimentos vegetales del Nuevo Mundo. Textos e imágenes españolas que los introdujeron en Europa*, Ministerio de Sanidad y Consumo (Madrid, 1992).

Friedman, John, *The Monstrous Races in Medieval Art and Thought*, Harvard University Press (Cambridge, 1981).

Fries, Lorenz, *Underweisung und uszlegunge Der Cartha Marina oder die mer cartē* (Strasburg, 1530).

Frisch, Andrea, 'In Sacramental Mode: Jean de Léry's Calvinist Ethnography', *Representations* 77 (2002).

Fuentes y Guzmán, Francisco Antonio de, *Historia de Guatemala o Recordación Florida*, 1690, ed. Justo Zaragoza, 2 vols., Biblioteca de los Americanistas (Madrid, 1882).

Fussell, Betty, *The Story of Corn*, Knopf (New York, 1992).

Gage, Thomas, *The English-American: A New Survey of the West Indies, 1648*, ed. A. P. Newton, El Patio (Guatemala, 1946).

Galen, *Galen on Food and Drink*, ed. Mark Grant, Routledge (New York, 2000).

Gallagher, Catherine, and Stephen Greenblatt, 'The Potato in the Materialist Imagination', in *Practicing New Historicism*, University of Chicago Press (2000).

Garcés, Julián, *De habilitate et capacitate gentium sive Indorum novi mundi nuncupati ad fidem Christi capessendam* (Rome, 1537).

García, Gregorio, *Orígen de los indios del Nuevo Mundo*, ed. Franklin Pease (Mexico City, 1981 [1607/1729]).

García Acosta, Virginia, 'El pan de maíz y el pan de trigo: una lucha por el dominio del panorama alimentario urbano colonial', in Long, ed., *Conquista y comida.*

García Ballester, Luis, *La búsqueda de la salud: sanadores y enfermos en la España medieval*, Península (Barcelona, 2001).

'The Circulation and Use of Medical Manuscripts in Arabic in Sixteenth-Century Spain', in Arrizabalaga *et al.*, eds., *Galen and Galenism.*

'Galenism and Medical Teaching at the University of Salamanca in the Fifteenth Century', in Arrizabalaga *et al.*, eds., *Galen and Galenism*.

García de Enterría, María Cruz, 'El cuerpo entre predicadores y copleros', in Redondo, ed., *Le corps dans la société espagnole*.

García Guillén, Diego, 'Judaism, Medicine and the Inquisitorial Mind in Sixteenth-Century Spain', in Angel Alcalá, ed., *The Spanish Inquisition and the Inquisitorial Mind*, Social Science Monographs (Boulder, 1987).

García Icazbalceta, Joaquín, ed., *Colección de documentos para la historia de México: versión actualizada* (Mexico City, 1858–66), Biblioteca Virtual Miguel de Cervantes, www.cervantesvirtual.com.

García Sanz, Ángel, 'Castile, 1580–1650: Economic Crisis and the Policy of "Reform"', in I.A.A. Thompson and Bartolomé Yun Casalilla, eds., *The Castilian Crisis of the Seventeenth Century: New Perspectives on the Economic and Social History of Seventeenth-Century Spain*, Cambridge University Press (1994).

Desarrollo y crisis del antiguo régimen en Castilla la Vieja, Akal (Madrid, 1986).

'Estudio preliminar', in Deza, *Gobierno político de agricultura*.

Garcilaso de la Vega, *Royal Commentaries of the Incas and General History of Peru*, trans. Harold Livermore, 2 vols., University of Texas Press (Austin, 1989 [1617]).

Garrido Aranda, Antonio, 'La revolución alimentaria del siglo XVI en América y Europa', in Garrido Aranda, ed., *Los sabores de España y América*.

Garrido Aranda, Antonio, ed., *Cultura alimentaria de España y América*, La Val de Onsera (Huesca, 1995).

Garrido Aranda, Antonio, ed., *Los sabores de España y América*, La Val de Onsera (Huesca, 1999).

Gavilan Vela, Diego, *Discurso contra los judios, traducido de lengua portuguesa en castellano* (Madrid, 1680).

Gemelli Careri, Giovanni Francesco, *Voyage du tour du monde*, 1699, trans. M.L.N., 6 vols. (Paris, 1776).

Gentilcore, David, *Pomodoro! A History of the Tomato in Italy*, Columbia University Press (New York, 2010).

Geraldini, Alessandro, *Itinerary to the Regions Located below the Equator*, in Symcock, ed., *Italian Reports on America*.

Gerard, John, *The Herbal or General History of Plants. The Complete 1633 Edition as Revised and Enlarged by Thomas Johnson*, Dover Publications (New York, 1975).

Gerbi, Antonello, *Nature in the New World: From Columbus to Gonzalo Fernández de Oviedo*, trans. Jeremy Moyle, Pittsburgh University Press (1985).

Gerson, Juan, *Tripartito del christianissimo y consolatorio doctor Juan Gerson, de doctrina christiana a qualquiera muy provechosa* (Mexico City, 1544).

Giamatti, A. Bartlett, *The Earthly Paradise and the Renaissance Epic*, Princeton University Press (1966).

Gibson, Charles, *The Aztecs under Spanish Rule: A History of the Indians of the Valley of Mexico, 1519–1810*, Stanford University Press (1964).

Gil, Juan, *Mitos y utopías del Descubrimiento*, vol. I, *Colón y su tiempo*, Alianza (Madrid, 1989).

Gil-Bermejo García, Juan, 'Tráfico de vinos en Sevilla para el comercio indiano', in Solano and Pino, eds., *América y la España del siglo XVI*, vol. II.

Gilberti, Maturino, *Thesoro spiritual de pobres en lengua de Michuacan* (Mexico City, 1575).

Gimmel, Millie, 'Reading Medicine in the Codex de la Cruz Badiano', *Journal of the History of Ideas* 69:2 (2008).

Glacken, Clarence, *Traces on the Rhodian Shore: Nature and Culture in Western Thought from Ancient Times to the End of the Eighteenth Century*, University of California Press (Berkeley, 1967).

Goldberg, Jonathan, *Sodometries: Renaissance Texts, Modern Sexualities*, Stanford University Press (1992).

González, Enrique, 'La enseñanza médica en la ciudad de México durante el siglo XVI', in Comas *et al.*, *El mestizaje cultural y la medicina novohispana del siglo XVI*.

Goodman, David, *Power and Penury: Government, Technology and Science in Philip II's Spain*, Cambridge University Press (1988).

Gootenberg, Paul, 'Carneros y chuño: Price Levels in Nineteenth-Century Peru', *Hispanic American Historical Review* 70:1 (1990).

Gordonio, Bernardo, *Lilio de medicina: Un manual básico de medicina medieval*, ed. John Cull and Brian Dutton, Hispanic Seminary of Medieval Studies (Madison, 1991 [1495]).

Graizbord, David, *Souls in Dispute: Converso Identities in Iberia and the Jewish Diaspora, 1580–1700*, University of Pennsylvania Press (Philadelphia, 2004).

Grangel, Luis, *La medicina española renacentista*, Universidad de Salamanca (1980).

Greenleaf, Richard. *The Mexican Inquisition of the Sixteenth Century*, University of New Mexico Press (Albuquerque, 1969).

Greer, Margaret, 'Imperialism and Anthropophagy in Early Modern Spanish Tragedy: The Unthought Known', in David Castillo and Massimo Lollini, eds., *Reason and Its Others: Italy, Spain and the New World*, Vanderbilt University Press (Nashville, 2006).

Greer, Margaret, Walter Mignolo and Maureen Quilligan, eds., *Rereading the Black Legend: The Discourses of Religious and Racial Difference in the Renaissances Empires*, University of Chicago Press (2007).

Grieco, Allen, 'The Social Politics of Pre-Linnaean Botanical Classification', *I Tatti Studies* 4 (1991).

Grijalva, Juan de, *Crónica de la orden de N.P.S. San Agustín en las provincias de Nueva España en cuatro edades desde el año de 1533 hasta el de 1592*, n.p. (Mexico City, 1924 [1624]).

Grove, Richard, *Green Imperialism: Colonial Expansion, Tropical Island Edens and the Origins of Environmentalism, 1600–1860*, Cambridge University Press (1995).

Gruzinski, Serge, *The Mestizo Mind: The Intellectual Dynamics of Colonization and Globalization*, trans. Deke Dusinberre, Routledge (London, 2002).

Guaman Poma de Ayala, Felipe, *El primer nueva corónica y buen gobierno*, 1615–16, www.kb.dk/permalink/2006/poma/info/en/frontpage.htm.

Guerra, Francisco, *Iconografía médica mexicana*, Imprenta Diario Español (Mexico City, 1955).

'La mutación de las bubas desde G. Fernández de Oviedo', in Solano and Pino, eds., *América y la España del siglo XVI*, vol. I.

Guerrini, Luigi, 'The "Accademia dei Lincei" and the New World', Max Planck Institute for the History of Science, preprint 348 (2008), www. mpiwg-berlin.mpg.de/Preprints/P348.PDF.

Gutiérrez, Ramón, *When Jesus Came, the Corn Mothers Went Away: Marriage, Sexuality, and Power in New Mexico, 1500–1846*, Stanford University Press (1991).

Guzmán Pinto, Zenón, 'Perspectiva urbana y cultura alimentaria, Cusco, 1545–1552', in Garrido Aranda, ed., *Cultura alimentaria de España y América*.

Hahn, Thomas, 'The Difference the Middle Ages Makes: Color and Race Mixture Before the Modern World', *Journal of Medieval and Early Modern Studies* 31:1 (2001).

Hamilton, Bernice, *Political Thought in Sixteenth-Century Spain: A Study of the Political Ideas of Vitoria, De Soto, Suárez, and Molina*, Oxford University Press (1963).

Hamilton, Earl J., *American Treasure and the Price Revolution in Spain, 1501–1650*, Octagon Books (New York, 1965 [1934]).

'Wages and Subsistence on Spanish Treasure Ships, 1503–1660', *Journal of Political Economy* 37:4 (1929).

Hamor, Ralph, *A True Discourse of the Present Estate of Virginia* (London, 1615).

Hanke, Lewis, *Aristotle and the American Indians: A Study in Race Prejudice in the Modern World*, Hollis & Carter (London, 1959).

The First Social Experiments in America: A Study in the Development of Spanish Indian Policy in the Sixteenth Century, Peter Smith (Gloucester, MA, 1964).

The Spanish Struggle for Justice in the Conquest of America, Southern Methodist University Press (Dallas, 2002 [1949]).

Hanke, Lewis, ed., *Los virreyes españoles en América durante el gobierno de la casa de Austria*, Editorial Atlas (Madrid, 1978).

Hanks, William, *Converting Words: Maya in the Age of the Cross*, University of California Press (Berkeley, 2010).

Haring, Clarence Henry, *Trade and Navigation between Spain and the Indies*, Peter Smith (Gloucester, 1964).

Harrison, Mark *Climates and Constitutions: Health, Race, Environment and British Imperialism in India, 1600–1850*, Oxford University Press (1999).

Harvey, L. P., 'Oral Composition and the Performance of Novels of Chivalry in Spain', in Joseph Duggan, ed., *Oral Literature: Seven Essays*, Scottish Academic Press (Edinburgh, 1975).

Hassig, Debra, 'Transplanting Medicine: Colonial Mexican Herbals of the Sixteenth Century', *Res: Anthropology and Aesthetics* 17 /18 (1989).

Hawkes, J. G., and J. Francisco-Ortega, 'The Potato in Spain during the Late 16th Century', *Economic Botany* 46 (1992).

Heng, Geraldine, *Empire of Magic: Medieval Romance and the Politics of Cultural Fantasy*, Columbia University Press (New York, 2003).

Hernández, Francisco, *Antigüedades de la Nueva España, c.* 1574, ed. Ascensión H. de León-Portilla, Historia 16 (Madrid, 1986).

The Mexican Treasury: The Writings of Dr. Francisco Hernández, ed. and trans. Simon Varey, Rafael Chabrán and Cynthia Chamberlain, Stanford University Press (2000).

Obras completas, ed. Germán Somolinos d'Ardois and José Miranda, 4 vols., Universidad Nacional Autónoma de México (Mexico City, 1959–).

Quatro libros de la naturaleza, y virtudes de las plantas, y animales que estan recividos en el uso de medicina en la Nueva España, trans. Francisco Ximénez (Mexico City, 1615).

Herrera, Antonio de, *Historia general de los hechos de los castellanos en las islas y tierrafirme del mar océano o 'decadas'*, ed. Mariano Cuesta Domingo, 4 vols., Universidad Complutense de Madrid (1991? [1605/1615]).

Herrera, Gabriel Alonso de, *Obra de agricultura*, 1513, ed. José Urbano Martínez, Editorial Atlas (Madrid, 1970).

Herrero García, Miguel, *Ideas de los españoles del siglo XVII*, Gredos (Madrid, 1966).

Herzog, Tamar, *Defining Nations: Immigrants and Citizens in Early Modern Spain and Spanish America*, Yale University Press (New Haven, 2003).

Hillgarth, J. N., *The Mirror of Spain, 1500–1700: The Formation of a Myth*, University of Michigan Press (Ann Arbor, 2000).

Hippocrates, *The Genuine Works of Hippocrates*, trans. Francis Adams (London, 1849).

Hippocrates, vol. IV, trans. W. H. S. Jones, Harvard University Press (Cambridge, 1998 [1931]).

Howell, James, *Instructions for Forreine Travell* (London, 1642).

Huarte [de San Juan], Juan, *Examen de Ingenios, or The Examination of Mens Wits* (London, 1594).

Examen de ingenios para las ciencias, ed. Eséban Torre, Promociones y Publicaciones Universitarias (Barcelona, 1988 [1575]).

Huet, Marie-Hélène, *Monstrous Imagination*, Harvard University Press (Cambridge, 1993).

Hulme, Peter, *Colonial Encounters: Europe and the Native Caribbean, 1492–1797*, Methuen (London, 1986).

Hutten, Felipe de, 'Diario', in Joaquín Gabaldón Márquez, ed., *Descubrimiento y conquista de Venezuela*, 2 vols., Academia Nacional de la Historia (Caracas, 1962).

Hutten, Ulrich von, *De Morbo Gallico, A Treatise on the French Disease*, 1519, trans. Daniel Turner (London, 1730).

Ibáñez Rodríguez, Santiago, 'La consolidación del vino de Rioja en el siglo XVII', *Historia agraria* 26 (2002).

Ibarra y Rodríguez, Eduardo, *El problema cerealista en España durante el reinado de los Reyes Católicos*, Consejo Superior de Investigaciones Científicas (Madrid, 1944).

Ife, W. B., *Don Quixote's Diet*, University of Bristol Hispanic Studies 34 (2001).

Isaac, Benjamin, *The Invention of Racism in Classical Antiquity*, Princeton University Press (2004).

Isaac, Benjamin, Joseph Ziegler and Miriam Eliav-Feldon, 'Introduction', in Eliav *et al.*, eds., *The Origins of Racism in the West*.

Isaac, Rhys, *The Transformation of Virginia, 1740–1790*, Norton (New York, 1988).

Isidore of Seville, *Traité de la nature, c.* 615, trans. Jacques Fontaine, Institut d'Études Augustiniennes (Paris, 2002).

The Etymologies of Isidore of Seville, ed. Stephen Barney, W. J. Lewis, J. A. Beach and Oliver Berghof, Cambridge University Press (2006).

Jackson, Robert, *Race, Caste, and Status: Indians in Colonial Spanish America*, University of New Mexico Press (Albuquerque, 1999).

Jamieson, Ross, 'The Essence of Commodification: Caffeine Dependencies in the Early Modern World', *Journal of Social History* 35:2 (2001).

Jarcho, Saul, 'Medicine in Sixteenth Century New Spain as Illustrated by the Writings of Bravo, Farfán and Vargas Machuca', *Bulletin of the History of Medicine* 31:5 (1957).

Jáuregui, Carlos, *Canibalia: Canibalismo, calibanismo, antropofagia cultural y consumo en América Latina*, Vervuert (Madrid, 2008).

'"El plato más sabroso": Eucaristía, plagio diabólico, y la traducción criolla del caníbal', *Colonial Latin American Review* 12:2 (2003).

Jiménez de la Espada, Marcos, ed., *Relaciones geográficas de las Indias: Perú*, 3 vols., Ediciones Atlas (Madrid, 1965).

Johnson, Hildegard Binder, *Carta Marina: World Geography in Strasburg, 1525*, Greenwood Press (Westport, 1974).

Joly, Barthélemy, 'Voyage en Espagne (1603–1604)', ed. L. Barrau-Dihigo, *Revue Hispanique* 20:58 (1909).

Jones, Hugh, *The Present State of Virginia*, ed. Richard Morton, University of North Carolina Press (Chapel Hill, 1956 [1724]).

Juan de la Anunciación, *Doctrina christiana muy cumplida, donde se contiene la exposición de todo lo necessario para doctrinar a los indios y administrarles los sanctos sacramentos, compuesta en lengua castellana y mexicana* (Mexico City, 1575).

Kagan, Richard, 'Clio and the Crown: Writing History in Habsburg Spain', in Kagan and Parker, eds., *Spain, Europe and the Atlantic World*.

Kagan, Richard, and Abigail Dyer, eds., *Inquisitorial Inquiries: Brief Lives of Secret Jews and Other Heretics*, Johns Hopkins University Press (Baltimore, 2004).

Kagan, Richard, and Geoffrey Parker, eds., *Spain, Europe and the Atlantic World: Essays in Honour of John H. Elliott*, Cambridge University Press (1995).

Kamen, Henry, *The Spanish Inquisition*, Weidenfeld and Nicolson (London, 1965).

Katzew, Ilona, *Casta Painting: Images of Race in Eighteenth-Century Mexico*, Yale University Press (New Haven, 2004).

Kidd, Colin, *The Forging of Races: Race and Scripture in the Protestant Atlantic World, 1600–2000*, Cambridge University Press (2006).

Klibansky, Raymond, Erwin Panofsky and Fritz Saxl, *Saturn and Melancholy: Studies in the History of Natural Philosophy, Religion and Art*, Nelson (London, 1964).

Konetzke, Richard, ed., *Colección de documentos para la historia de la formación social de Hispanoamérica, 1493–1810*, 3 vols., Consejo Superior de Investigaciones Científicas (Madrid, 1953).

Kruger, Steven, 'Becoming Christian, Becoming Male?', in Jeffrey Jerome Cohen and Bonnie Wheeler, eds., *Becoming Male in the Middle Ages*, Garland (New York, 1997).

'The Bodies of Jews in the Late Middle Ages', in James Dean and Christian Zacher, eds., *The Idea of Medieval Literature*, University of Delaware Press (Newark, 1992).

'Conversion and Medieval Sexual, Religious and Racial Categories', in Karma Lochrie, Peggy McCracken and James Schultz, eds., *Constructing Medieval Sexuality*, University of Minnesota Press (Minneapolis, 1997).

Kupperman, Karen Ordahl, 'Fear of Hot Climates in the Anglo-American Colonial Experience', *William and Mary Quarterly* 41:2 (1984).

Lafaye, Jacques, *Quetzalcóatl and Guadalupe: The Formation of Mexican National Consciousness, 1531–1813*, trans. Benjamin Keen, University of Chicago Press (1987).

Laín Entralgo, Pedro, *Doctor and Patient*, trans. Frances Partridge, Weidenfeld and Nicolson (London, 1969).

Enfermedad y pecado, Ediciones Toras (Barcelona, 1961).

Landa, Diego de, *Relación de las cosas de Yucatán*, ed. Angel María Garibay, Editorial Porrua (Mexico City, 1959 [1574]).

Lanning, John Tate, *The Royal Protomedicato: The Regulation of the Medical Professions in the Spanish Empire*, ed. John TePaske, Duke University Press (Durham, 1985).

Laqueur, Thomas, *Making Sex: Body and Gender from the Greeks to Freud*, Harvard University Press (Cambridge, 1990).

Lara, Jaime, *Christian Texts for Aztecs: Art and Liturgy in Colonial Mexico*, University of Notre Dame Press (2008).

Las Casas, Bartolomé de, *Breve relación de la destrucción de las Indias Occidentales* (Philadelphia, 1821 [1542]).

Obras escogidas, ed. Juan Pérez de Tudela Bueso, 5 vols., Editorial Atlas (Madrid, 1957–8).

Lavallé, Bernard, *Las promesas ambiguas. Criollismo colonial en los Andes*, Pontífica Universidad Católica del Perú (Lima, 1993).

Lázaro de Arregui, Domingo, *Descripción de la Nueva Galicia, 1621*, ed. François Chavalier, Consejo Superior de Investigaciones Científicas (Seville, 1946).

Lechner, J., 'El concepto de "policía" y su presencia en la obra de los primeros historiadores de Indias', *Revista de Indias* 41:165–6 (1981).

Lemnius, Levinus, *The Touchstone of Complexions*, trans. T.N. (London, 1633).

Leon, Martín de, *Camino del cielo en lengua mexicana, con todos los requisitos necesarios para conseguir este fin, con todo le que un christiano deve creer, saber, y obrar, desde el punto que tiene uso de razon, hasta que muere* (Mexico City, 1611).

Leon Pinelo, Antonio de, *Question moral si el chocolate quebranta el ayuno eclesiástico* (Madrid, 1638).

El paraíso en el Nuevo Mundo: comentario apologético, historia natural y peregrina de las Indias Occidentales, Islas de Tierra Firme del Mar Oceano, ed. Raul Porras Barrenechea (Lima, 1943 [c. 1656]).

Leonard, Irving, *Books of the Brave: Being an Account of Books and of Men in the Spanish Conquest and Settlement of the Sixteenth-Century New World*, University of California Press (Berkeley, 1992).

Léry, Jean de, *History of a Voyage to the Land of Brazil, otherwise called America*, trans. Janet Whatley, University of California Press (Berkeley, 1990 [1578]).

Lestringant, Frank, 'Le canibale et ses paradoxes', *Mentalités/Mentalities* 1–2 (1983).

Cannibals: The Discovery and Representation of the Cannibal from Columbus to Jules Verne, University of California Press (Berkeley, 1997).

Levin, Harry, *The Myth of the Golden Age in the Renaissance*, Faber and Faber (London, 1969).

Lévi-Strauss, Claude, *The Raw and the Cooked: Introduction to the Science of Mythology*, trans. John and Doreen Weightman, Cape (London, 1970 [1964]).

Lewis, Laura, *Hall of Mirrors: Power, Witchcraft, and Caste in Colonial Mexico*, Duke University Press (Durham, 2003).

'The "Weakness" of Women and the Feminization of the Indian in Colonial Mexico', *Colonial Latin American Review* 5:1 (1996).

Libro de medicina llamado tesoro de los pobres con un regimiento de sanidad (Seville, 1547).

Lindberg, David, *The Beginnings of Western Science: The European Scientific Tradition in Philosophical, Religious, and Institutional Context, 600 B.C. to A.D. 1450*, University of Chicago Press (1992).

Lindman, Janet, and Michele Tarter, eds., *A Center of Wonders: The Body in Early America*, Cornell University Press (Ithaca, 2001).

Lindorfer, Bianca, 'Discovering Taste: Spain, Austria, and the Spread of Chocolate Consumption among the Austrian Aristocracy, 1650–1700', *Food and History* 7:1 (2010).

Liss, Peggy, *Mexico under Spain, 1521–1556: Society and the Origins of Nationality*, University of Chicago Press (1975).

Livi-Bacci, Massimo, *Conquest: The Destruction of the American Indios*, trans. Carl Ipsen, Polity Press (Cambridge, 2008).

'Return to Hispaniola: Reassessing a Demographic Catastrophe', *Hispanic American Historical Review* 83:1 (2003).

Lizárraga, Reginaldo de, *Descripción breve de toda la tierra del Perú, Tucumán, Río de la Plata y Chile*, c. 1609, ed. Toribio de Ortiguera, Editorial Atlas (Madrid, 1968).

Lobera de Avila, Luis, *Banquete de nobles caballeros compuesto por Luis Lobera de Avila (1530)*, Ediciones Castilla (Madrid, 1952).

Vergel de sanidad que por otro nombre se llamaba banquete de caballeros y orden de vivir (Alcalá de Henares, 1542).

Lockhart, James, *The Nahuas after the Spanish Conquest: A Social and Cultural History of the Indians of Central Mexico, Sixteenth through Eighteenth Centuries*, Stanford University Press (1992).

Lockhart, James, and Enrique Otte, eds., *Letters and People of the Spanish Indies: Sixteenth Century*, Cambridge University Press (1976).

Lomnitz, Claudio, 'Nationalism as a Practical System: Benedict Anderson's Theory of Nationalism from the Vantage Point of Spanish America', in Miguel Angel Centeno and Fernando López-Alves, eds., *The Other Mirror: Grand Theory through the Lens of Latin America*, Princeton University Press (2001).

Long, Janet, ed., *Conquista y comida. Consecuencias del encuentro de dos mundos*, Universidad Nacional Autónoma de México (Mexico City, 1997).

'El tomate: de hierba silvestre de las Américas a denominador común en las cocinas mediterráneas', in Garrido Aranda, ed., *Cultura alimentaria de España y América*.

Lope de Vega y Carpio, Félix Arturo, *La Dorotea: acción en prosa*, Castalia (Madrid, 1988 [1632]), www.scribd.com/doc/7942182/Vega-Lope-de-La-Dorotea.

El nuevo mundo descubierto por Cristóbal Colón, c. 1596–1603, ed. J. Lemartinel and Charles Minguet, Presses Universitaires de Lille (Paris, 1980).

Obras completas de Lope de Vega, ed. Jesús Gómez y Paloma Cuenca, vol. X, *Comedias*, Biblioteca Castro (Madrid, 1994).

López, Gregorio, *Tesoro de medicina para diversos enfermedades* (Madrid, 1708 [1673]).

López Austin, Alfredo, 'Equilibrio y desequilibrio del cuerpo humano, las concepciones de los antiguos nahuas', in Comas *et al.*, *El mestizaje cultural y la medicina novohispana del siglo XVI*.

Human Body and Ideology. Concepts of the Ancient Nahua, trans. Thelma and Bernard Ortiz de Montellano, University of Utah Press (Salt Lake City, 1988).

López Beltrán, Carlos, 'Hippocratic Bodies: Temperament and Castas in Spanish America (1570–1820)', *Journal of Spanish Cultural Studies* 8:2 (2007).

López de Gómara, Francisco, *Historia general de las Indias*, Linkgua (Barcelona, 2006 [1552]).

López de Hinojoso, Alonso, *Summa, y recopilacion de chirugia, con un arte para sa[n]grar muy util y provechosa* (Mexico City, 1578).

López de Velasco, Juan, *Geografía y descripción universal de las Indias, c.* 1574, ed. Cesáreo Fernández-Duro (Madrid, 1894), Biblioteca Virtual Luis Angel Arango, www.banrepcultural.org/blaavirtual/historia/india/indice.htm.

López de Villalobos, Francisco, *Libro intitulado los problemas de Villalobos que trata de cuerpos naturales y morales* (Seville, 1574).

The Medical Works of Francisco López de Villalobos, trans. George Gaskoin, John Churchill (London, 1870).

López Medel, Tomás, *De los tres elementos: Tratado sobre la naturaleza y el hombre en el nuevo mundo, c.* 1570, ed. Berta Ares Queija, Alianza (Madrid, 1990).

Visita de la gobernación de Popayán. Libro de tributos (1558–1559), ed. Berta Ares Queija, Consejo Superior de Investigaciones Científicas (Madrid, 1989).

López Piñero, José María, *Ciencia y técnica en la sociedad española de los siglos XVI y XVII*, Editorial Labor (Barcelona, 1979).

'The Faculty of Medicine of Valencia: Its Position in Renaissance Europe', in Mordechai Feingold and Victor Navarrro-Brotons, eds., *Universities and Science in the Early Modern Period*, Springer (Dordrecht, 2006).

'Paracelsus and His Work in Sixteenth- and Seventeenth-Century Spain', *Clio Medica* 8:2 (1973).

López Piñero José María, ed. *El 'Vanquete de Nobles Caballeros' (1530) de Luis Lobera de Avila y la higiene individual de siglo XVI*, Ministerio de Sanidad y consumo (Madrid, 1991).

López Piñero, José María, and José Pardo Tomás, 'The Contribution of Hernández to European Botany and Materia Medica', in Varey *et al.*, eds., *Searching for the Secrets of Nature.*

Nuevos materiales y noticias sobre la Historia de las plantas de Nueva España, de Francisco Hernández, Universitat de València (1994).

López-Salazar, Jerónimo, and Manuel Martín Galan, 'La producción cerealista en el Arzobispado de Toledo, 1463–1699', *Cuadernos de historia moderna y contemporánea* 2 (1981).

López Terrada, María José, 'Hernández and Spanish Painting in the Seventeenth Century', in Varey *et al.*, eds., *Searching for the Secrets of Nature.*

Loreto López, Rosalva, 'Prácticas alimenticias en los conventos de mujeres en la Puebla del siglo XVIII', in Long, ed., *Conquista y comida.*

Lovera, José Rafael, 'Intercambios y transformaciones alimentarias en Venezuela colonial: diversidad de panes y de gente', in Long, ed., *Conquista y comida.*

Lutz, Christopher, *Santiago de Guatemala, 1541–1773. City, Caste and the Colonial Experience*, University of Oklahoma Press (Norman, 1994).

Lynch, John, *Spain under the Hapsburgs*, 2 vols., Blackwell (Oxford, 1969).

Lyon, Eugene, 'Spain's Sixteenth-Century North American Settlement Attempts: A Neglected Aspect', *Florida Historical Quarterly* 59:1 (1981).

Mandeville, John, *The Travels of Sir John Mandeville*, c. 1356, ed. C. W. R. D. Moseley, Penguin Books (Harmondsworth, 1983).

Maravall, José Antonio, *El concepto de España en la Edad Media*, Centro de Estudios Constitucionales (Madrid, 1997 [1954]).

Estado moderno y mentalidad social, siglos XV a XVII, 2 vols., Ediciones de la Revista de Occidente (Madrid, 1972).

Mariscal, George, 'The Figure of the *Indiano* in Early Modern Spanish Culture', *Journal of Spanish Cultural Studies* 2:1 (2001).

Marradón, Barthelemy, 'Dialogue du chocolate entre un medecin, un indien et un bourgeois', in Philippe Sylvestre Dufour, *Traitez nouveaux et curieux du café, du the et du chocolate* (The Hague, 1685).

Martin, Lynn, 'National Reputations for Drinking in Traditional Europe', *Parergon: Bulletin of the Australian and New Zealand Association for Medieval and Early Modern Studies* 17:1 (1999).

Martínez, Henrico, *Reportorio de los tiempos e historia natural desta Nueva España*, Consejo Nacional para la Cultura y las Artes (Mexico City, 1991 [1606]).

Martínez, María Elena, *Genealogical Fictions: Limpieza de Sangre, Religion, and Gender in Colonial Mexico*, Stanford University Press (2008).

Marx, Leo, *The Machine in the Garden: Technology and the Pastoral Idea in America*, Oxford University Press (New York, 1964).

Matienzo, Juan de, *Gobierno del Perú*, ed. Guillermo Lohmann Villena, Institut Français d'Études Andines (Paris and Lima, 1967 [1567]).

Máynez, Pilar, ed., *Hechicerías e idolatrías del México antiguo*, Cien de México (Mexico City, 2008).

Mazumdar, Sucheta, 'The Impact of New World Food Crops on the Diet and Economy of China and India, 1600–1900', in Raymond Grew, ed., *Food in Global History*, Westview Press (Boulder, 1999).

McCann, James, *Maize and Grace: Africa's Encounter with a New World Crop, 1500–2000*, Harvard University Press (Cambridge, MA, 2005).

McClintock, Anne, *Imperial Leather: Race, Gender and Sexuality in the Colonial Contest*, Routledge (London, 1995).

McVaugh, Michael, *Medicine before the Plague: Practitioners and Their Patients in the Crown of Aragon, 1285–1345*, Cambridge University Press (1993).

Medina, Pedro de, *Primera y segunda parte de las grandezas y cosas notables de España* (Alcalá de Henares, 1595).

Meléndez, Carlos, 'Aspectos sobre la historia del cultivo del trigo durante la época colonial', in *Costa Rica: Tierra y problemamiento en la colonia*, Editorial Costa Rica (San José, 1977).

Melville, Elinor, *A Plague of Sheep: Environmental Consequences of the Conquest of Mexico*, Cambridge University Press (1997).

Mena García, Carmen, 'Nuevos datos sobre bastamentos y envases en armadas y flotas de la carrera', *Revista de Indias* 64:231 (2004).

Méndez, Cristóbal, *Libro de ejercicio corporal y de sus provechos*, ed. Juan Somolinos Palencia, Academia Nacional de Medicina (Mexico City, 1991 [1553]).

Méndez Nieto, Juan, *Discursos medicinales*, c. 1611, in *Documentos inéditos para la historia de España*, vol. XIII, Imprenta Góngora (Madrid, 1957).

Mendieta, Gerónimo de, *Historia eclesiástica indiana*, c. 1596, ed. Joaquín García Icazbalceta, Editorial Porrua (Mexico City, 1971 [1870]).

Mercado, Pedro de, *Diálogos de philosophia natural y moral* (Granada, 1574).

Mexía, Pedro, *Silva de varia lección*, ed. Antonio Castro, 2 vols., Catedra (Madrid, 1989 [1540]).

Minchom, Martin, *The People of Quito, 1690–1810: Change and Unrest in the Underclass*, Westview Press (Boulder, 1994).

Minsheu, John, *A Dictionary in Spanish and English* (London, 1599), www.ems.kcl.ac.uk/content/proj/anglo/dict/pro-anglo-dict-main.html.

Molina, Alonso de, *Confessionario mayor en la lengua mexicana y castellana*, ed. Roberto Moreno, Universidad Nacional Autónoma de México (Mexico City, 1984 [1569]).

Monardes, Nicolás, *Joyfull News out of the New-found Worlde* (London, 1596).

Moncada, Sancho de, *Restauración política de España, primera parte* (Madrid, 1619).

Montanari, Massimo, 'Food Models and Culinary Identity', in Flandrin *et al.*, eds., *Food: A Culinary History*.

'Food Systems and Models of Civilization', in Flandrin *et al.*, eds., *Food: A Culinary History*.

Montrose, Luis, 'The Work of Gender in the Discourse of Discovery', *Representations* 33 (1991).

Mörner, Magnus, *La corona española y los foráneos en los pueblos de indios de América*, Almquist and Wiksell (Stockholm, 1970).

Race Mixture in the History of Latin America, Little, Brown (Boston, 1967).

'The Rural Economy and Society in Colonial Spanish South America', in Bethell, ed., *The Cambridge History of Latin America*, vol. II.

Motolinía, Toribio de, *Historia de los Indios de la Nueva España*, 1541, in García Icazbalceta, ed., *Colección de documentos para la historia de México*.

Memoriales o libro de las cosas de la Nueva España y de los naturales de Ella, ed. Eduardo O'Gorman, Universidad Nacional Autónoma de México (Mexico City, 1971).

Muldoon, James, *The Americas in the Spanish World Order: The Justification for Conquest in the Seventeenth Century*, University of Pennsylvania Press (Philadelphia, 1994).

Munger, Robert, 'Guaiacum, the Holy Wood from the New World', *Journal of the History of Medicine and Allied Sciences* 4:2 (1949).

Murúa, Martín de, *Historia general del Perú, c.* 1612, ed. Manuel Ballesteros, Historia 16 (Madrid, 1986).

Myers, Kathleen, *Fernández de Oviedo's Chronicle of America: A New History for a New World*, University of Texas Press (Austin, 2007).

Nagera Yanguas, Diego de, *Doctrina y enseñanza en la lengua maçahua de cosas muy utiles y provechosos para los ministros de doctrina y para los naturales que hablan la lengua maçahua* (Mexico City, 1637).

Newson, Linda, 'Medical Practice in Early Colonial Spanish America: A Prospectus', *Bulletin of Latin American Research* 25:3 (2006).

Newson, Linda, and Susie Minchin, 'Diets, Food Supplies and the African Slave Trade in Early Seventeenth-Century Spanish America', *The Americas* 63 :4 (2007).

Nieremberg, Juan Eusebio, *Curiosa y oculta filosofia. Primera y segunda parte de las maravillas de la naturaleza, examinadas en varias questiones naturales* (Madrid, 1643).

Nirenberg, David, 'El concepto de raza en el estudio del antijudaísmo ibérico medieval', *Edad media: revista de historia* 3 (2000).

'Race and the Middle Ages: The Case of Spain and Its Jews', in Greer *et al.*, eds., *Rereading the Black Legend*.

'Religious and Sexual Boundaries in the Medieval Crown of Aragon', in Mark Meyerson and Edward English, eds., *Christians, Muslims, and Jews in Medieval and Early Modern Spain: Interaction and Cultural Change*, University of Notre Dame Press (Notre Dame, 1999).

Norton, Marcy, *Sacred Gifts, Profane Pleasures: A History of Tobacco and Chocolate in the Atlantic World*, Cornell University Press (Ithaca, 2008).

'Tasting Empire: Chocolate and the European Internalization of Mesoamerican Aesthetics', *American Historical Review* 111:3 (2006).

Noticias sobre el Río de la Plata: Montevideo en el siglo XVIII, ed. Nelson Martínez Díaz, Historia 16 (Madrid, 1988).

Nuñez de Oria, Francisco, *Regimiento y aviso de sanidad, que trata de todos los generos de alimentos y del regimiento della* (Medina del Campo, 1586).

Nutton, Vivian, 'Medicine in the Greek World, 800–50 BC', in Conrad *et al.*, *The Western Medical Tradition.*

Olabarrieta Medrano, Miguel de, *Recuerdo de las obligaciones del ministerio apostólico en la cura de las almas* (Lima, 1717).

Olschki, Leonardo, *Storia letteraria delle scoperte geografiche*, Olschki Editore (Florence, 1937).

Olson, Julius, and Edward Bourne, eds., *The Voyages of Columbus and of John Cabot*, Charles Scribner's Sons (New York, 1906).

Ore, Luis Heironymo de, *Symbolo catholico indiano, en el qual se declaran los mysterios de la Fe* (Lima, 1598).

Ortiz de Montellano, Bernard, *Aztec Medicine, Health and Nutrition*, Rutgers University Press (New Brunswick, 1990).

Otte, Enrique, ed., *Cartas privadas de emigrantes a Indias, 1540–1616*, Fondo de Cultura Económica (Mexico City, 1996).

Ovalle, Alonso de, *Histórica relación del Reyno de Chile*, Instituto de Literatura Chilena (Santiago, 1969 [1646]).

Pacheco, Joaquín, Francisco de Cárdenas and Luís Torres de Mendoza, eds., *Colección de documentos inéditos relativos al descubrimiento, conquista y colonización de las posesiones españolas en América y Ocanía*, 42 vols. (Madrid, 1864–).

Pacheco, Juan Francisco, *Question médica nuevamente ventilada si la variedad de la comida es dañosa para la conservación de la salud* (Jaen, 1646).

Padrón, Ricardo, *The Spacious Word: Cartography, Literature and Empire in Early Modern Spain*, University of Chicago Press (2004).

Pagden, Anthony, *European Encounters with the New World: From Renaissance to Romanticism*, Yale University Press (New Haven, 1993).

The Fall of Natural Man: The American Indian and the Origins of Comparative Ethnology, Cambridge University Press (1982).

'The Forbidden Food: Francisco de Vitoria and José de Acosta on Cannibalism', *Terrae Incognitae* 13 (1981).

Spanish Imperialism and the Political Imagination: Studies in European and Spanish-American Social and Political Theory, 1513–1830, Yale University Press (New Haven, 1990).

Palencia-Roth, Michael, 'The Cannibal Law of 1503', in Jerry Williams and Robert Lewis, eds., *Early Images of the Americas: Transfer and Invention*, University of Arizona Press (Tucson, 1993).

Paniagua, Juan Antonio, *El Doctor Chanca y su obra médica*, Ediciones Cultura Hispánica (Madrid, 1977).

Pardo Tomás, José, 'Physicians' and Inquisitors' Stories: Circumcision and Crypto-Judaism in Sixteenth–Eighteenth-Century Spain', in Florike Egmond and Robert Zwijnenberg, eds., *Bodily Extremities: Preoccupations with the Human Body in Early Modern European Culture*, Ashgate (Aldershot, 2003).

Pardo Tomás, José, and María Luz López Terrada, *Las primeras noticias sobre plantas americanas en las relaciones de viajes y crónicas de Indias (1493– 1533)*, Instituto de Estudios Documentales e Históricos sobre la Ciencia (Valencia, 1993).

Pareja, Francisco de, *Doctrina cristiana muy útil y necesaria, México, 1578*, ed. Luis Resines, Universidad de Salamanca (1990).

Parets, Miquel, *A Journal of the Plague Year: The Diary of the Barcelona Tanner Miquel Parets, 1651*, ed. J. S. Amelang, Oxford University Press (New York, 1991).

Parrish, Susan Scott, *American Curiosity: Cultures of Natural History in the Colonial British Atlantic World*, University of North Carolina Press (Chapel Hill, 2006).

Paso y Troncoso, Francisco del, ed., *Relaciones geográficas de México, segunda serie: geografía y estadística*, Editorial Cosmos (Mexico City, 1979 [1890]).

Paster, Gail Kern, *The Body Embarrassed: Drama and the Disciplines of Shame in Early Modern England*, Cornell University Press (Ithaca, 1993).

Paul III, 'Sublimus Dei', 29 May 1537, Papal Encyclicals Online, www. papalencyclicals.net.

Peña, Carmen, and Fernando Girón, *La prevención de la enfermedad en la España bajo medieval*, Universidad de Granada (2006).

Peña Montenegro, Alonso de la, *Itinerario para parochos de indios en que se tratan las materias mas particulares, tocantes a ellos, para su buena administración* (Madrid, 1668).

Peñaloza y Mondragón, Benito de, *Libro de las cinco excelencias del español que despueblan a España para su mayor potencia y dilatición* (Pamplona, 1629).

Perceval, José María, 'Asco y asquerosidad del morisco según los apologistas cristianos del Siglo de Oro', *La Torre: Revista de Ciencias Sociales de la Universidad de Puerto Rico* 13 (1990).

Pérez Bocanegra, Ivan, *Ritual, formulario e institución de curas, para administrar a los naturales de este reyno los santos sacramentos* (Lima, 1631).

Pérez de Herrera, Christoval, *Proverbios morales y consejos christianos muy prove- chosos para concierto y espejo de la vida* (Madrid, 1618).

Pérez Samper, Maria Angeles, *La alimentación en la España del siglo de oro: Domingo Hernández de Maceras, 'Libro del arte de cocina'*, La Val de Onsera/ Artes Gráficas (Huesca, 1998).

Peset, José Luis, 'La enseñanza de la medicina y la cirugía en el antiguo régi- men', in *Historia y medicina en España*, Junta de Castilla y León (Valladolid, 1994).

Peset, José Luis, and Manuel Almela Navarro, 'Mesa y clase en el siglo de oro español: la alimentación en "el Quijote"', *Cuadernos de Historia de la medicina española* 14 (1975).

Peter Martyr D'Anghera, *De Orbe Novo: The Eight Decades of Peter Martyr D'Anghera*, trans. Francis Augustus MacNutt, 2 vols. (New York, 1912), Project Gutenberg, www.gutenberg.org.

Epistolario, ed. José López de Tori, Imprenta Góngora (Madrid, 1953).

Phelan, John Leddy, *The Millennial Kingdom of the Franciscans in the New World*, University of California Press (Berkeley, 1970).

Phillips, Carla Rahn, *Ciudad Real, 1500–1750. Growth, Crisis and Readjustment in the Spanish Economy*, Harvard University Press (Cambridge, 1979).

'The Growth and Composition of Trade in the Iberian Empires, 1450–1750', in James Tracy, ed., *The Rise of Merchant Empires: Long-Distance Trade in the Early Modern World, 1450–1750*, Cambridge University Press (1990).

Pilcher, Jeffrey, *¡Que vivan los tamales! Food and the Making of Mexican Identity*, University of New Mexico Press (Albuquerque, 1998).

Pineda, Juan de, *Primera parte de los 35 dialogos familiares de la agricultura cristiana*, 2 vols. (Salamanca, 1589).

Pleij, Herman, *Dreaming of Cockaigne: Medieval Fantasies of the Perfect Life*, trans. Diane Webb, Columbia University Press (New York, 2001).

Pol, Nicholas, *On the Method of Healing with the Indian Wood called Guaiac the Bodies of Germans who have Contracted the French Disease*, 1517, in *Nicholas Pol Doctor 1494*, trans. Max Fisch (New York, 1947).

Polo, Marco, *Travels*, c. 1307, trans. William Marsden, Wordsworth (Ware, 1997).

Pomata, Gianna, 'Menstruating Men: Similarity and Difference of the Sexes in Early Modern Medicine', in Finucci and Brownlee, eds., *Generation and Degeneration*.

Popol Vuh: The Sacred Book of the Ancient Quiché Maya, trans. Delia Goetz and Sylvanus G. Morley, University of Oklahoma Press (Norman, 1950).

Pouchelle, Marie-Christine, *The Body and Surgery in the Middle Ages*, trans. Rosemary Morris, Polity Press (Cambridge, 1990).

Price, Merrall Llewelyn, *Consuming Passions: The Uses of Cannibalism in Late Medieval and Early Modern Europe*, Routledge (New York, 2003).

Prieto Carrasco, Castro, 'La medicina en la Universidad de Salamanca: lo que se sabe y lo que se puede suponer de sus origenes y periodo floreciente y de su decadencia', 1936, in *Dos Estudios sobre la enseñanza de la medicina en la Universidad de Salamanca*, Universidad de Salamanca (1986).

Puente, Juan de la, *Tomo primero de la conveniencia de las dos monarquías católicas, la de la Iglesia Romana y la del Imperio Español, y defensa de la precedencia de los reyes católicos de España a todos los reyes del mundo* (Madrid, 1612).

Purchas, Samuel, *Purchas His Pilgrimage, Or Relations of the World* (London, 1613).

Quiroga, Vasco de, *Don Vasco de Quiroga. Documentos*, ed. Rafael Aguayo Spencer, Acción Moderna Mercantil (Mexico City, 1939).

Qusta ibn Luqa, *Qusta ibn Luqa's Medical Regime for the Pilgrims to Mecca. The risala fi tadbir safar al-hajj*, ed. and trans. Gerrit Bos, Brill (Leiden, 1992).

Raleigh, Walter, *The Discovery of the Large, Rich and Beautiful Empire of Guiana* (London, 1596).

Recarte, Gaspar de, 'Tratado del servicio personal y repartimiento de los indios de Nueva España', 3 Oct. 1584, in Mariano Cuevas, ed., *Documentos inéditos del siglo XVI para la historia de México*, Museo Nacional de Antropología, Historia y Etnología (Mexico City, 1914).

Recetario novohispano, México, siglo XVIII, Introduction by Elisa Vargas Lugo, Conaculta (Mexico City, 2004).

Recinos, Adrián, *Doña Leonor de Alvarado y otros estudios*, Editorial Universitaria (Guatemala, 1958).

Recopilación de leyes de los reynos de las Indias, 3 vols., Ediciones Cultura Hispánica (Madrid, 1943 [1791]).

Redondo, Agustín, ed., *Le corps dans la société espagnole des XVI et XVII siècles*, Publications de la Sorbonne (Paris, 1990).

Refranes famosísimos y provechosos, glosados, Gráficas Reunidos (Madrid, 1923 [1509]).

Regueiro y González-Barros, Antonio, 'La flora americana en la España del siglo XVI', in Solano and Pino, eds., *América y la España del siglo XVI*, vol. I.

Reitz, Elizabeth, 'The Spanish Colonial Experience and Domestic Animals', *Historical Archaeology* 26:2 (1992).

Reitz, Elizabeth, and Bonnie McEwan, 'Animals, Environment and the Spanish Diet at Puerto Real', in Kathleen Deagan, ed., *Puerto Real: The Archaeology of a Sixteenth-Century Spanish Town in Hispaniola*, University of Florida Press (Gainesville, 1995).

Reitz, Elizabeth, and C. Margaret Scarry, *Reconstructing Historic Subsistence with an Example from Sixteenth-Century Spanish Florida*, Society for Historical Archaeology, Special Publication Series 3 (Pleasant Hill, 1985).

'Relación de la religión y ritos del Perú hecha por los padres agustinos', *c.* 1560, in *Relación de los agustinos de Huamachuco*, ed. Lucila Castro de Trelles, Pontífica Universidad Católica del Perú (Lima, 1992).

Restall, Matthew, *The Black Middle: Africans, Mayas, and Spaniards in Colonial Yucatan*, Stanford University Press (2009).

Rice, Prudence, 'Wine and Brandy Production in Colonial Peru: A Historical and Archaeological Investigation', *Journal of Interdisciplinary History* 27:3 (1997).

Río Moreno, Justo L. del, 'El cerdo. Historia de un elemento esencial de la cultura castellana en la conquista y colonización de América (siglo XVI)', *Anuario de Estudios Americanos* 53 (1996).

Río Moreno, Justo L. del, and Lorenzo López y Sebastián, 'El trigo en la ciudad de México. Industria y comercio de un cultivo importado (1521–1564)', *Revista Complutense de Historia de América* 22 (1996).

Ríos, Gregorio de los, *Agricultura de jardines*, Sociedad de Bibliófilos Españoles (Madrid, 1951 [1592]).

Ripalda, Jerónimo de, *Doctrina cristiana*, ed. Juan M. Sánchez (Madrid, 1909 [1591]).

Risse, Guenther, 'Medicine in New Spain', in Roland Numbers, ed., *Medicine in the New World: New Spain, New France and New England*, University of Tennessee Press (Knoxville, 1987).

'Shelter and Care for Natives and Colonists: Hospitals in Sixteenth-Century New Spain', in Varey *et al.*, eds., *Searching for the Secrets of Nature*.

Rocha, Diego Andrés, *El origen de los indios*, ed. José Alcina Franch, Historia 16 (Madrid, 1988 [1681]).

Rodríguez-Alegría, Enrique, 'Eating Like an Indian: Negotiating Social Relations in the Spanish Colonies', *Current Anthropology* 46:4 (2005).

Rodríguez de Almela, Diego, *Valerio de las historias escolásticas*, ed. Fernan Pérez de Guzman (Salamanca, 1587 [1462]).

Rodríguez Demorizi, Emilio, ed., *Los dominicos y las encomiendas de indios de la isla Española*, Academia Dominicana de la Historia (Santo Domingo, 1971).

Root, Deborah, 'Speaking Christian: Orthodoxy and Difference in Sixteenth-Century Spain', *Representations* 23 (1988).

Rubin, Miri, *Corpus Christi: The Eucharist in Late Medieval Culture*, Cambridge University Press (1991).

Ruderman, David, *Jewish Thought and Scientific Discovery in Early Modern Europe*, Yale University Press (New Haven, 1995).

Rueda, Lope de, *Pasos completos*, ed. F. García Pavón, Tauris (Madrid, 1981).

Ruiz de Alarcón, Hernando, *Tratado de las supersticiones y costumbres gentílicas que hoy viven entre los indios naturales de esta Nueva España*, digital edition based on F. del Paso y Troncoso, ed., *Tratado de las idolatrías, supersticiones, dioses, ritos, hechicerías y otras costumbres gentílicas de las razas aborígenes de México*, Biblioteca Virtual Miguel de Cervantes, www.cervantesvirtual. com.

Russell-Wood, A.J.R., 'Before Columbus: Portugal's African Prelude to the Middle Passage and Contribution to Discourse on Race and Slavery', in Vera Lawrence and Rex Nettleford, eds., *Race, Discourse, and the Origin of the Americas: A New World View*, Smithsonian Institution Press (Washington, DC, 1995).

Ruyz, Antonio, *Catecismo de la lengua guarani* (Madrid, 1640).

Sabuco Barrera, Oliva, *Nueva filosofía de la naturaleza del hombre, no conocida ni alcançada de los grande filósofos antiguos* (Braga, 1622).

Sahagún, Bernardino de, 'The *Exercicio quotidiana*', 1574, in *Codex Chamalpahin. Society and Politics in Mexico Tenochtitlan, Tlatelolco, Texcoco, Culhuacan, and other Nahua Altepetl in Central Mexico*, ed. and trans. Arthur J.O. Anderson and Susan Schroeder, 2 vols., University of Oklahoma Press (Norman, 1997).

Historia general de las cosas de Nueva España, 1577, ed. Alfredo López Austin and Josefina García Quintana, 2 vols., Fomento Cultural Banamex (Mexico City, 1982).

Salaman, Redcliffe, *History and Social Influence of the Potato*, Cambridge University Press (1985 [1949]).

Salazar, Esteban de, *Veinte discursos sobre el credo, en declaración de nuestra sancta fe catholica, y doctrina chrisitina muy necessarios a todos los fieles en este tiempo* (Seville, 1586).

Salinas y Córdova, Buenaventura de, *Memorial de las historias del Nuevo Mundo Pirú*, ed. Luis Valcárcel, Universidad Nacional Mayor de San Marcos (Lima, 1957 [1630]).

Memorial, informe y manifiesto (Madrid?, c. 1646).

Sampson Vera Tudela, Elisa, *Colonial Angels: Narratives of Gender and Spirituality in Mexico, 1580–1750*, University of Texas Press (Austin, 2000).

Sánchez, Juan, *Corónica y historia general del hombre* (Madrid, 1598).

Sánchez-Albornoz, Nicolás, 'The Population of Colonial Spanish America', in Bethell, ed., *The Cambridge History of Latin America*, vol. I.

Sánchez-Moscoso Hermida, Angustias, 'Concepto científico de nutrición en un texto médico del siglo XVI: "De regimine cibi atque potus", de Enrique Jorge Enriques', in Solano and Pino, eds., *América y la España del siglo XVI*, vol. I.

Sánchez Rubio, Rocío, and Isabel Testón Núñez, eds., *El hilo que une: las relaciones epistolares en el viejo y el nuevo mundo (siglos XVI–XVIII)*, Universidad de Extremadura (Mérida, 1999).

Sandoval, Alonso de, *De Instauranda aethiopum salute: El mundo de la esclavitud negra en América*, ed. Angel Valtierra, Biblioteca de la Presidencia de Colombia (Bogotá, 1956 [1627]).

Sandoval, Prudencio de, *Historia de la vida y hechos del Emperador Carlos V*, 3 vols., Atlas (Madrid, 1955–6 [1604–6]).

Saravia Viejo, María Justina and Isabel Arenas Frutos, '¿Olla Común? El problema de la alimentación en la reforma monarcal feminina. México, siglo XVIII', in Garrido Aranda, ed., *Los sabores de España y América*.

Schiebinger, Londa, *Nature's Body: Sexual Politics and the Making of Modern Science*, Pandora (London, 1994).

Schoenfeldt, Michael, *Bodies and Selves in Early Modern England: Physiology and Inwardness in Spenser, Shakespeare, Herbert, and Milton*, Cambridge University Press (1999).

'Fables of the Belly in Early Modern England', in David Hillman and Carla Mazzio, eds., *The Body in Parts: Fantasies of Corporeality in Early Modern Europe*, Routledge (London, 1997).

Schorsch, Jonathan, *Jews and Blacks in the Early Modern World*, Cambridge University Press (2004).

Swimming the Christian Atlantic: Judeoconversos, Afroiberians and Amerindians in the Seventeenth Century, Brill (Leiden, 2009).

Schwartz, Stuart, and Frank Salomon, 'New Peoples and New Kinds of People: Adaptation, Readjustment, and Ethnogenesis in South American Indigenous Societies (Colonial Era)', in Frank Salomon and Stuart Schwartz, eds., *The Cambridge History of the Native Peoples of the Americas*, vol. III:ii: *South America*, ed., Cambridge University Press (1999).

Sepúlveda, Juan Ginés de, *Demócrates segundo o De las justas causas de la guerra contra los indios*, 1548, ed. Angel Losada, Consejo Superior de Investigaciones Científicas (Madrid, 1951).

Serrano y Sanz, Manuel, ed., *Orígenes de la dominación española en América*, vol. I, Casa Editorial Bailly (Madrid, 1918).

Sheller, Mimi, *Consuming the Caribbean: From Arawaks to Zombies*, Routledge (London and New York, 2003).

Sierra, Justo, 'México social y político, apuntes para un libro', 1889, in *Obras completas*, ed. Manuel Mestre Ghigliazza, vol. IX, *Ensayos*, Universidad Nacional Autónoma de México (Mexico City, 1991).

Sigüenza, José de, *Historia de la Orden de San Gerónimo*, ed. Juan Catalina García, 2 vols., Casa Editorial Bailly (Madrid, 1907 [1600–05]).

Silverblatt, Irene, 'The Black Legend and Global Conspiracies: Spain, the Inquisition, and the Emerging Modern World', in Greer *et al.*, eds., *Rereading the Black Legend*.

'Foreword', in Fisher and O'Hara, eds., *Imperial Subjects*.

Modern Inquisitions: Peru and the Colonial Origins of the Civilized World, Duke University Press (Durham, 2004).

Simón, Pedro, *Noticias historiales de las conquistas de Tierra Firme en las Indias Occidentales*, ed. Juan Friede, Biblioteca Banco Popular (Bogotá, 1981 [1627]).

Siraisi, Nancy, *Avicenna in Renaissance Italy. The Canon and Medical Teaching in Italian Universities after 1500*, Princeton University Press (1987).

Medieval and Early Renaissance Medicine: An Introduction to Knowledge and Practice, University of Chicago Press (1990).

Slicher van Bath, B. H., *The Agrarian History of Western Europe, A.D. 500–1850*, trans. Olive Ordish, Edward Arnold (London, 1963).

Smith, Andrew, *The Tomato in America: Early History, Culture, and Cookery*, University of South Carolina Press (Columbia, 1994).

Socolow, Susan, *The Women of Colonial Latin America*, Cambridge University Press (2000).

Solano, Francisco de, ed., *Cuestionarios para la formación de las relaciones geográficas de Indias: siglos XVI/XIX*, Consejo Superior de Investigaciones Científicas (Madrid, 1988).

Solano, Francisco de, and Fermín del Pino, eds., *América y la España del siglo XVI*, 2 vols., Consejo Superior de Investigaciones Científicas (Madrid, 1983).

Solomon, Michael, *Fictions of Well-Being: Sickly Readers and Vernacular Medical Writing in Late Medieval and Early Modern Spain*, University of Pennsylvania Press (Philadelphia, 2010).

Solórzano Pereira, Juan de, *Política indiana*, 2 vols. (Madrid, 1736 [1647]).

Somolinos d'Ardois, Germán, 'Los impresos médicos mexicanos (1553–1618)', in Comas *et al.*, *El mestizaje cultural y la medicina novohispana del siglo XVI*.

Sorapan de Rieros, Juan, *Medicina española contenida en proverbios vulgares de nuestra lengua* ([Madrid], 1616).

Soufas, Teresa Scott, *Melancholy and the Secular Mind in Spanish Golden Age Literature*, University of Missouri Press (Columbia, 1990).

Spalding, Karen, *Huarochirí: An Andean Society under Inca and Spanish Rule*, Stanford University Press (1984).

Spearing, A. C., *Medieval Dream-Poetry*, Cambridge University Press (1967).

Stein, Claudia, *Negotiating the French Pox in Early Modern Germany*, Ashgate (Farnham, 2009).

Stepan, Nancy Leys, *'The Hour of Eugenics': Race, Gender and Nation in Latin America*, Cornell University Press (Ithaca, 1991).

Stoler, Ann Laura, *Carnal Knowledge and Imperial Power: Race and the Intimate in Colonial Rule*, University of California Press (Berkeley, 2002).

Race and the Education of Desire: Foucault's History of Sexuality and the Colonial Order of Things, Duke University Press (Durham, 1995).

'Racial Histories and Their Regimes of Truth', *Political Power and Social Theory* 11 (1997).

Suarez de Figueroa, Christoval, *El passagero: advertencias utilíssimas a la vida humana* (Barcelona, 1618).

Super, John, 'Spanish Diet in the Atlantic Crossing, the 1570s', *Terra Incognita* 16 (1984).

Stuurman, Siep, 'François Bernier and the Invention of Racial Classification', *History Workshop Journal* 50 (2000).

Sweet, James, 'The Iberian Roots of American Racist Thought', *William and Mary Quarterly* 54:1 (1997).

Symcox, Geoffrey, ed., *Italian Reports on America, 1493–1522*, Brepols (Turnhout, 2002).

Talbot, Charles, 'America and the European Drug Trade', in Fredi Chiappelli, ed., *First Images of America: The Impact of the New World on the Old*, University of California Press (Berkeley, 1976).

Taube, Karl, 'The Maize Tamale in Classic Maya Diet, Epigraphy and Art', *American Antiquity* 54:1 (1989).

Tauste, Francisco de, *Arte y bocabulario de la lengua de los indios chaymas, cumanagotos, cores, parias, y otros diversos de la provincia de Cumaná, o Nueva Andalucía* (Madrid, 1680).

Tavárez, David, 'Legally Indian: Inquisitorial Readings of Indigenous Identity in New Spain', in Fisher and O'Hara, eds., *Imperial Subjects.*

Taylor, William, *Drinking, Homicide, and Rebellion in Colonial Mexican Villages*, Stanford University Press (1979).

Tercero cathecismo y exposición de la doctrina christiana (Lima, 1585).

Third Lateran Council, 1179, e-text based on *Decrees of the Ecumenical Councils*, ed. Norman Tanner, Georgetown University Press (Washington, DC, 1990), www.intratext.com/IXT/ENG0064/_INDEX.HTM.

Thompson, I. A. A., 'Castile, Spain and the Monarchy: The Political Community from *Patria Natural* to *Patria Nacional*', in Kagan and Parker, eds., *Spain, Europe and the Atlantic World.*

Torquemada, Antonio de, *Jardín de flores curiosas*, ed. Giovanni Allegra, Castalia (Madrid, 1982 [1570]).

Torquemada, Juan de, *Monarchia yndiana*, 3 vols. (Seville, 1615).

Torrejoncillo, Francisco de, *Centinela contra judios, puesta en la torre de la iglesia de dios* (Pamplona, 1691).

Torres, Juan de, *Philosophia moral de príncipes para su buena crianca y govierno: y para personas de todo estado* (Burgos, 1596).

Torres, Pedro de, *Libro que trata de la enfermedad de las bubas* (Madrid, 1600).

Torres Rubio, Diego de, *Arte de la lengua aymara* (Lima, 1616).

Trachtenberg, Joshua, *The Devil and the Jews: The Medieval Conception of the Jew and Its Relation to Modern Anti-Semitism*, Jewish Publication Society (Philadelphia, 1983).

Trueba, Eduardo, *Sevilla: tribunal de océanos (siglo XVI)*, Gráficas del Sur (Seville, 1988).

Tudela de la Orden, José, 'Economía', in Tudela de la Orden, ed., *El legado de España a América*, vol. II.

Tudela de la Orden, José, ed., *Codice Tudela*, 2 vols., Ediciones Cultura Hispánica (Madrid, 1980).

El legado de España a América, 2 vols., Ediciones Pegaso (Madrid, 1954).

Twinam, Ann, 'Purchasing Whiteness: Conversations on the Essence of Pardoness and Mulatto-ness at the End of Empire', in Fisher and O'Hara, eds., *Imperial Subjects*.

'Racial Passing: Informal and Official "Whiteness" in Colonial Spanish America', in John Smolenski and Thomas Humphries, eds., *New World Orders: Violence, Sanctions, and Authority in the Colonial Americas*, University of Pennsylvania Press (Philadelphia, 2005).

Valadés, Diego, *Retórica cristiana*, ed. Esteban Palomera, Alfonso Castro Pallares and Tarsicio Herrera Zapién, Fondo de Cultura Económica (Mexico City, 1989 [1579]).

Valdés, Juan de, *Diálogo de la lengua*, ed. Angel Alcalá Galve, Biblioteca de la Universidad de Alicante (Madrid, 1997 [1535]).

Varey, Simon, Rafael Chabrán and Dora Weiner, eds., *Searching for the Secrets of Nature: The Life and Works of Dr. Francisco Hernández*, Stanford University Press (2000).

Vargas Machuca, Bernardo de, *Milicia y descripción de las Indias*, 2 vols. (Madrid, 1892 [1599]).

Vargas Machuca, Francisco de, *Médicos discursos y prácticas de curar el sarampion, y el fatal morbo, que sobrevino en estado de convalecencia a los que lo padecieron el año pasado de 93* (Lima, 1694).

Vásquez de Espinosa, Antonio, *Compendio y descripción de las Indias occidentales*, ed. B. Velasco Bayon, Editorial Atlas (Madrid, 1969).

Vassberg, David, 'Concerning Pigs, the Pizarros, and the Agro-Pastoral Background of the Conquerors of Peru', *Latin American Research Review* 13:3 (1978).

Land and Society in Golden Age Castile, Cambridge University Press (1984).

Vespucci, Amerigo, *The First Four Voyages of Amerigo Vespucci*, trans. Michael Kearney (London, 1885).

The Letters of Amerigo Vespucci and Other Documents Illustrative of His Career, ed. Clements R. Markham, Hakluyt Society (London, 1894).

Vetancurt, Agustín de, *Teatro mexicano*, Porrua (Mexico City, 1971 [1698]).

Vicens Vives, Jaime, *An Economic History of Spain*, trans. Frances López-Morillas, Princeton University Press (1969).

Vigneras, Louis-André, 'La búsqueda del Paraíso y las legendarias islas del Atlántico', *Cuadernos colombinos* 6, Universidad de Valladolid (1976).

The Discovery of South America and the Andalusian Voyages, University of Chicago Press (1976).

Vilanova, Arnand de, *El maravilloso regimiento y orden de vivir*, ed. Juan Paniagua Arellano, Universidad de Zaragoza (1980).

Vilchis, Jaime, 'Globalizing the *Natural History*', in Varey et al., eds., *Searching for the Secrets of Nature*.

Villalón, Cristóbal de, *El scholástico*, 1538–41, ed. José Miguel Martínez Torrejón, Crítica (Barcelona, 1997).

Viñas Mey, Carmelo, 'Datos para la historia económica de la colonización española', *Revista nacional de economía* 44 (Madrid, 1923).

Vincent of Beauvais, *Speculum doctrinale* (Venice, 1494).

Vitoria, Francisco de, *Political Writings*, ed. Anthony Pagden and Jeremy Lawrence, Cambridge University Press (1991).

Vivero, Rodrigo de, *Tratado ecónomico político, c.* 1609, in *Documentos inéditos para la historia de España*, vol. V, *Papeles de Indias*, ed. M. Ballesteros Gaibrois, Editorial Maestre (Madrid, 1947).

Vos, Paula de, 'Research, Development, and Empire: State Support of Science in the Later Spanish Empire', *Colonial Latin American Review* 15:1 (2006).

Wade, Peter, 'Afterword. Race and Nation in Latin America: An Anthropological View', in Nancy Appelbaum, Anne Macpherson and Karin Alejandra Rosemblatt, eds., *Race and Nation in Modern Latin America*, University of North Carolina Press (Chapel Hill and London, 2003).

Wadsworth, James, *The Present Estate of Spayne* (London, 1630).

Wandel, Lee Palmer, *The Eucharist in the Reformation: Incarnation and History*, Cambridge University Press (2006).

Warman, Arturo, *Corn and Capitalism: How a Botanical Bastard Grew to Global Dominance*, trans. Nancy Westrate, University of North Carolina Press (Chapel Hill, 2003).

Watts, Pauline Moffitt, 'Prophecy and Discovery: On the Spiritual Origins of Christopher Columbus' "Enterprise of the Indies"', *American Historical Review* 90:1 (1985).

Weismantel, Mary, *Food, Gender, and Poverty in the Ecuadorian Andes*, University of Pennsylvania Press (Philadelphia, 1988).

Wey Gómez, Nicolás, *The Tropics of Empire: Why Columbus Sailed South to the Indies*, MIT Press (Cambridge, 2008).

Whitmore, Thomas, and B. L. Turner II, 'Landscapes of Cultivation in Mesoamerica on the Eve of the Conquest', in Michael Smith and Marilyn Masson, eds., *The Ancient Civilizations of Mesoamerica: A Reader*, Blackwell (Oxford, 2000).

Wilson, Kathleen, *The Island Race: Englishness, Empire and Gender in the Eighteenth Century*, Routledge (London, 2003).

Wolf, Kenneth Baxter, 'The "Moors" of West Africa and the Beginnings of the Portuguese Slave Trade', *Journal of Medieval and Renaissance Studies* 24:3 (1994).

Xerez, Francisco de, *Verdadera relación de la conquista del Perú* (Madrid, 1891 [1534]).

Young, Robert, *Colonial Desire: Hybridity in Theory, Culture and Race*, Routledge (London, 1995).

Yun Casalilla, Bartolomé, *Marte contra Minerva: el precio del imperio español, c. 1450–1600*, Críticia (Barcelona, 2004).

Yupanqui, Titu Cusi, *History of How the Spaniards Arrived in Peru*, 1570, ed. Catherine Julien, Hackett (Indianapolis, 2006).

Zamora, Margarita, *Reading Columbus*, University of California Press (Berkeley, 1993).

Zárate, Agustín de, *Historia del descubrimiento y conquista del Perú*, ed. Franklin Pease and Teodoro Hampe Martínez, Pontífica Universidad Católica del Perú (Lima, 1995 [1555]).

A History of the Discovery and Conquest of Peru, trans. Thomas Nicholas, Norwood (London, 1977 [1581]).

Zurara, Gomes Eanes de, *Chronica do descobrimento e conquisita de Guiné*, ed. Viscount of Santarém (Paris, 1841).

Index

CPSIA information can be obtained
at www.ICGtesting.com
Printed in the USA
LVOW12s0846060816

499279LV00016B/353/P